D1060844

KAMANDI

ARCHIVES ▼ VOLUME 2

JACK KIRBY

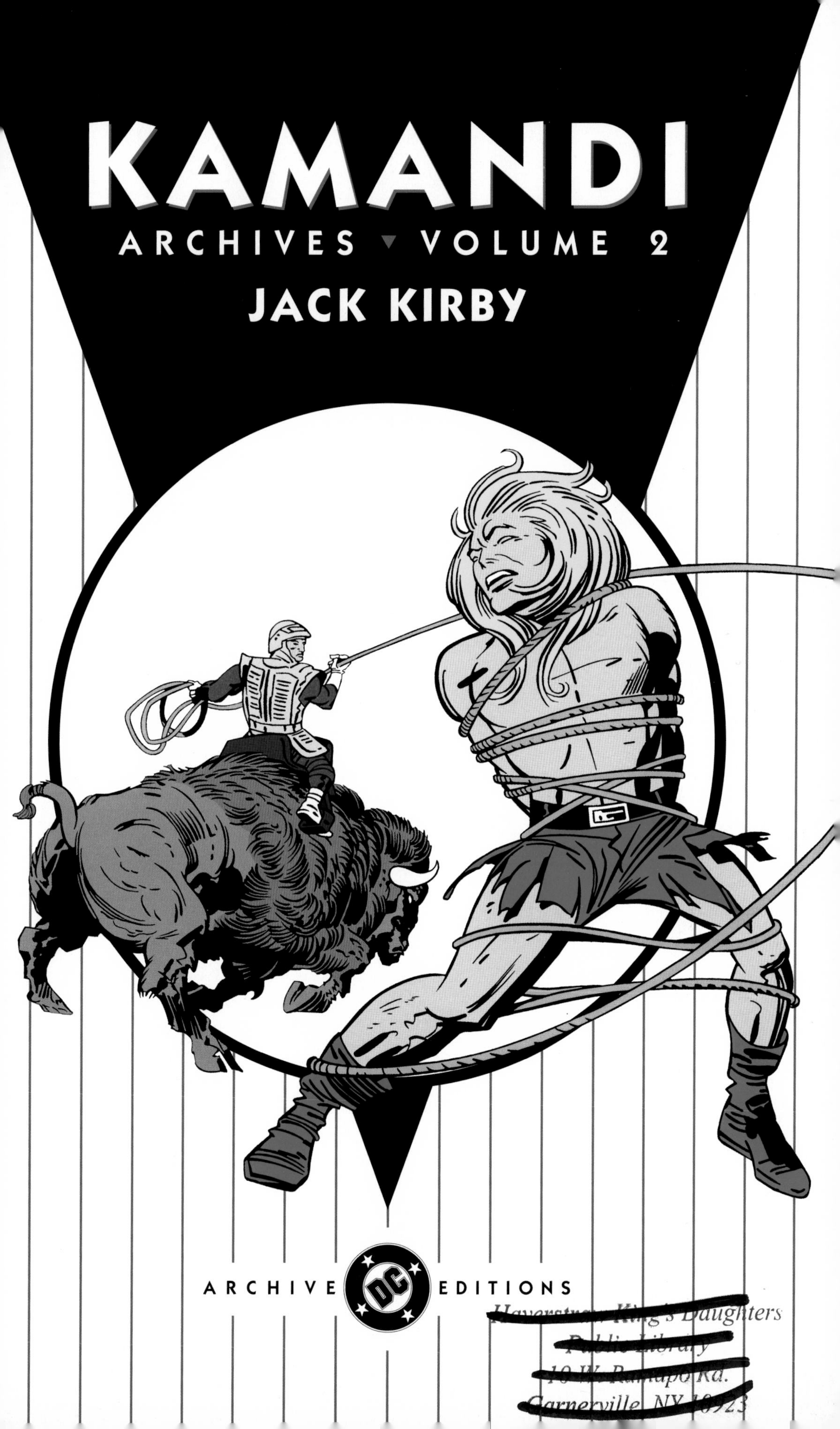

ARCHIVE EDITIONS

KAMANDI
THE LAST BOY ON EARTH!

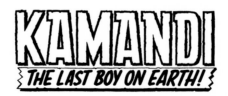

KAMANDI CREATED BY JACK KIRBY.

KAMANDI ARCHIVES
VOLUME 2

ISBN 1-4012-1208-5
ISBN 13: 978-1-4012-1208-7

DC COMICS
1700 BROADWAY
NEW YORK, NY 10019

A WARNER BROS. ENTERTAINMENT COMPANY

PRINTED IN HONG KONG.
FIRST PRINTING.

THE DC ARCHIVE EDITIONS

COVER ILLUSTRATION BY JACK KIRBY AND MIKE ROYER.

COLOR RECONSTRUCTION ON COVER AND INTERIOR PAGES BY JAMISON.

BLACK-AND-WHITE RECONSTRUCTION ON SELECTED INTERIOR PAGES BY DALE CRAIN

SERIES DESIGN BY ALEX JAY/STUDIO J.

PUBLICATION DESIGN BY ROBBIE BIEDERMAN

TABLE OF CONTENTS

ALL STORIES WRITTEN AND PENCILLED BY
JACK KIRBY.

TABLE OF CONTENTS

FOREWORD

WHEN KIRBY CALLED!

It was a dark and stormy night... not a fit night out for man nor beast... it was... all right, it was a night like any other night, except that this was the night Kirby called!

For one young cartoonist in his late twenties and only three years into his comic book career, getting that phone call would have a profound effect on his life from that day forward. That young cartoonist was, of course, myself.

Growing up in rural farm country near a small town in the Pacific Northwest, I looked forward to the weekly trip with my father into town where, in "our" grocery store, the latest issues of my favorite early 1950s comic books were found. I would enthusiastically escape into the adventurous worlds of Jack Kirby and Joe Simon's *Boys' Ranch* and *Bulls-Eye*, as well as delighting in the frustrations of a certain duck drawn by Carl Barks.

Back in the country, I would walk on the county highway a quarter mile east of our home to the little mom-and-pop "trading post" where one could find, in a corner at the rear of the store, a shelf piled high with hundreds of coverless comic books from the 1940s, all priced at a mere five cents each. Between these two sources, I had the best of two decades' worth of comics, and could enjoy the old (i.e., BOY COMMANDOS, the Newsboy Legion, etc.) and the new work of Jack Kirby simultaneously.

In the mid-'50s our family moved into town, and attending high school, going to the movies and discovering the opposite sex — not necessarily in that order — to a great extent replaced the four-color adventures of cowboys, super-heroes and adventurous ducks. It was nearly a decade before I rediscovered their colorful pulp pages and began to truly examine the genius of Kirby's work. This was all before Kirby called.

Accepting the reality that pursuing my dream of a career in syndicated newspaper strips — nurtured in grammar school, then practiced in high school art classes and bolstered by Kirby's impressive newspaper strip from the late 1950s, *Sky Masters* (featuring a lead character named Dr. Royer!) — was quickly fading due to the Fourth Estate's trend away from adventure content, I returned to a place where high adventure was being reborn, first with Carmine Infantino's THE FLASH and then with Kirby's marvelous new creations: comic books!

It was probably inevitable that Jack Kirby would return to the company where he had enjoyed success with such titles as GREEN ARROW and CHALLENGERS OF THE UNKNOWN. His creative well was overflowing with fresh ideas and characters, and he wanted to have more personal control over the directions in which their adventures would lead them. Although Sherlock Holmes always advised us never to assume, I feel that Kirby believed DC Comics could provide the right environment for the peoples and worlds he wished to develop. But before this historic event, the foundation for a decade-long professional association and an even-longer friendship was about to have its groundbreaking — and it would begin the night Kirby called.

Jack Kirby had moved to California at the end of the 1960s, and when he wasn't producing pages of dynamic storytelling for the four-color presses he busied himself with creating graphics for a merchandising licensee in Los Angeles. His comic book art was still being inked and lettered on the east coast, however,

and he began to look for someone closer to home to ink his other work. Having moved to the Los Angeles area in the mid-'60s, I was pursuing my new comic book ambitions by assisting artist Russ Manning on the titles *Magnus, Robot Fighter* and *Tarzan*, as well as picking up other assignments from his editor at the west coast's only (at the time) comic book house, Western Publishing Company. A young Mark Evanier, whom I'd met at one of the many southern California fan gatherings, was toiling at the aforementioned merchandising company and suggested my name to Kirby as a possible local inker. In a conversation with fellow east coast transplant Alex Toth, Jack got confirmation of Mark's recommendation, and so... Kirby called!

My wife and three offspring were at their nightly AAU swim workout of several thousand laps, and just after 7:00 P.M., while crossing the yard between my studio and the house and anticipating the imminent arrival of my wet family, I heard the phone ringing in the kitchen, and ran to answer it.

Cue drum roll...

"Mike Royer?! This is Jack Kirby! Alex Toth says you're a pretty good inker!"

You have to understand: having seen Kirby's uninked pencils reproduced in fanzines, I had dreamed of one day having the opportunity to "complete" his pencil statements with ink in the way I felt he would have wanted it — something I had not, in my humble opinion, seen done by anyone other than Kirby himself. And now here he was, on the telephone, asking if I'd be interested in trying my hand at inking his merchandising art!

What followed was a baptism of fire in which I inked my first assignment for the King of Comics at his very own drawing board, with him looking over my shoulder all the while. He was — and I am again assuming here — pleased enough with the results that he decided to offer me a role in his next big career move. And so, Kirby called again!

"I'm going to be doing some big things I can't talk about right now, but you are definitely a part of them!" Jack informed me shortly before departing on a flight to New York City. Soon after returning to California, he told me that he was now creating work for DC Comics and that he planned on taking me with him. He'd found someone to complete his pencil statements faithfully in ink, and it was his intent that I should letter and ink all of his "Fourth World" creations. DC, however, was at first reluctant to try this unknown part of Kirby's equation. It took four issues each of his new titles (THE NEW GODS, THE FOREVER PEOPLE and MISTER MIRACLE) before his plan was realized and I was indeed inking and lettering Jack Kirby for DC, the company that — with the help of a couple of teenagers — had created the world of super-hero comic books more than three decades earlier.

You now hold in your hands the second volume collecting the KAMANDI saga, which for me represents one of Kirby's greatest creations and which I recall with great fondness and pride. Jack was a never-ending fount of wonderful storytelling, and the Last Boy on Earth allowed his creative juices to flow in a river of anthropomorphic character creations that rival any super-villain.

Kirby's approach to visual storytelling was simple and direct. A fan of Hollywood's Golden Age (the films of Warner Bros. in particular), he equated the shape of the comic book panel with that of the motion picture screen, and often remarked that it was what goes on inside the panel, or the screen, that matters, and not the panel itself. "The storytelling is the important thing, not the space it occupies!"

If you've eagerly awaited this collection, I don't have to say anything further about the power of Kirby's art. You know what I mean. If you're new to the topsy-turvy world he created for young Kamandi's struggle for survival, I need only say, "Welcome aboard, pilgrim!"

It has now been over thirty years since I was privileged to ink and letter most of the pages that follow. Of those days, there are two things that I recall most vividly: the intoxicating aroma of Roi-Tan cigars, which issued forth from the packages of completed pencils which Jack would send to me via Special Delivery; and the awful dread I would feel, after drinking in the beauty of his superb design and storytelling, that I wouldn't be able to give those magic pencils their due. I'll let you be the judge of my success.

It's been great fun reliving these classic and timeless adventures, which I can finally, after more than twenty years, enjoy with a certain detachment unavailable to me when they were originally being produced. Back then, I had to letter a complete book in less than two days and ink three pages a day! I would guess that I hold the record as an inker for keeping up with Kirby's prolific creative output, though of course I could not sustain this level indefinitely. A hint of the toll that working to Kirby's pace demanded can be found on page 119, in the credits for issue #16 (the last of my KAMANDI issues in this volume): "Mountain-climbing" Mike Royer, after eight days in the wilderness, stood almost 15,000 feet high atop majestic Mt. Whitney in the Sierra Nevada range, filled his lungs with crisp, icy air and said, "Do I really need to be working this hard?" So, this time Royer called Kirby.

Happily, my professional association with Jack did not end there. After a short break, it continued through the end of the 1970s — but that's a story for a different time. Right now, let's all sit back and witness the power, charm, excitement and humor of Kamandi, the Last Boy on Earth, as he deals with the allure of lovely young Spirit, the ruthlessness of the leopards, the fellowship of his human friends Ben and company, the business acumen of the crafty Sacker, the giant grasshoppers,

and all of the other wonders to be found in this crazy, frighteningly upside-down world where humans are called animals and animals rule with a brutal iron paw!

This time, Kirby's call is for *you* — so answer it and enjoy!

— Mike Royer
September, 2006

Following his famous collaborations with Jack Kirby on such titles as THE NEW GODS, THE FOREVER PEOPLE, MIRACLE MAN, OMAC, THE DEMON and KAMANDI, Mike Royer began a long association with Disney Productions, where he worked both on staff and as a freelancer, and he continues to do creative work for a variety of clients from his home in Medford, Oregon. While on the road in southern California, he scribbled a rough draft of this foreword beneath a mighty oak tree, just a short distance from Jack Kirby's final home in Thousand Oaks. Long live the King!

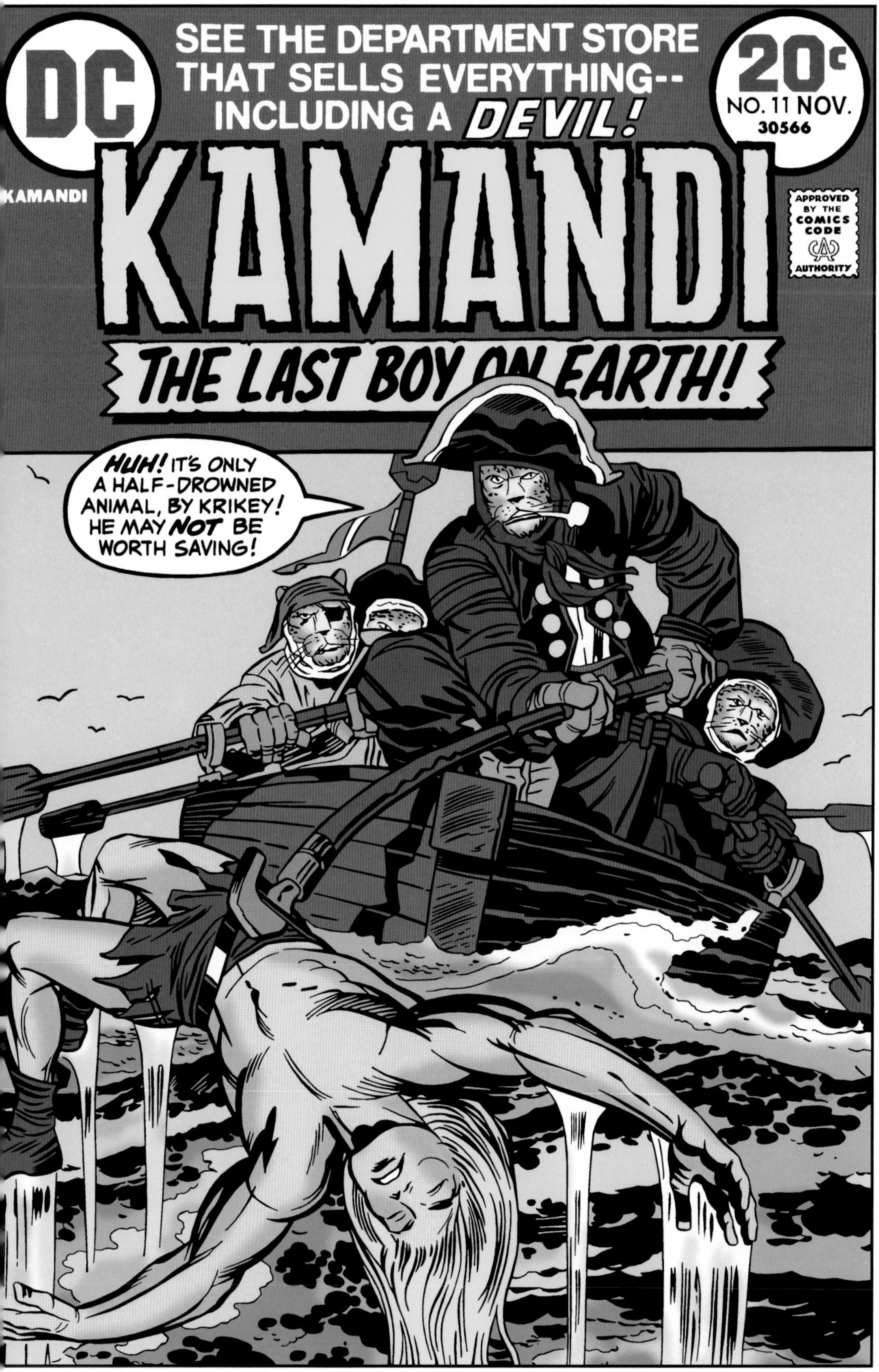
SEE THE DEPARTMENT STORE THAT SELLS EVERYTHING-- INCLUDING A DEVIL!
DC
20¢
NO. 11 NOV.
30566
KAMANDI
KAMANDI
APPROVED BY THE COMICS CODE AUTHORITY
THE LAST BOY ON EARTH!
HUH! IT'S ONLY A HALF-DROWNED ANIMAL, BY KRIKEY! HE MAY NOT BE WORTH SAVING!

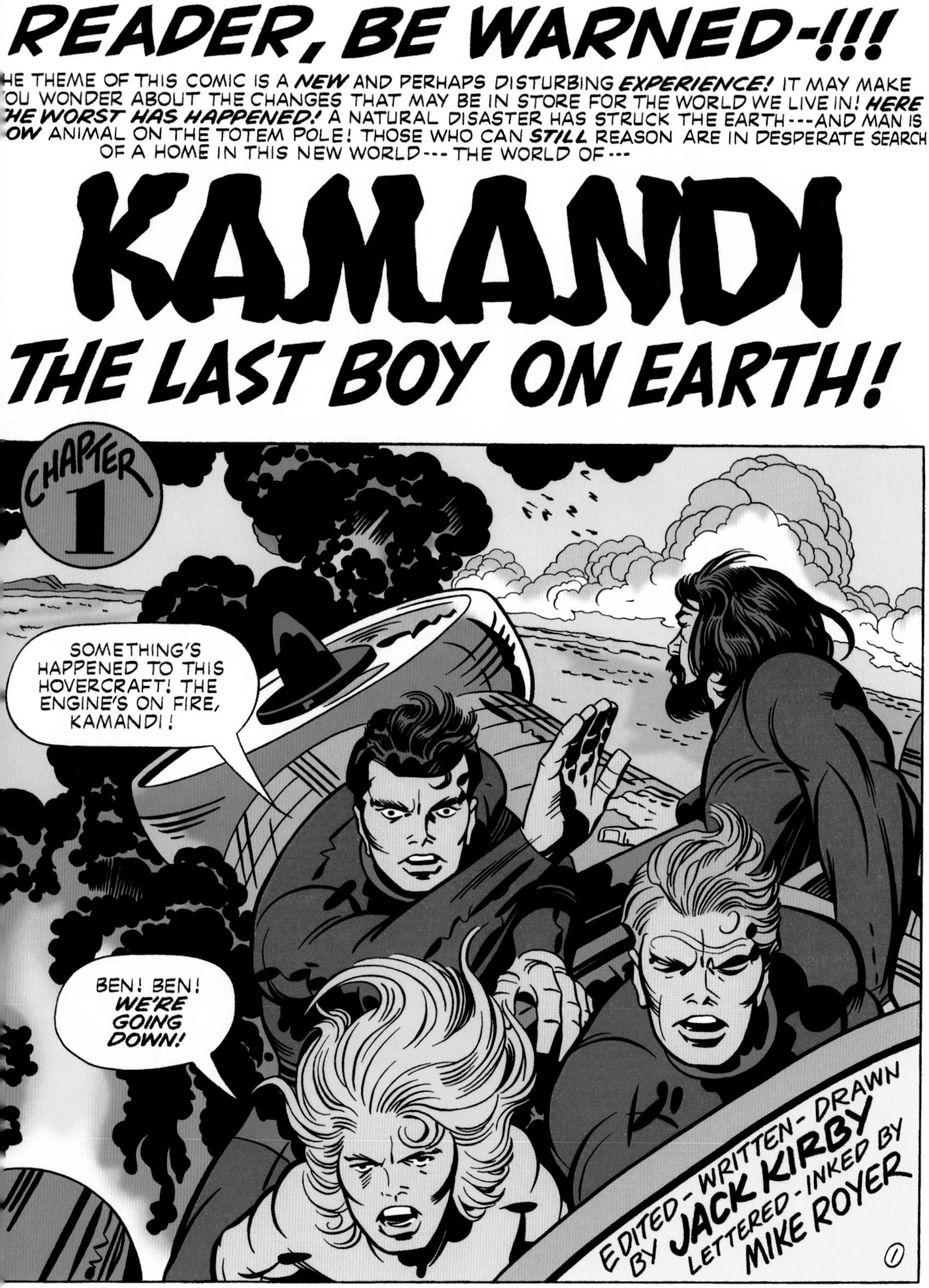
READER, BE WARNED-!!!
HE THEME OF THIS COMIC IS A NEW AND PERHAPS DISTURBING EXPERIENCE! IT MAY MAKE OU WONDER ABOUT THE CHANGES THAT MAY BE IN STORE FOR THE WORLD WE LIVE IN! HERE HE WORST HAS HAPPENED! A NATURAL DISASTER HAS STRUCK THE EARTH---AND MAN IS OW ANIMAL ON THE TOTEM POLE! THOSE WHO CAN STILL REASON ARE IN DESPERATE SEARCH OF A HOME IN THIS NEW WORLD--- THE WORLD OF---
KAMANDI
THE LAST BOY ON EARTH!
CHAPTER 1
SOMETHING'S HAPPENED TO THIS HOVERCRAFT! THE ENGINE'S ON FIRE, KAMANDI!
BEN! BEN! WE'RE GOING DOWN!
EDITED-WRITTEN-DRAWN BY JACK KIRBY
LETTERED-INKED BY MIKE ROYER
1

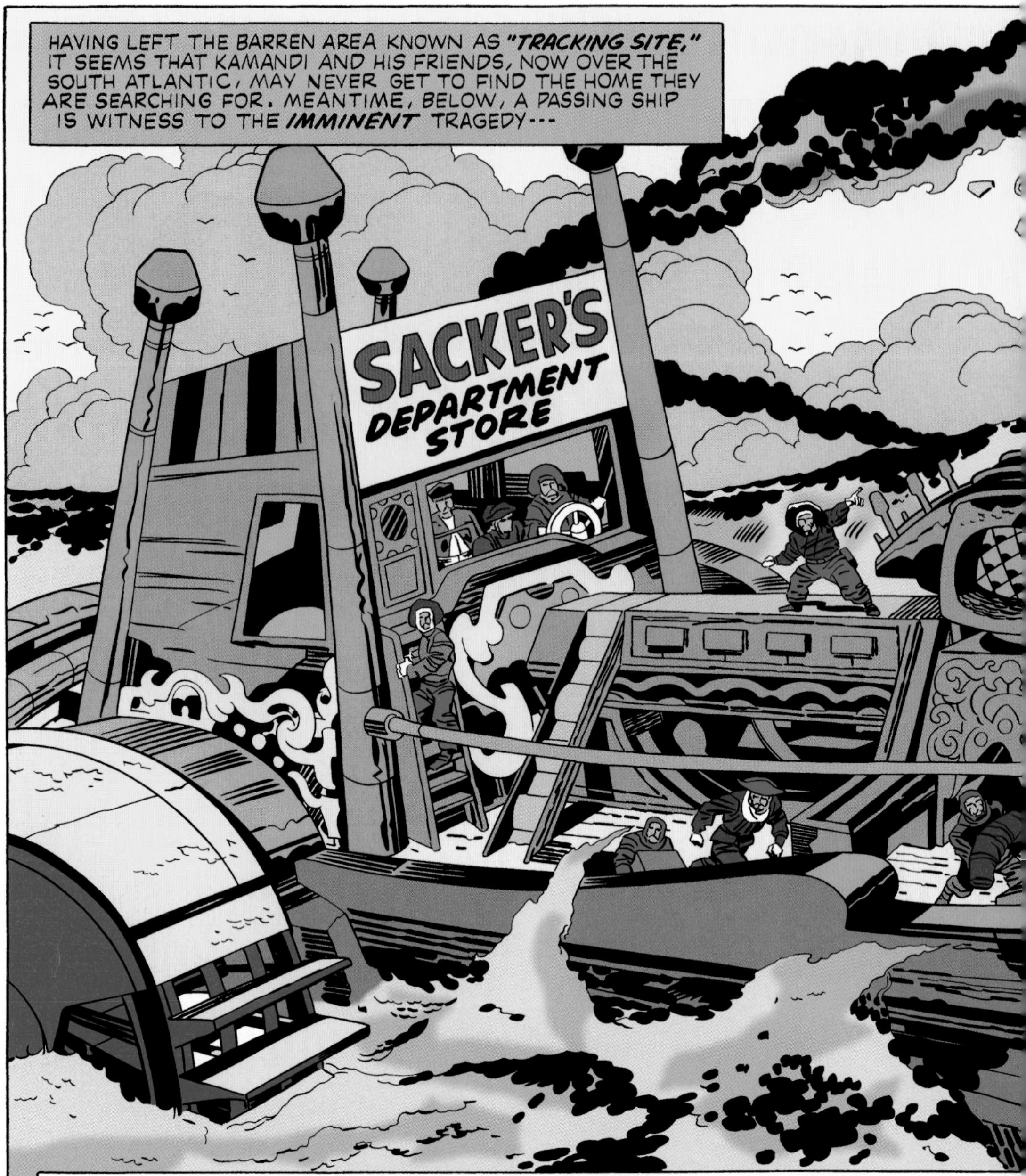
HAVING LEFT THE BARREN AREA KNOWN AS "TRACKING SITE," IT SEEMS THAT KAMANDI AND HIS FRIENDS, NOW OVER THE SOUTH ATLANTIC, MAY NEVER GET TO FIND THE HOME THEY ARE SEARCHING FOR. MEANTIME, BELOW, A PASSING SHIP IS WITNESS TO THE IMMINENT TRAGEDY---
SACKER'S DEPARTMENT STORE

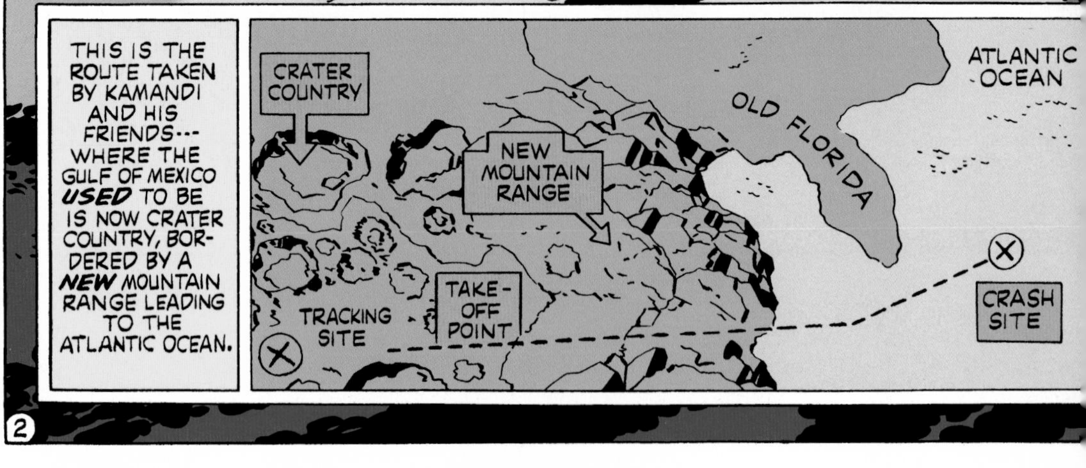
THIS IS THE ROUTE TAKEN BY KAMANDI AND HIS FRIENDS--- WHERE THE GULF OF MEXICO USED TO BE IS NOW CRATER COUNTRY, BORDERED BY A NEW MOUNTAIN RANGE LEADING TO THE ATLANTIC OCEAN.
CRATER COUNTRY
NEW MOUNTAIN RANGE
OLD FLORIDA
ATLANTIC OCEAN
TRACKING SITE
TAKE-OFF POINT
CRASH SITE
2

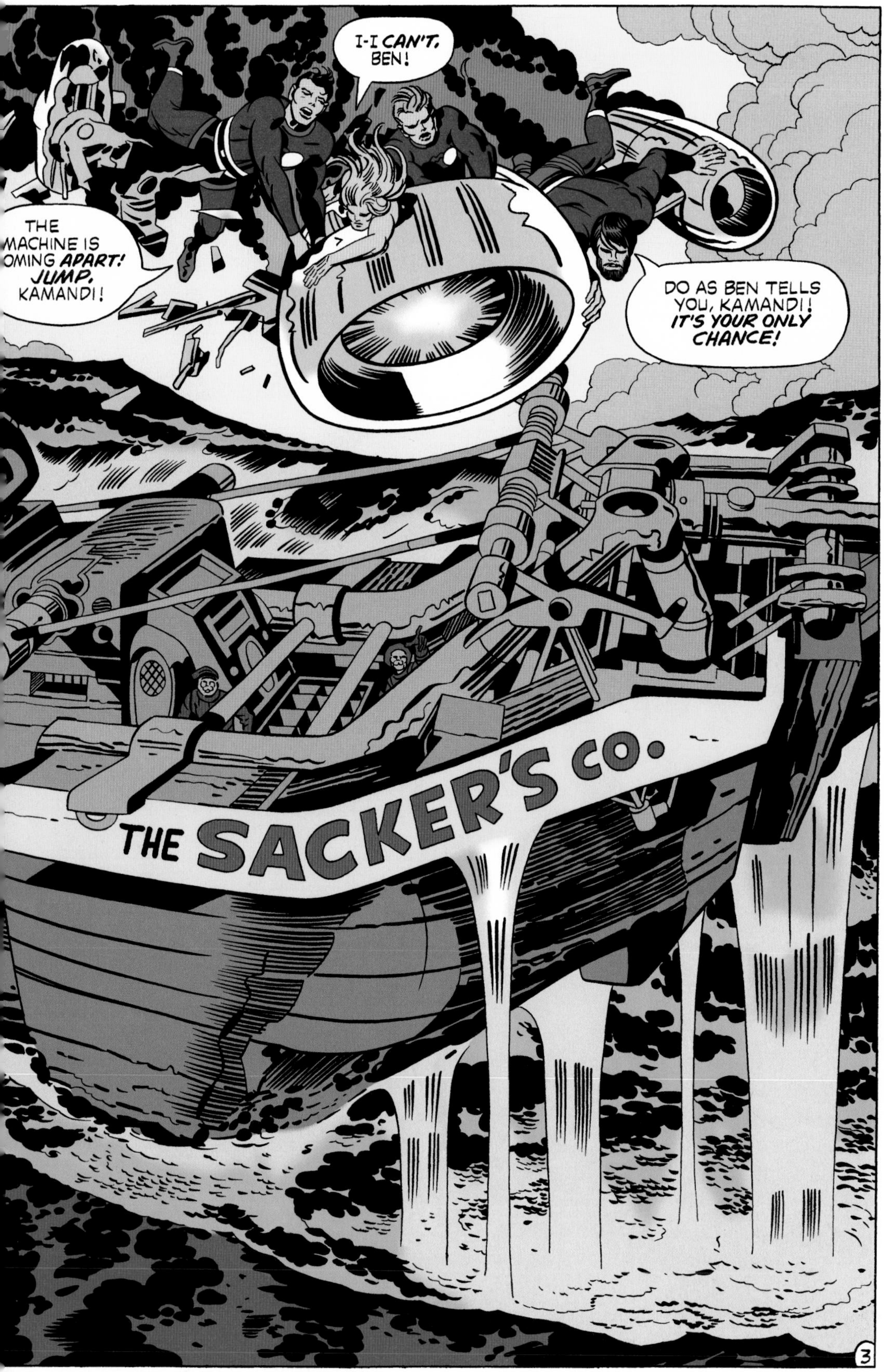
THE MACHINE IS OMING APART! JUMP, KAMANDI!
I-I CAN'T, BEN!
DO AS BEN TELLS YOU, KAMANDI! IT'S YOUR ONLY CHANCE!
THE SACKER'S CO.
3

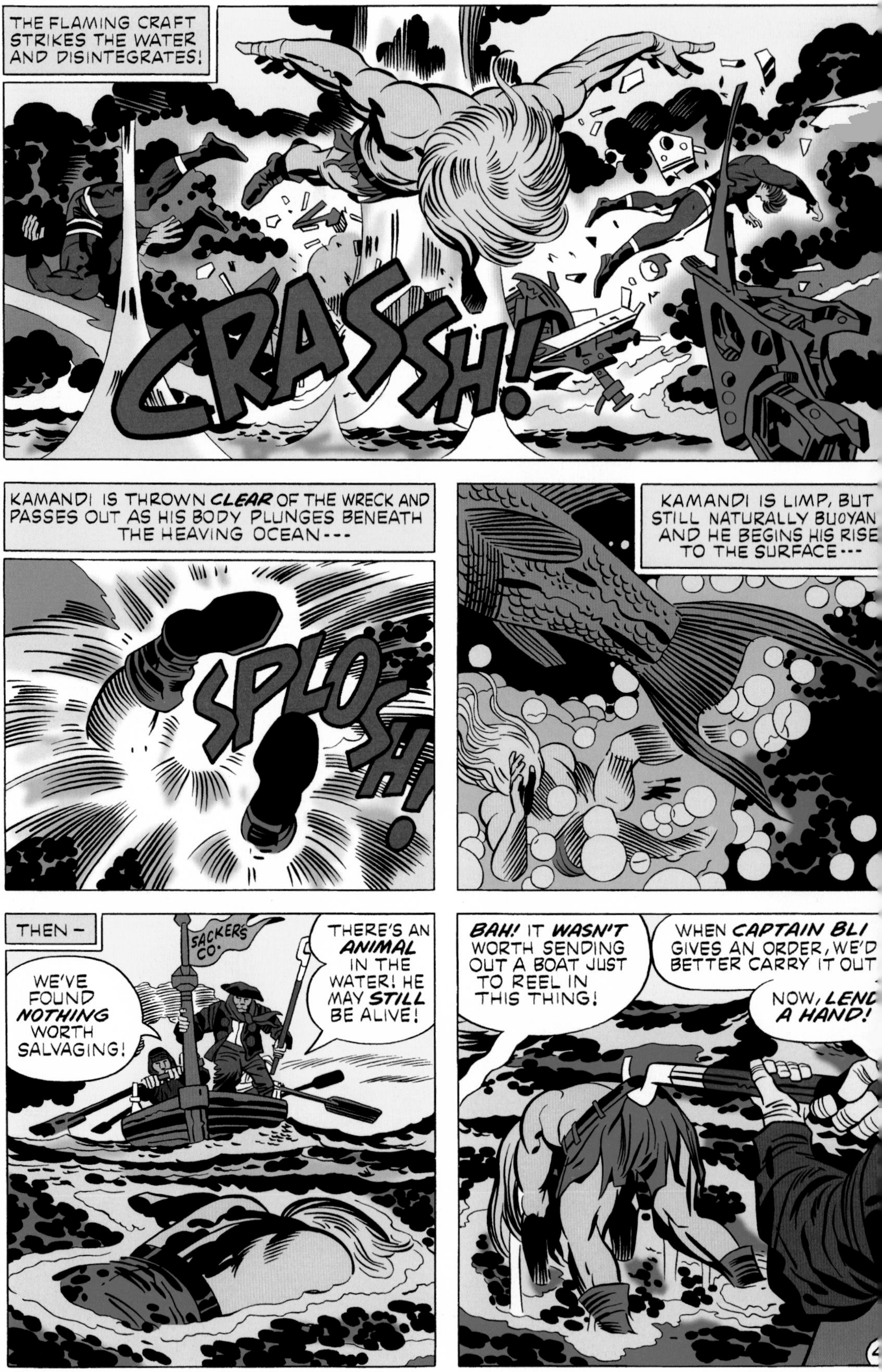
THE FLAMING CRAFT STRIKES THE WATER AND DISINTEGRATES!
CRASSH!
KAMANDI IS THROWN CLEAR OF THE WRECK AND PASSES OUT AS HIS BODY PLUNGES BENEATH THE HEAVING OCEAN---
SPLOSH!
KAMANDI IS LIMP, BUT STILL NATURALLY BUOYAN AND HE BEGINS HIS RISE TO THE SURFACE---
THEN -
SACKER'S CO.
WE'VE FOUND NOTHING WORTH SALVAGING!
THERE'S AN ANIMAL IN THE WATER! HE MAY STILL BE ALIVE!
BAH! IT WASN'T WORTH SENDING OUT A BOAT JUST TO REEL IN THIS THING!
WHEN CAPTAIN BLI GIVES AN ORDER, WE'D BETTER CARRY IT OUT
NOW, LEND A HAND!

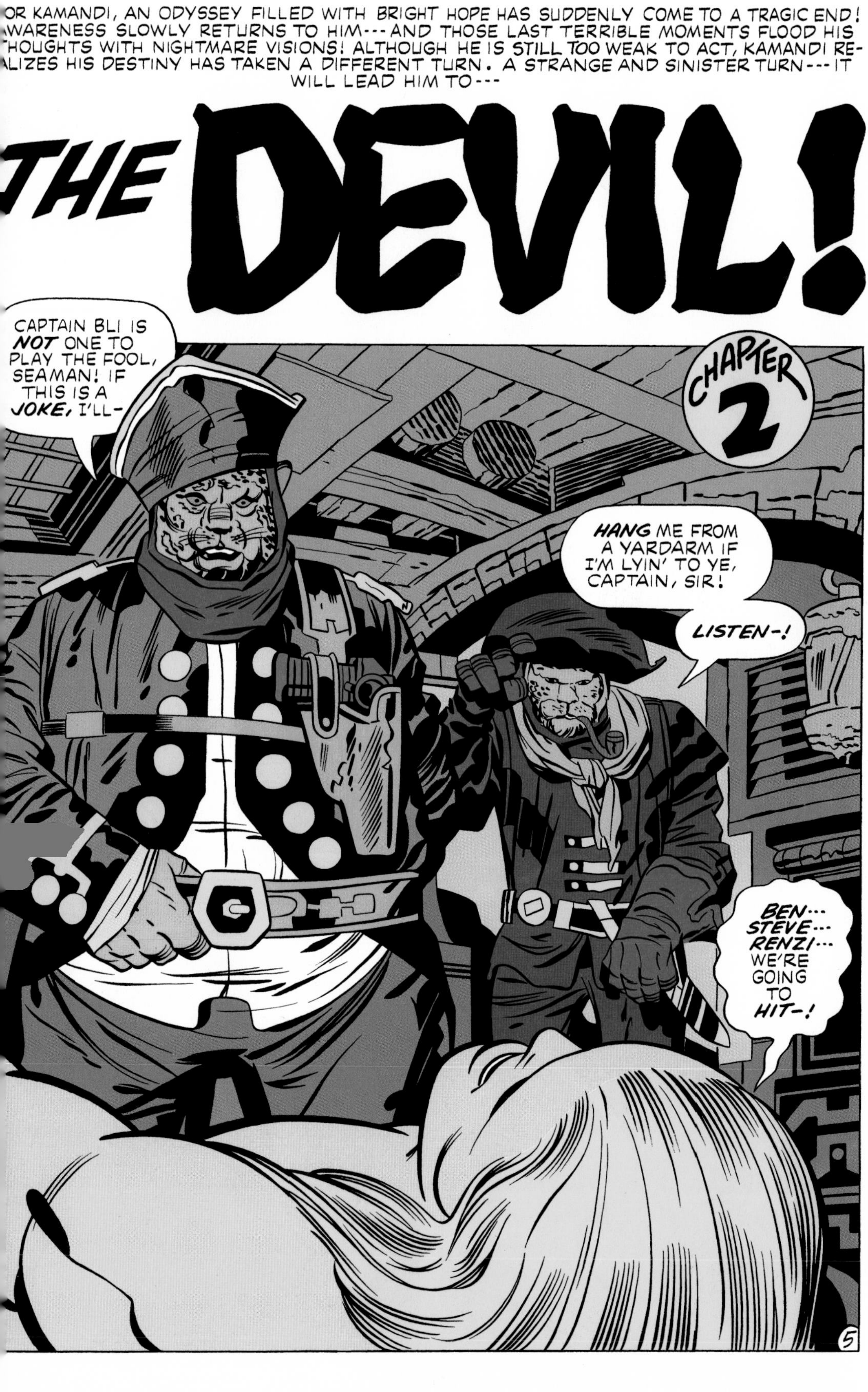
OR KAMANDI, AN ODYSSEY FILLED WITH BRIGHT HOPE HAS SUDDENLY COME TO A TRAGIC END! WARENESS SLOWLY RETURNS TO HIM--- AND THOSE LAST TERRIBLE MOMENTS FLOOD HIS HOUGHTS WITH NIGHTMARE VISIONS! ALTHOUGH HE IS STILL TOO WEAK TO ACT, KAMANDI RE- LIZES HIS DESTINY HAS TAKEN A DIFFERENT TURN. A STRANGE AND SINISTER TURN--- IT WILL LEAD HIM TO---
THE DEVIL!
CAPTAIN BLI IS NOT ONE TO PLAY THE FOOL, SEAMAN! IF THIS IS A JOKE, I'LL-
CHAPTER 2
HANG ME FROM A YARDARM IF I'M LYIN' TO YE, CAPTAIN, SIR!
LISTEN-!
BEN... STEVE... RENZI... WE'RE GOING TO HIT-!
5

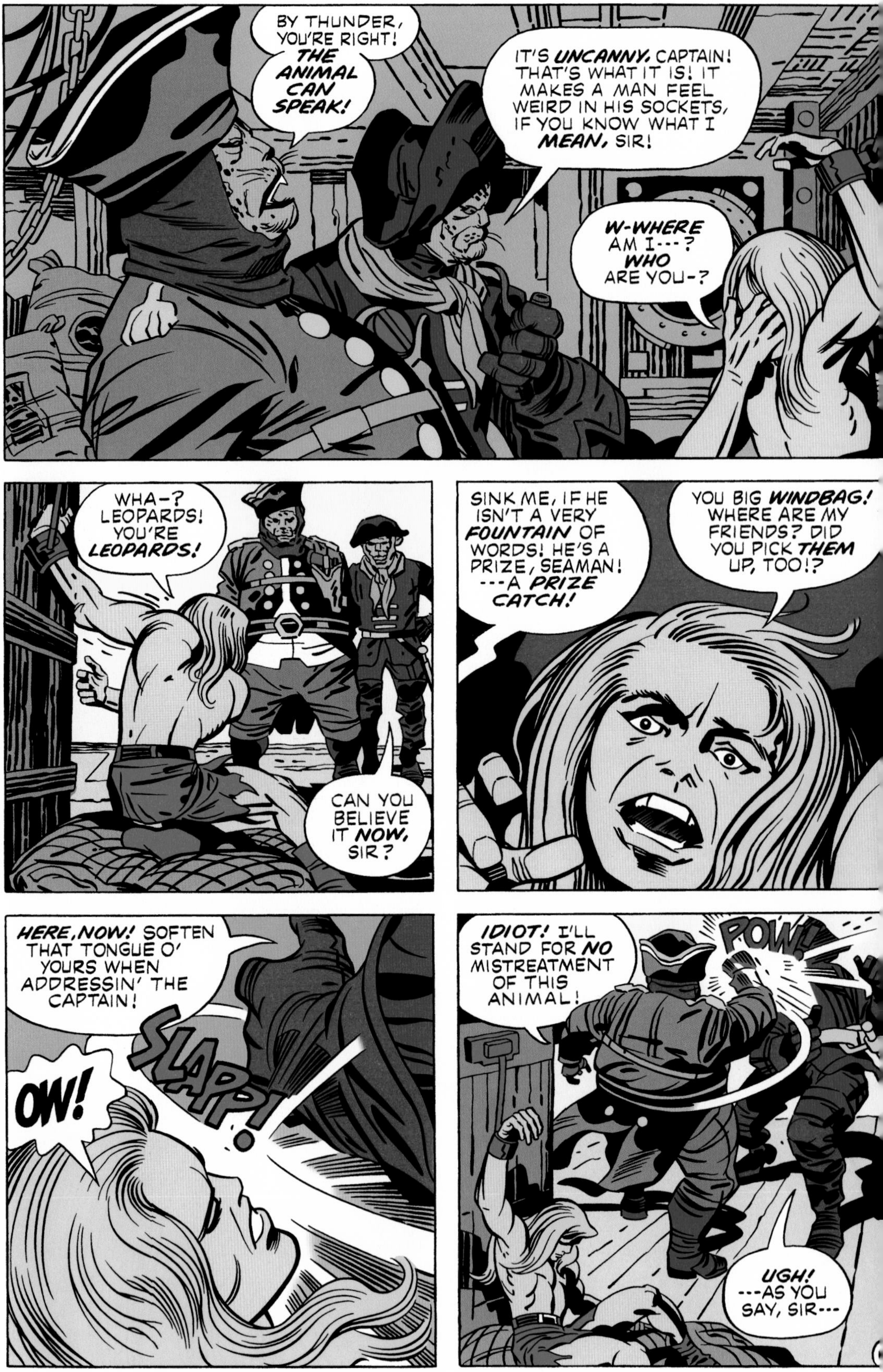
BY THUNDER, YOU'RE RIGHT! THE ANIMAL CAN SPEAK!
IT'S UNCANNY, CAPTAIN! THAT'S WHAT IT IS! IT MAKES A MAN FEEL WEIRD IN HIS SOCKETS, IF YOU KNOW WHAT I MEAN, SIR!
W-WHERE AM I---? WHO ARE YOU-?
WHA-? LEOPARDS! YOU'RE LEOPARDS!
CAN YOU BELIEVE IT NOW, SIR?
SINK ME, IF HE ISN'T A VERY FOUNTAIN OF WORDS! HE'S A PRIZE, SEAMAN! ---A PRIZE CATCH!
YOU BIG WINDBAG! WHERE ARE MY FRIENDS? DID YOU PICK THEM UP, TOO!?
HERE, NOW! SOFTEN THAT TONGUE O' YOURS WHEN ADDRESSIN' THE CAPTAIN!
SLAP!
OW!
IDIOT! I'LL STAND FOR NO MISTREATMENT OF THIS ANIMAL!
POW!
UGH! ---AS YOU SAY, SIR---

HERE'S **NO** [TE]LLING HOW [M]UCH HE'S [W]ORTH IN [C]OLD **CASH!**

[T]HE **LASH** [W]AITS FOR [A]NY SWAB [WH]O HARMS THIS [A]NIMAL!

AYE AYE, SIR---

AT THAT MOMENT, A **STRANGE,** UNNERVING **SOUND** RISES FROM SOMEWHERE ON THE SHIP---

KKK'KLIGGIGIK'

W-WHAT'S **THAT**-?

I-IT'S **HIM** AGAIN, SIR! ---THE **DEVIL!**

SAY, WHAT KIND OF [S]HIP IS THIS? WHAT [KI]ND OF **CARGO** ARE [Y]OU CARRYING?

HEH-HEH! LIKE **YOURSELF,** ANIMAL, I'D SAY IT'S **MOSTLY LIVE CARGO!**

TALKING WITH AN ANIMAL IS ENOUGH TO **SHAKE** A MAN!

LET'S CHECK ON THE **DEVIL,** SEAMAN!

---GOT TO **FREE** MYSELF! ---GOT TO---!

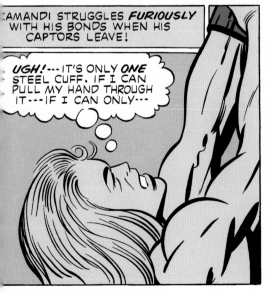

[K]AMANDI STRUGGLES **FURIOUSLY** WITH HIS BONDS WHEN HIS CAPTORS LEAVE!

UGH!---IT'S ONLY **ONE** STEEL CUFF. IF I CAN PULL MY HAND THROUGH IT---IF I CAN ONLY---

STOICALLY ENDURING THE PRESSURE, KAMANDI **SLOWLY** MANAGES TO SQUEEZE HIS HAND OUT OF ITS METAL PRISON---

I-I'M--- **MAKING** ---IT---!

7

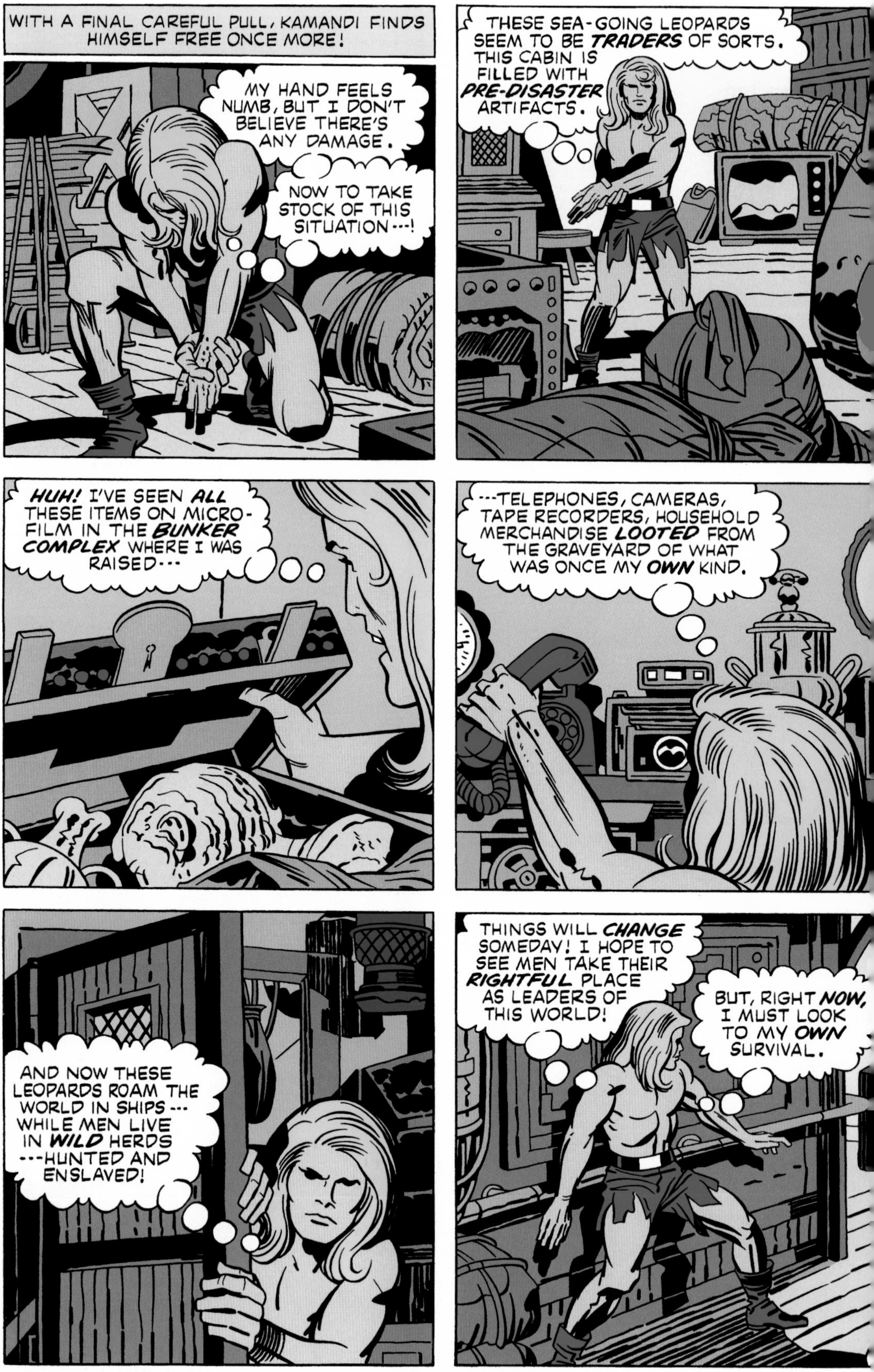
WITH A FINAL CAREFUL PULL, KAMANDI FINDS HIMSELF FREE ONCE MORE!
MY HAND FEELS NUMB, BUT I DON'T BELIEVE THERE'S ANY DAMAGE.
NOW TO TAKE STOCK OF THIS SITUATION---!
THESE SEA-GOING LEOPARDS SEEM TO BE TRADERS OF SORTS. THIS CABIN IS FILLED WITH PRE-DISASTER ARTIFACTS.
HUH! I'VE SEEN ALL THESE ITEMS ON MICRO-FILM IN THE BUNKER COMPLEX WHERE I WAS RAISED---
---TELEPHONES, CAMERAS, TAPE RECORDERS, HOUSEHOLD MERCHANDISE LOOTED FROM THE GRAVEYARD OF WHAT WAS ONCE MY OWN KIND.
AND NOW THESE LEOPARDS ROAM THE WORLD IN SHIPS--- WHILE MEN LIVE IN WILD HERDS ---HUNTED AND ENSLAVED!
THINGS WILL CHANGE SOMEDAY! I HOPE TO SEE MEN TAKE THEIR RIGHTFUL PLACE AS LEADERS OF THIS WORLD!
BUT, RIGHT NOW, I MUST LOOK TO MY OWN SURVIVAL.

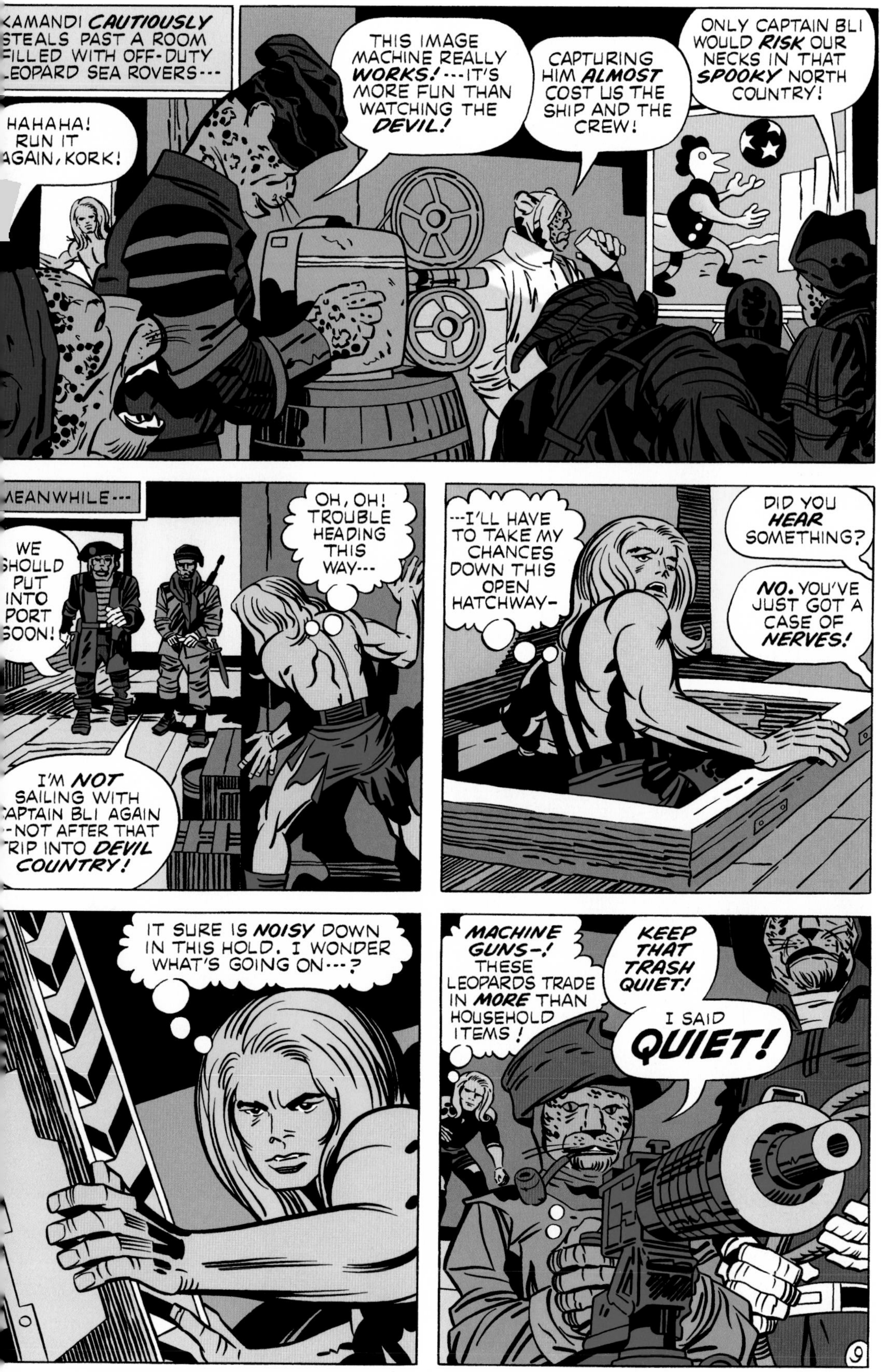
KAMANDI CAUTIOUSLY STEALS PAST A ROOM FILLED WITH OFF-DUTY LEOPARD SEA ROVERS---
HAHAHA! RUN IT AGAIN, KORK!
THIS IMAGE MACHINE REALLY WORKS! ---IT'S MORE FUN THAN WATCHING THE DEVIL!
CAPTURING HIM ALMOST COST US THE SHIP AND THE CREW!
ONLY CAPTAIN BLI WOULD RISK OUR NECKS IN THAT SPOOKY NORTH COUNTRY!
MEANWHILE---
WE SHOULD PUT INTO PORT SOON!
I'M NOT SAILING WITH CAPTAIN BLI AGAIN --NOT AFTER THAT TRIP INTO DEVIL COUNTRY!
OH, OH! TROUBLE HEADING THIS WAY---
---I'LL HAVE TO TAKE MY CHANCES DOWN THIS OPEN HATCHWAY-
DID YOU HEAR SOMETHING?
NO. YOU'VE JUST GOT A CASE OF NERVES!
IT SURE IS NOISY DOWN IN THIS HOLD. I WONDER WHAT'S GOING ON---?
MACHINE GUNS-! THESE LEOPARDS TRADE IN MORE THAN HOUSEHOLD ITEMS!
KEEP THAT TRASH QUIET!
I SAID QUIET!
9

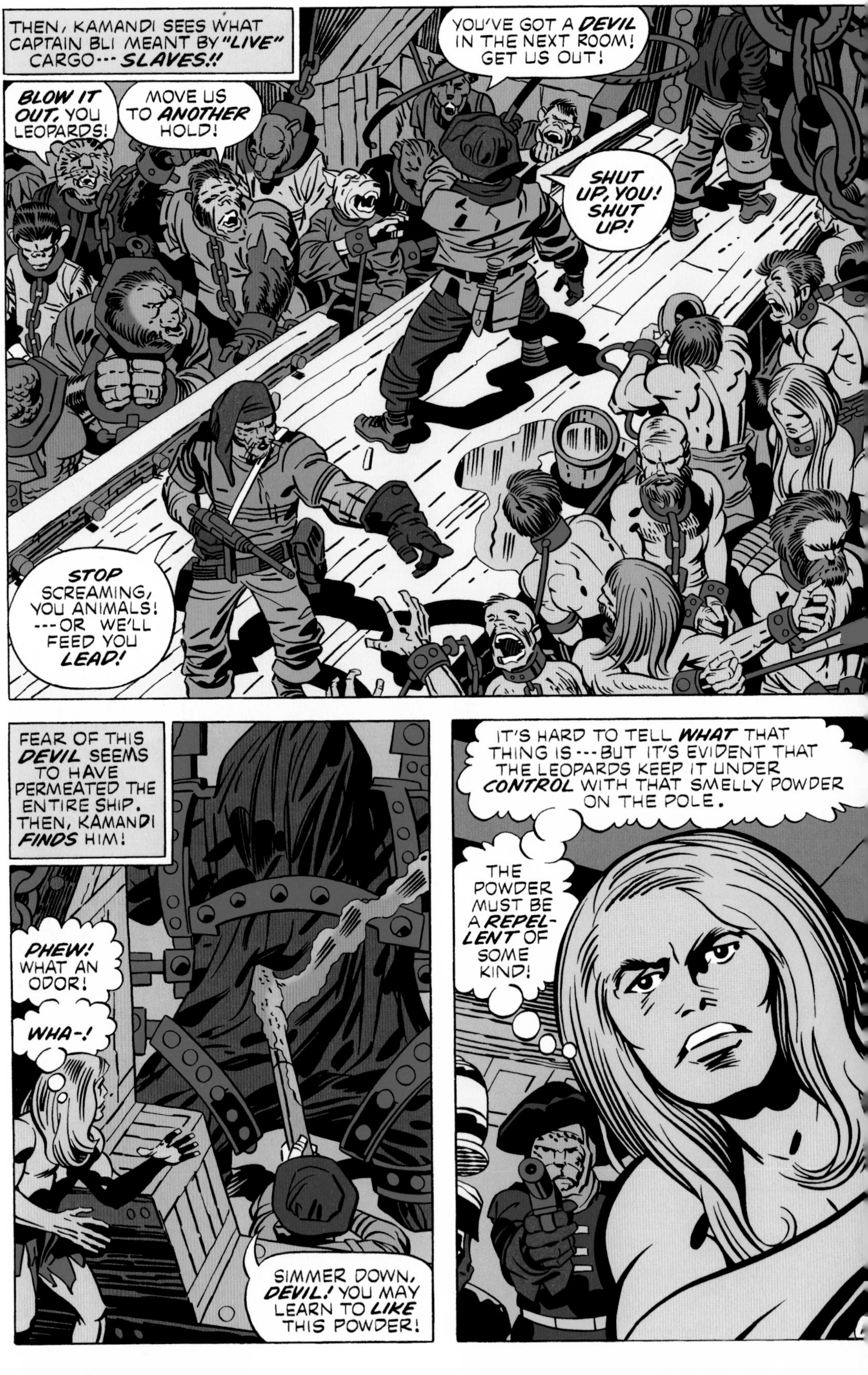
THEN, KAMANDI SEES WHAT CAPTAIN BLI MEANT BY "LIVE" CARGO--- SLAVES!!
YOU'VE GOT A DEVIL IN THE NEXT ROOM! GET US OUT!
BLOW IT OUT, YOU LEOPARDS!
MOVE US TO ANOTHER HOLD!
SHUT UP, YOU! SHUT UP!
STOP SCREAMING, YOU ANIMALS! ---OR WE'LL FEED YOU LEAD!
FEAR OF THIS DEVIL SEEMS TO HAVE PERMEATED THE ENTIRE SHIP. THEN, KAMANDI FINDS HIM!
PHEW! WHAT AN ODOR!
WHA-!
SIMMER DOWN, DEVIL! YOU MAY LEARN TO LIKE THIS POWDER!
IT'S HARD TO TELL WHAT THAT THING IS---BUT IT'S EVIDENT THAT THE LEOPARDS KEEP IT UNDER CONTROL WITH THAT SMELLY POWDER ON THE POLE.
THE POWDER MUST BE A REPEL-LENT OF SOME KIND!

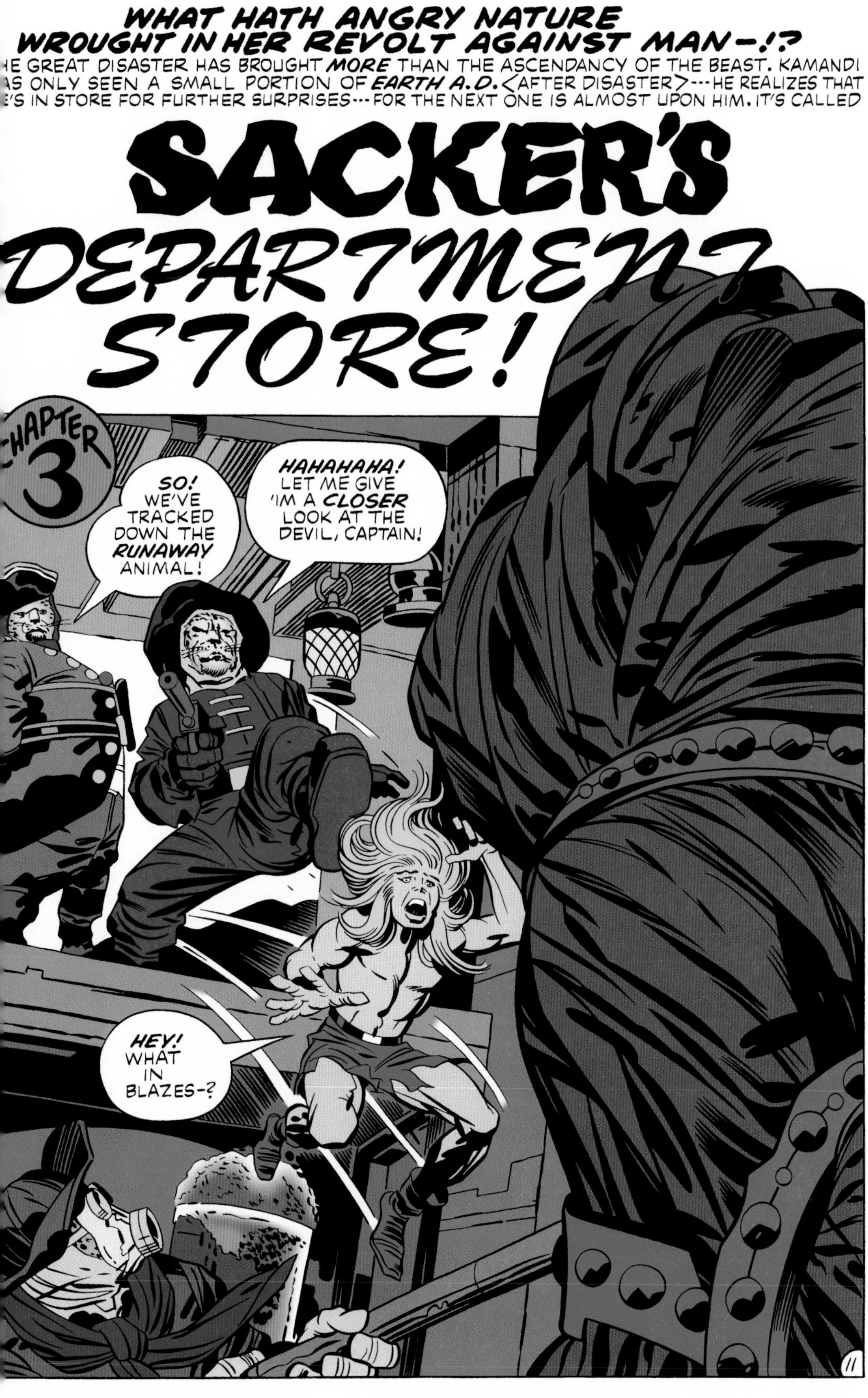
WHAT HATH ANGRY NATURE WROUGHT IN HER REVOLT AGAINST MAN-!?
GREAT DISASTER HAS BROUGHT MORE THAN THE ASCENDANCY OF THE BEAST. KAMANDI
ONLY SEEN A SMALL PORTION OF EARTH A.D. <AFTER DISASTER>--- HE REALIZES THAT
IN STORE FOR FURTHER SURPRISES--- FOR THE NEXT ONE IS ALMOST UPON HIM. IT'S CALLED
SACKER'S DEPARTMENT STORE!
CHAPTER 3
SO! WE'VE TRACKED DOWN THE RUNAWAY ANIMAL!
HAHAHAHA! LET ME GIVE 'IM A CLOSER LOOK AT THE DEVIL, CAPTAIN!
HEY! WHAT IN BLAZES-?
11

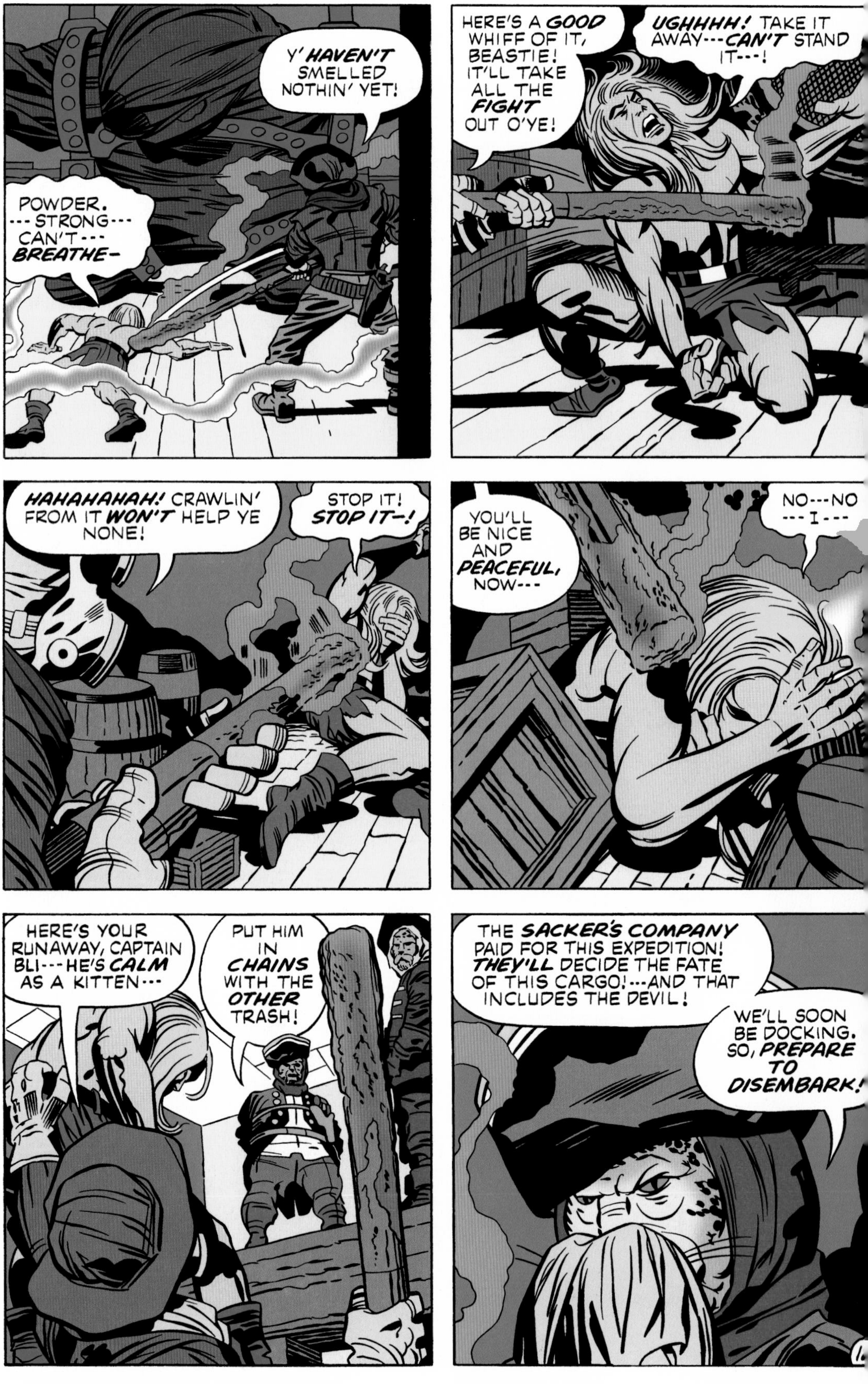
Y' HAVEN'T SMELLED NOTHIN' YET!
POWDER. --- STRONG--- CAN'T--- BREATHE-
HERE'S A GOOD WHIFF OF IT, BEASTIE! IT'LL TAKE ALL THE FIGHT OUT O'YE!
UGHHHH! TAKE IT AWAY---CAN'T STAND IT---!
HAHAHAHAH! CRAWLIN' FROM IT WON'T HELP YE NONE!
STOP IT! STOP IT-!
YOU'LL BE NICE AND PEACEFUL, NOW---
NO---NO ---I---
HERE'S YOUR RUNAWAY, CAPTAIN BLI---HE'S CALM AS A KITTEN---
PUT HIM IN CHAINS WITH THE OTHER TRASH!
THE SACKER'S COMPANY PAID FOR THIS EXPEDITION! THEY'LL DECIDE THE FATE OF THIS CARGO!---AND THAT INCLUDES THE DEVIL!
WE'LL SOON BE DOCKING. SO, PREPARE TO DISEMBARK!

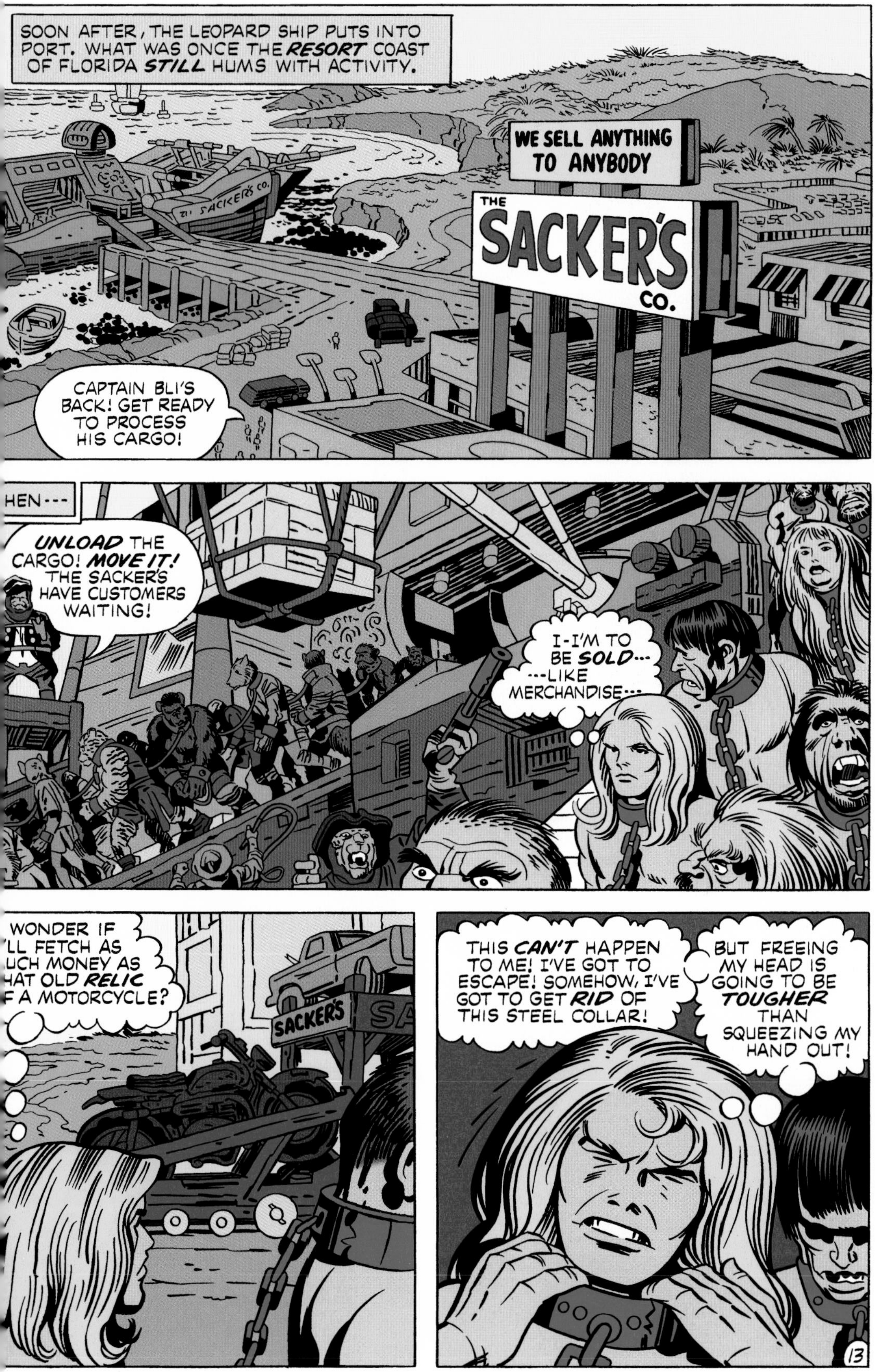
SOON AFTER, THE LEOPARD SHIP PUTS INTO PORT. WHAT WAS ONCE THE RESORT COAST OF FLORIDA STILL HUMS WITH ACTIVITY.
WE SELL ANYTHING TO ANYBODY
THE SACKER'S CO.
CAPTAIN BLI'S BACK! GET READY TO PROCESS HIS CARGO!
HEN---
UNLOAD THE CARGO! MOVE IT! THE SACKER'S HAVE CUSTOMERS WAITING!
I-I'M TO BE SOLD--- ---LIKE MERCHANDISE---
WONDER IF 'LL FETCH AS UCH MONEY AS HAT OLD RELIC F A MOTORCYCLE?
SACKER'S
THIS CAN'T HAPPEN TO ME! I'VE GOT TO ESCAPE! SOMEHOW, I'VE GOT TO GET RID OF THIS STEEL COLLAR!
BUT FREEING MY HEAD IS GOING TO BE TOUGHER THAN SQUEEZING MY HAND OUT!
13

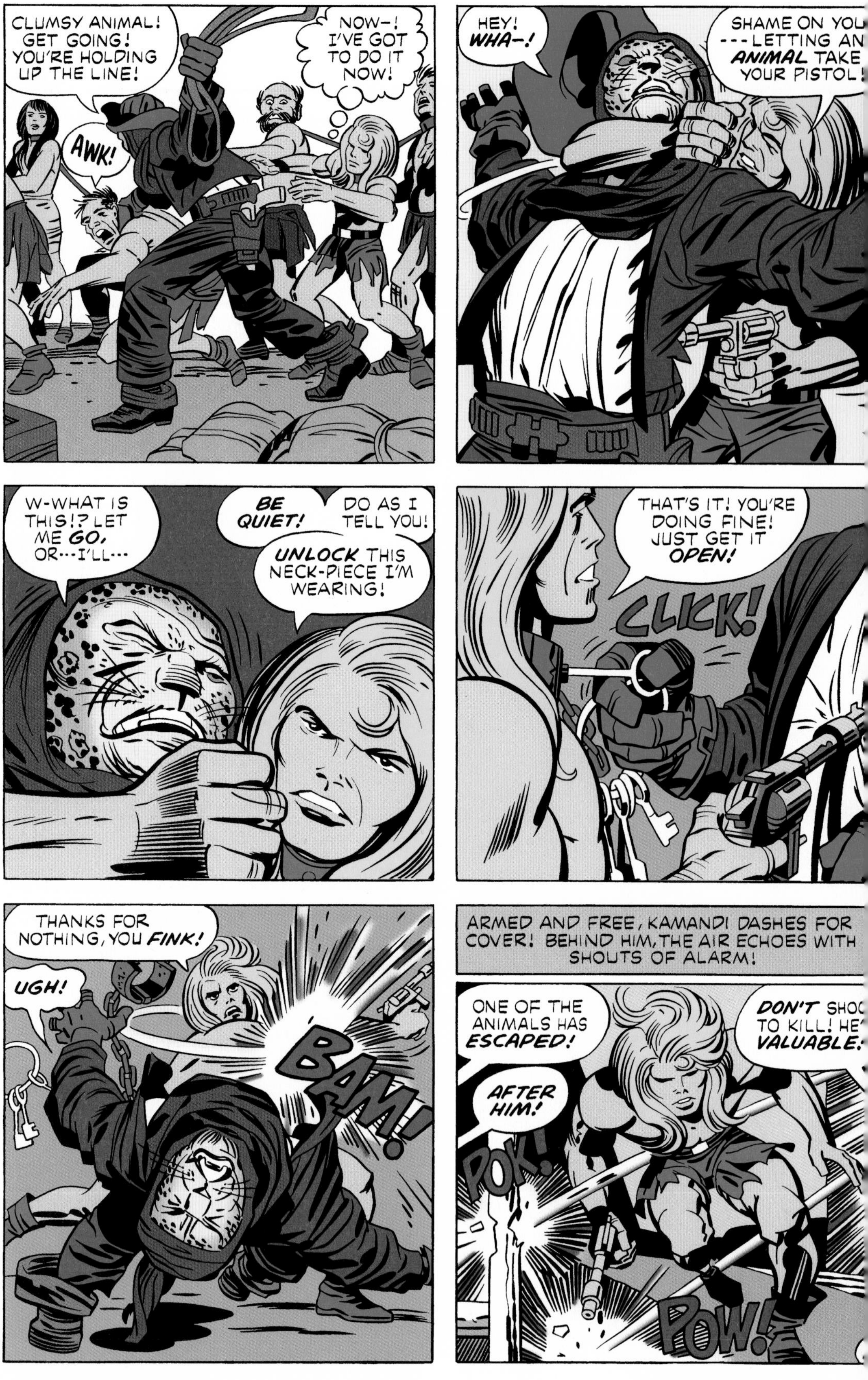
CLUMSY ANIMAL! GET GOING! YOU'RE HOLDING UP THE LINE!
AWK!
NOW-! I'VE GOT TO DO IT NOW!
HEY! WHA-!
SHAME ON YOU ---LETTING AN ANIMAL TAKE YOUR PISTOL!
W-WHAT IS THIS!? LET ME GO, OR···I'LL···
BE QUIET!
DO AS I TELL YOU!
UNLOCK THIS NECK-PIECE I'M WEARING!
THAT'S IT! YOU'RE DOING FINE! JUST GET IT OPEN!
CLICK!
THANKS FOR NOTHING, YOU FINK!
UGH!
BAM!
ARMED AND FREE, KAMANDI DASHES FOR COVER! BEHIND HIM, THE AIR ECHOES WITH SHOUTS OF ALARM!
ONE OF THE ANIMALS HAS ESCAPED!
DON'T SHOO TO KILL! HE' VALUABLE.
AFTER HIM!
POK!
POW!

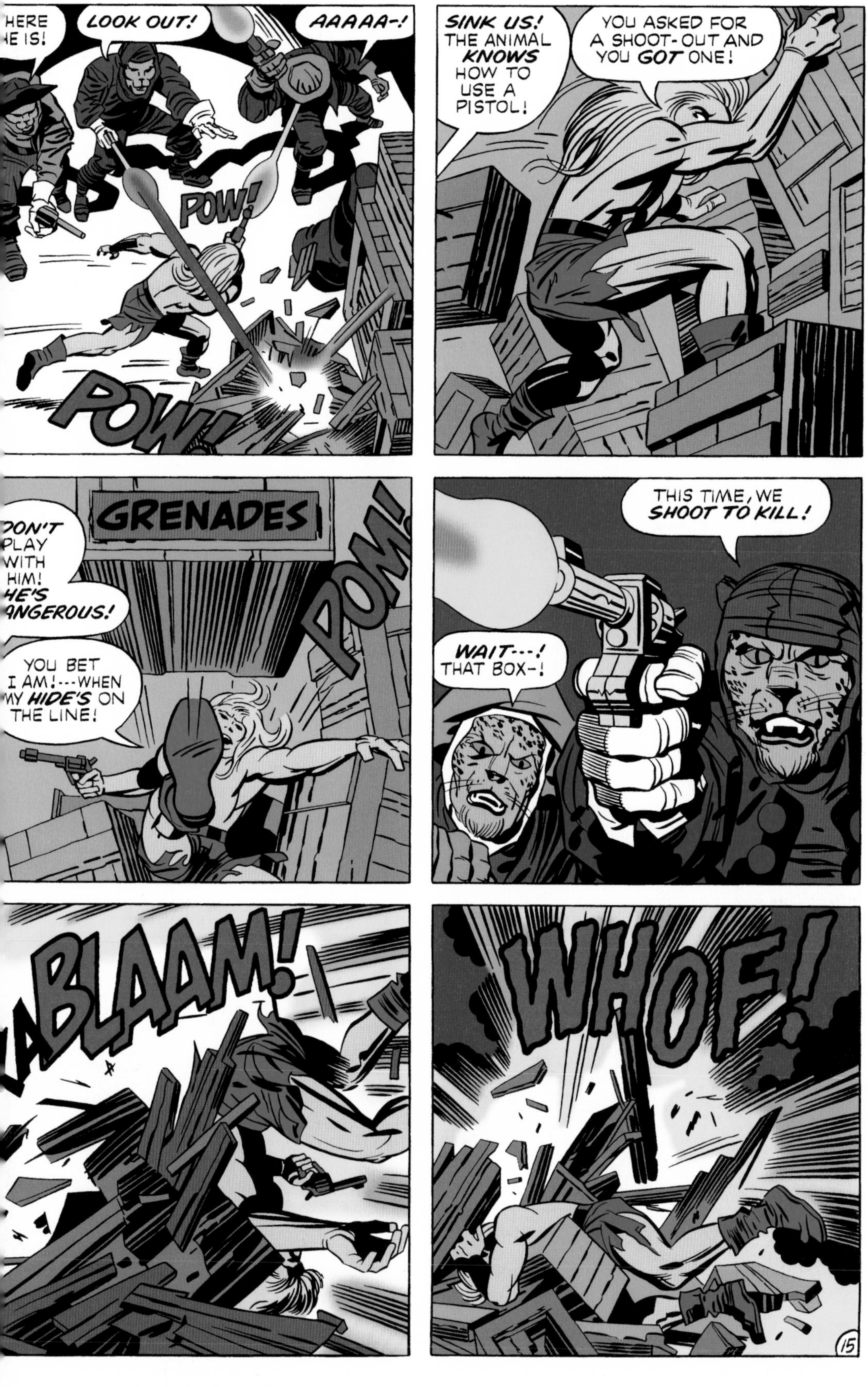
HERE
HE IS!
LOOK OUT!
AAAAA-!
POW!
POW!
SINK US! THE ANIMAL KNOWS HOW TO USE A PISTOL!
YOU ASKED FOR A SHOOT-OUT AND YOU GOT ONE!
GRENADES
DON'T PLAY WITH HIM! HE'S DANGEROUS!
YOU BET I AM!---WHEN MY HIDE'S ON THE LINE!
POM!
THIS TIME, WE SHOOT TO KILL!
WAIT---! THAT BOX-!
KABLAAM!
WHOF!
15

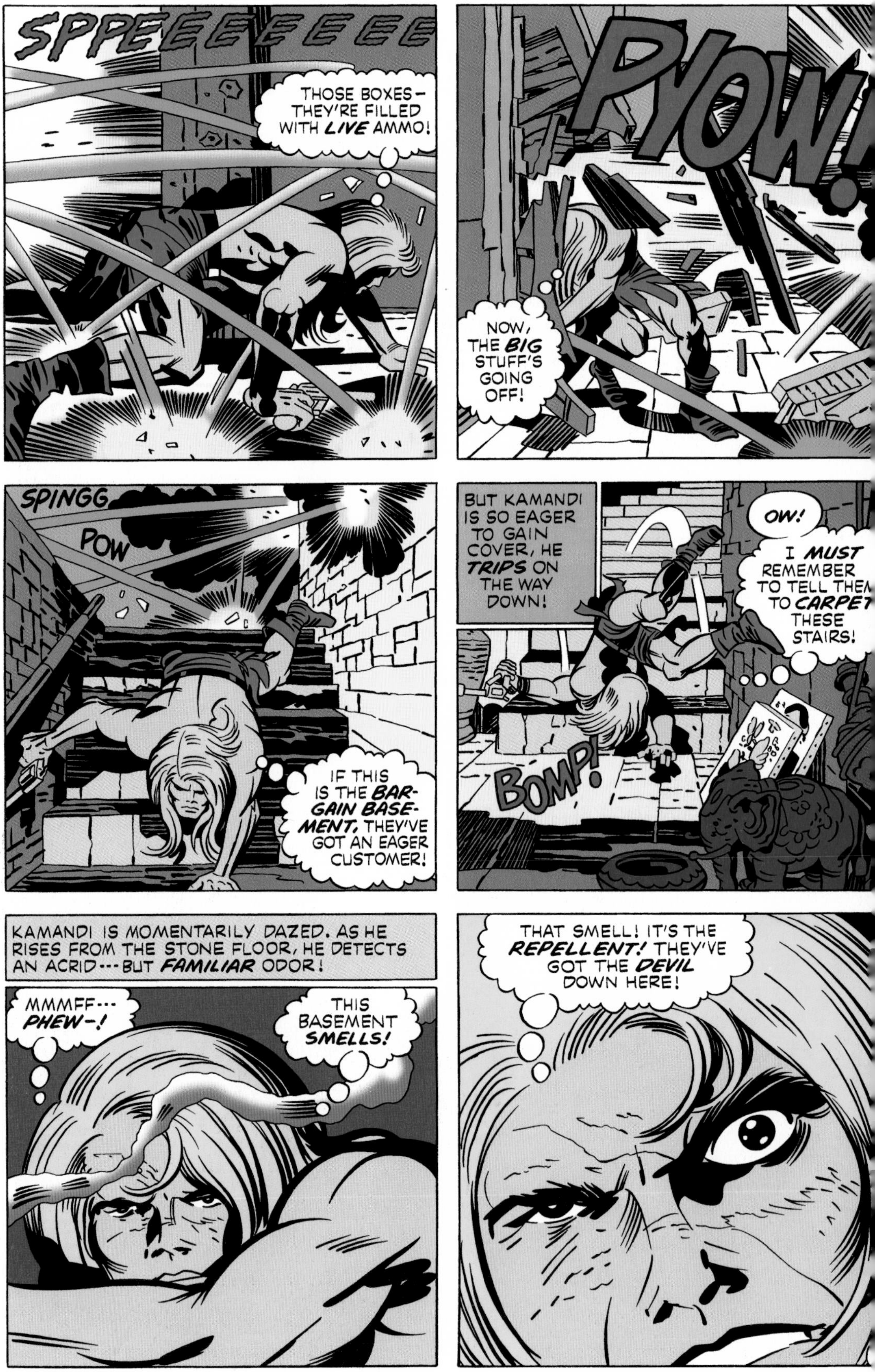
SPPEEEEEEEEE
THOSE BOXES— THEY'RE FILLED WITH LIVE AMMO!
PYOW!
NOW, THE BIG STUFF'S GOING OFF!
SPINGG
POW
IF THIS IS THE BARGAIN BASEMENT, THEY'VE GOT AN EAGER CUSTOMER!
BUT KAMANDI IS SO EAGER TO GAIN COVER, HE TRIPS ON THE WAY DOWN!
OW!
I MUST REMEMBER TO TELL THEM TO CARPET THESE STAIRS!
BOMP!
KAMANDI IS MOMENTARILY DAZED. AS HE RISES FROM THE STONE FLOOR, HE DETECTS AN ACRID--- BUT FAMILIAR ODOR!
MMMFF--- PHEW-!
THIS BASEMENT SMELLS!
THAT SMELL! IT'S THE REPELLENT! THEY'VE GOT THE DEVIL DOWN HERE!

HE WAY TO FREEDOM CAN LEAD THROUGH THE JAWS OF *FEAR* AND *SUPERSTITION* AND KILL A
AN BEFORE HE SEES THE LIGHT. KAMANDI WILL HAVE TO MAKE THAT *DEADLY* RUN, BECAUSE
TE WILL GIVE HIM NO CHOICE! SHE WILL THRUST HIS BACK AGAINST THE WALL AND FACE HIM
WITH THE---

UNMASKED TERROR! CHAPTER 4

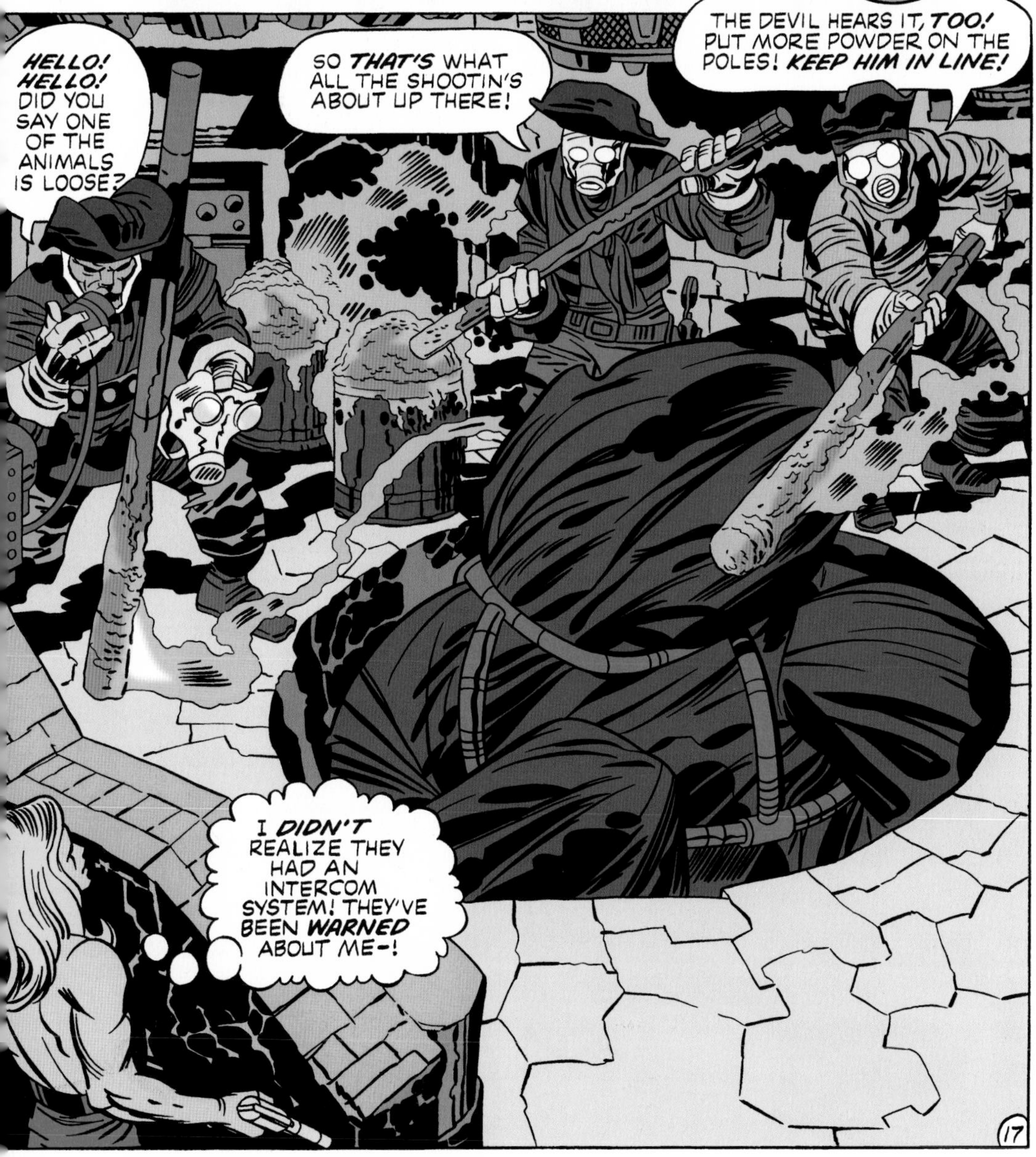
HELLO! HELLO! DID YOU SAY ONE OF THE ANIMALS IS LOOSE?
SO THAT'S WHAT ALL THE SHOOTIN'S ABOUT UP THERE!
THE DEVIL HEARS IT, TOO! PUT MORE POWDER ON THE POLES! KEEP HIM IN LINE!
I DIDN'T REALIZE THEY HAD AN INTERCOM SYSTEM! THEY'VE BEEN WARNED ABOUT ME-!
17

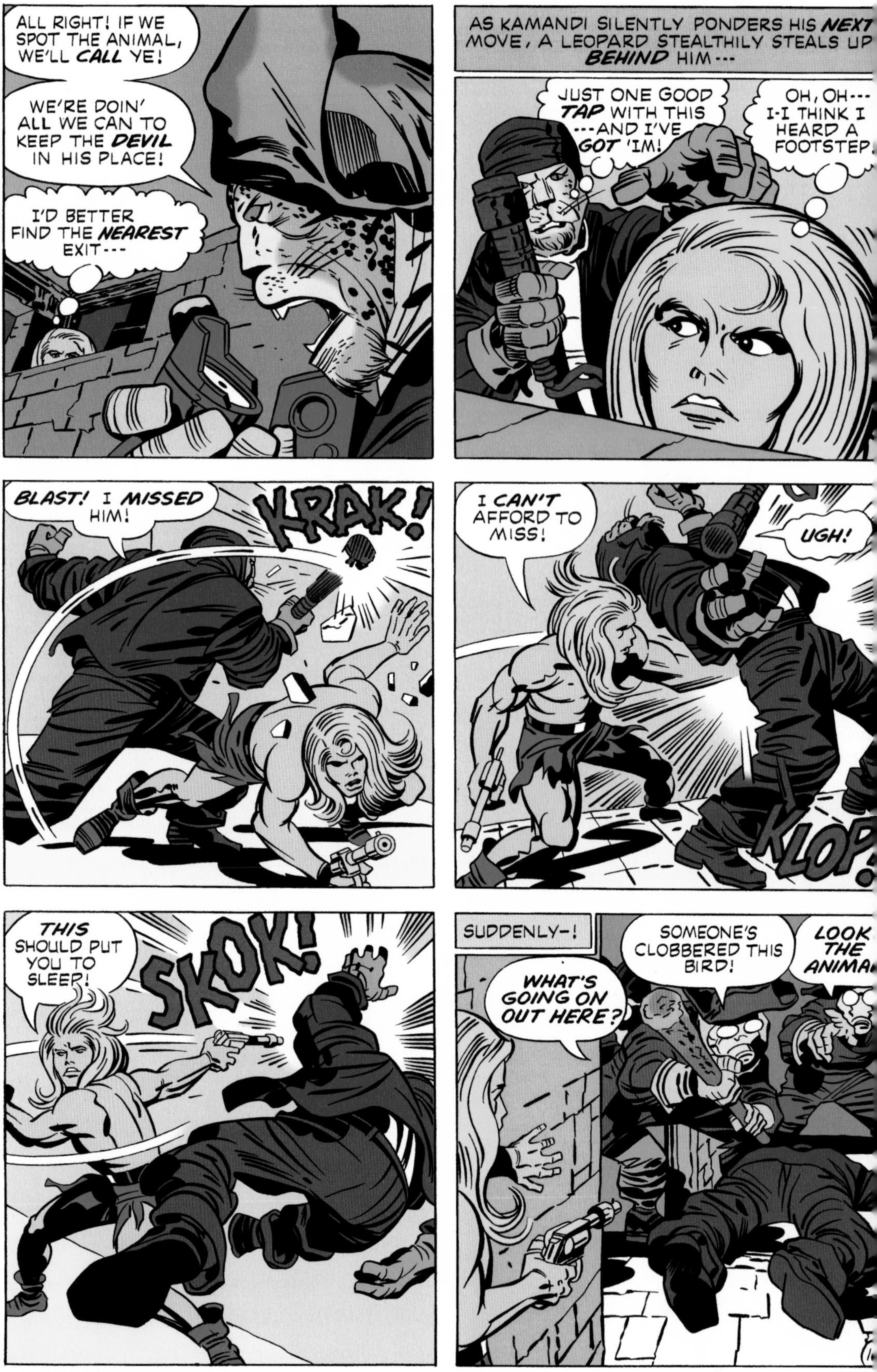

ALL RIGHT! IF WE SPOT THE ANIMAL, WE'LL CALL YE!
WE'RE DOIN' ALL WE CAN TO KEEP THE DEVIL IN HIS PLACE!
I'D BETTER FIND THE NEAREST EXIT---
AS KAMANDI SILENTLY PONDERS HIS NEXT MOVE, A LEOPARD STEALTHILY STEALS UP BEHIND HIM---
JUST ONE GOOD TAP WITH THIS ---AND I'VE GOT 'IM!
OH, OH--- I-I THINK I HEARD A FOOTSTEP!
BLAST! I MISSED HIM!
KRAK!
I CAN'T AFFORD TO MISS!
UGH!
KLOP!
THIS SHOULD PUT YOU TO SLEEP!
SKOK!
SUDDENLY-!
WHAT'S GOING ON OUT HERE?
SOMEONE'S CLOBBERED THIS BIRD!

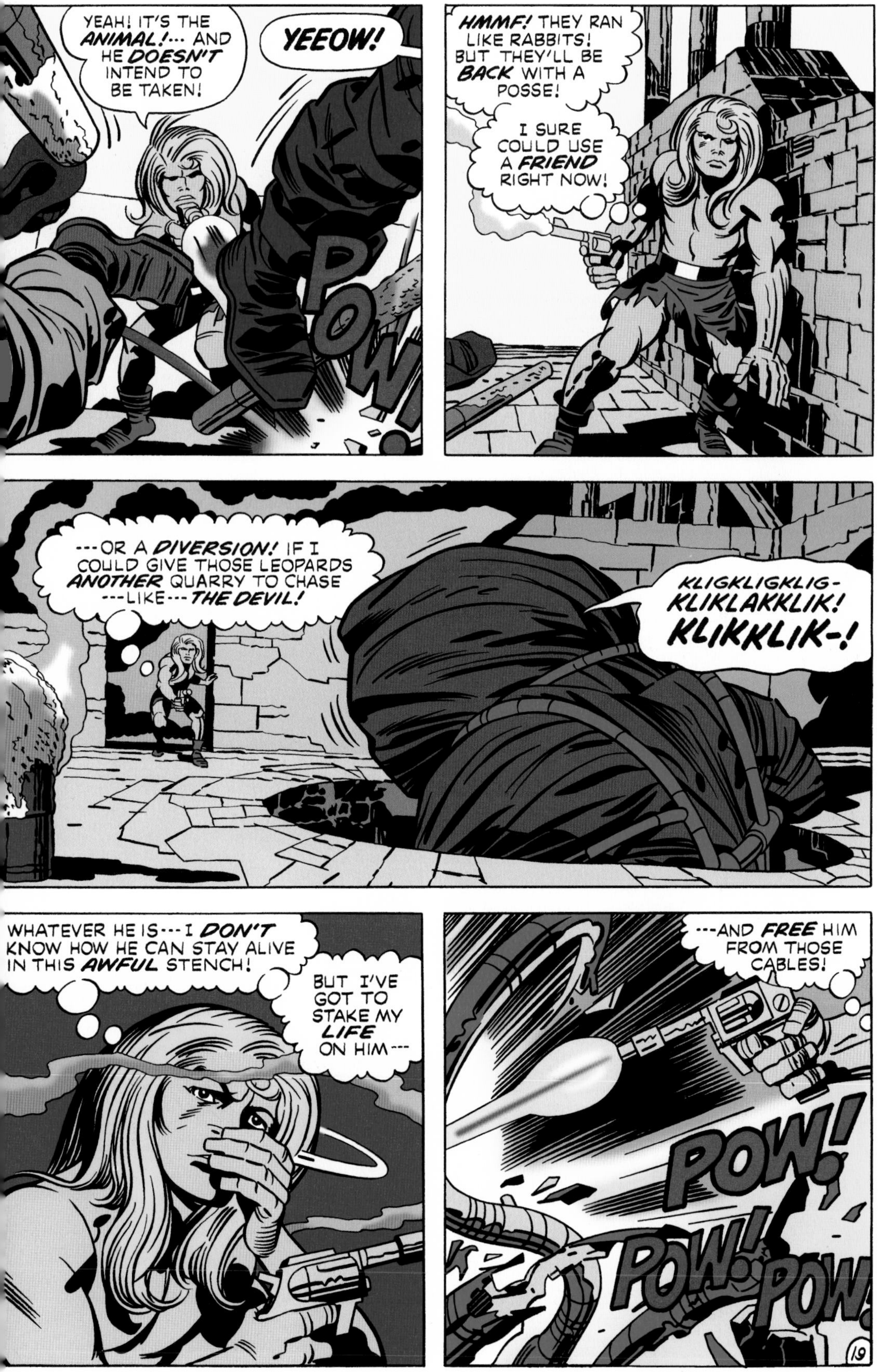
YEAH! IT'S THE ANIMAL!--- AND HE DOESN'T INTEND TO BE TAKEN!
YEEOW!
POW!
HMMF! THEY RAN LIKE RABBITS! BUT THEY'LL BE BACK WITH A POSSE!
I SURE COULD USE A FRIEND RIGHT NOW!
---OR A DIVERSION! IF I COULD GIVE THOSE LEOPARDS ANOTHER QUARRY TO CHASE ---LIKE--- THE DEVIL!
KLIGKLIGKLIG-KLIKLAKKLIK! KLIKKLIK-!
WHATEVER HE IS--- I DON'T KNOW HOW HE CAN STAY ALIVE IN THIS AWFUL STENCH!
BUT I'VE GOT TO STAKE MY LIFE ON HIM---
---AND FREE HIM FROM THOSE CABLES!
POW!
POW!
POW!
19

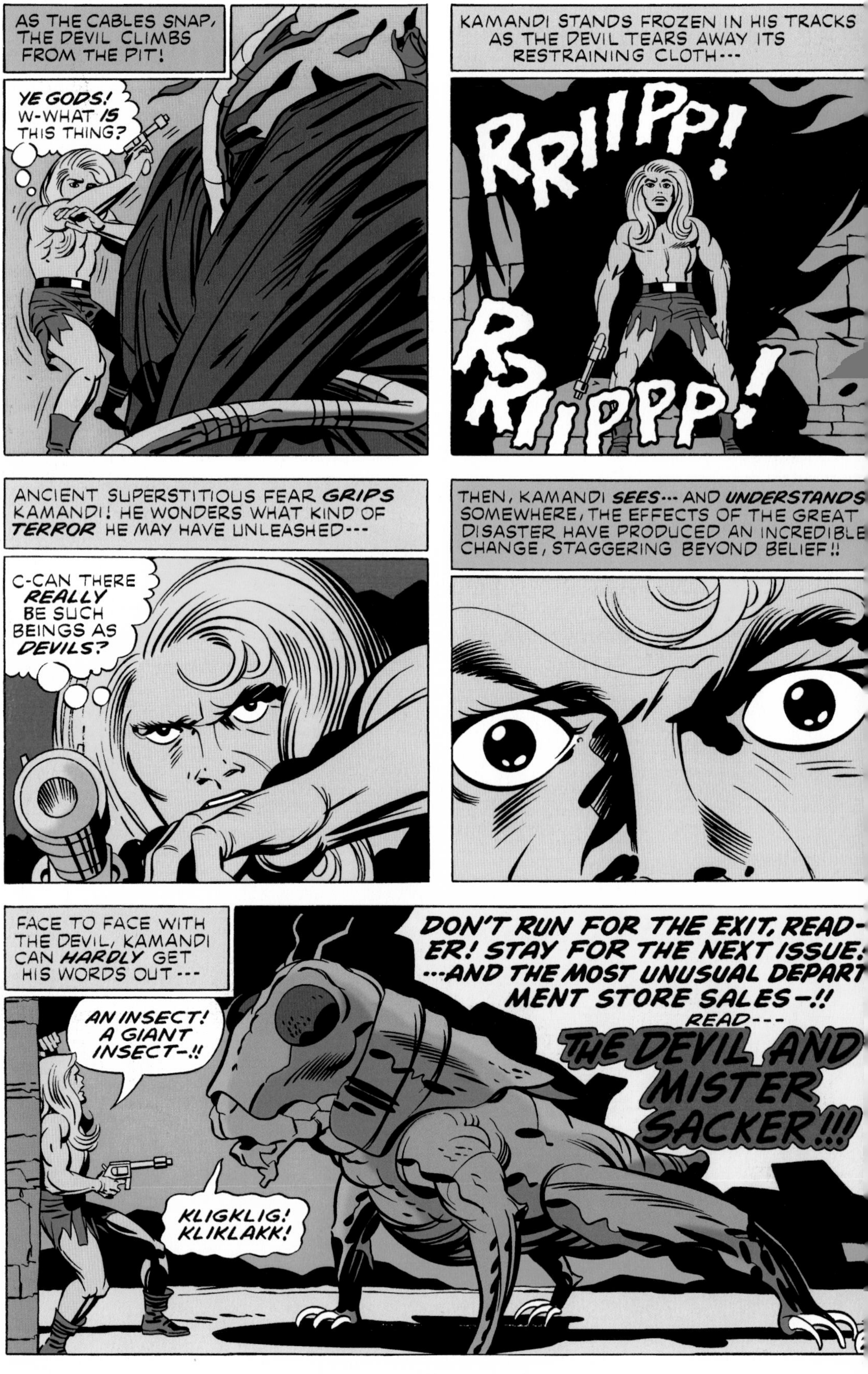
AS THE CABLES SNAP, THE DEVIL CLIMBS FROM THE PIT!
YE GODS! W-WHAT IS THIS THING?
KAMANDI STANDS FROZEN IN HIS TRACKS AS THE DEVIL TEARS AWAY ITS RESTRAINING CLOTH---
RRIIPP!
RRIIPPP!
ANCIENT SUPERSTITIOUS FEAR GRIPS KAMANDI! HE WONDERS WHAT KIND OF TERROR HE MAY HAVE UNLEASHED---
C-CAN THERE REALLY BE SUCH BEINGS AS DEVILS?
THEN, KAMANDI SEES--- AND UNDERSTANDS SOMEWHERE, THE EFFECTS OF THE GREAT DISASTER HAVE PRODUCED AN INCREDIBLE CHANGE, STAGGERING BEYOND BELIEF!!
FACE TO FACE WITH THE DEVIL, KAMANDI CAN HARDLY GET HIS WORDS OUT---
AN INSECT! A GIANT INSECT-!!
KLIGKLIG! KLIKLAKK!
DON'T RUN FOR THE EXIT, READER! STAY FOR THE NEXT ISSUE! ---AND THE MOST UNUSUAL DEPARTMENT STORE SALES-!!
READ---
THE DEVIL AND MISTER SACKER!!!

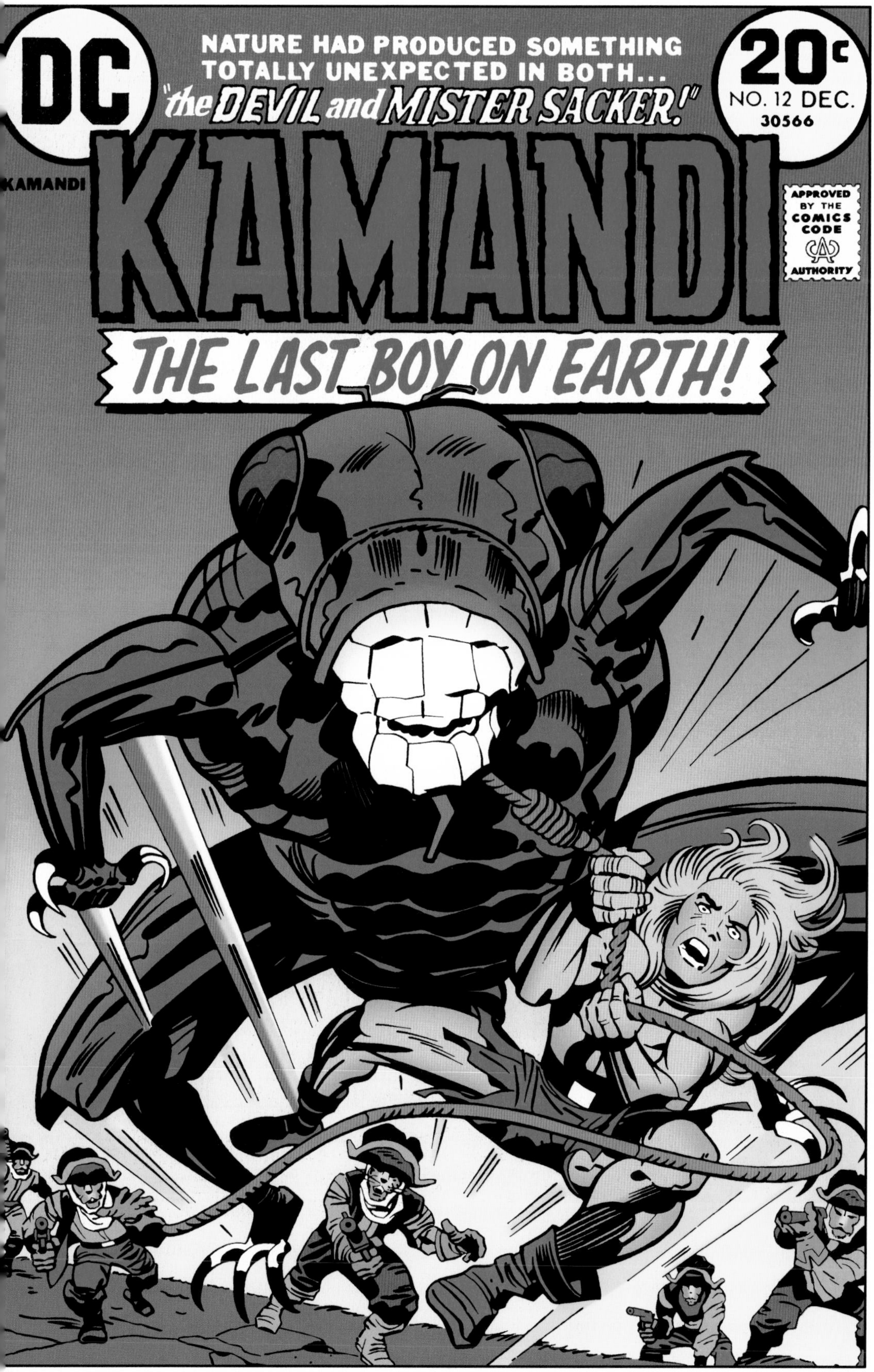
DC
NATURE HAD PRODUCED SOMETHING TOTALLY UNEXPECTED IN BOTH...
"the DEVIL and MISTER SACKER!"
20¢
NO. 12 DEC.
30566
KAMANDI
KAMANDI
APPROVED BY THE COMICS CODE AUTHORITY
THE LAST BOY ON EARTH!

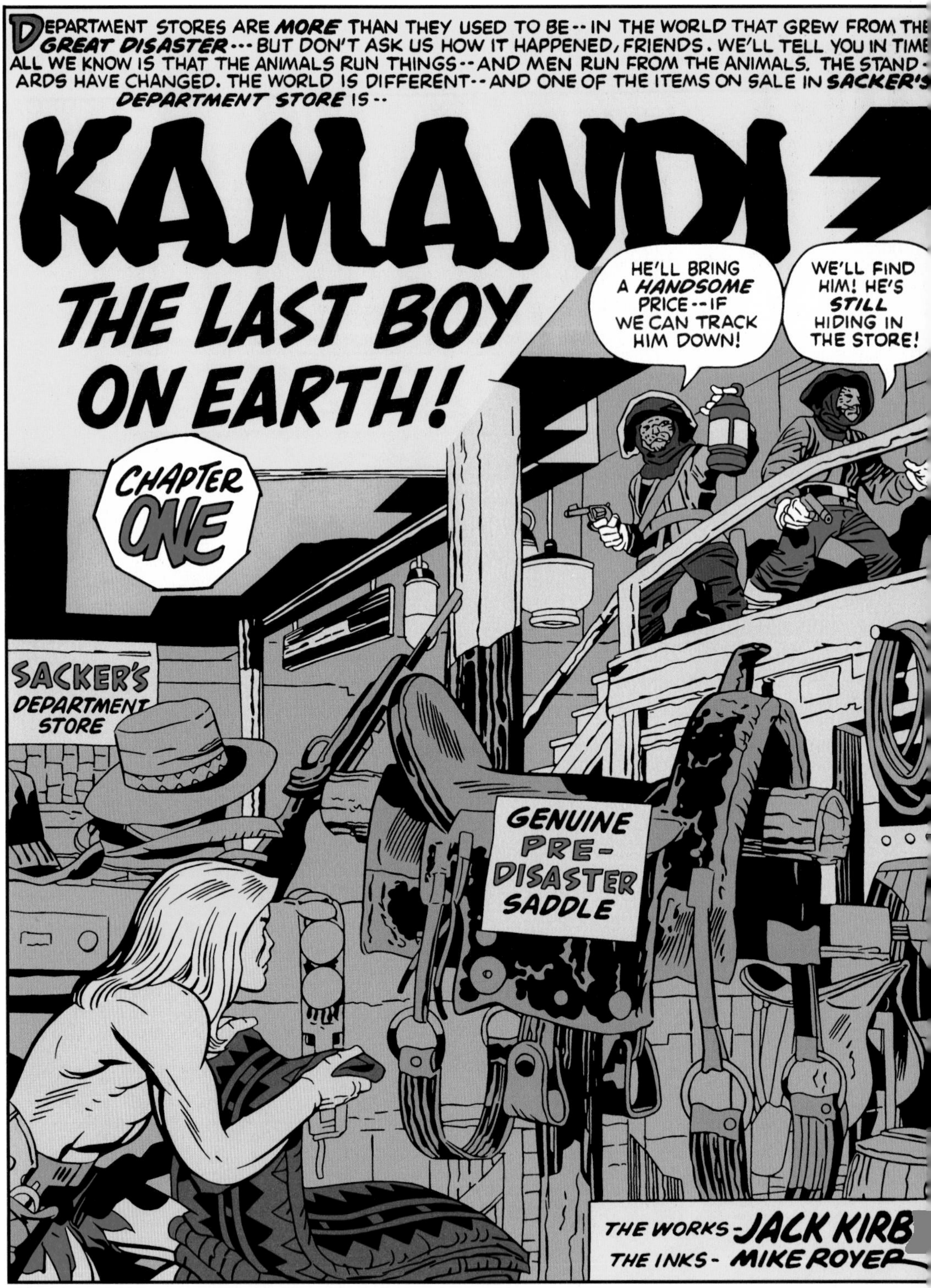
DEPARTMENT STORES ARE MORE THAN THEY USED TO BE -- IN THE WORLD THAT GREW FROM THE GREAT DISASTER --- BUT DON'T ASK US HOW IT HAPPENED, FRIENDS. WE'LL TELL YOU IN TIME. ALL WE KNOW IS THAT THE ANIMALS RUN THINGS -- AND MEN RUN FROM THE ANIMALS. THE STANDARDS HAVE CHANGED. THE WORLD IS DIFFERENT -- AND ONE OF THE ITEMS ON SALE IN SACKER'S DEPARTMENT STORE IS --
KAMANDI
THE LAST BOY ON EARTH!
CHAPTER ONE
HE'LL BRING A HANDSOME PRICE -- IF WE CAN TRACK HIM DOWN!
WE'LL FIND HIM! HE'S STILL HIDING IN THE STORE!
SACKER'S DEPARTMENT STORE
GENUINE PRE-DISASTER SADDLE
THE WORKS - JACK KIRB
THE INKS - MIKE ROYER

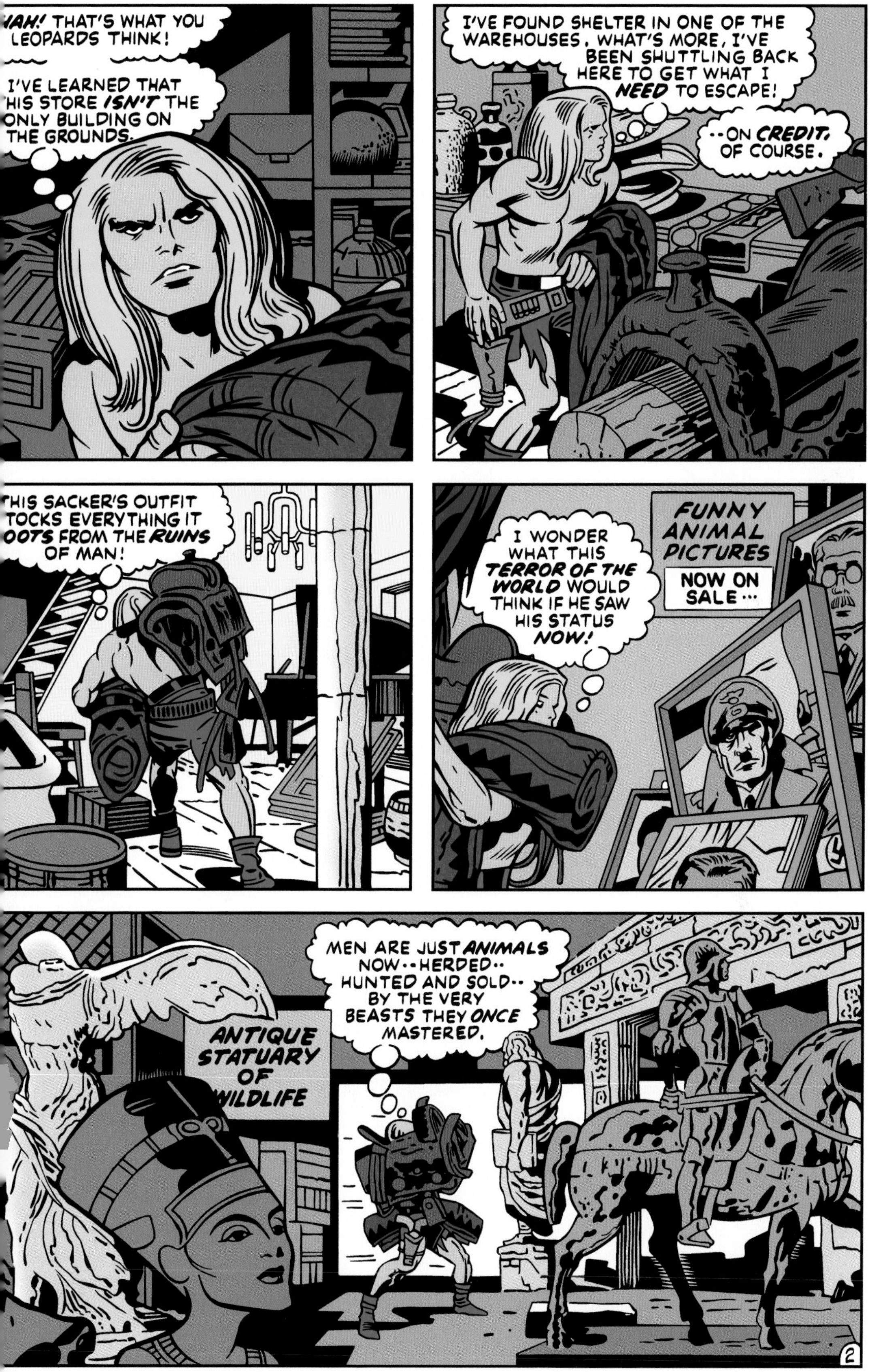

HAH! THAT'S WHAT YOU LEOPARDS THINK!
I'VE LEARNED THAT THIS STORE ISN'T THE ONLY BUILDING ON THE GROUNDS.
I'VE FOUND SHELTER IN ONE OF THE WAREHOUSES. WHAT'S MORE, I'VE BEEN SHUTTLING BACK HERE TO GET WHAT I NEED TO ESCAPE!
--ON CREDIT, OF COURSE.
THIS SACKER'S OUTFIT STOCKS EVERYTHING IT LOOTS FROM THE RUINS OF MAN!
I WONDER WHAT THIS TERROR OF THE WORLD WOULD THINK IF HE SAW HIS STATUS NOW!
FUNNY ANIMAL PICTURES
NOW ON SALE...
MEN ARE JUST ANIMALS NOW--HERDED--HUNTED AND SOLD--BY THE VERY BEASTS THEY ONCE MASTERED.
ANTIQUE STATUARY OF WILDLIFE
2

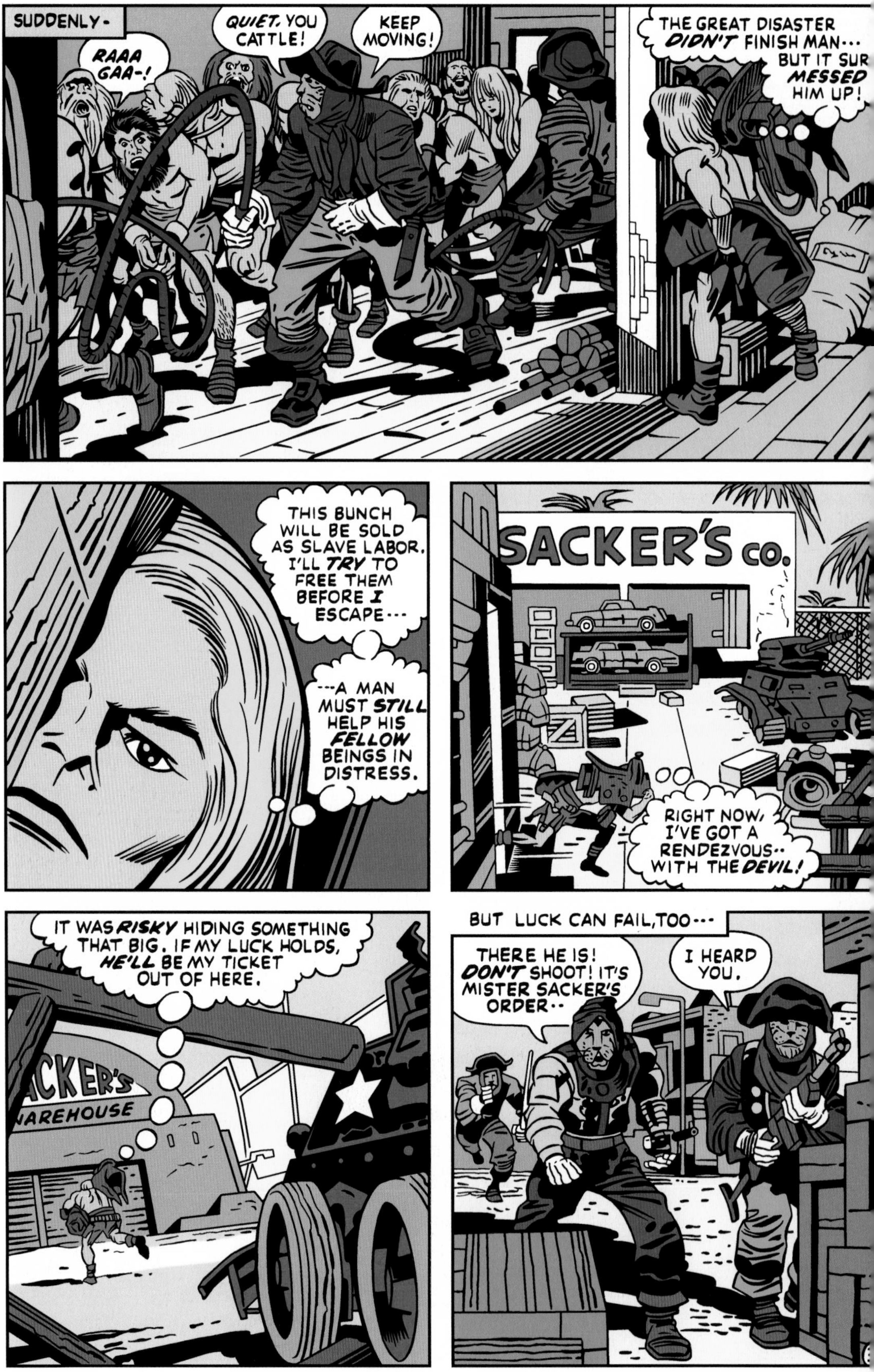
SUDDENLY-
RAAA GAA-!
QUIET, YOU CATTLE!
KEEP MOVING!
THE GREAT DISASTER DIDN'T FINISH MAN... BUT IT SUR MESSED HIM UP!
THIS BUNCH WILL BE SOLD AS SLAVE LABOR. I'LL TRY TO FREE THEM BEFORE I ESCAPE---
---A MAN MUST STILL HELP HIS FELLOW BEINGS IN DISTRESS.
SACKER'S co.
RIGHT NOW, I'VE GOT A RENDEZVOUS.. WITH THE DEVIL!
IT WAS RISKY HIDING SOMETHING THAT BIG. IF MY LUCK HOLDS, HE'LL BE MY TICKET OUT OF HERE.
ACKER'S
AREHOUSE
BUT LUCK CAN FAIL, TOO---
THERE HE IS! DON'T SHOOT! IT'S MISTER SACKER'S ORDER..
I HEARD YOU.

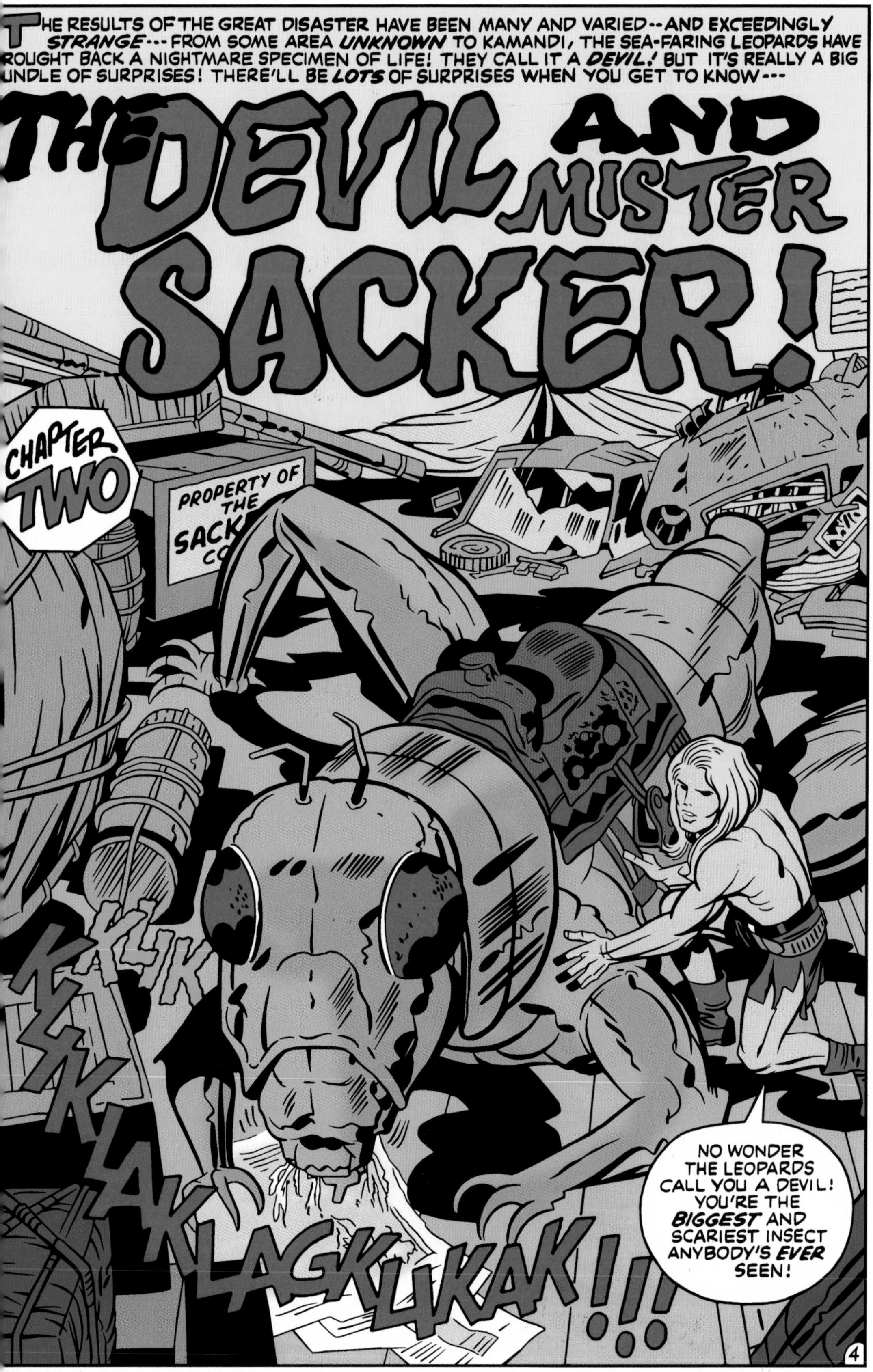
THE RESULTS OF THE GREAT DISASTER HAVE BEEN MANY AND VARIED--AND EXCEEDINGLY STRANGE--- FROM SOME AREA UNKNOWN TO KAMANDI, THE SEA-FARING LEOPARDS HAVE ROUGHT BACK A NIGHTMARE SPECIMEN OF LIFE! THEY CALL IT A DEVIL! BUT IT'S REALLY A BIG UNDLE OF SURPRISES! THERE'LL BE LOTS OF SURPRISES WHEN YOU GET TO KNOW---
THE DEVIL AND MISTER SACKER!
CHAPTER TWO
PROPERTY OF THE SACK CO
KLIK KLIK KLAK KLAGKLIKAK!!!
NO WONDER THE LEOPARDS CALL YOU A DEVIL! YOU'RE THE BIGGEST AND SCARIEST INSECT ANYBODY'S EVER SEEN!
4

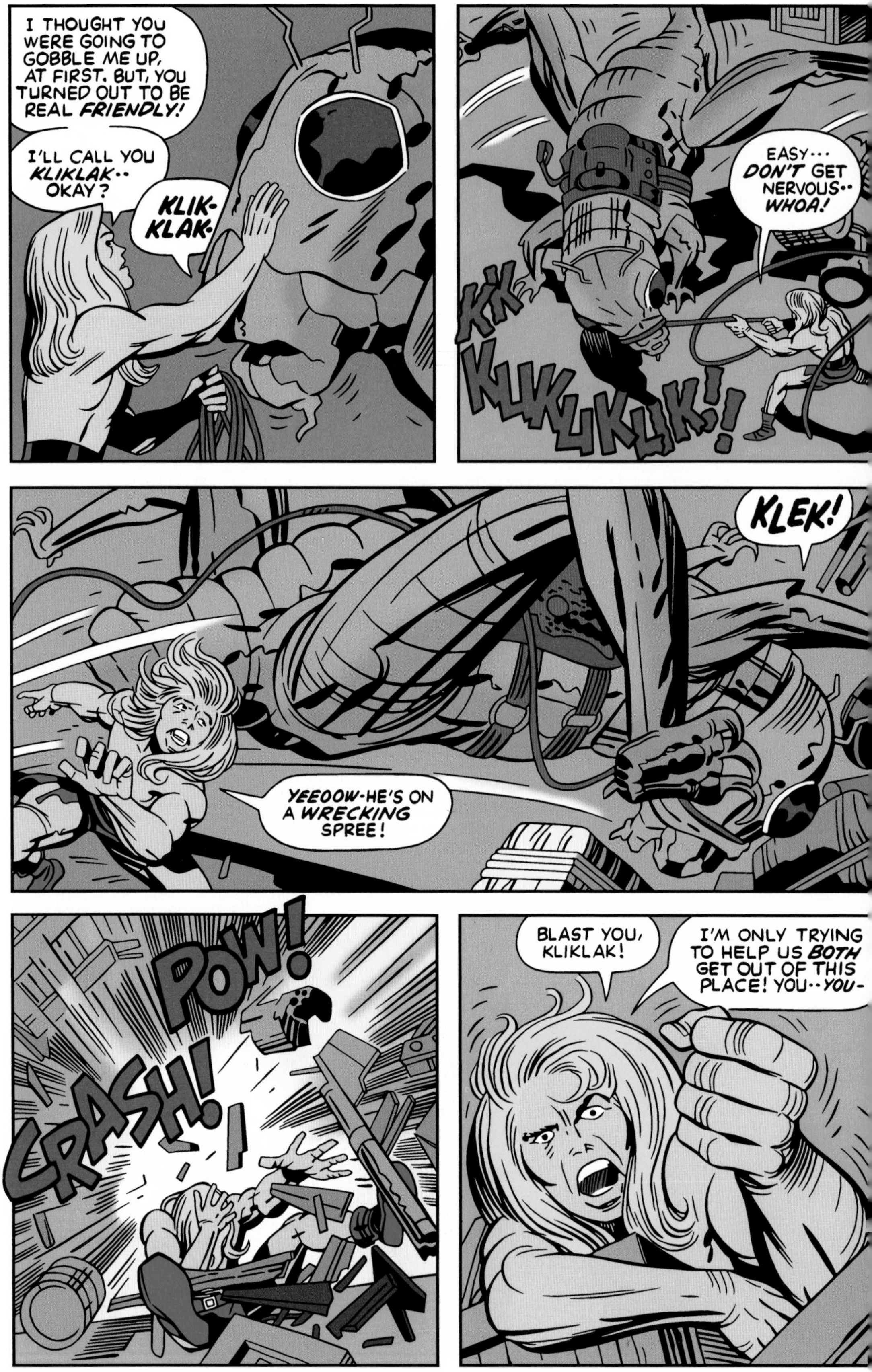
I THOUGHT YOU WERE GOING TO GOBBLE ME UP, AT FIRST. BUT, YOU TURNED OUT TO BE REAL FRIENDLY!
I'LL CALL YOU KLIKLAK.. OKAY?
KLIK-KLAK-
EASY... DON'T GET NERVOUS.. WHOA!
KK
KLIKLIKLIKLIK!!
KLEK!
YEEOOW-HE'S ON A WRECKING SPREE!
POW!
CRASH!
BLAST YOU, KLIKLAK!
I'M ONLY TRYING TO HELP US BOTH GET OUT OF THIS PLACE! YOU..YOU-

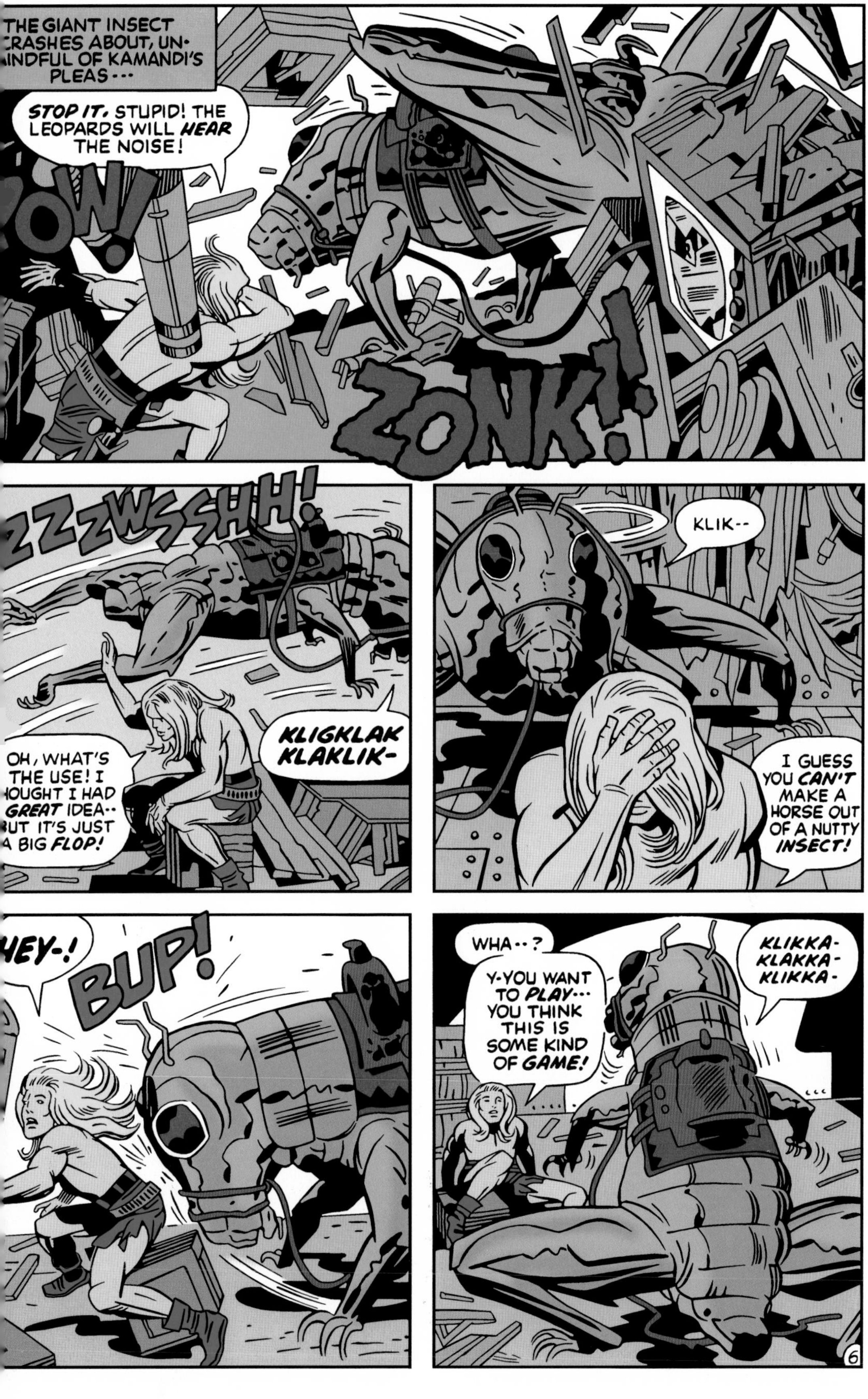
THE GIANT INSECT CRASHES ABOUT, UN-MINDFUL OF KAMANDI'S PLEAS---
STOP IT, STUPID! THE LEOPARDS WILL HEAR THE NOISE!
POW!
ZONK!!
ZZZZWSSHH!
OH, WHAT'S THE USE! I THOUGHT I HAD GREAT IDEA-- BUT IT'S JUST A BIG FLOP!
KLIGKLAK KLAKLIK-
KLIK--
I GUESS YOU CAN'T MAKE A HORSE OUT OF A NUTTY INSECT!
HEY-!
BUP!
WHA--?
Y-YOU WANT TO PLAY--- YOU THINK THIS IS SOME KIND OF GAME!
KLIKKA-KLAKKA-KLIKKA-
6

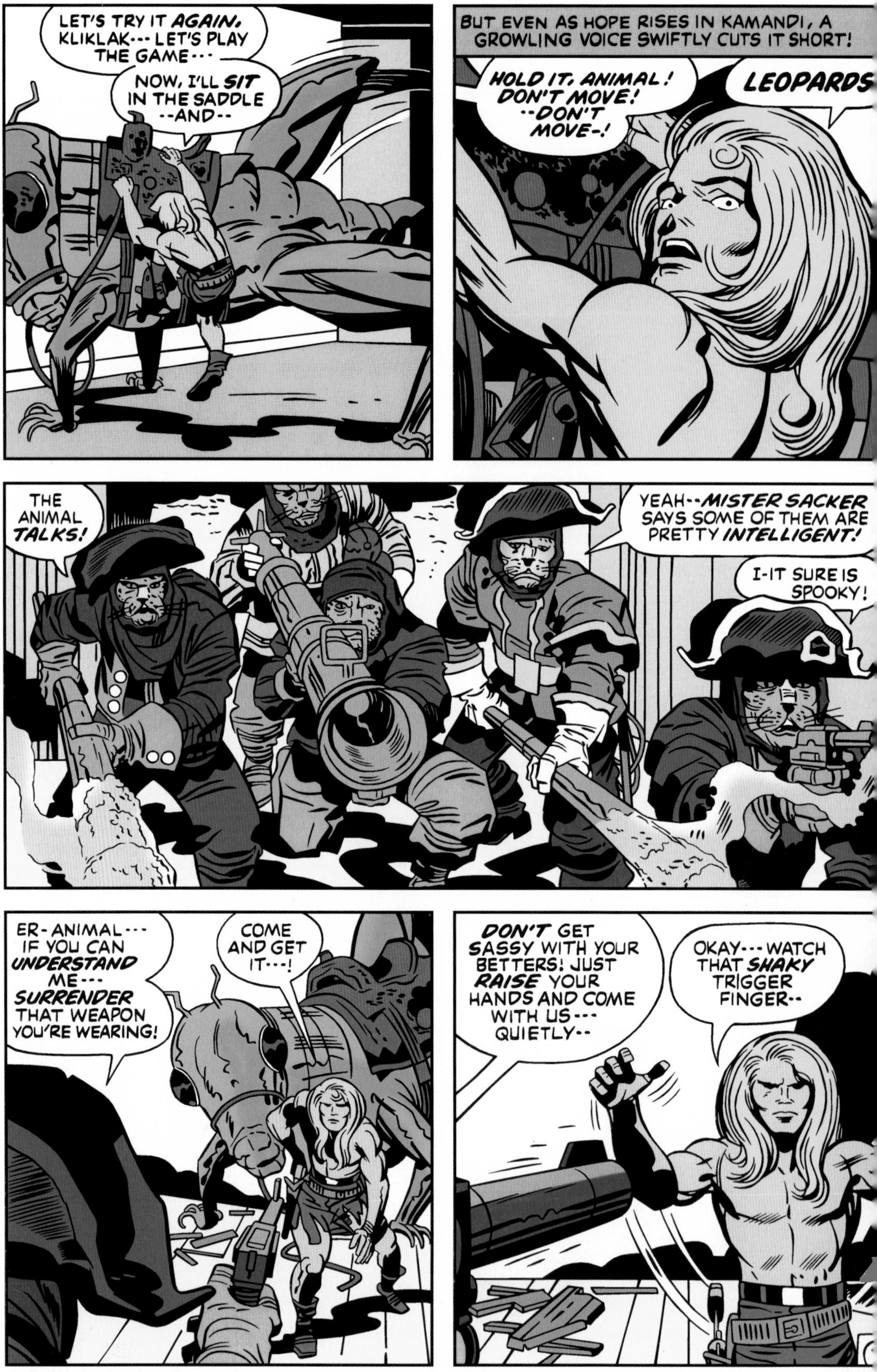
LET'S TRY IT AGAIN, KLIKLAK--- LET'S PLAY THE GAME---
NOW, I'LL SIT IN THE SADDLE --AND--
BUT EVEN AS HOPE RISES IN KAMANDI, A GROWLING VOICE SWIFTLY CUTS IT SHORT!
HOLD IT, ANIMAL! DON'T MOVE! --DON'T MOVE-!
LEOPARDS
THE ANIMAL TALKS!
YEAH--MISTER SACKER SAYS SOME OF THEM ARE PRETTY INTELLIGENT!
I-IT SURE IS SPOOKY!
ER-ANIMAL--- IF YOU CAN UNDERSTAND ME--- SURRENDER THAT WEAPON YOU'RE WEARING!
COME AND GET IT---!
DON'T GET SASSY WITH YOUR BETTERS! JUST RAISE YOUR HANDS AND COME WITH US--- QUIETLY--
OKAY--- WATCH THAT SHAKY TRIGGER FINGER--

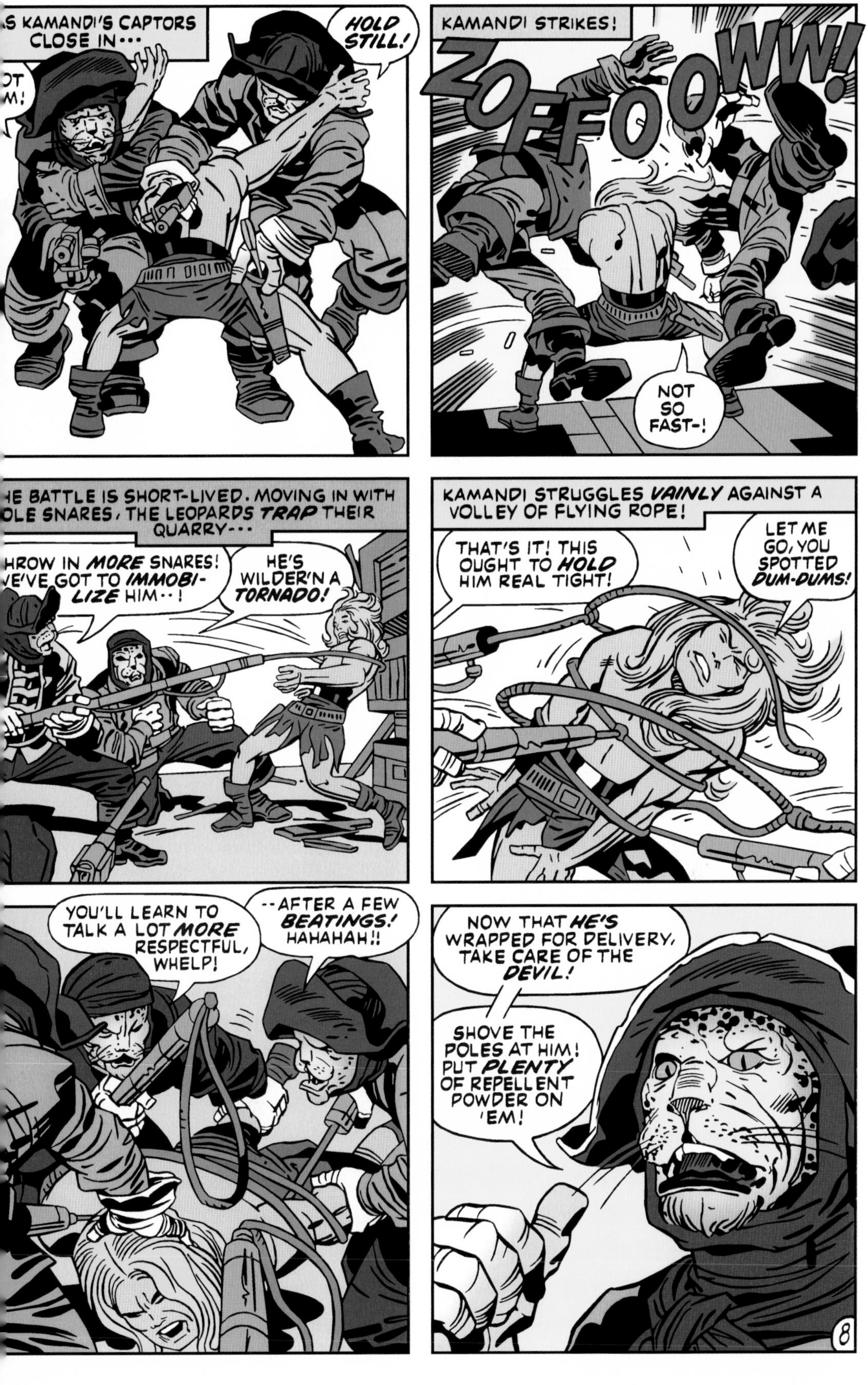
S KAMANDI'S CAPTORS CLOSE IN···
HOLD STILL!
KAMANDI STRIKES!
ZOFFOOWW!
NOT SO FAST-!
E BATTLE IS SHORT-LIVED. MOVING IN WITH OLE SNARES, THE LEOPARDS TRAP THEIR QUARRY···
HROW IN MORE SNARES! VE'VE GOT TO IMMOBI-LIZE HIM··!
HE'S WILDER'N A TORNADO!
KAMANDI STRUGGLES VAINLY AGAINST A VOLLEY OF FLYING ROPE!
THAT'S IT! THIS OUGHT TO HOLD HIM REAL TIGHT!
LET ME GO, YOU SPOTTED DUM-DUMS!
YOU'LL LEARN TO TALK A LOT MORE RESPECTFUL, WHELP!
--AFTER A FEW BEATINGS! HAHAHAH!!
NOW THAT HE'S WRAPPED FOR DELIVERY, TAKE CARE OF THE DEVIL!
SHOVE THE POLES AT HIM! PUT PLENTY OF REPELLENT POWDER ON 'EM!
8

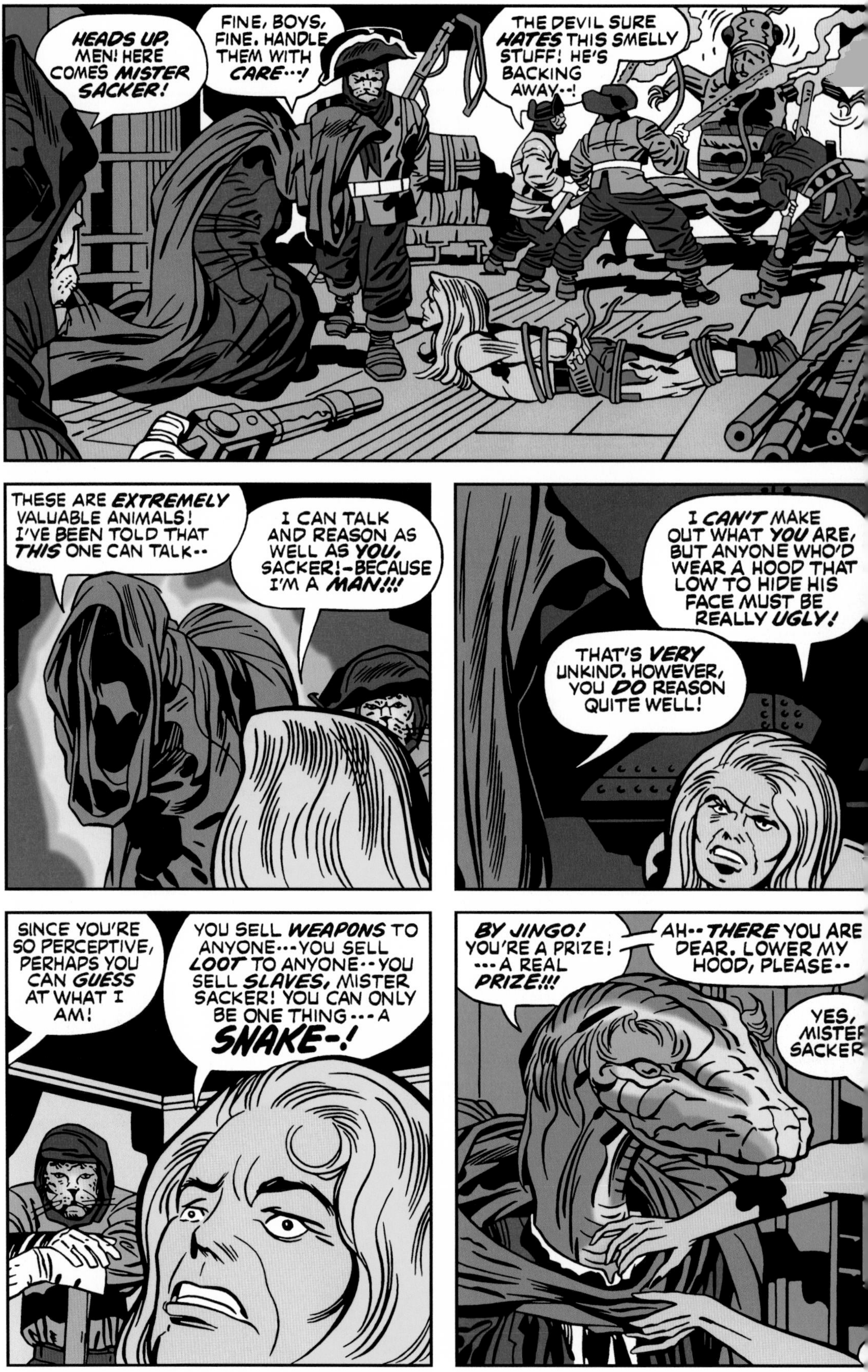
HEADS UP, MEN! HERE COMES MISTER SACKER!
FINE, BOYS, FINE. HANDLE THEM WITH CARE--!
THE DEVIL SURE HATES THIS SMELLY STUFF! HE'S BACKING AWAY--!
THESE ARE EXTREMELY VALUABLE ANIMALS! I'VE BEEN TOLD THAT THIS ONE CAN TALK--
I CAN TALK AND REASON AS WELL AS YOU, SACKER!--BECAUSE I'M A MAN!!!
I CAN'T MAKE OUT WHAT YOU ARE, BUT ANYONE WHO'D WEAR A HOOD THAT LOW TO HIDE HIS FACE MUST BE REALLY UGLY!
THAT'S VERY UNKIND. HOWEVER, YOU DO REASON QUITE WELL!
SINCE YOU'RE SO PERCEPTIVE, PERHAPS YOU CAN GUESS AT WHAT I AM!
YOU SELL WEAPONS TO ANYONE---YOU SELL LOOT TO ANYONE--YOU SELL SLAVES, MISTER SACKER! YOU CAN ONLY BE ONE THING--- A SNAKE--!
BY JINGO! YOU'RE A PRIZE! ---A REAL PRIZE!!!
AH--THERE YOU ARE DEAR. LOWER MY HOOD, PLEASE--
YES, MISTEF SACKER

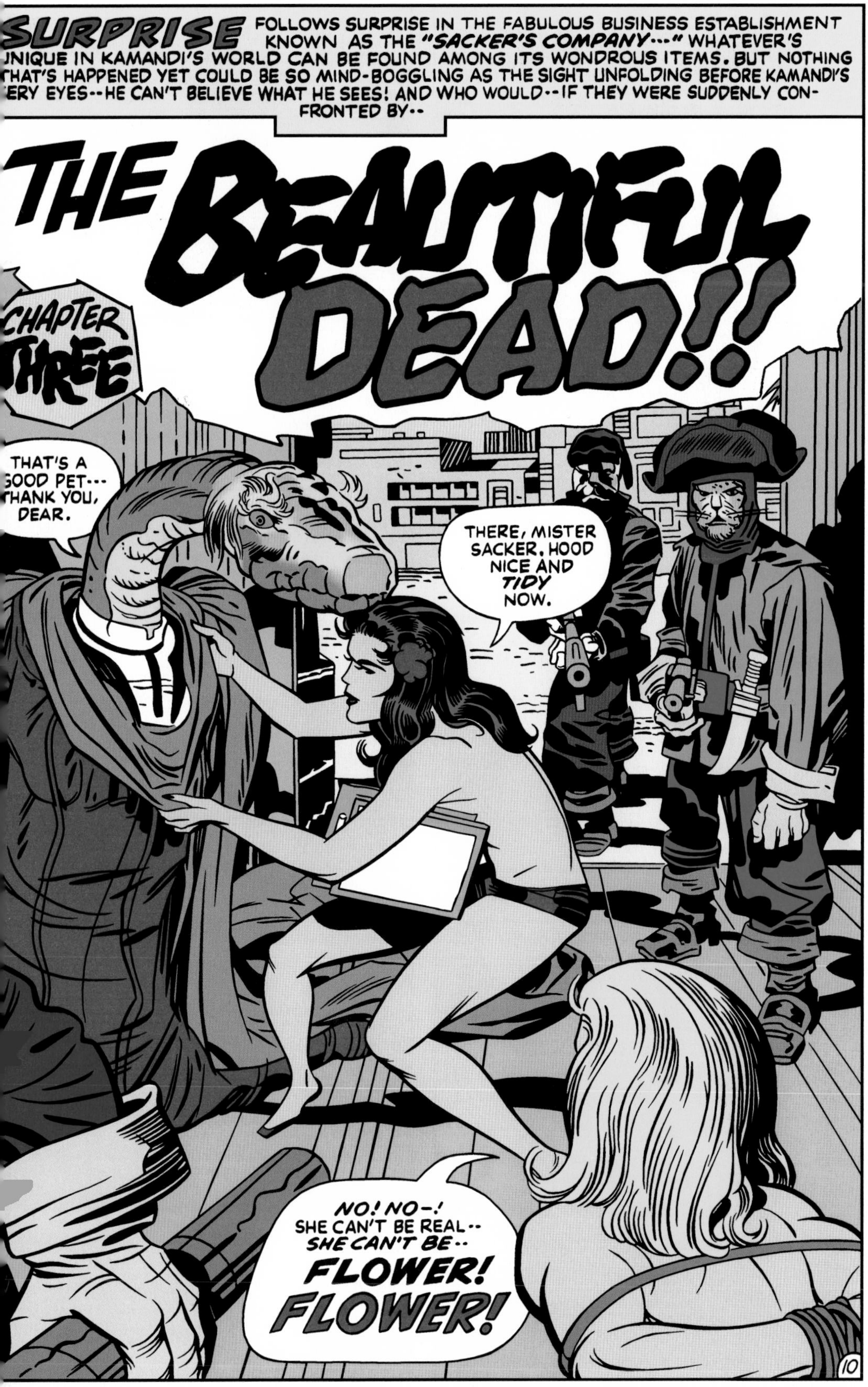
SURPRISE FOLLOWS SURPRISE IN THE FABULOUS BUSINESS ESTABLISHMENT KNOWN AS THE "SACKER'S COMPANY---" WHATEVER'S UNIQUE IN KAMANDI'S WORLD CAN BE FOUND AMONG ITS WONDROUS ITEMS. BUT NOTHING THAT'S HAPPENED YET COULD BE SO MIND-BOGGLING AS THE SIGHT UNFOLDING BEFORE KAMANDI'S VERY EYES--HE CAN'T BELIEVE WHAT HE SEES! AND WHO WOULD--IF THEY WERE SUDDENLY CONFRONTED BY--
THE BEAUTIFUL DEAD!!
CHAPTER THREE
THAT'S A GOOD PET--- THANK YOU, DEAR.
THERE, MISTER SACKER, HOOD NICE AND TIDY NOW.
NO! NO-! SHE CAN'T BE REAL-- SHE CAN'T BE-- FLOWER! FLOWER!
10

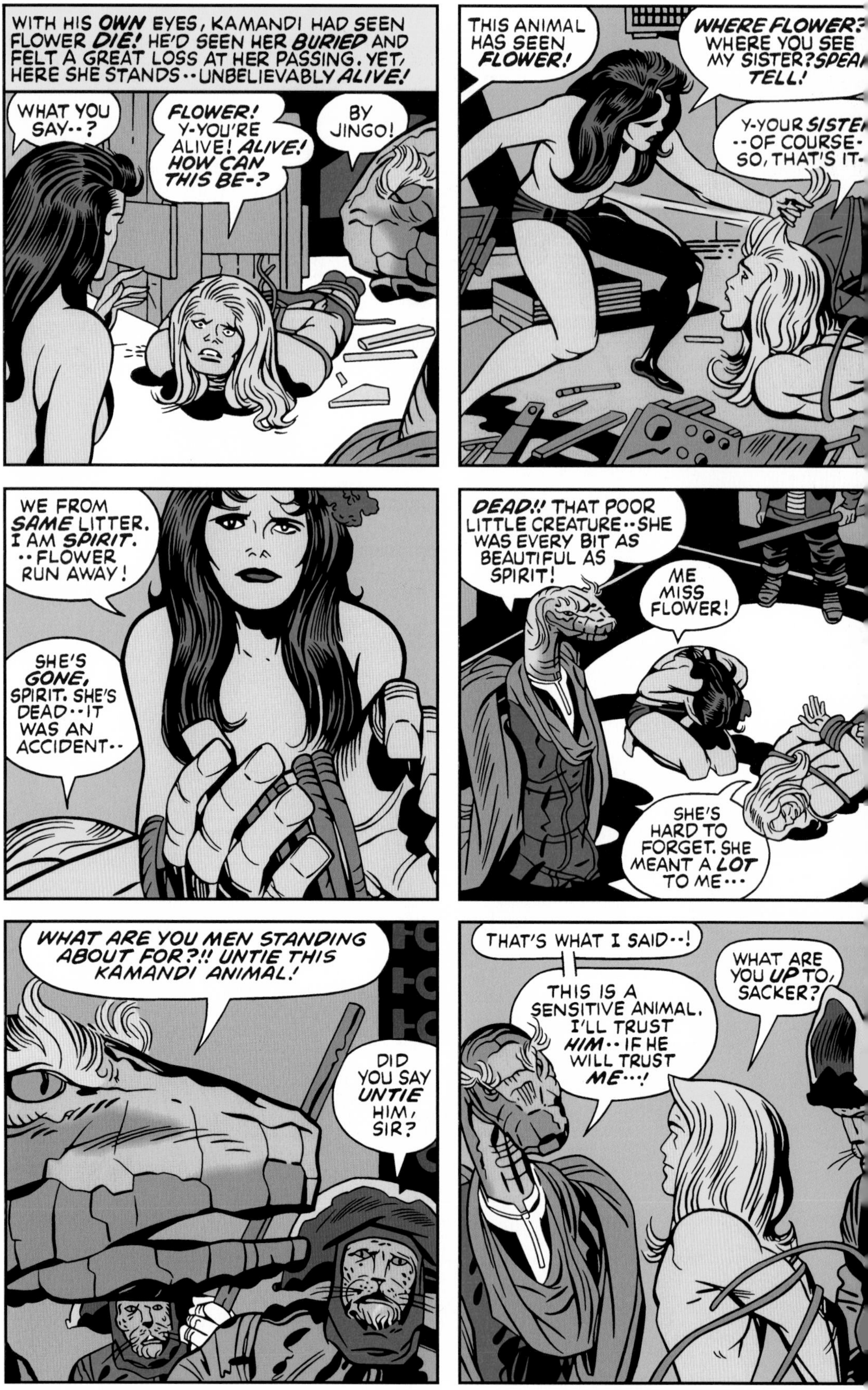
WITH HIS OWN EYES, KAMANDI HAD SEEN FLOWER DIE! HE'D SEEN HER BURIED AND FELT A GREAT LOSS AT HER PASSING. YET, HERE SHE STANDS -- UNBELIEVABLY ALIVE!
WHAT YOU SAY--?
FLOWER! Y-YOU'RE ALIVE! ALIVE! HOW CAN THIS BE-?
BY JINGO!
THIS ANIMAL HAS SEEN FLOWER!
WHERE FLOWER? WHERE YOU SEE MY SISTER? SPEA TELL!
Y-YOUR SISTE --OF COURSE- SO, THAT'S IT-
WE FROM SAME LITTER. I AM SPIRIT. --FLOWER RUN AWAY!
SHE'S GONE, SPIRIT. SHE'S DEAD--IT WAS AN ACCIDENT--
DEAD!! THAT POOR LITTLE CREATURE--SHE WAS EVERY BIT AS BEAUTIFUL AS SPIRIT!
ME MISS FLOWER!
SHE'S HARD TO FORGET. SHE MEANT A LOT TO ME...
WHAT ARE YOU MEN STANDING ABOUT FOR?!! UNTIE THIS KAMANDI ANIMAL!
DID YOU SAY UNTIE HIM, SIR?
THAT'S WHAT I SAID--!
THIS IS A SENSITIVE ANIMAL. I'LL TRUST HIM--IF HE WILL TRUST ME...!
WHAT ARE YOU UP TO, SACKER?

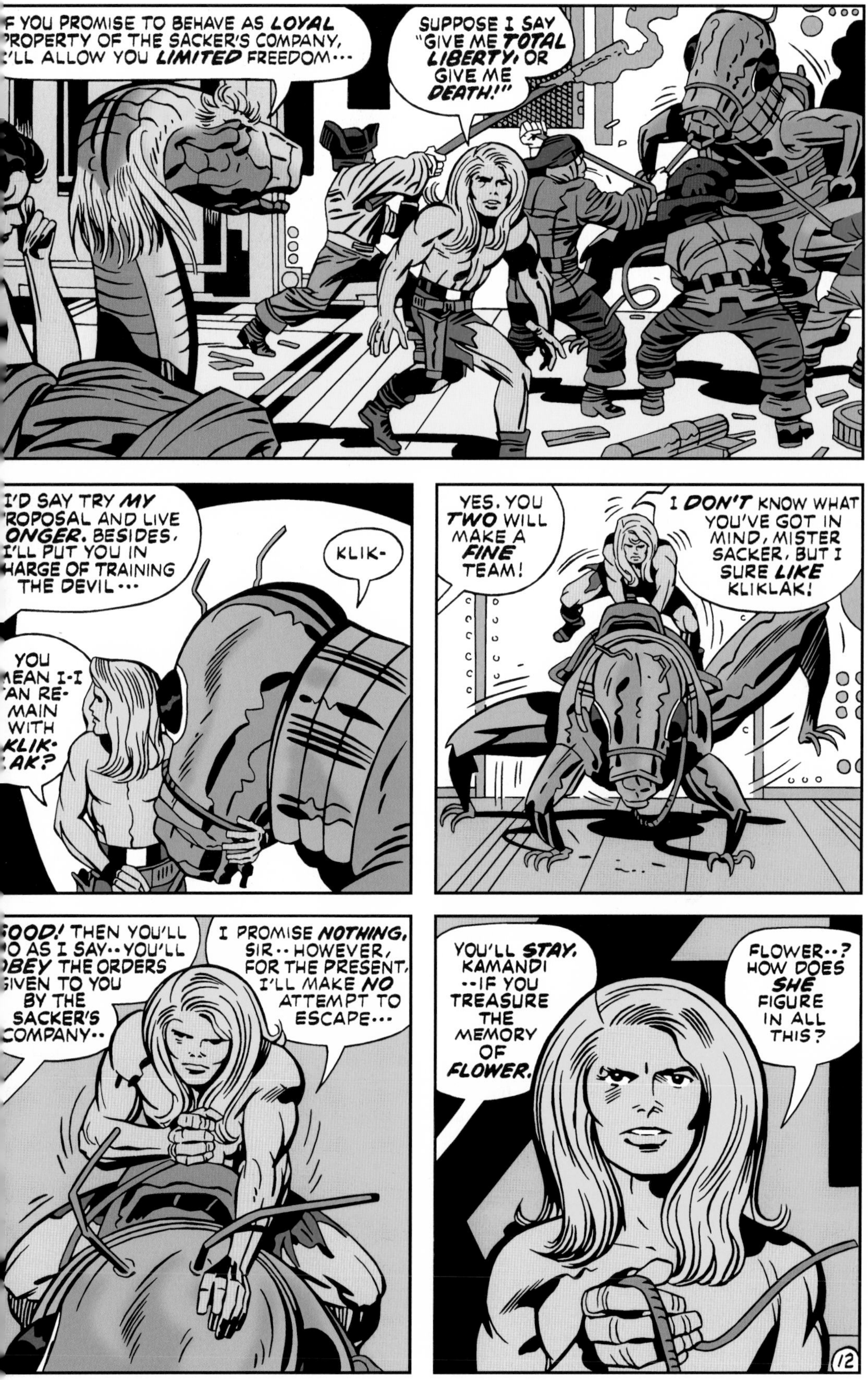
F YOU PROMISE TO BEHAVE AS LOYAL PROPERTY OF THE SACKER'S COMPANY, I'LL ALLOW YOU LIMITED FREEDOM···
SUPPOSE I SAY "GIVE ME TOTAL LIBERTY, OR GIVE ME DEATH!"
I'D SAY TRY MY ROPOSAL AND LIVE ONGER. BESIDES, I'LL PUT YOU IN HARGE OF TRAINING THE DEVIL···
KLIK-
YOU MEAN I-I AN RE-MAIN WITH KLIK-AK?
YES. YOU TWO WILL MAKE A FINE TEAM!
I DON'T KNOW WHAT YOU'VE GOT IN MIND, MISTER SACKER, BUT I SURE LIKE KLIKLAK!
OOD! THEN YOU'LL O AS I SAY·· YOU'LL BEY THE ORDERS IVEN TO YOU BY THE SACKER'S COMPANY··
I PROMISE NOTHING, SIR·· HOWEVER, FOR THE PRESENT, I'LL MAKE NO ATTEMPT TO ESCAPE···
YOU'LL STAY, KAMANDI ··IF YOU TREASURE THE MEMORY OF FLOWER.
FLOWER··? HOW DOES SHE FIGURE IN ALL THIS?
12

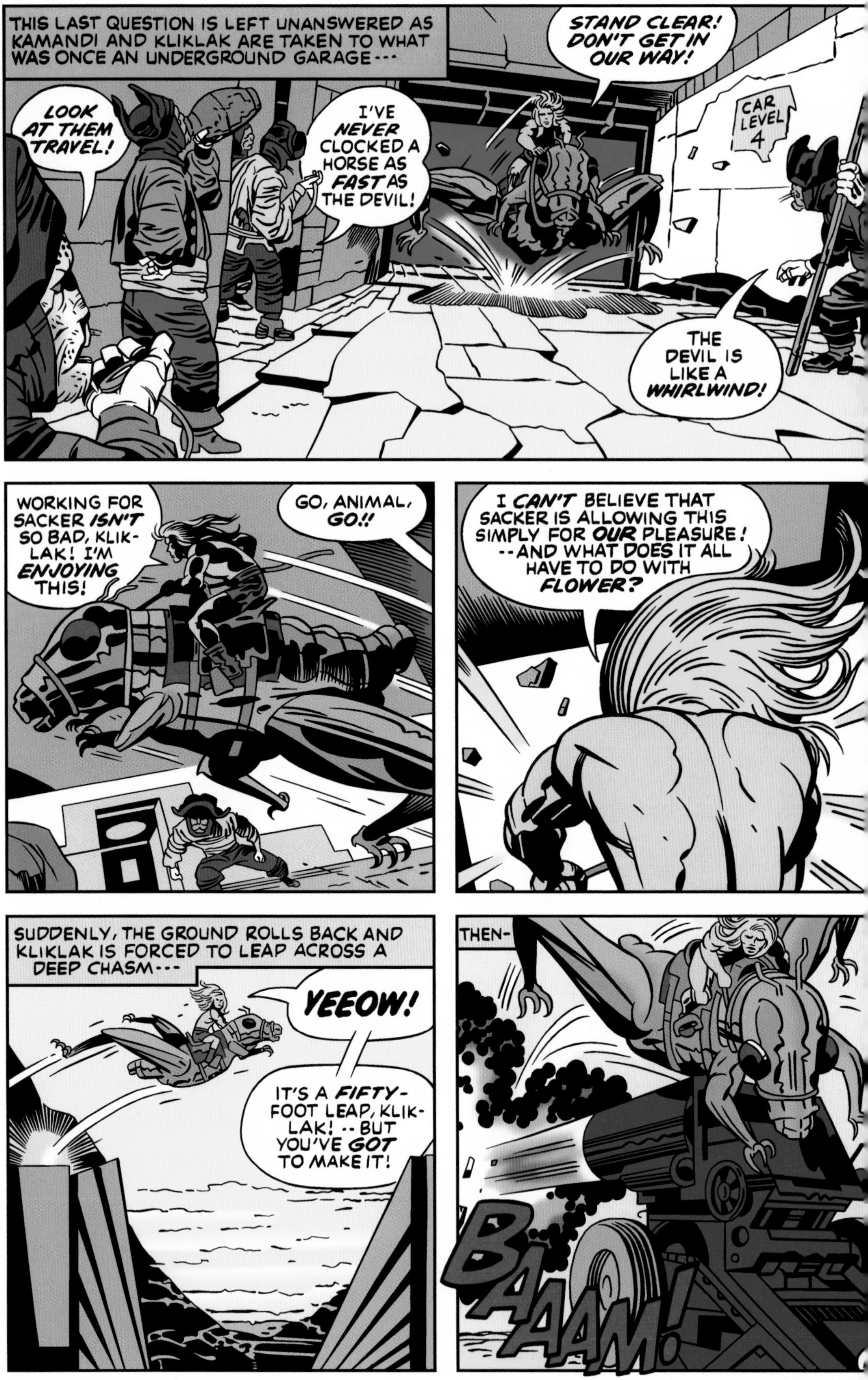
THIS LAST QUESTION IS LEFT UNANSWERED AS KAMANDI AND KLIKLAK ARE TAKEN TO WHAT WAS ONCE AN UNDERGROUND GARAGE---
STAND CLEAR! DON'T GET IN OUR WAY!
LOOK AT THEM TRAVEL!
I'VE NEVER CLOCKED A HORSE AS FAST AS THE DEVIL!
CAR LEVEL 4
THE DEVIL IS LIKE A WHIRLWIND!
WORKING FOR SACKER ISN'T SO BAD, KLIK-LAK! I'M ENJOYING THIS!
GO, ANIMAL, GO!!
I CAN'T BELIEVE THAT SACKER IS ALLOWING THIS SIMPLY FOR OUR PLEASURE! --AND WHAT DOES IT ALL HAVE TO DO WITH FLOWER?
SUDDENLY, THE GROUND ROLLS BACK AND KLIKLAK IS FORCED TO LEAP ACROSS A DEEP CHASM---
YEEOW!
IT'S A FIFTY-FOOT LEAP, KLIK-LAK! --BUT YOU'VE GOT TO MAKE IT!
THEN-
BAAAM!

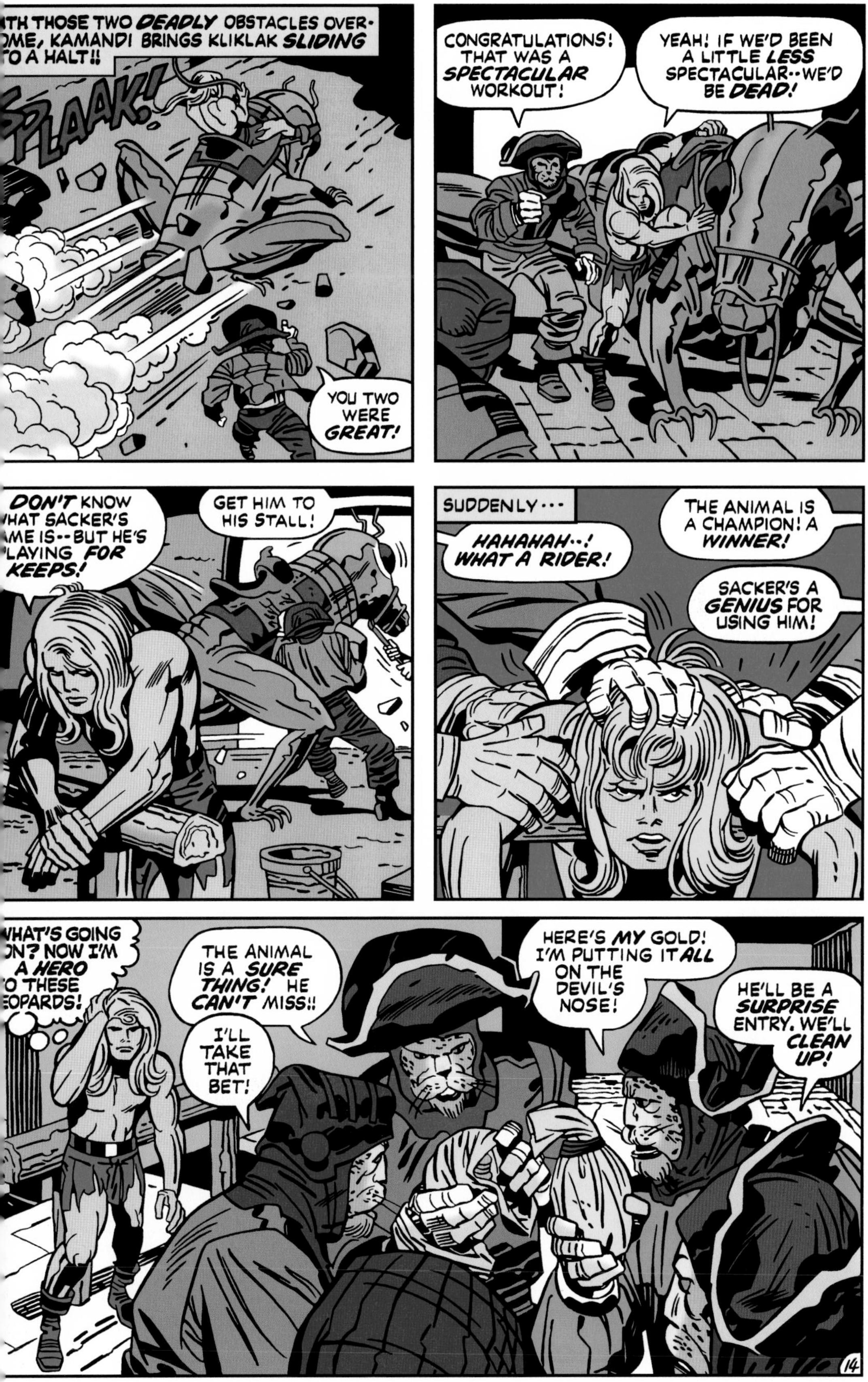

ITH THOSE TWO DEADLY OBSTACLES OVER-OME, KAMANDI BRINGS KLIKLAK SLIDING TO A HALT!!
SPLAAK!
YOU TWO WERE GREAT!
CONGRATULATIONS! THAT WAS A SPECTACULAR WORKOUT!
YEAH! IF WE'D BEEN A LITTLE LESS SPECTACULAR--WE'D BE DEAD!
DON'T KNOW HAT SACKER'S ME IS--BUT HE'S LAYING FOR KEEPS!
GET HIM TO HIS STALL!
SUDDENLY...
HAHAHAH--! WHAT A RIDER!
THE ANIMAL IS A CHAMPION! A WINNER!
SACKER'S A GENIUS FOR USING HIM!
HAT'S GOING ON? NOW I'M A HERO O THESE EOPARDS!
THE ANIMAL IS A SURE THING! HE CAN'T MISS!!
I'LL TAKE THAT BET!
HERE'S MY GOLD! I'M PUTTING IT ALL ON THE DEVIL'S NOSE!
HE'LL BE A SURPRISE ENTRY. WE'LL CLEAN UP!
14

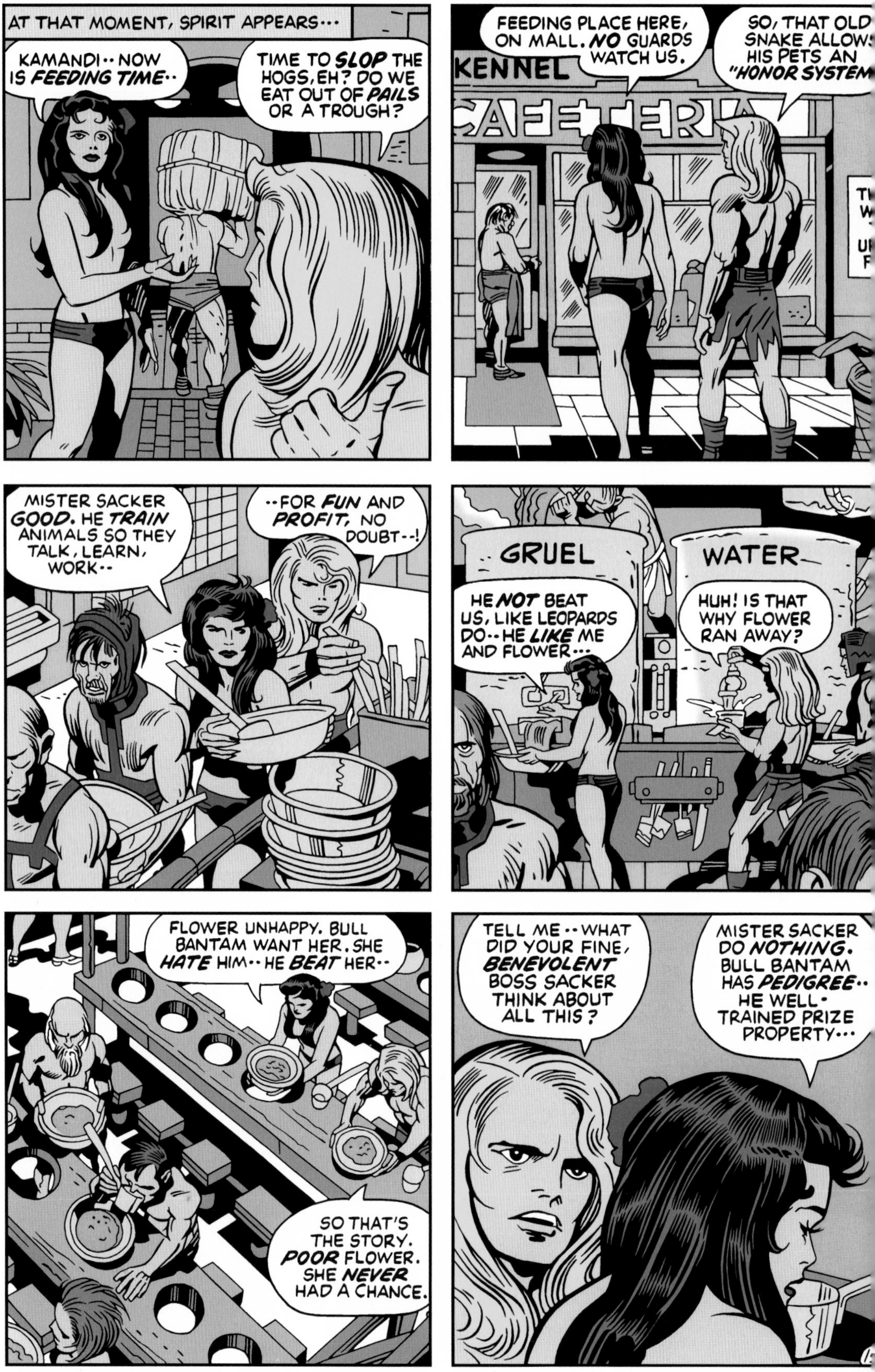
AT THAT MOMENT, SPIRIT APPEARS...
KAMANDI.. NOW IS FEEDING TIME..
TIME TO SLOP THE HOGS, EH? DO WE EAT OUT OF PAILS OR A TROUGH?
FEEDING PLACE HERE, ON MALL. NO GUARDS WATCH US.
KENNEL
SO, THAT OLD SNAKE ALLOWS HIS PETS AN "HONOR SYSTEM
MISTER SACKER GOOD. HE TRAIN ANIMALS SO THEY TALK, LEARN, WORK..
..FOR FUN AND PROFIT, NO DOUBT--!
GRUEL
WATER
HE NOT BEAT US, LIKE LEOPARDS DO.. HE LIKE ME AND FLOWER...
HUH! IS THAT WHY FLOWER RAN AWAY?
FLOWER UNHAPPY. BULL BANTAM WANT HER. SHE HATE HIM.. HE BEAT HER..
SO THAT'S THE STORY. POOR FLOWER. SHE NEVER HAD A CHANCE.
TELL ME.. WHAT DID YOUR FINE, BENEVOLENT BOSS SACKER THINK ABOUT ALL THIS?
MISTER SACKER DO NOTHING. BULL BANTAM HAS PEDIGREE.. HE WELL-TRAINED PRIZE PROPERTY...

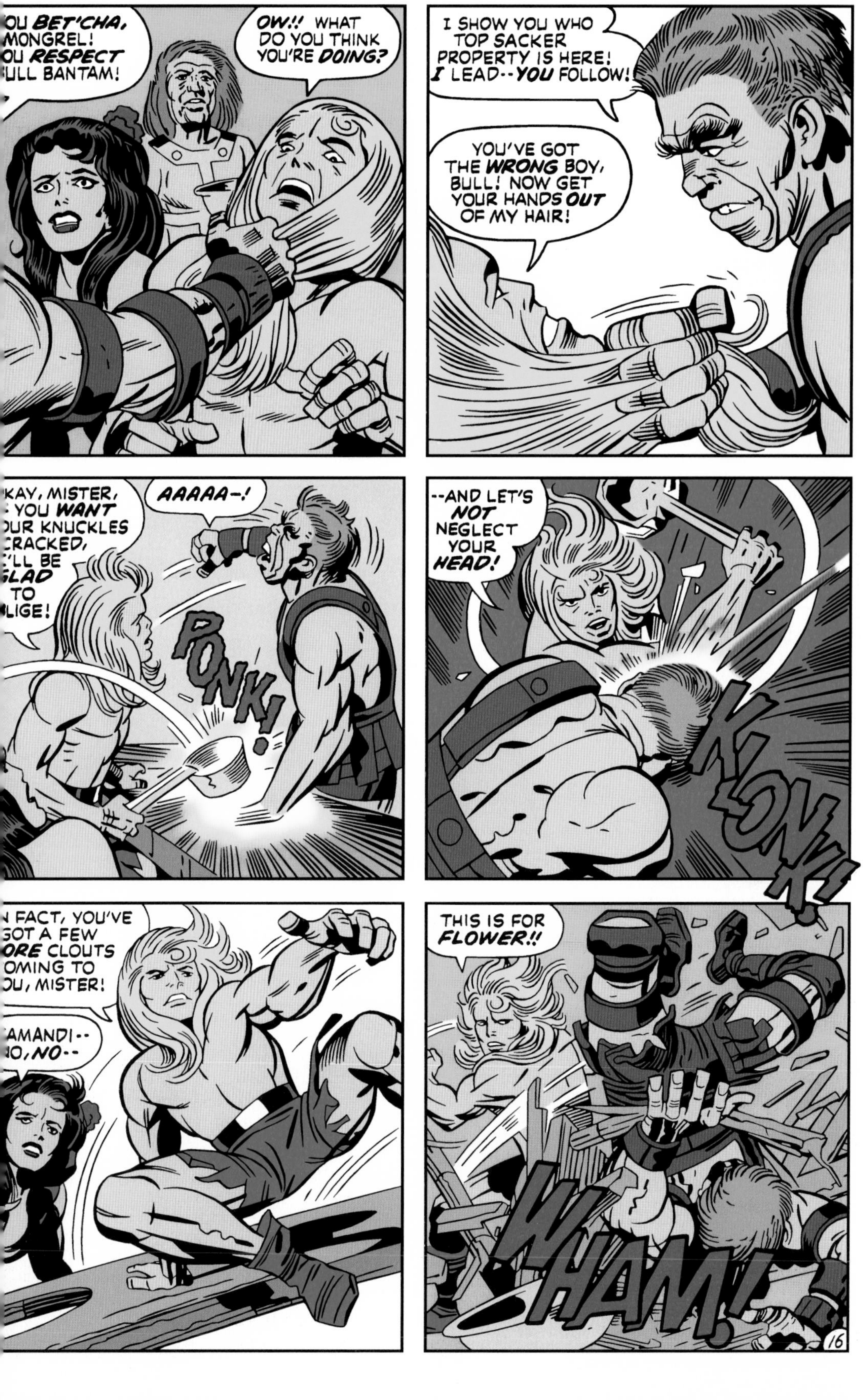
OU BET'CHA, MONGREL! OU RESPECT ULL BANTAM!
OW!! WHAT DO YOU THINK YOU'RE DOING?
I SHOW YOU WHO TOP SACKER PROPERTY IS HERE! I LEAD--YOU FOLLOW!
YOU'VE GOT THE WRONG BOY, BULL! NOW GET YOUR HANDS OUT OF MY HAIR!
KAY, MISTER, YOU WANT OUR KNUCKLES CRACKED, 'LL BE GLAD TO LIGE!
AAAAA-!
PONK!
--AND LET'S NOT NEGLECT YOUR HEAD!
KLONK!
N FACT, YOU'VE GOT A FEW ORE CLOUTS OMING TO OU, MISTER!
AMANDI-- O, NO--
THIS IS FOR FLOWER!!
WHAM!
16

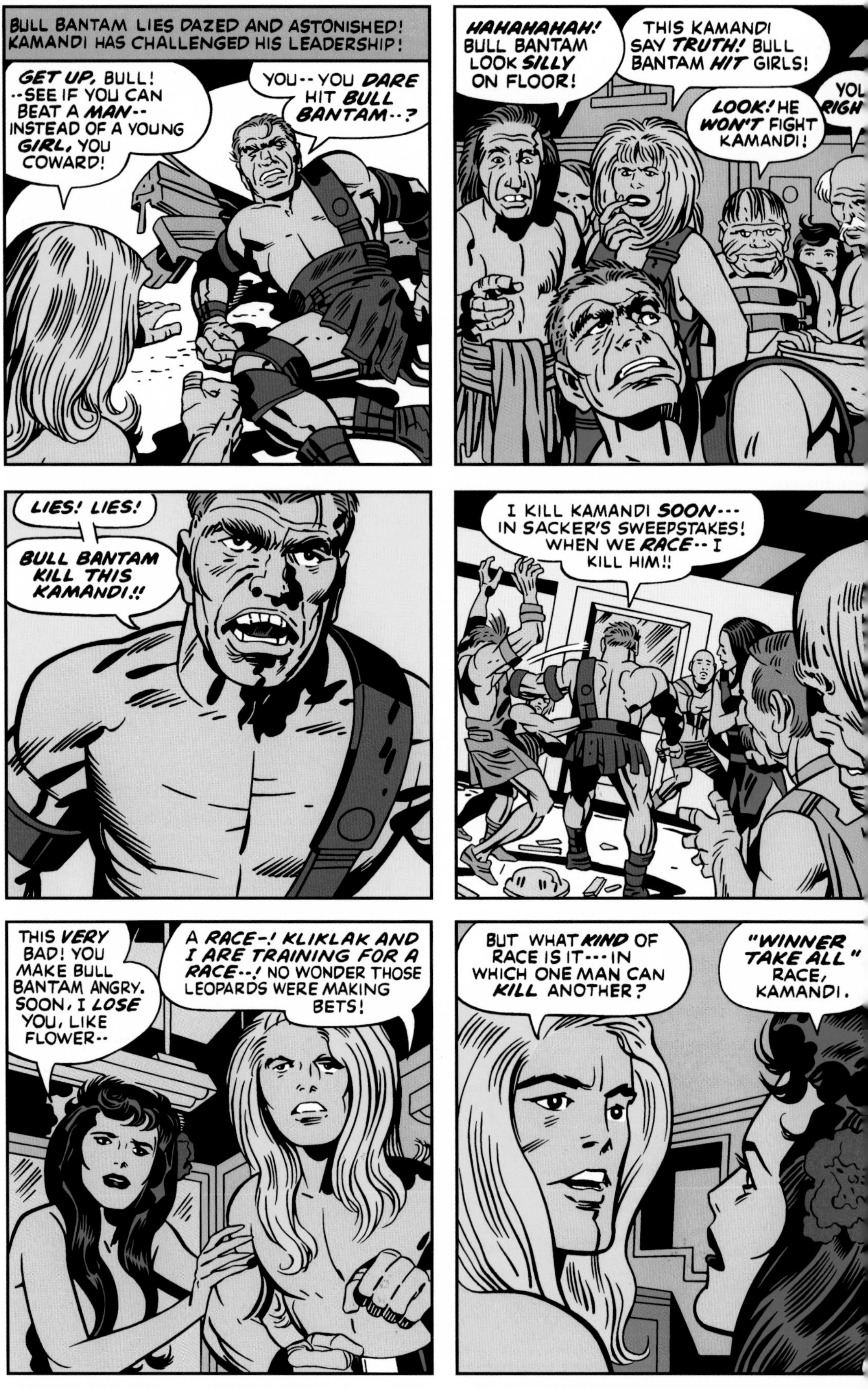
BULL BANTAM LIES DAZED AND ASTONISHED! KAMANDI HAS CHALLENGED HIS LEADERSHIP!
GET UP, BULL! --SEE IF YOU CAN BEAT A MAN-- INSTEAD OF A YOUNG GIRL, YOU COWARD!
YOU--YOU DARE HIT BULL BANTAM--?
HAHAHAHAH! BULL BANTAM LOOK SILLY ON FLOOR!
THIS KAMANDI SAY TRUTH! BULL BANTAM HIT GIRLS!
LOOK! HE WON'T FIGHT KAMANDI!
LIES! LIES!
BULL BANTAM KILL THIS KAMANDI!!
I KILL KAMANDI SOON--- IN SACKER'S SWEEPSTAKES! WHEN WE RACE-- I KILL HIM!!
THIS VERY BAD! YOU MAKE BULL BANTAM ANGRY. SOON, I LOSE YOU, LIKE FLOWER--
A RACE-! KLIKLAK AND I ARE TRAINING FOR A RACE--! NO WONDER THOSE LEOPARDS WERE MAKING BETS!
BUT WHAT KIND OF RACE IS IT--- IN WHICH ONE MAN CAN KILL ANOTHER?
"WINNER TAKE ALL" RACE, KAMANDI.

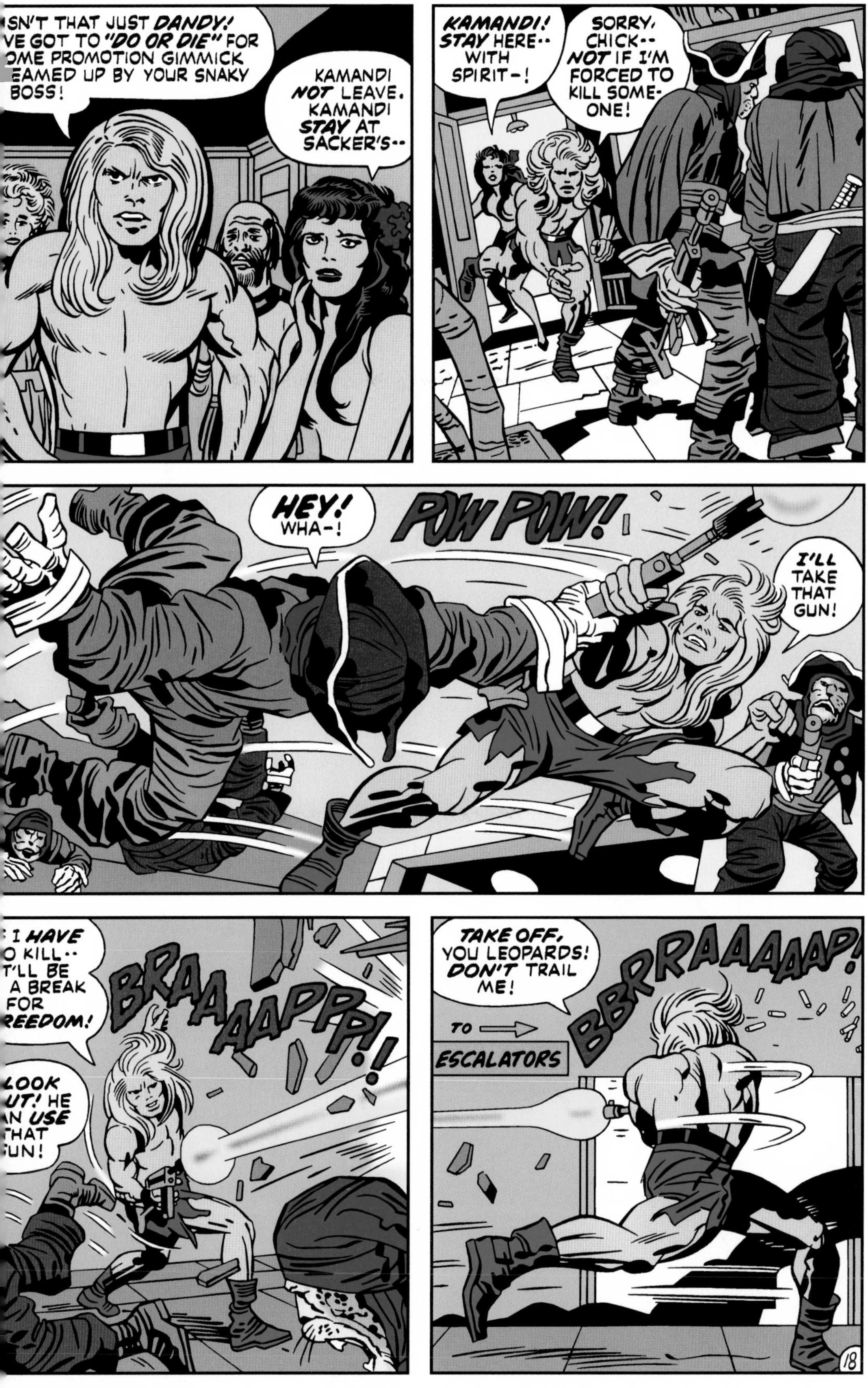
ISN'T THAT JUST DANDY! VE GOT TO "DO OR DIE" FOR OME PROMOTION GIMMICK EAMED UP BY YOUR SNAKY BOSS!
KAMANDI NOT LEAVE. KAMANDI STAY AT SACKER'S--
KAMANDI! STAY HERE-- WITH SPIRIT-!
SORRY, CHICK-- NOT IF I'M FORCED TO KILL SOMEONE!
HEY! WHA-!
POW POW!
I'LL TAKE THAT GUN!
I HAVE O KILL-- T'LL BE A BREAK FOR REEDOM!
BRAAAAPPP!!
LOOK UT! HE N USE THAT UN!
TAKE OFF, YOU LEOPARDS! DON'T TRAIL ME!
TO
ESCALATORS
BBRRAAAAAP!
18

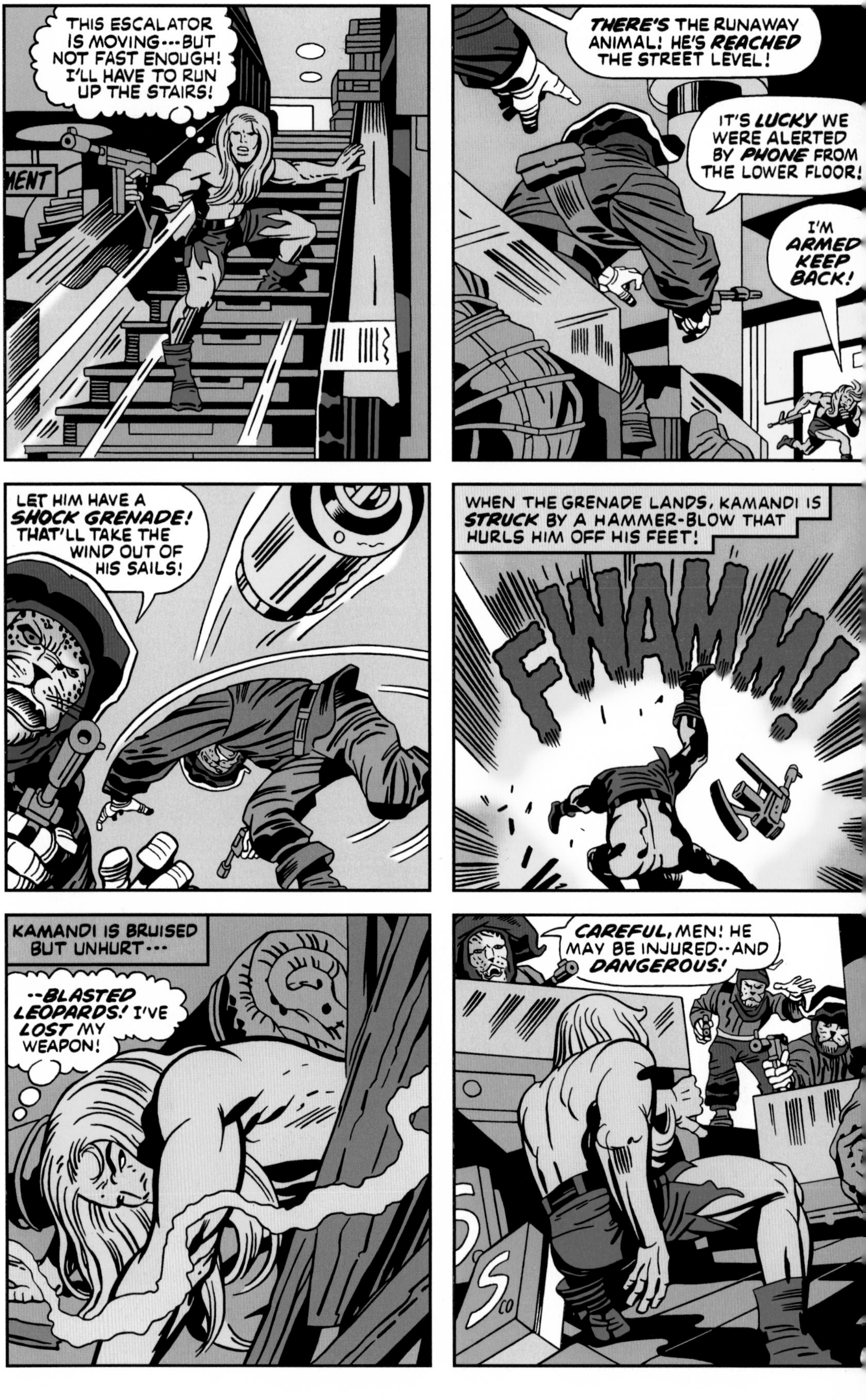
THIS ESCALATOR IS MOVING---BUT NOT FAST ENOUGH! I'LL HAVE TO RUN UP THE STAIRS!
MENT
THERE'S THE RUNAWAY ANIMAL! HE'S REACHED THE STREET LEVEL!
IT'S LUCKY WE WERE ALERTED BY PHONE FROM THE LOWER FLOOR!
I'M ARMED KEEP BACK!
LET HIM HAVE A SHOCK GRENADE! THAT'LL TAKE THE WIND OUT OF HIS SAILS!
WHEN THE GRENADE LANDS, KAMANDI IS STRUCK BY A HAMMER-BLOW THAT HURLS HIM OFF HIS FEET!
FWAMM!
KAMANDI IS BRUISED BUT UNHURT---
--BLASTED LEOPARDS! I'VE LOST MY WEAPON!
CAREFUL, MEN! HE MAY BE INJURED--AND DANGEROUS!

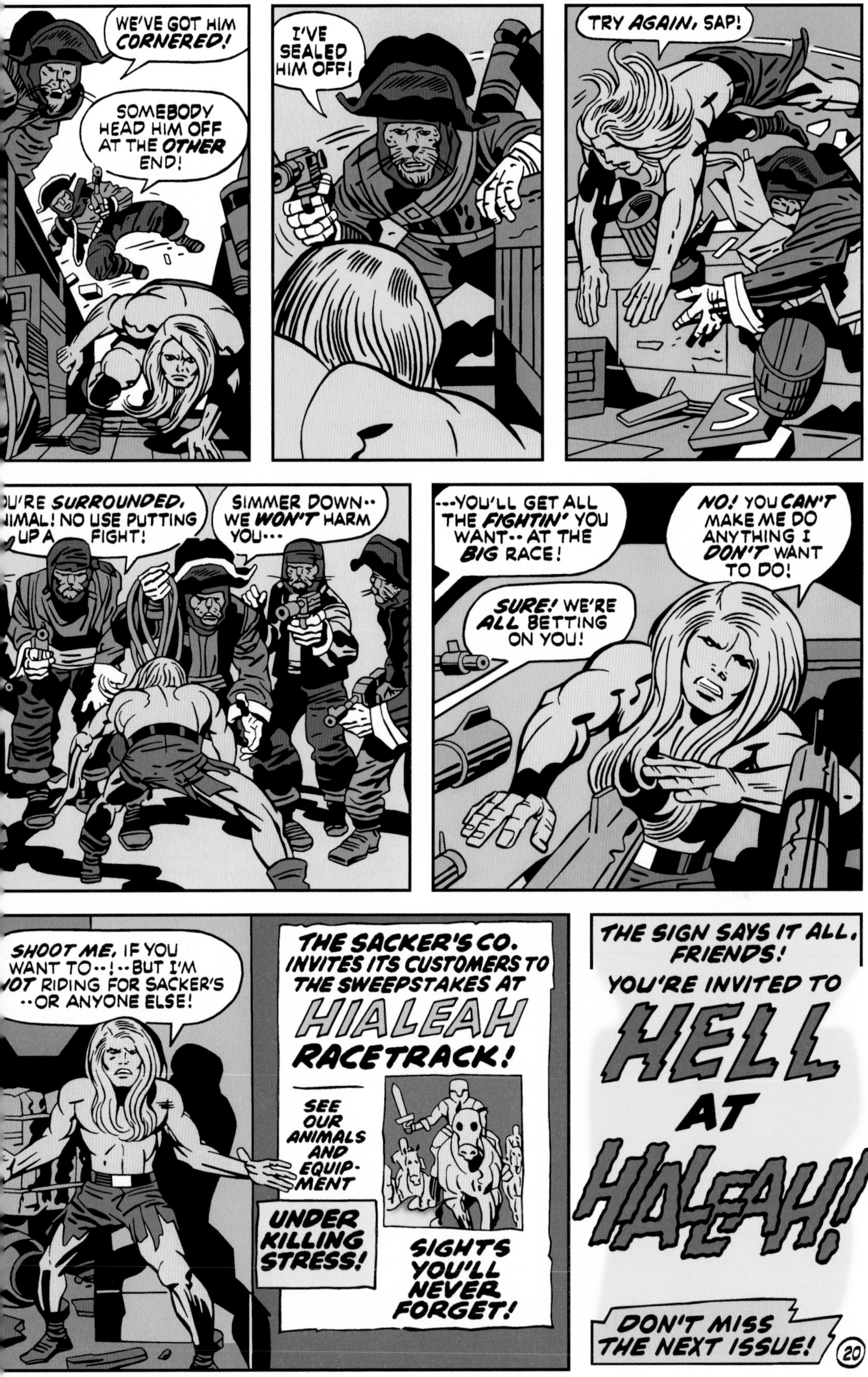
WE'VE GOT HIM CORNERED!
SOMEBODY HEAD HIM OFF AT THE OTHER END!
I'VE SEALED HIM OFF!
TRY AGAIN, SAP!
U'RE SURROUNDED, IMAL! NO USE PUTTING UP A FIGHT!
SIMMER DOWN-- WE WON'T HARM YOU---
---YOU'LL GET ALL THE FIGHTIN' YOU WANT-- AT THE BIG RACE!
NO! YOU CAN'T MAKE ME DO ANYTHING I DON'T WANT TO DO!
SURE! WE'RE ALL BETTING ON YOU!
SHOOT ME, IF YOU WANT TO--!--BUT I'M OT RIDING FOR SACKER'S --OR ANYONE ELSE!
THE SACKER'S CO. INVITES ITS CUSTOMERS TO THE SWEEPSTAKES AT
HIALEAH RACETRACK!
SEE OUR ANIMALS AND EQUIPMENT
UNDER KILLING STRESS!
SIGHTS YOU'LL NEVER FORGET!
THE SIGN SAYS IT ALL, FRIENDS!
YOU'RE INVITED TO
HELL AT HIALEAH!
DON'T MISS THE NEXT ISSUE!
20

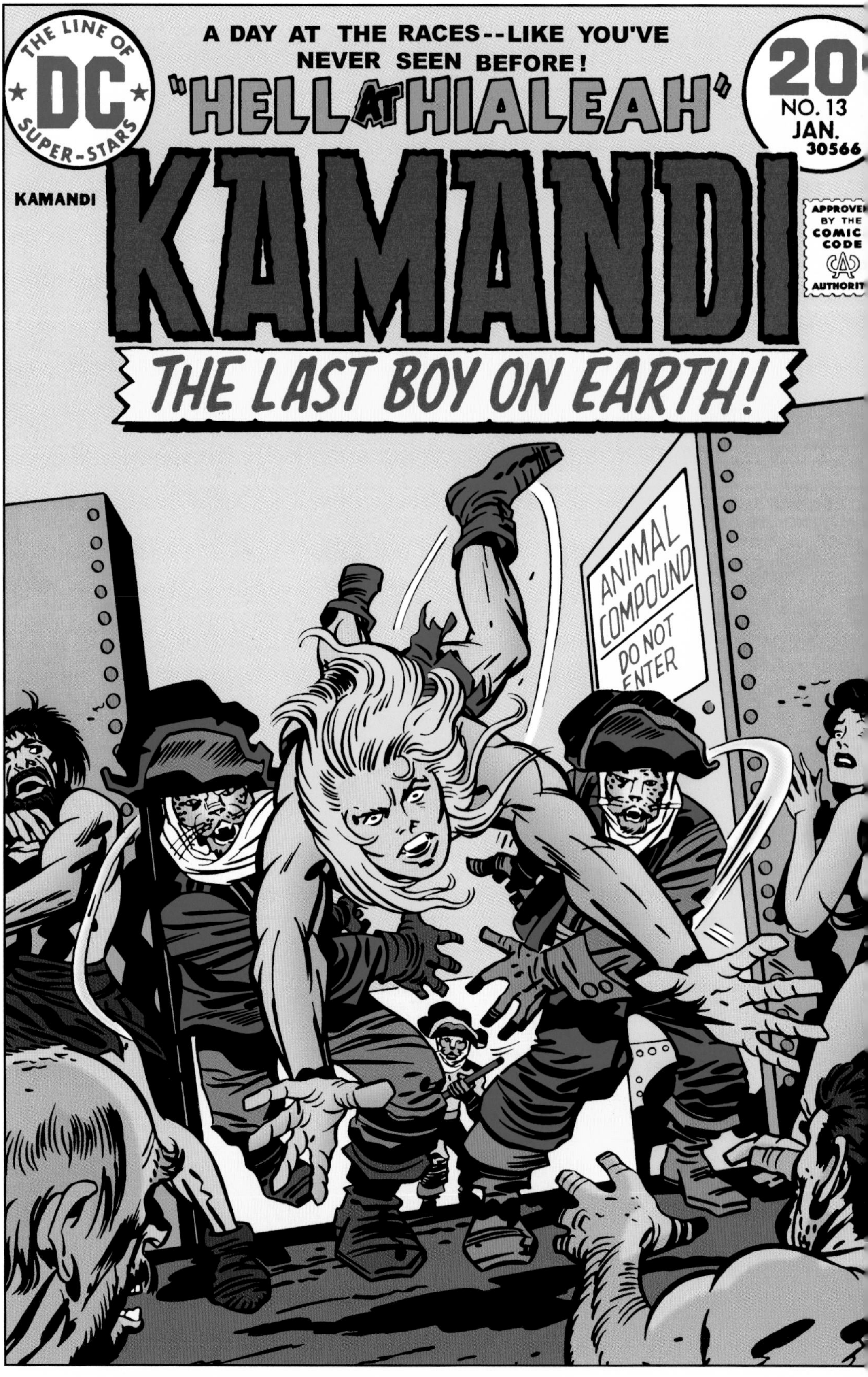
THE LINE OF DC SUPER-STARS
A DAY AT THE RACES--LIKE YOU'VE NEVER SEEN BEFORE!
"HELL AT HIALEAH"
20¢
NO. 13
JAN.
30566
KAMANDI
KAMANDI
APPROVED BY THE COMIC CODE AUTHORITY
THE LAST BOY ON EARTH!
ANIMAL COMPOUND
DO NOT ENTER

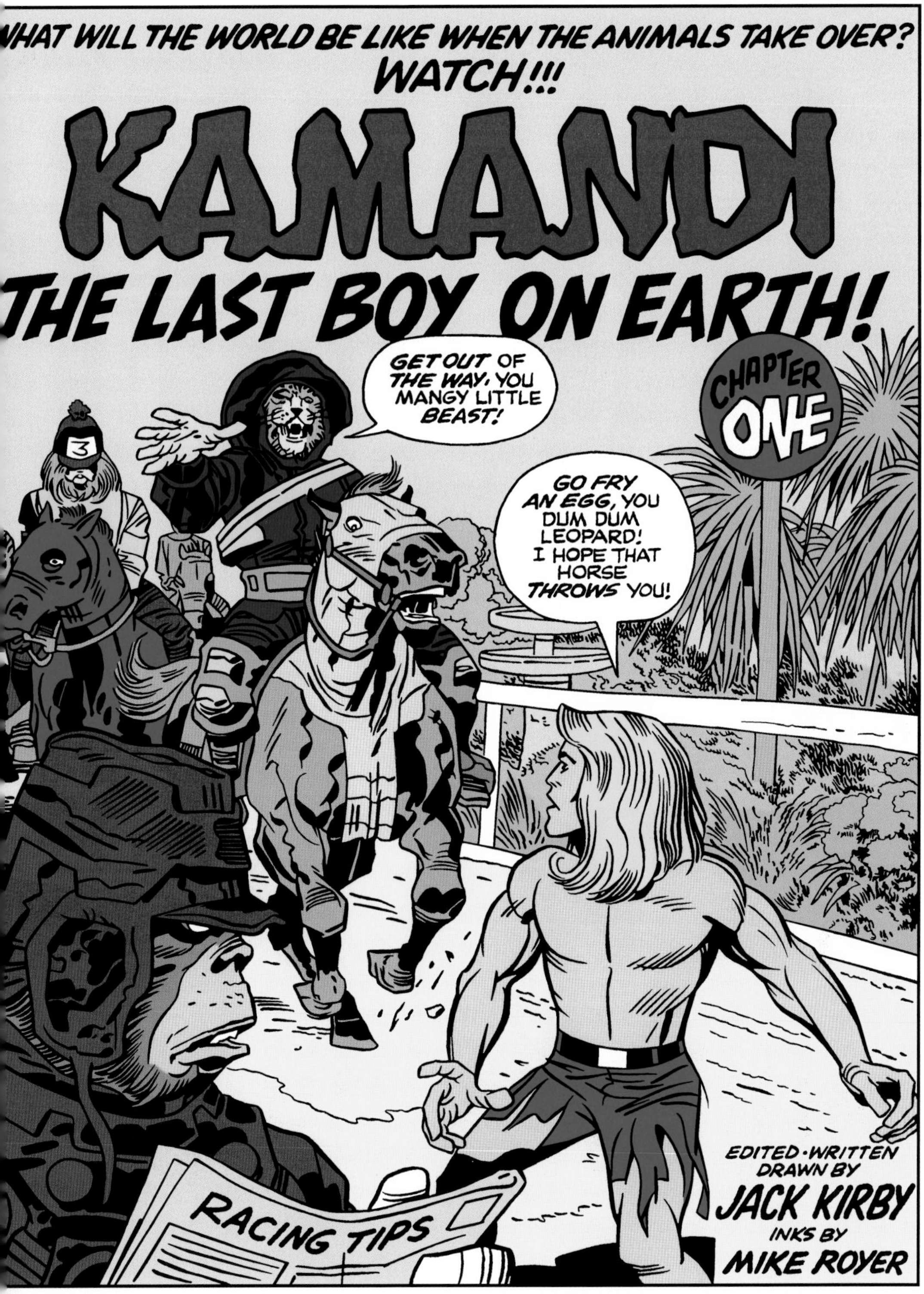
WHAT WILL THE WORLD BE LIKE WHEN THE ANIMALS TAKE OVER?
WATCH!!!
KAMANDI
THE LAST BOY ON EARTH!
GET OUT OF THE WAY, YOU MANGY LITTLE BEAST!
CHAPTER ONE
GO FRY AN EGG, YOU DUM DUM LEOPARD! I HOPE THAT HORSE THROWS YOU!
RACING TIPS
EDITED · WRITTEN DRAWN BY
JACK KIRBY
INKS BY
MIKE ROYER

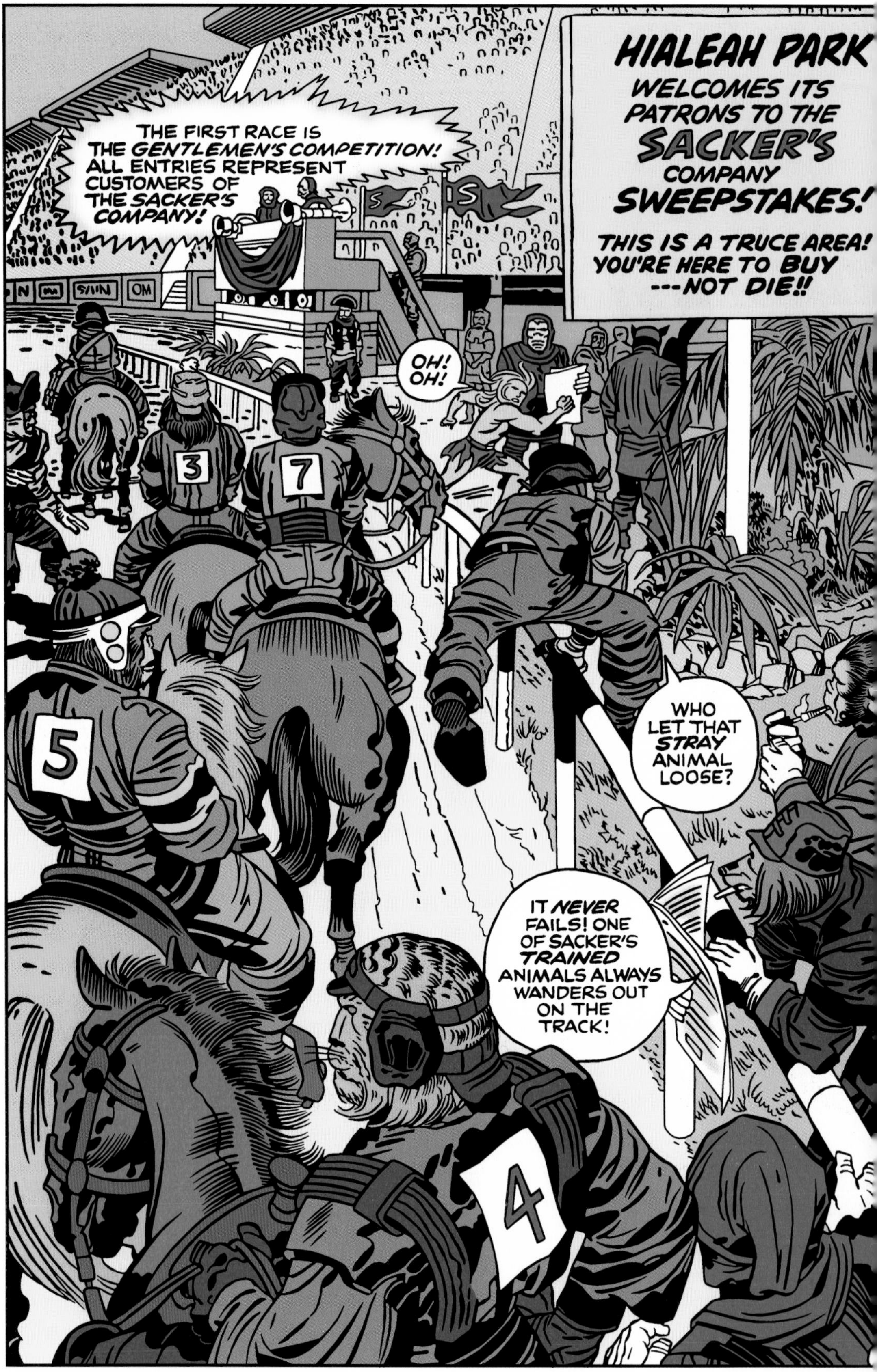
HIALEAH PARK WELCOMES ITS PATRONS TO THE SACKER'S COMPANY SWEEPSTAKES!
THIS IS A TRUCE AREA! YOU'RE HERE TO BUY ---NOT DIE!!
THE FIRST RACE IS THE GENTLEMEN'S COMPETITION! ALL ENTRIES REPRESENT CUSTOMERS OF THE SACKER'S COMPANY!
OH! OH!
WHO LET THAT STRAY ANIMAL LOOSE?
IT NEVER FAILS! ONE OF SACKER'S TRAINED ANIMALS ALWAYS WANDERS OUT ON THE TRACK!

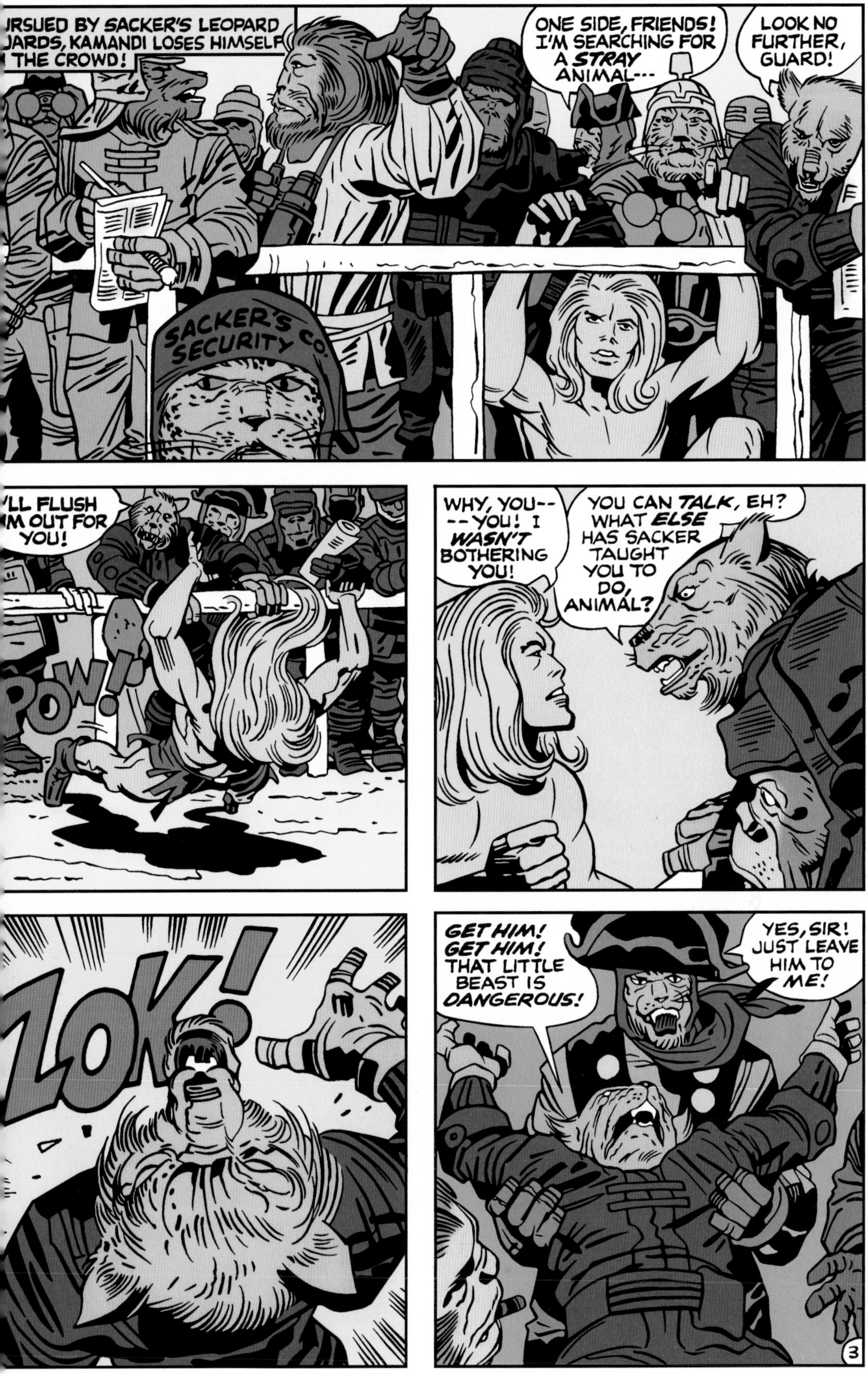

RSUED BY SACKER'S LEOPARD
JARDS, KAMANDI LOSES HIMSELF
THE CROWD!
SACKER'S CO. SECURITY
ONE SIDE, FRIENDS! I'M SEARCHING FOR A STRAY ANIMAL---
LOOK NO FURTHER, GUARD!
'LL FLUSH M OUT FOR YOU!
POW!
WHY, YOU-- --YOU! I WASN'T BOTHERING YOU!
YOU CAN TALK, EH? WHAT ELSE HAS SACKER TAUGHT YOU TO DO, ANIMAL?
ZOK!
GET HIM! GET HIM! THAT LITTLE BEAST IS DANGEROUS!
YES, SIR! JUST LEAVE HIM TO ME!
3

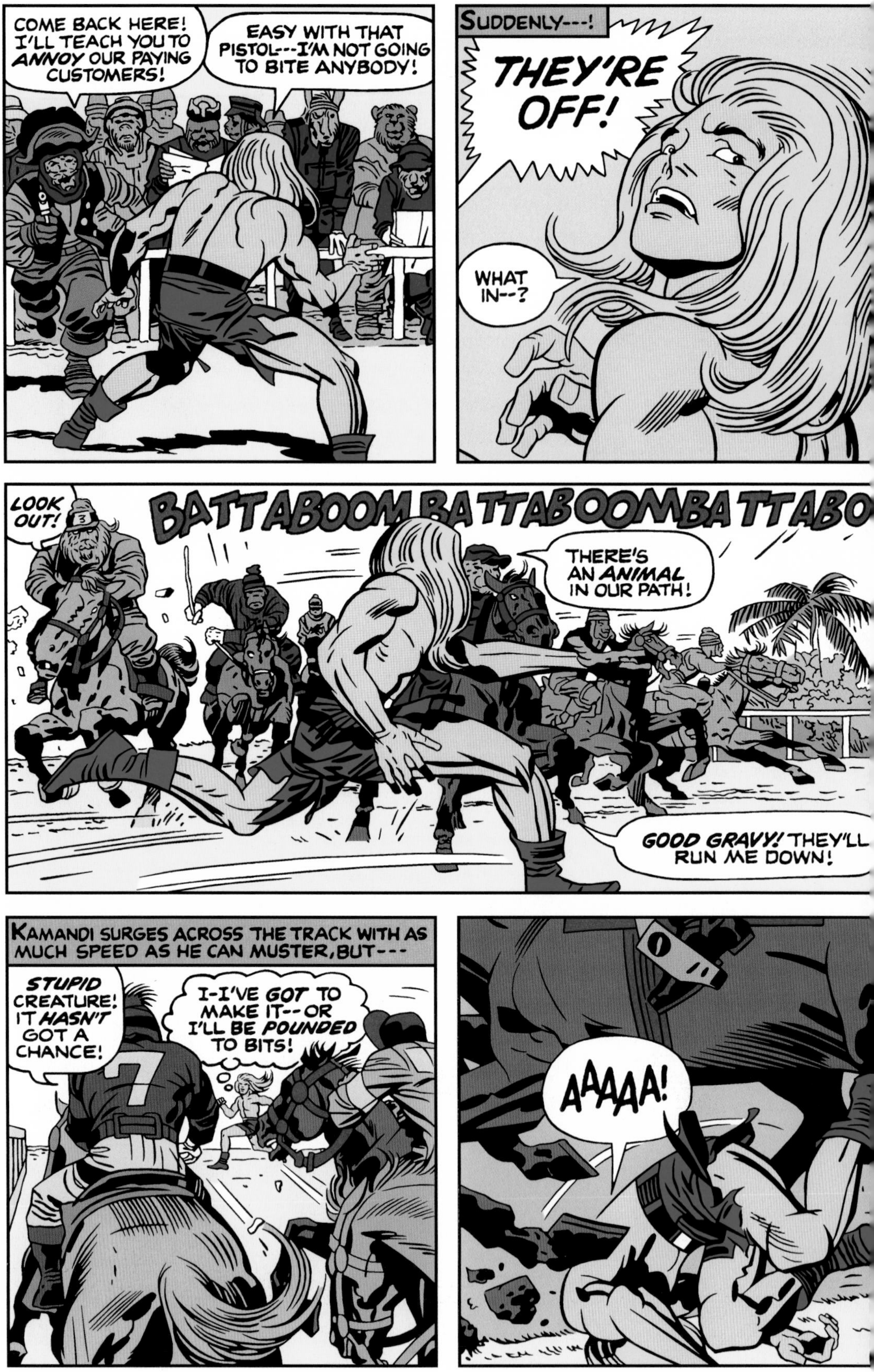
COME BACK HERE! I'LL TEACH YOU TO ANNOY OUR PAYING CUSTOMERS!
EASY WITH THAT PISTOL--I'M NOT GOING TO BITE ANYBODY!
SUDDENLY---!
THEY'RE OFF!
WHAT IN--?
LOOK OUT!
BATTABOOM BATTABOOM BATTABO
THERE'S AN ANIMAL IN OUR PATH!
GOOD GRAVY! THEY'LL RUN ME DOWN!
KAMANDI SURGES ACROSS THE TRACK WITH AS MUCH SPEED AS HE CAN MUSTER, BUT---
STUPID CREATURE! IT HASN'T GOT A CHANCE!
I-I'VE GOT TO MAKE IT--OR I'LL BE POUNDED TO BITS!
AAAAA!

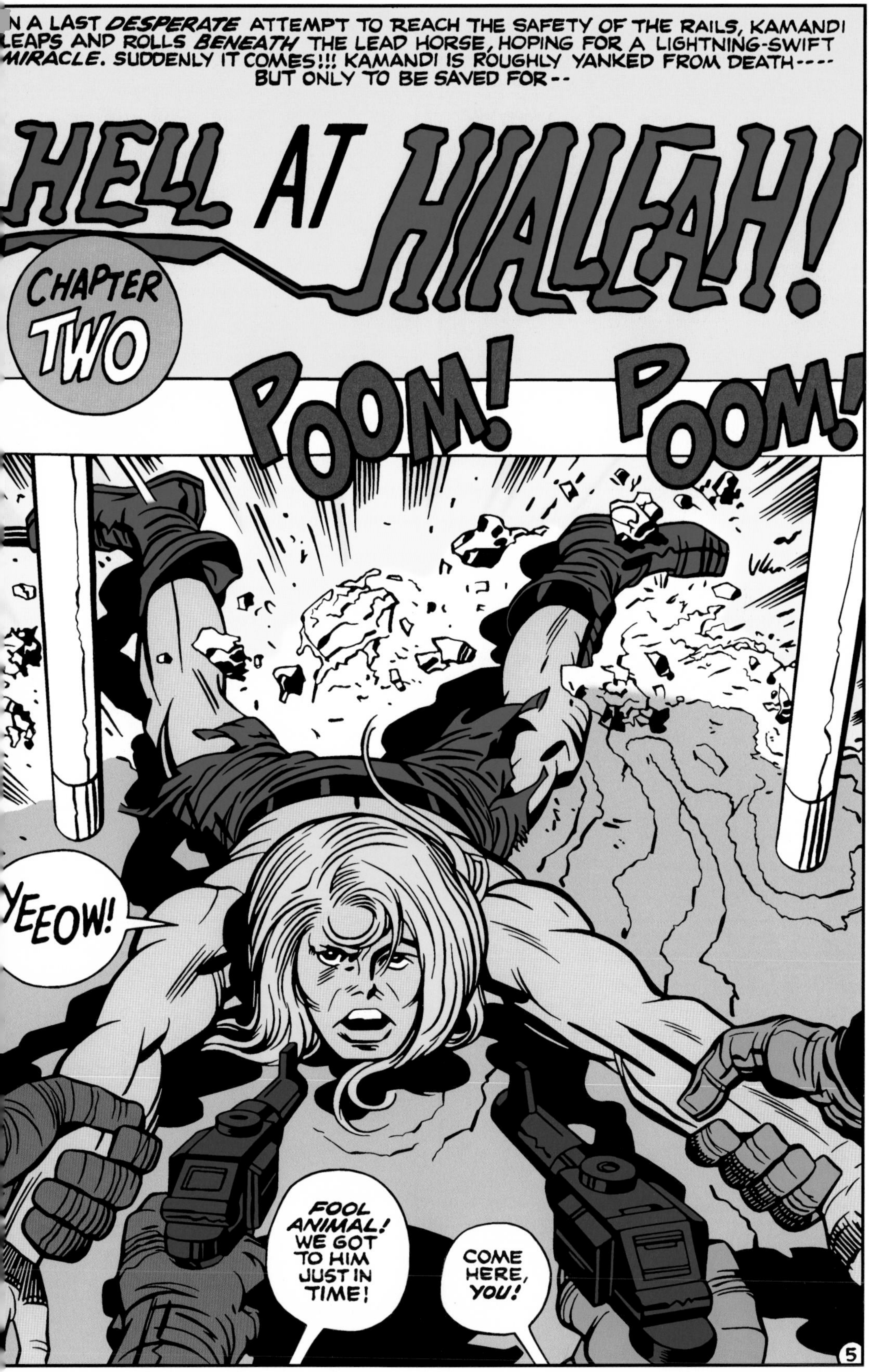
IN A LAST DESPERATE ATTEMPT TO REACH THE SAFETY OF THE RAILS, KAMANDI LEAPS AND ROLLS BENEATH THE LEAD HORSE, HOPING FOR A LIGHTNING-SWIFT MIRACLE. SUDDENLY IT COMES!!! KAMANDI IS ROUGHLY YANKED FROM DEATH---- BUT ONLY TO BE SAVED FOR--
HELL AT HIALEAH!
CHAPTER TWO
POOM! POOM!
YEEOW!
FOOL ANIMAL! WE GOT TO HIM JUST IN TIME!
COME HERE, YOU!
5

NUMB AND SHAKEN, KAMANDI ALLOWS HIMSELF TO BE DRAGGED OFF BY THE SACKER'S COMPANY LEOPARD GUARDS---

SOMEONE'S GONNA GET *CHEWED OUT* FOR LETTING HIM *ESCAPE* FROM THE ANIMAL COMPOUND!

THIS IS THE ONE CALLED *KAMANDI*--

--A *REAL* TROUBLE-MAKER!

I CAN *STILL* DISH OUT PLENTY OF IT!

OOF--!

POW

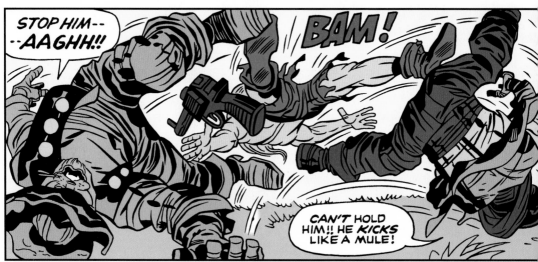

STOP HIM-- --*AAGHH!!*

BAM!

CAN'T HOLD HIM!! HE *KICKS* LIKE A MULE!

SLIPPERY LITTLE FIEND! WE'LL TOSS YOU IN A *CAGE* AND THROW THE KEY AWAY!

YOU'LL HAVE TO *CATCH* ME FIRST, LOOSE-LIPS!

I'LL GET HIM!

KAMANDI SUDDENLY FEELS A *STRONG* HAND CLOSE ON HIS ANKLE!

LET ME GO! LET ME GO, --OR *I'LL*--!

YOU'V HAD IT WHE

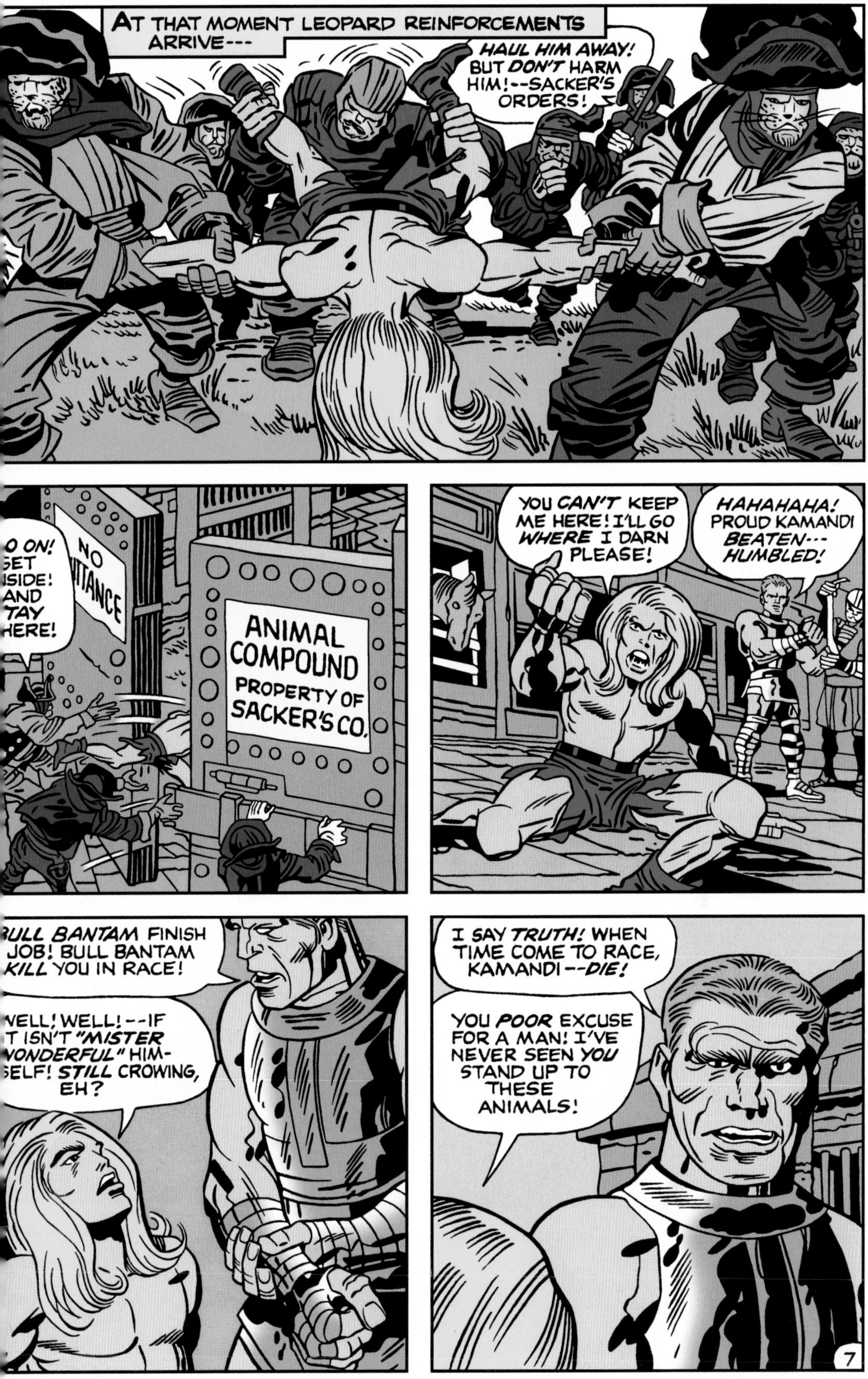
AT THAT MOMENT LEOPARD REINFORCEMENTS ARRIVE---
HAUL HIM AWAY! BUT DON'T HARM HIM!--SACKER'S ORDERS!
O ON! ET NSIDE! AND TAY HERE!
NO ITTANCE
ANIMAL COMPOUND PROPERTY OF SACKER'S CO.
YOU CAN'T KEEP ME HERE! I'LL GO WHERE I DARN PLEASE!
HAHAHAHA! PROUD KAMANDI BEATEN--- HUMBLED!
ULL BANTAM FINISH JOB! BULL BANTAM KILL YOU IN RACE!
VELL! WELL! --IF T ISN'T "MISTER VONDERFUL" HIM-SELF! STILL CROWING, EH?
I SAY TRUTH! WHEN TIME COME TO RACE, KAMANDI --DIE!
YOU POOR EXCUSE FOR A MAN! I'VE NEVER SEEN YOU STAND UP TO THESE ANIMALS!
7

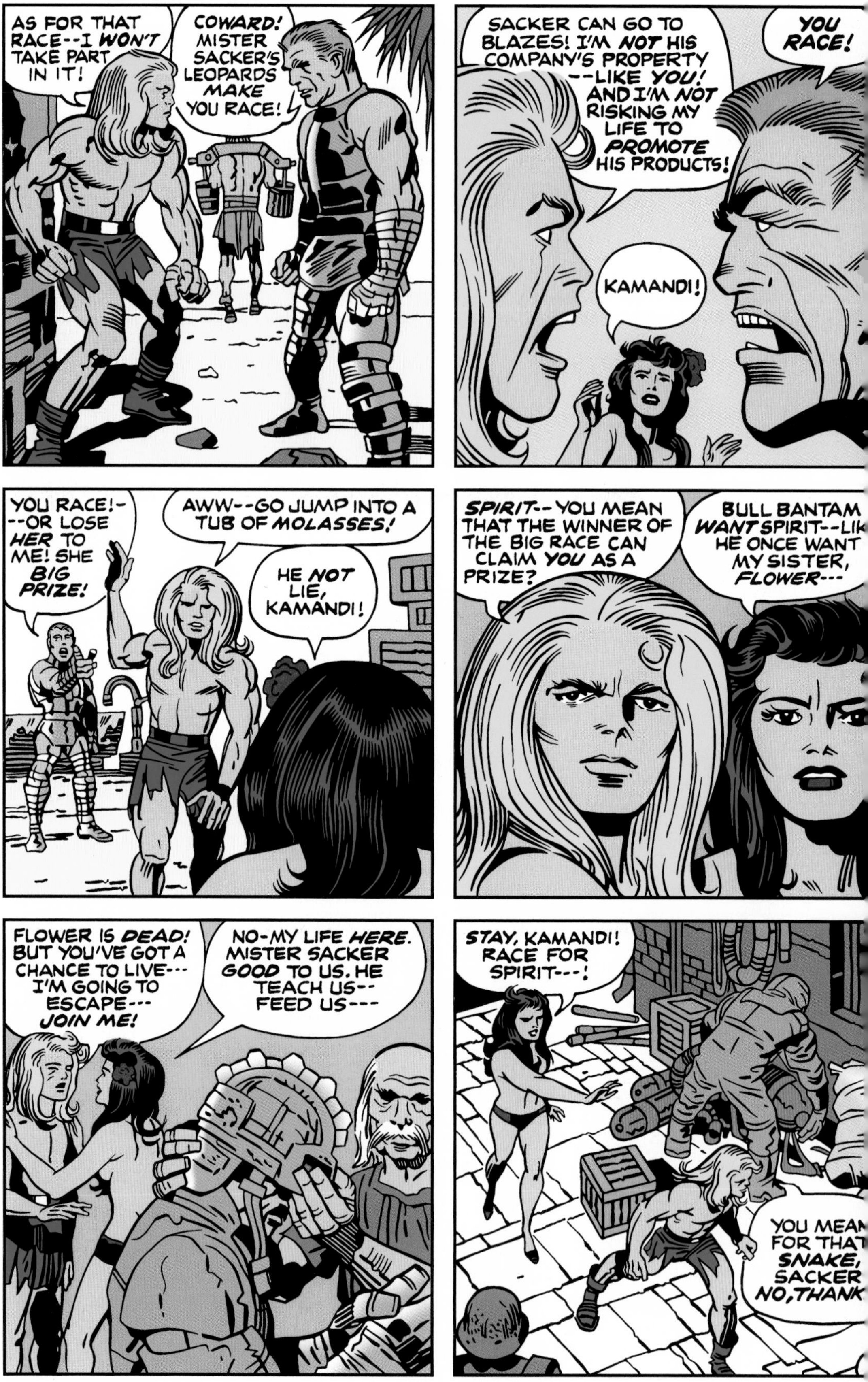
AS FOR THAT RACE--I WON'T TAKE PART IN IT!
COWARD! MISTER SACKER'S LEOPARDS MAKE YOU RACE!
SACKER CAN GO TO BLAZES! I'M NOT HIS COMPANY'S PROPERTY --LIKE YOU! AND I'M NOT RISKING MY LIFE TO PROMOTE HIS PRODUCTS!
YOU RACE!
KAMANDI!
YOU RACE!- --OR LOSE HER TO ME! SHE BIG PRIZE!
AWW--GO JUMP INTO A TUB OF MOLASSES!
HE NOT LIE, KAMANDI!
SPIRIT--YOU MEAN THAT THE WINNER OF THE BIG RACE CAN CLAIM YOU AS A PRIZE?
FLOWER IS DEAD! BUT YOU'VE GOT A CHANCE TO LIVE--- I'M GOING TO ESCAPE--- JOIN ME!
NO-MY LIFE HERE. MISTER SACKER GOOD TO US. HE TEACH US-- FEED US---
STAY, KAMANDI! RACE FOR SPIRIT---!

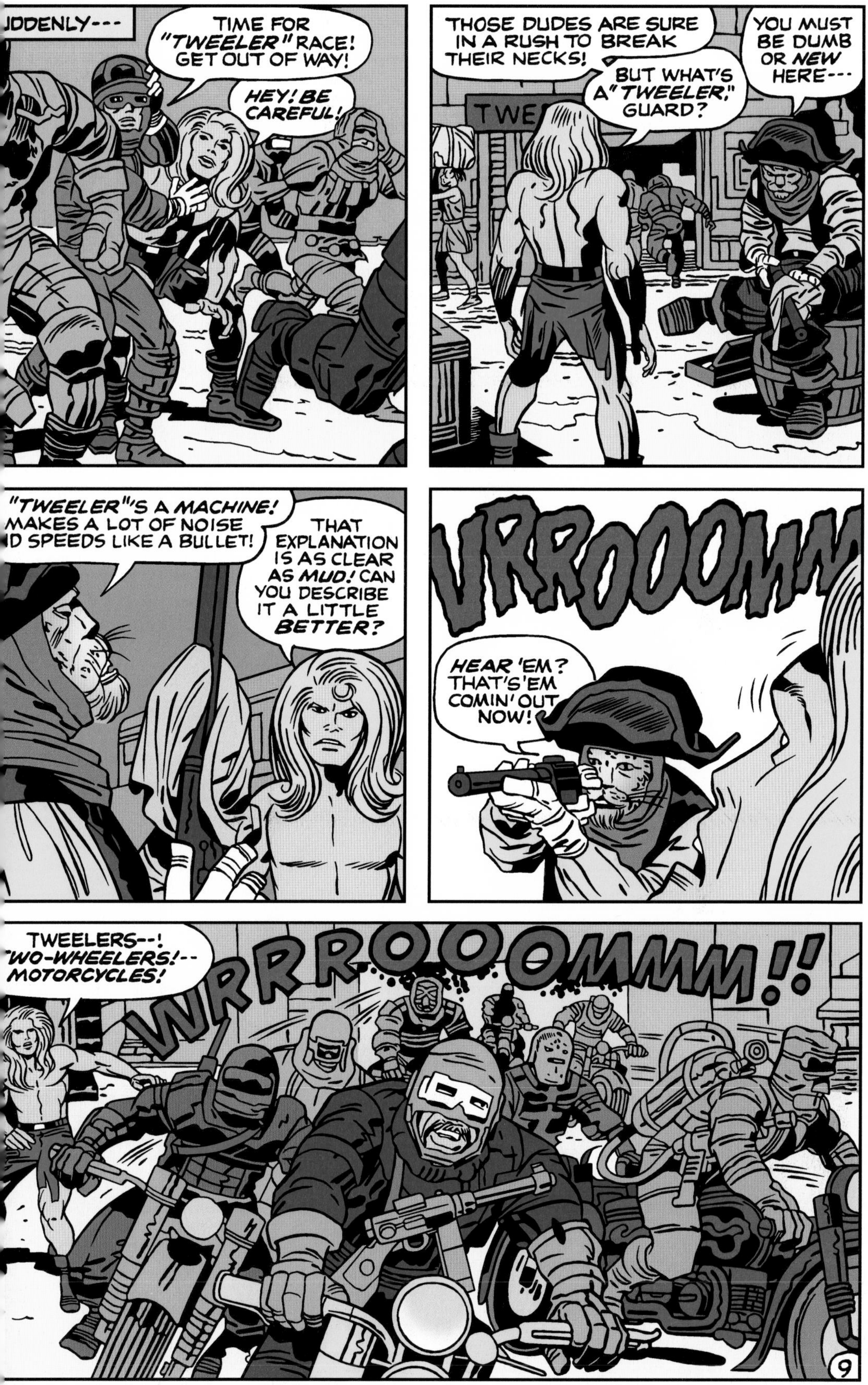
UDDENLY---
TIME FOR "TWEELER" RACE! GET OUT OF WAY!
HEY! BE CAREFUL!
THOSE DUDES ARE SURE IN A RUSH TO BREAK THEIR NECKS!
BUT WHAT'S A "TWEELER," GUARD?
YOU MUST BE DUMB OR NEW HERE---
TWE
"TWEELER"'S A MACHINE! MAKES A LOT OF NOISE ID SPEEDS LIKE A BULLET!
THAT EXPLANATION IS AS CLEAR AS MUD! CAN YOU DESCRIBE IT A LITTLE BETTER?
VRROOOMM
HEAR 'EM? THAT'S'EM COMIN' OUT NOW!
TWEELERS--! 'WO-WHEELERS!-- MOTORCYCLES!
WRRROOOMMM!!
9

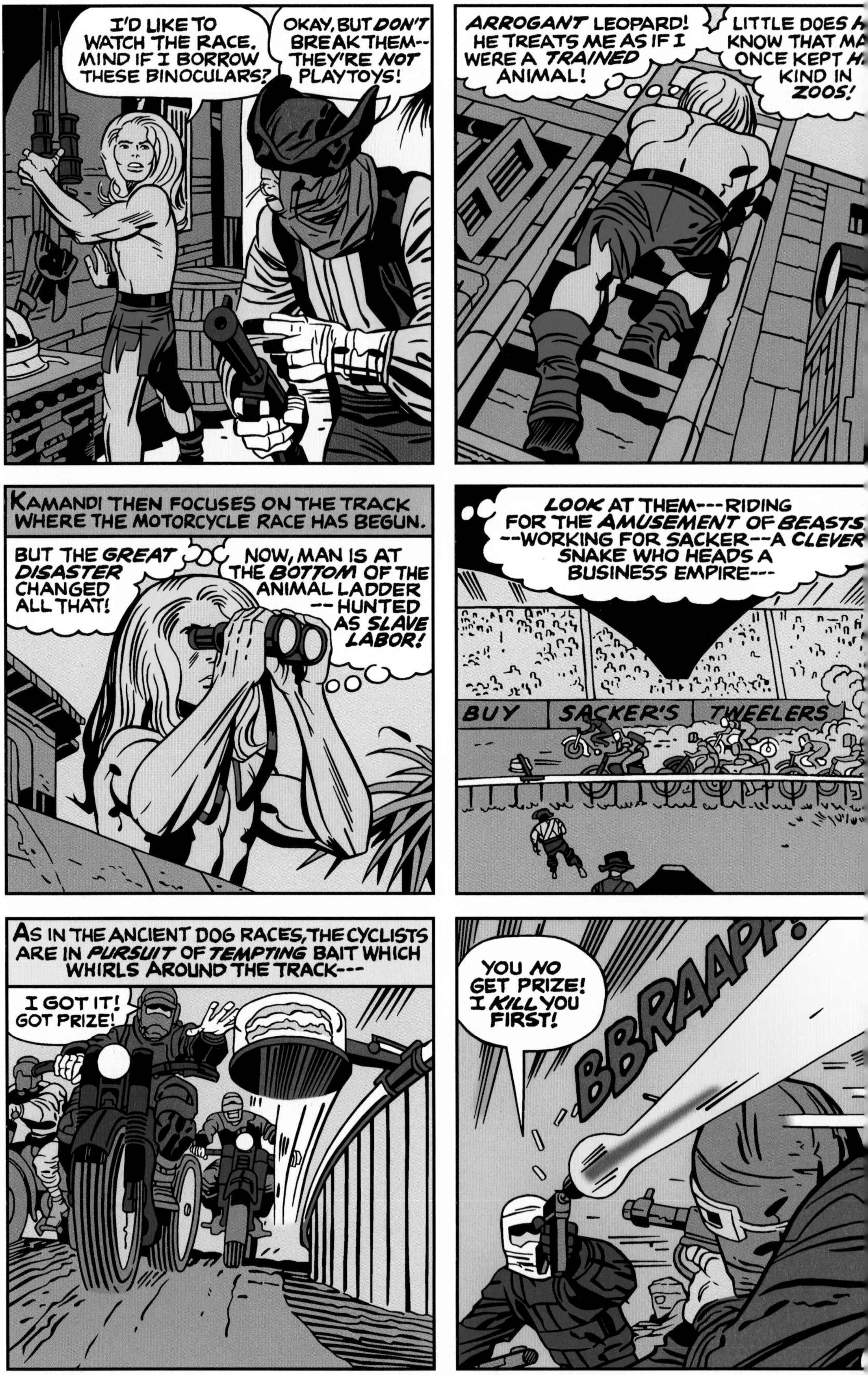
I'D LIKE TO WATCH THE RACE. MIND IF I BORROW THESE BINOCULARS?
OKAY, BUT DON'T BREAK THEM-- THEY'RE NOT PLAYTOYS!
ARROGANT LEOPARD! HE TREATS ME AS IF I WERE A TRAINED ANIMAL!
LITTLE DOES KNOW THAT MA ONCE KEPT KIND IN ZOOS!
KAMANDI THEN FOCUSES ON THE TRACK WHERE THE MOTORCYCLE RACE HAS BEGUN.
BUT THE GREAT DISASTER CHANGED ALL THAT!
NOW, MAN IS AT THE BOTTOM OF THE ANIMAL LADDER --HUNTED AS SLAVE LABOR!
LOOK AT THEM---RIDING FOR THE AMUSEMENT OF BEASTS --WORKING FOR SACKER--A CLEVER SNAKE WHO HEADS A BUSINESS EMPIRE---
BUY SACKER'S TWEELERS
AS IN THE ANCIENT DOG RACES, THE CYCLISTS ARE IN PURSUIT OF TEMPTING BAIT WHICH WHIRLS AROUND THE TRACK---
I GOT IT! GOT PRIZE!
YOU NO GET PRIZE! I KILL YOU FIRST!
BBRAAPP

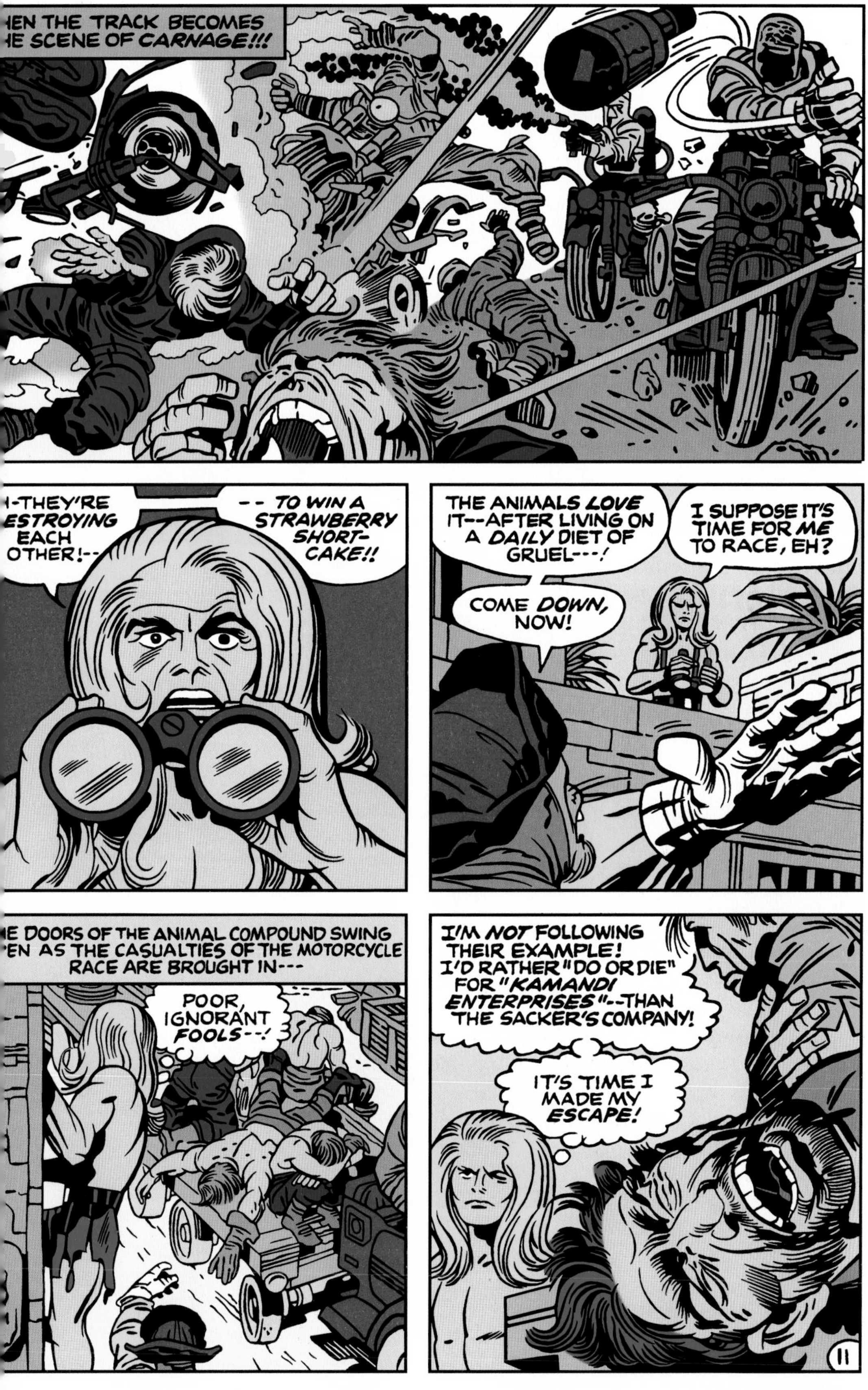
EN THE TRACK BECOMES
E SCENE OF *CARNAGE!!!*
-THEY'RE *ESTROYING* EACH OTHER!--
-- *TO WIN A STRAWBERRY SHORT-CAKE!!*
THE ANIMALS *LOVE* IT--AFTER LIVING ON A *DAILY* DIET OF GRUEL---!
I SUPPOSE IT'S TIME FOR *ME* TO RACE, EH?
COME *DOWN,* NOW!
E DOORS OF THE ANIMAL COMPOUND SWING
EN AS THE CASUALTIES OF THE MOTORCYCLE RACE ARE BROUGHT IN---
POOR, IGNORANT *FOOLS*--!
I'M *NOT* FOLLOWING THEIR EXAMPLE! I'D RATHER "DO OR DIE" FOR "*KAMANDI ENTERPRISES*"--THAN THE SACKER'S COMPANY!
IT'S TIME I MADE MY *ESCAPE!*
11

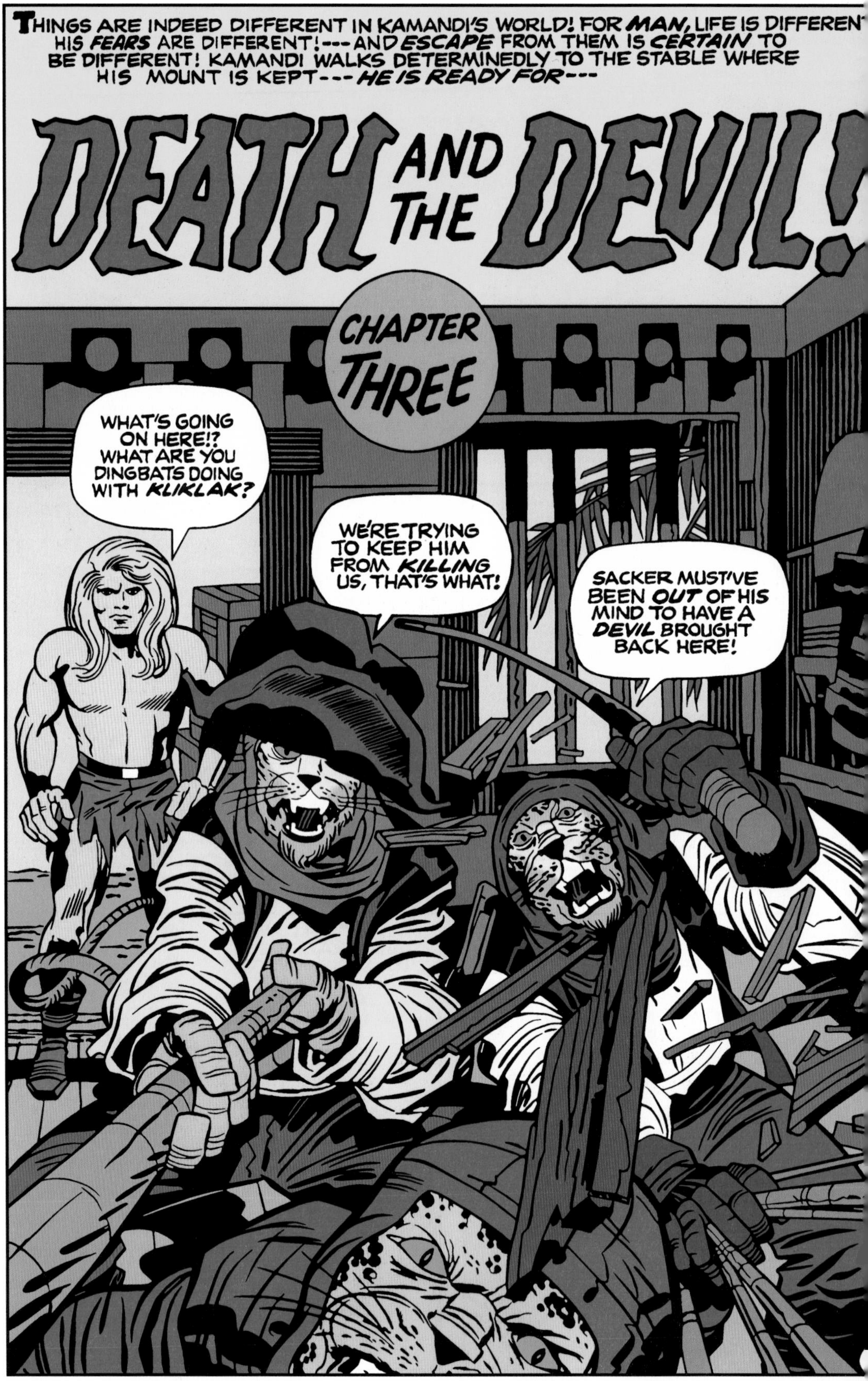
THINGS ARE INDEED DIFFERENT IN KAMANDI'S WORLD! FOR MAN, LIFE IS DIFFERENT HIS FEARS ARE DIFFERENT! --- AND ESCAPE FROM THEM IS CERTAIN TO BE DIFFERENT! KAMANDI WALKS DETERMINEDLY TO THE STABLE WHERE HIS MOUNT IS KEPT --- HE IS READY FOR---
DEATH AND THE DEVIL!
CHAPTER THREE
WHAT'S GOING ON HERE!? WHAT ARE YOU DINGBATS DOING WITH KLIKLAK?
WE'RE TRYING TO KEEP HIM FROM KILLING US, THAT'S WHAT!
SACKER MUST'VE BEEN OUT OF HIS MIND TO HAVE A DEVIL BROUGHT BACK HERE!

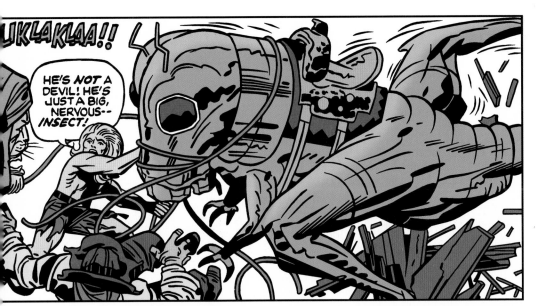

UKLAKLAA!!

HE'S *NOT* A DEVIL! HE'S JUST A BIG, NERVOUS-- *INSECT!*

...LLING ON HIM ...TH ROPES ONLY ...AKES HIM *MORE* JITTERY!

THEN YOU'D BETTER CALM HIM DOWN FOR THE BIG RACE!

WHAT RACE?

...KLIKLAK AND I ...RE *DUMPING* THE ...G RACE IN FAVOR OF A *BIGGER* PRIZE--

FREEDOM! GO, BOY-- GO!

CRAASHH!

IT'S A BREAK-OUT!

THE DEVIL'S LOOSE!

13

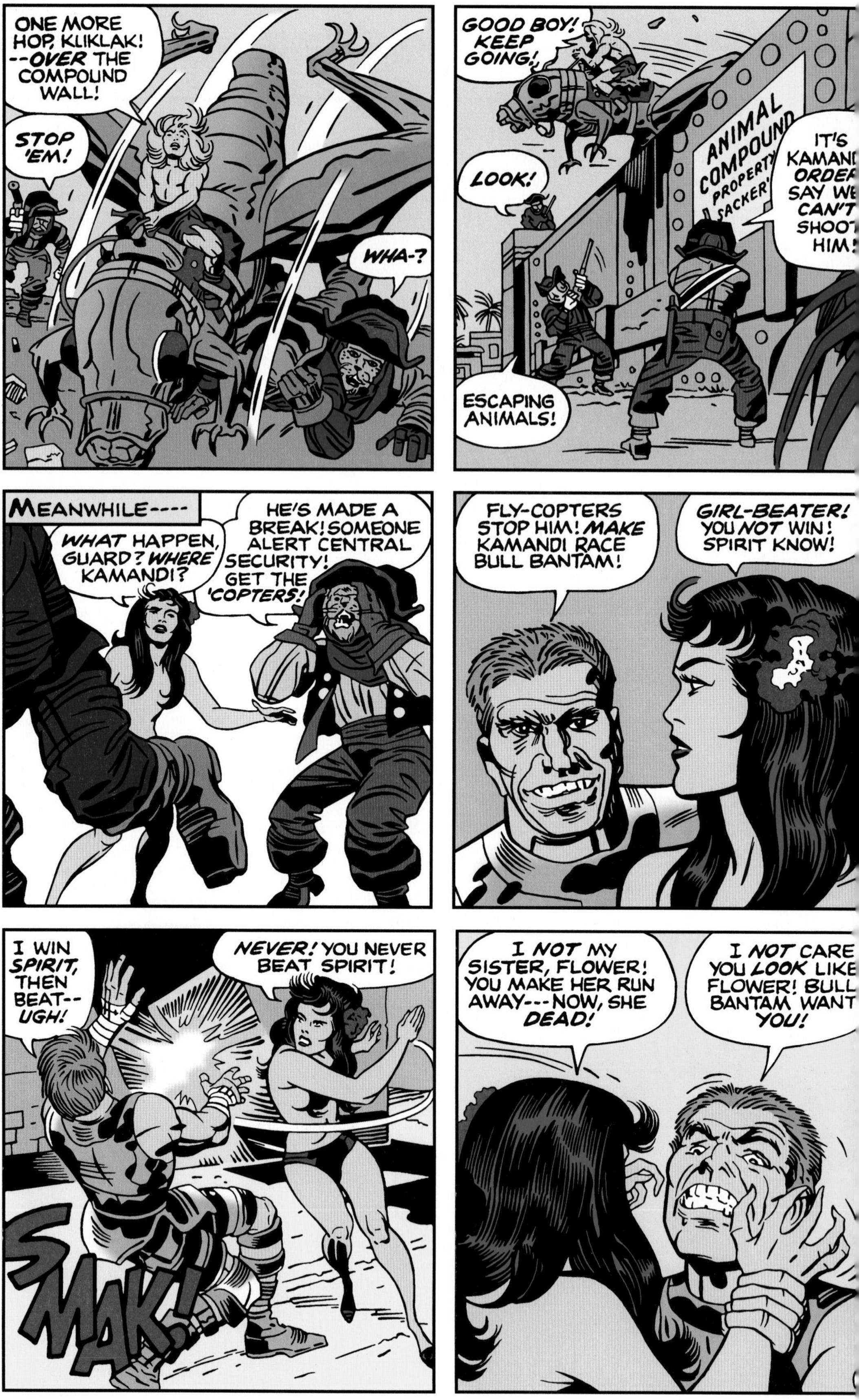
ONE MORE HOP, KLIKLAK! --OVER THE COMPOUND WALL!
STOP 'EM!
WHA-?
GOOD BOY! KEEP GOING!
LOOK!
ANIMAL COMPOUND
IT'S KAMANDI ORDER SAY WE CAN'T SHOOT HIM!
ESCAPING ANIMALS!
MEANWHILE----
WHAT HAPPEN, GUARD? WHERE KAMANDI?
HE'S MADE A BREAK! SOMEONE ALERT CENTRAL SECURITY! GET THE 'COPTERS!
FLY-COPTERS STOP HIM! MAKE KAMANDI RACE BULL BANTAM!
GIRL-BEATER! YOU NOT WIN! SPIRIT KNOW!
I WIN SPIRIT, THEN BEAT-- UGH!
NEVER! YOU NEVER BEAT SPIRIT!
SMAK!
I NOT MY SISTER, FLOWER! YOU MAKE HER RUN AWAY---NOW, SHE DEAD!
I NOT CARE YOU LOOK LIKE FLOWER! BULL BANTAM WANT YOU!

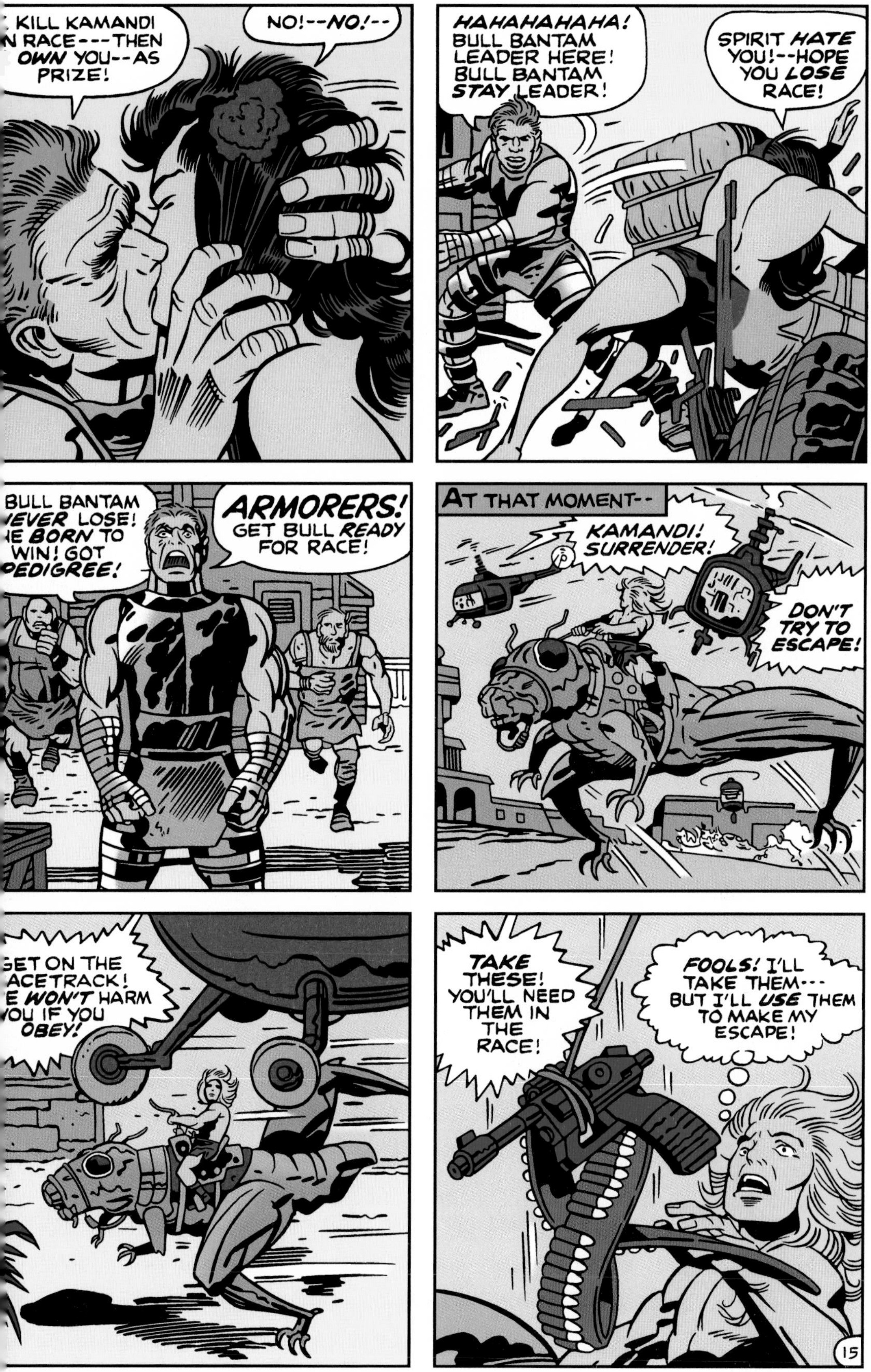
KILL KAMANDI
N RACE---THEN
OWN YOU--AS
PRIZE!
NO!--NO!--
HAHAHAHAHA!
BULL BANTAM
LEADER HERE!
BULL BANTAM
STAY LEADER!
SPIRIT HATE
YOU!--HOPE
YOU LOSE
RACE!
BULL BANTAM
VEVER LOSE!
IE BORN TO
WIN! GOT
PEDIGREE!
ARMORERS!
GET BULL READY
FOR RACE!
AT THAT MOMENT--
KAMANDI!
SURRENDER!
DON'T
TRY TO
ESCAPE!
GET ON THE
ACETRACK!
E WON'T HARM
YOU IF YOU
OBEY!
TAKE
THESE!
YOU'LL NEED
THEM IN
THE
RACE!
FOOLS! I'LL
TAKE THEM---
BUT I'LL USE THEM
TO MAKE MY
ESCAPE!
15

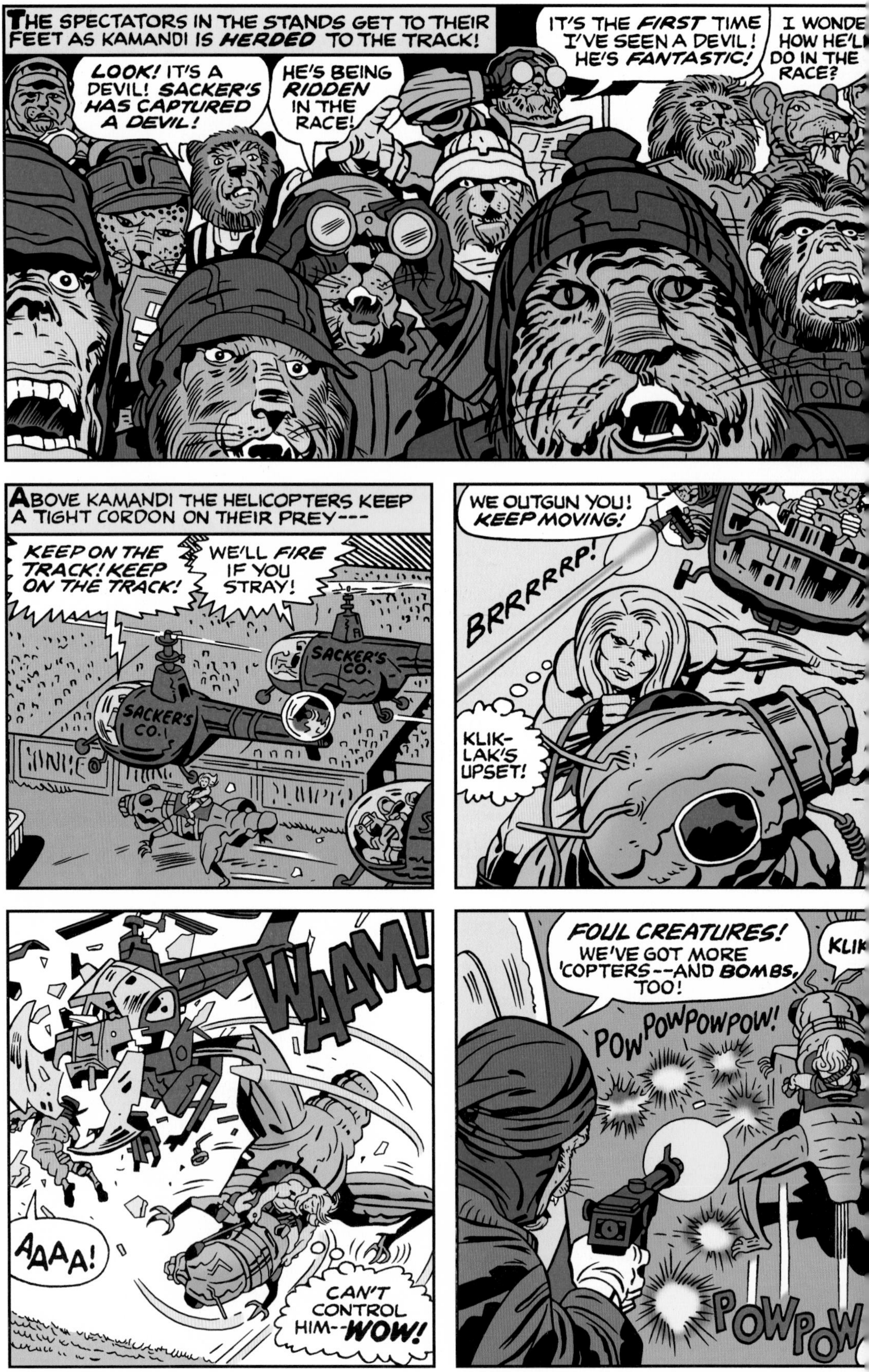
THE SPECTATORS IN THE STANDS GET TO THEIR FEET AS KAMANDI IS HERDED TO THE TRACK!
LOOK! IT'S A DEVIL! SACKER'S HAS CAPTURED A DEVIL!
HE'S BEING RIDDEN IN THE RACE!
IT'S THE FIRST TIME I'VE SEEN A DEVIL! HE'S FANTASTIC!
ABOVE KAMANDI THE HELICOPTERS KEEP A TIGHT CORDON ON THEIR PREY---
KEEP ON THE TRACK! KEEP ON THE TRACK!
WE'LL FIRE IF YOU STRAY!
SACKER'S CO.
SACKER'S CO.
WE OUTGUN YOU! KEEP MOVING!
BRRRRRP!
KLIK-LAK'S UPSET!
WAAM!
AAAA!
CAN'T CONTROL HIM--WOW!
FOUL CREATURES! WE'VE GOT MORE 'COPTERS--AND BOMBS, TOO!
POWPOWPOWPOW!

O YOU SEE THAT? THE DEVIL CKED OFF A 'COPTER!

THEY'RE OFF!

A HORSE COULDN'T DO IT!

WELL, IT LOOKS LIKE WE'RE *IN* THE RACE, KLIKLAK!

THAT DEVIL HAS *SPEED!*

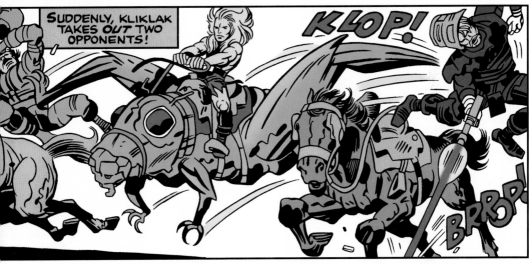

SUDDENLY, KLIKLAK TAKES *OUT* TWO OPPONENTS!

KLOP!

BRRRP!

HEN, AS KAMANDI BEGINS TO *CROWD* HE OTHERS--

RRAAAAP!

STAY OFF MY TAIL, YOU--

THE FIRING SPURS KLIKLAK TO LEAP CLEAR OVER THE LINE OF RIDERS--

STOP THE DEVIL! HE'S OUT IN FRONT!

BAM!

BAM!

17

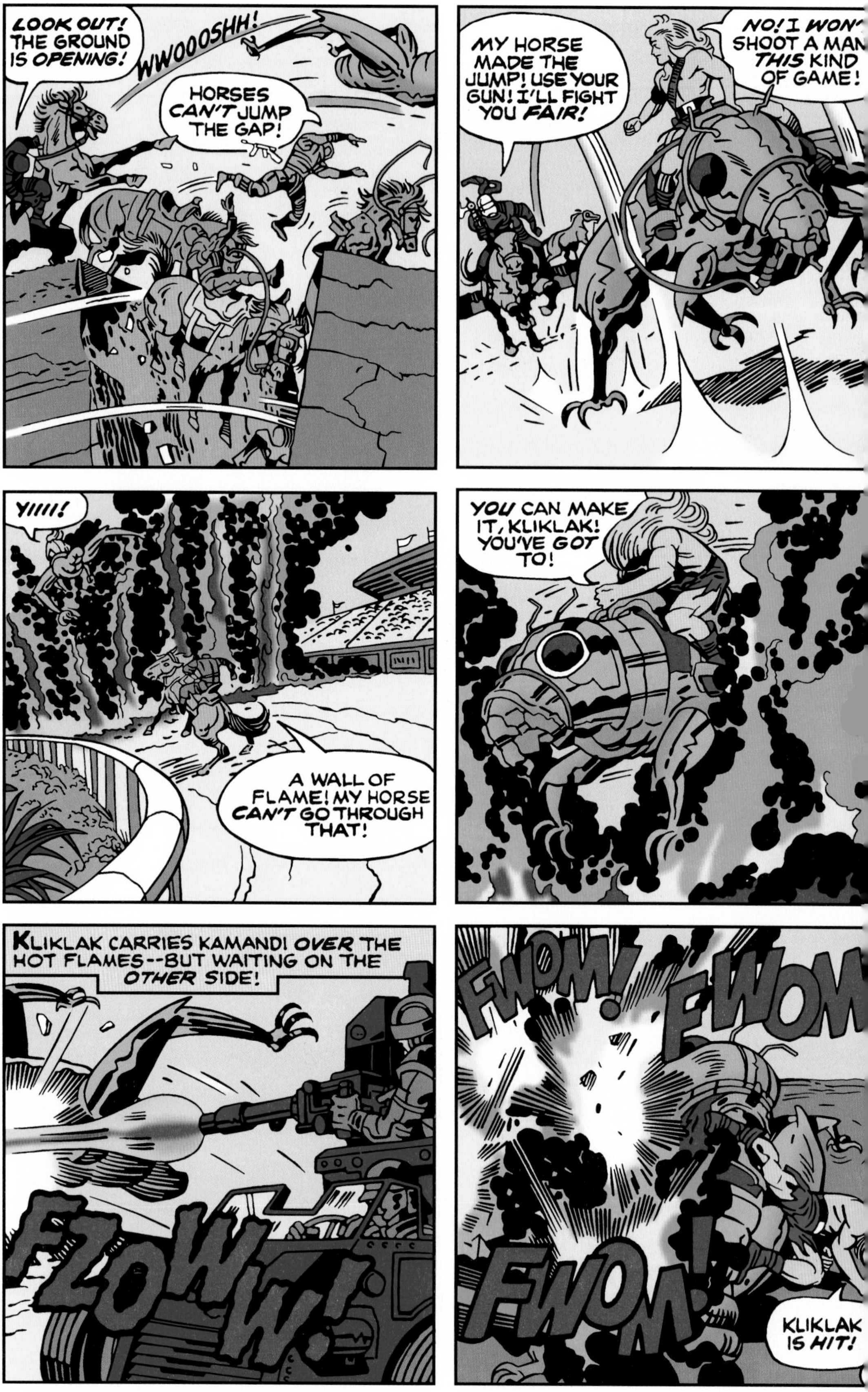
LOOK OUT! THE GROUND IS OPENING!
WWOOOSHH!
HORSES CAN'T JUMP THE GAP!
MY HORSE MADE THE JUMP! USE YOUR GUN! I'LL FIGHT YOU FAIR!
NO! I WON' SHOOT A MAN THIS KIND OF GAME!
YIIII!
A WALL OF FLAME! MY HORSE CAN'T GO THROUGH THAT!
YOU CAN MAKE IT, KLIKLAK! YOU'VE GOT TO!
KLIKLAK CARRIES KAMANDI OVER THE HOT FLAMES--BUT WAITING ON THE OTHER SIDE!
FZOWW!
FWOM!
FWOM
FWOM!
KLIKLAK IS HIT!

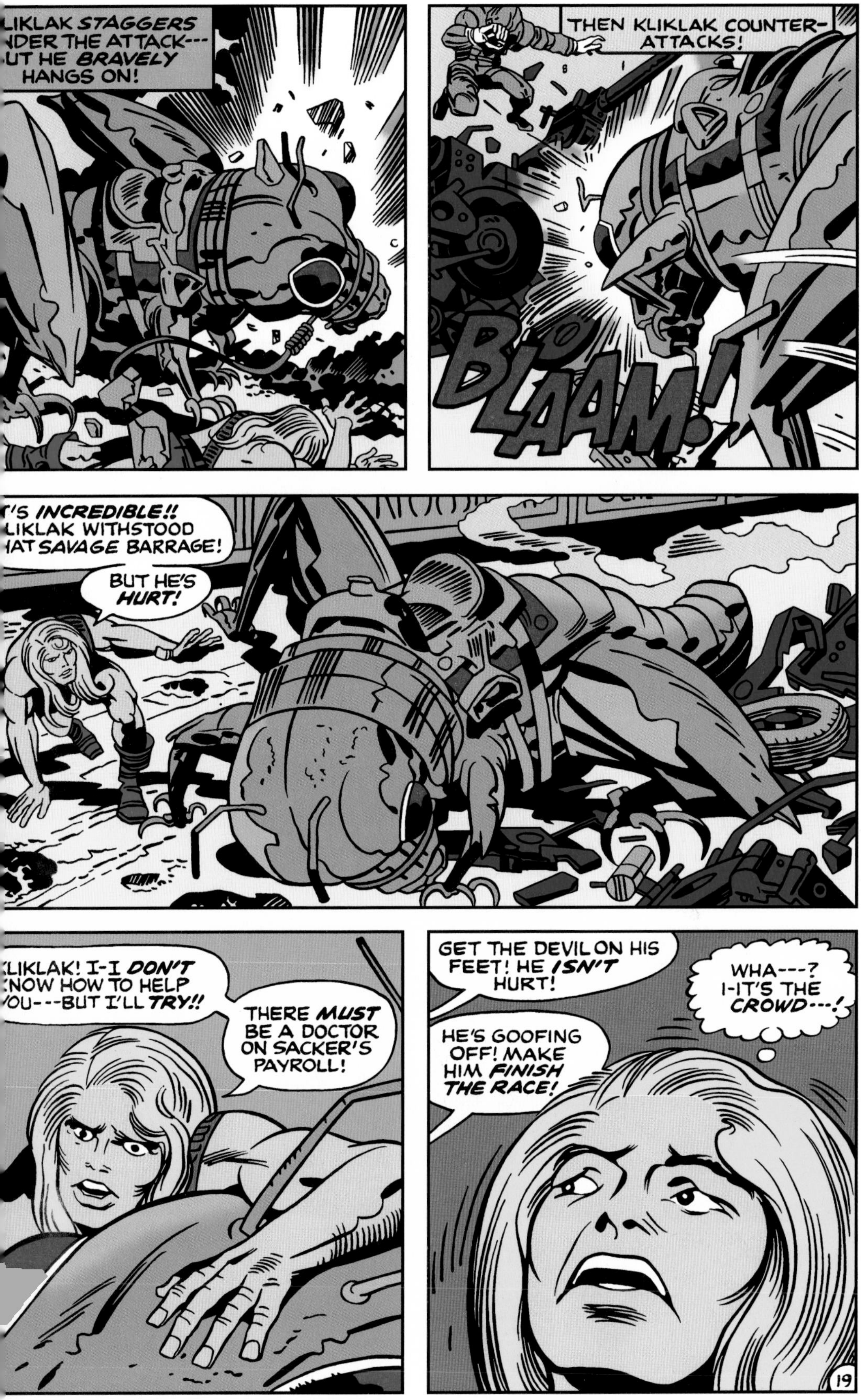
LIKLAK STAGGERS
NDER THE ATTACK---
UT HE BRAVELY
HANGS ON!
THEN KLIKLAK COUNTER-
ATTACKS!
BLAAM!
'S INCREDIBLE!!
LIKLAK WITHSTOOD
IAT SAVAGE BARRAGE!
BUT HE'S
HURT!
LIKLAK! I-I DON'T
NOW HOW TO HELP
OU---BUT I'LL TRY!!
THERE MUST
BE A DOCTOR
ON SACKER'S
PAYROLL!
GET THE DEVIL ON HIS
FEET! HE ISN'T
HURT!
HE'S GOOFING
OFF! MAKE
HIM FINISH
THE RACE!
WHA---?
I-IT'S THE
CROWD---!
19

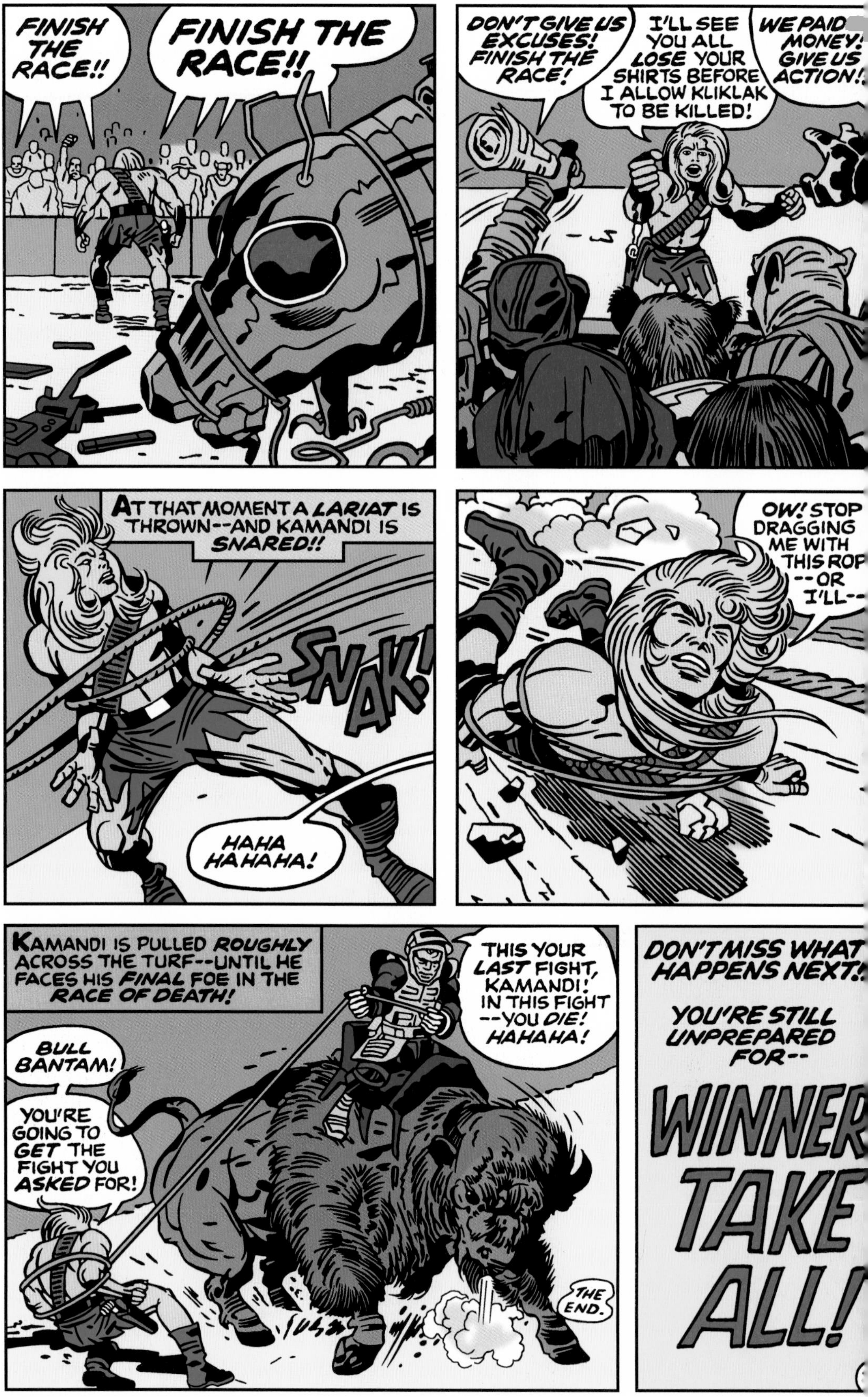
FINISH THE RACE!!
FINISH THE RACE!!
DON'T GIVE US EXCUSES! FINISH THE RACE!
I'LL SEE YOU ALL LOSE YOUR SHIRTS BEFORE I ALLOW KLIKLAK TO BE KILLED!
WE PAID MONEY! GIVE US ACTION!
AT THAT MOMENT A LARIAT IS THROWN--AND KAMANDI IS SNARED!!
SNAK!
HAHA HAHAHA!
OW! STOP DRAGGING ME WITH THIS ROP --OR I'LL--
KAMANDI IS PULLED ROUGHLY ACROSS THE TURF--UNTIL HE FACES HIS FINAL FOE IN THE RACE OF DEATH!
BULL BANTAM!
YOU'RE GOING TO GET THE FIGHT YOU ASKED FOR!
THIS YOUR LAST FIGHT, KAMANDI! IN THIS FIGHT --YOU DIE! HAHAHA!
THE END.
DON'T MISS WHAT HAPPENS NEXT!
YOU'RE STILL UNPREPARED FOR--
WINNER TAKE ALL!

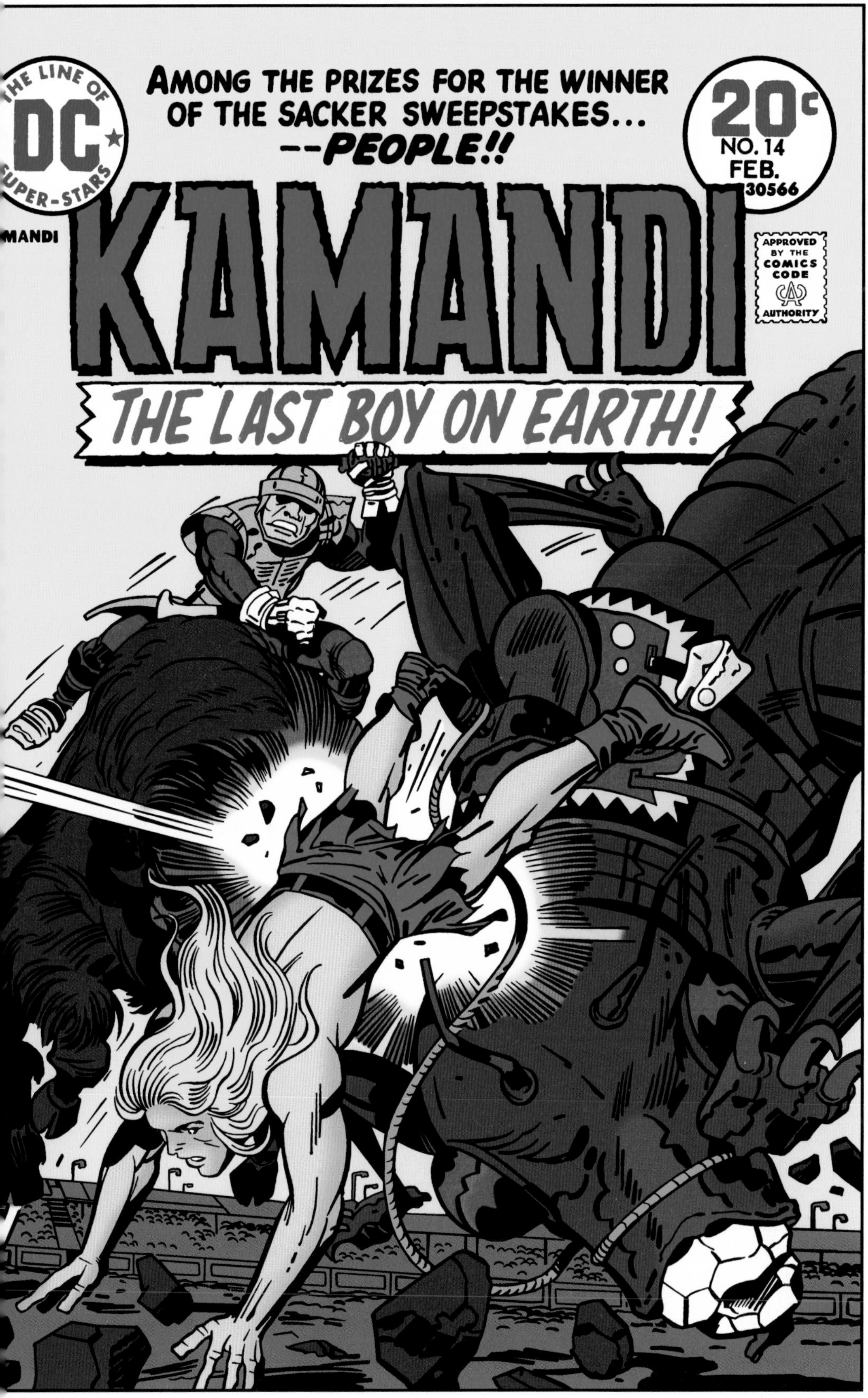
AMONG THE PRIZES FOR THE WINNER OF THE SACKER SWEEPSTAKES... --PEOPLE!!
THE LINE OF DC SUPER-STARS
20¢ NO. 14 FEB. 30566
KAMANDI
APPROVED BY THE COMICS CODE AUTHORITY
KAMANDI
THE LAST BOY ON EARTH!

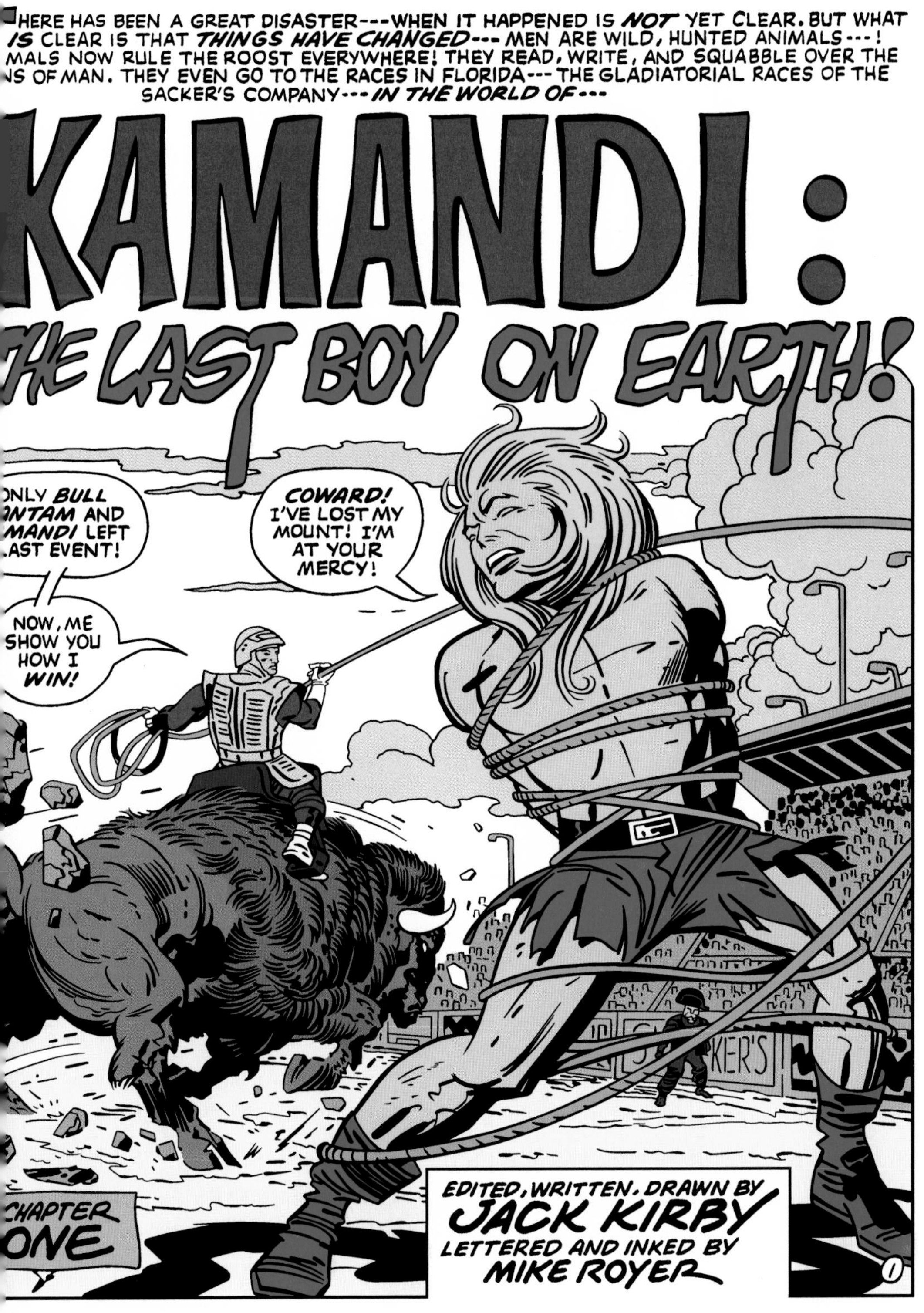
HERE HAS BEEN A GREAT DISASTER---WHEN IT HAPPENED IS NOT YET CLEAR. BUT WHAT IS CLEAR IS THAT THINGS HAVE CHANGED--- MEN ARE WILD, HUNTED ANIMALS---! MALS NOW RULE THE ROOST EVERYWHERE! THEY READ, WRITE, AND SQUABBLE OVER THE NS OF MAN. THEY EVEN GO TO THE RACES IN FLORIDA--- THE GLADIATORIAL RACES OF THE SACKER'S COMPANY--- IN THE WORLD OF---
KAMANDI:
THE LAST BOY ON EARTH!
NLY BULL NTAM AND MANDI LEFT AST EVENT!
NOW, ME SHOW YOU HOW I WIN!
COWARD! I'VE LOST MY MOUNT! I'M AT YOUR MERCY!
KER'S
CHAPTER ONE
EDITED, WRITTEN, DRAWN BY JACK KIRBY
LETTERED AND INKED BY MIKE ROYER
1

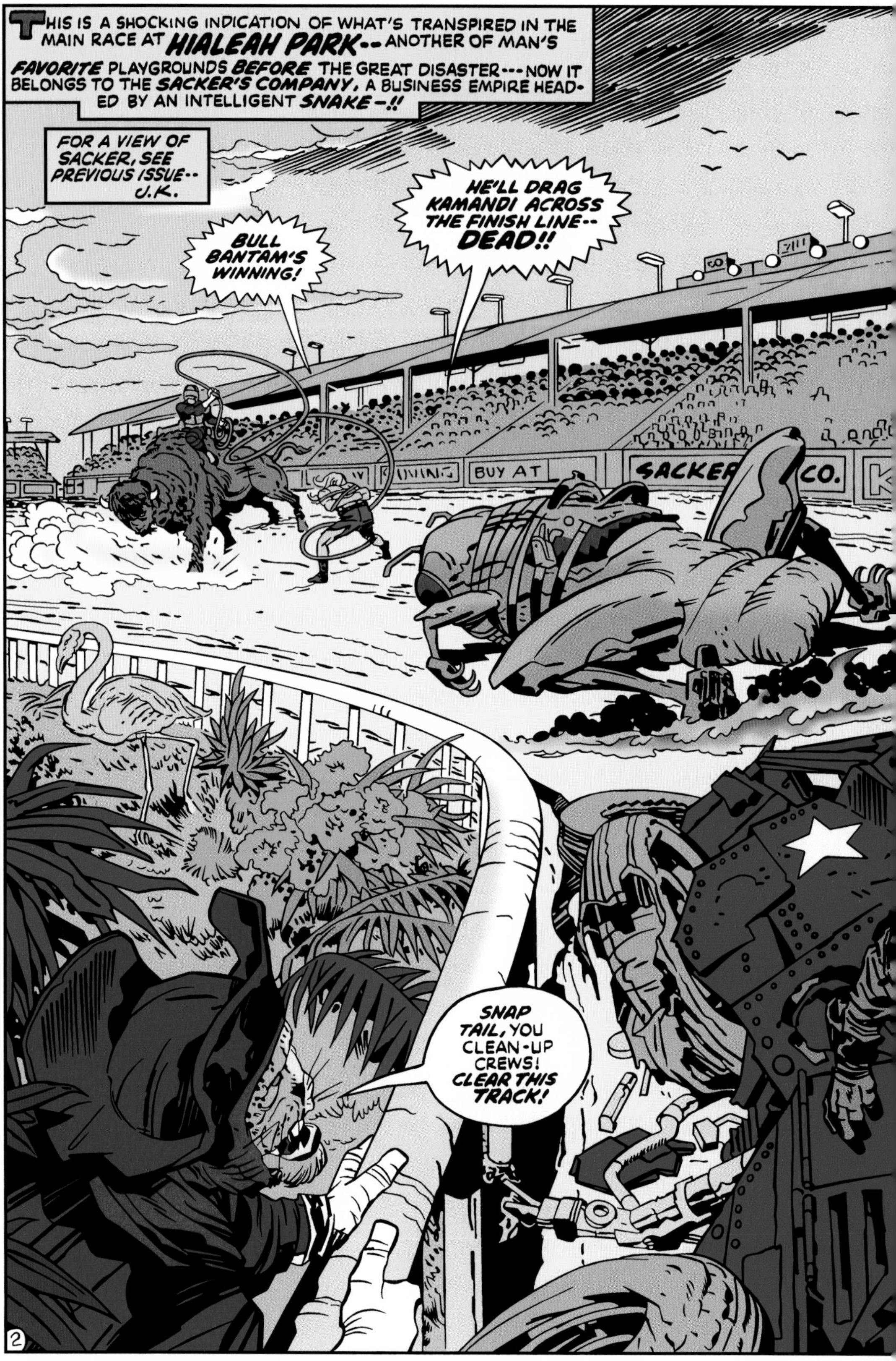
THIS IS A SHOCKING INDICATION OF WHAT'S TRANSPIRED IN THE MAIN RACE AT HIALEAH PARK-- ANOTHER OF MAN'S FAVORITE PLAYGROUNDS BEFORE THE GREAT DISASTER---NOW IT BELONGS TO THE SACKER'S COMPANY, A BUSINESS EMPIRE HEADED BY AN INTELLIGENT SNAKE-!!
FOR A VIEW OF SACKER, SEE PREVIOUS ISSUE-- J.K.
BULL BANTAM'S WINNING!
HE'LL DRAG KAMANDI ACROSS THE FINISH LINE-- DEAD!!
BUY AT
SACKER CO.
SNAP TAIL, YOU CLEAN-UP CREWS! CLEAR THIS TRACK!
2

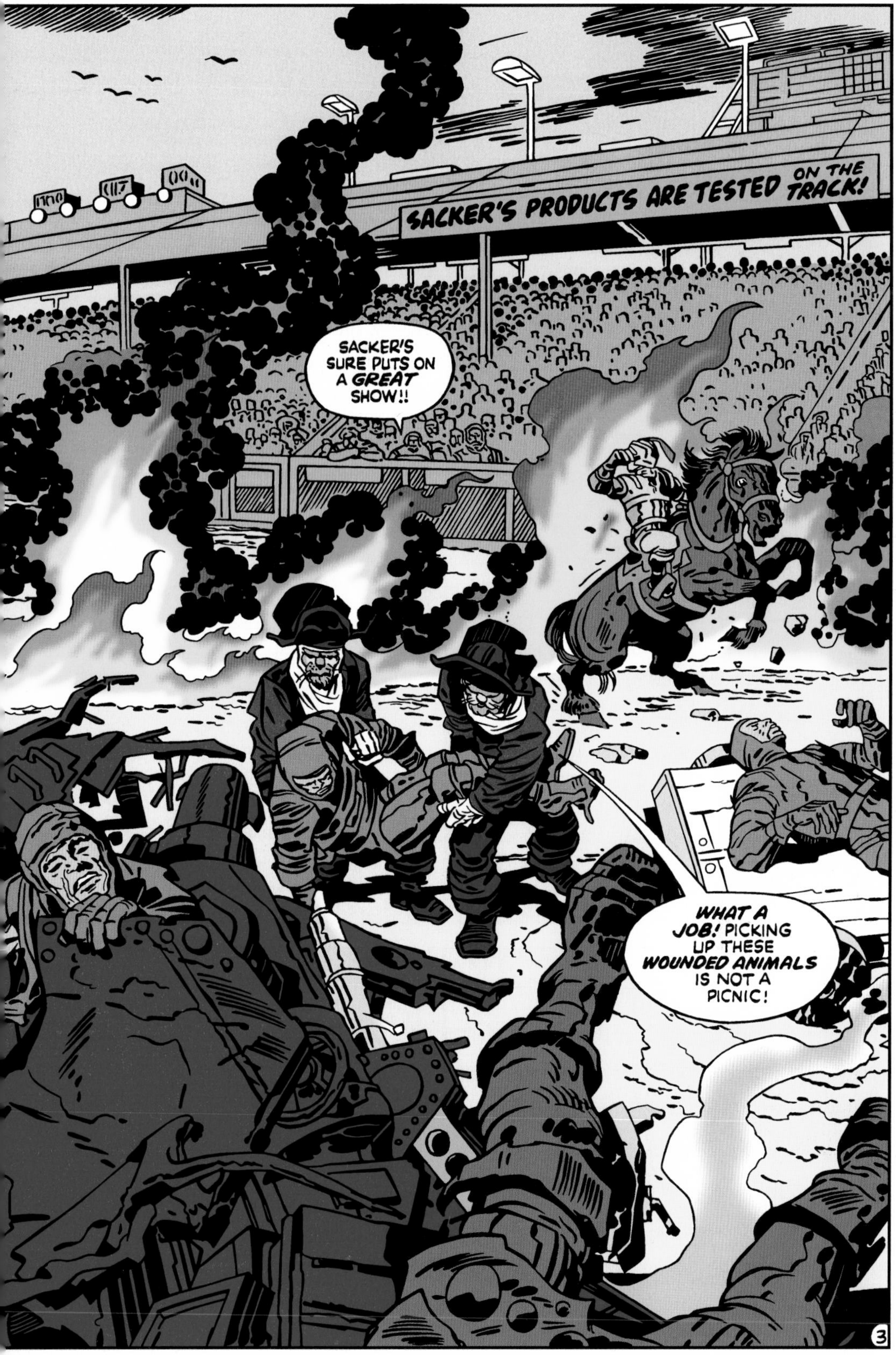
SACKER'S PRODUCTS ARE TESTED ON THE TRACK!
SACKER'S SURE PUTS ON A GREAT SHOW!!
WHAT A JOB! PICKING UP THESE WOUNDED ANIMALS IS NOT A PICNIC!
3

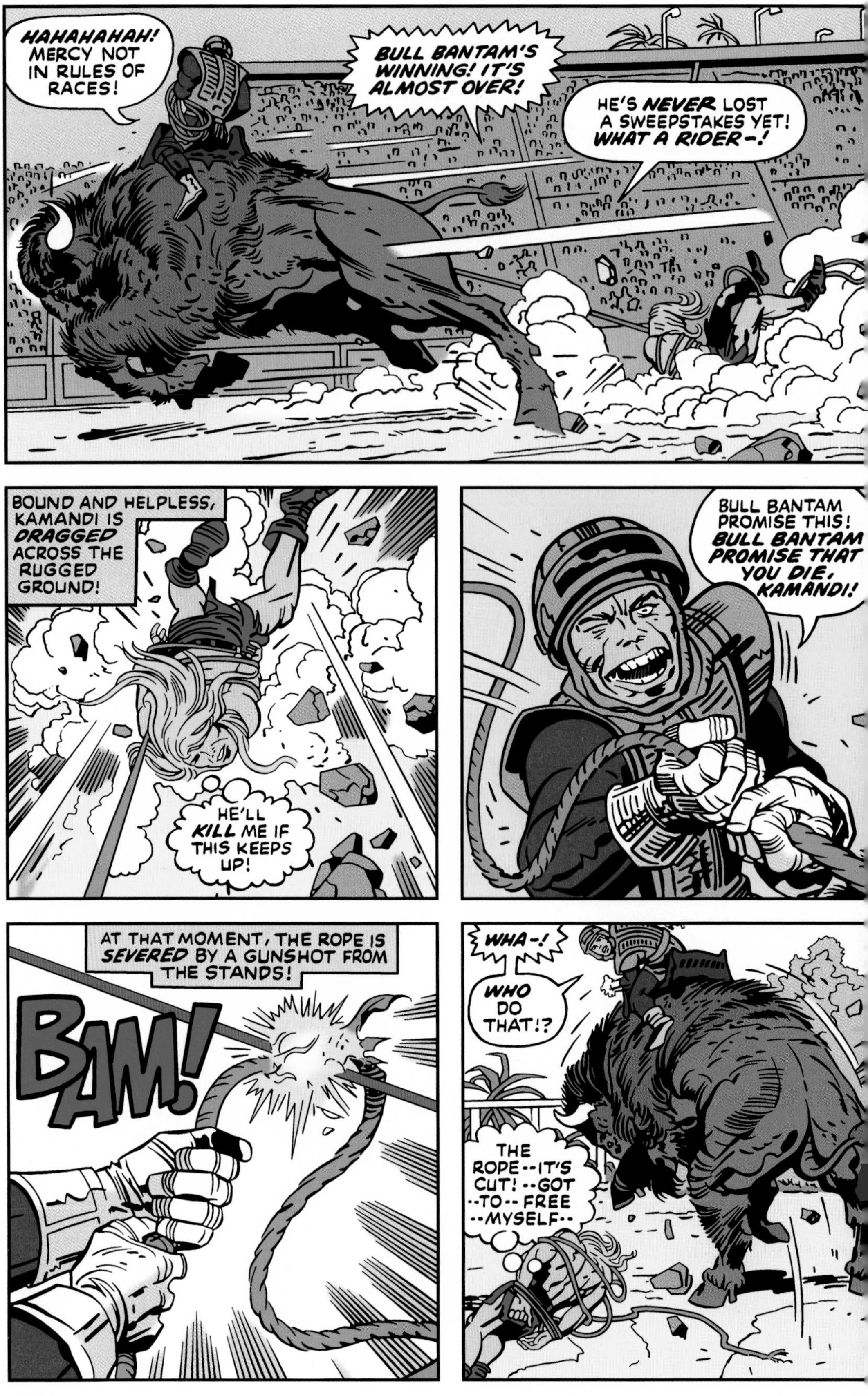
HAHAHAHAH! MERCY NOT IN RULES OF RACES!
BULL BANTAM'S WINNING! IT'S ALMOST OVER!
HE'S NEVER LOST A SWEEPSTAKES YET! WHAT A RIDER--!
BOUND AND HELPLESS, KAMANDI IS DRAGGED ACROSS THE RUGGED GROUND!
HE'LL KILL ME IF THIS KEEPS UP!
BULL BANTAM PROMISE THIS! BULL BANTAM PROMISE THAT YOU DIE, KAMANDI!
AT THAT MOMENT, THE ROPE IS SEVERED BY A GUNSHOT FROM THE STANDS!
BAM!
WHA--!
WHO DO THAT!?
THE ROPE--IT'S CUT! --GOT --TO-- FREE --MYSELF--

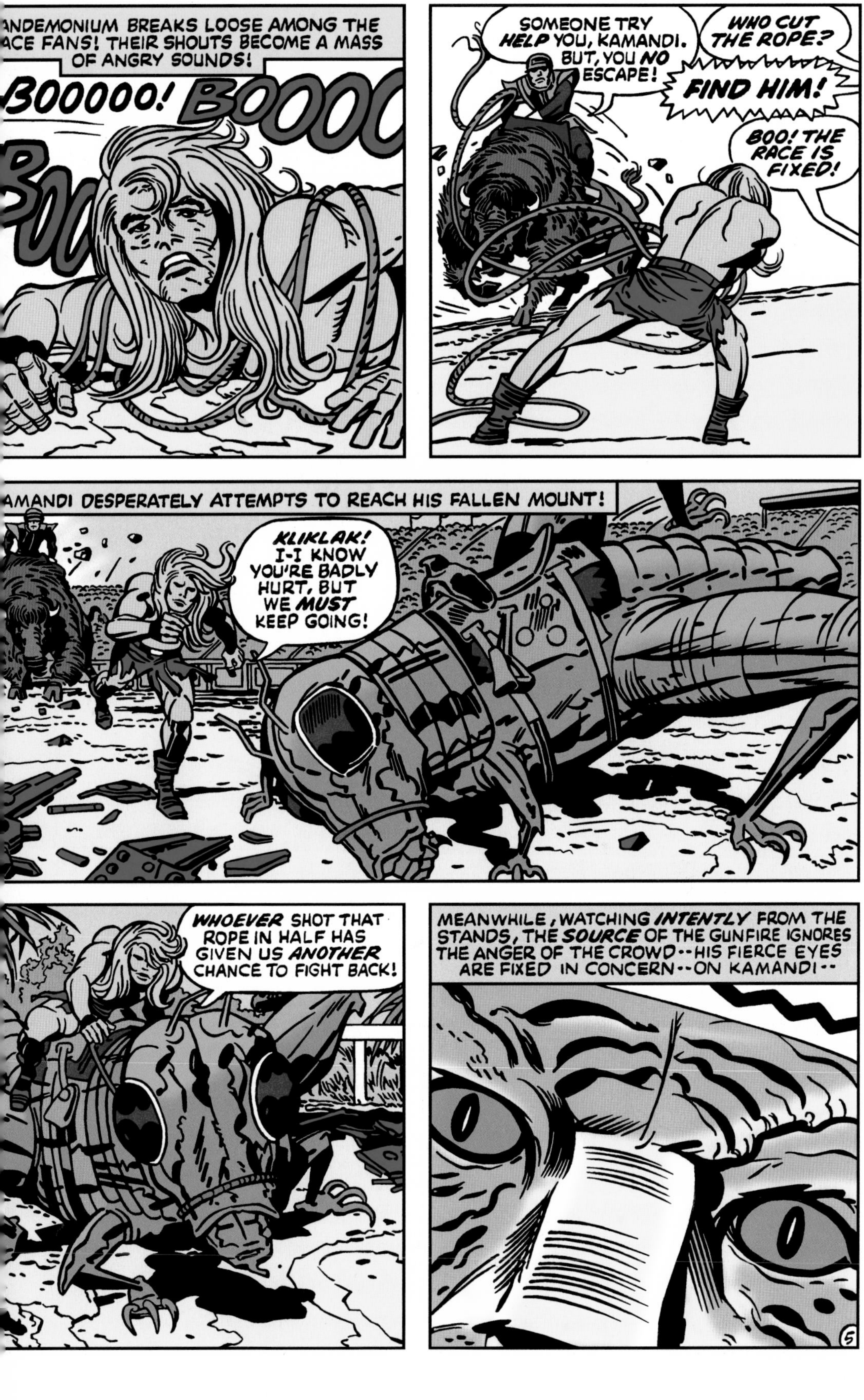
ANDEMONIUM BREAKS LOOSE AMONG THE ACE FANS! THEIR SHOUTS BECOME A MASS OF ANGRY SOUNDS!
BOOOOO! BOOOO
SOMEONE TRY HELP YOU, KAMANDI. BUT, YOU NO ESCAPE!
WHO CUT THE ROPE?
FIND HIM!
BOO! THE RACE IS FIXED!
AMANDI DESPERATELY ATTEMPTS TO REACH HIS FALLEN MOUNT!
KLIKLAK! I-I KNOW YOU'RE BADLY HURT, BUT WE MUST KEEP GOING!
WHOEVER SHOT THAT ROPE IN HALF HAS GIVEN US ANOTHER CHANCE TO FIGHT BACK!
MEANWHILE, WATCHING INTENTLY FROM THE STANDS, THE SOURCE OF THE GUNFIRE IGNORES THE ANGER OF THE CROWD--HIS FIERCE EYES ARE FIXED IN CONCERN--ON KAMANDI--
5

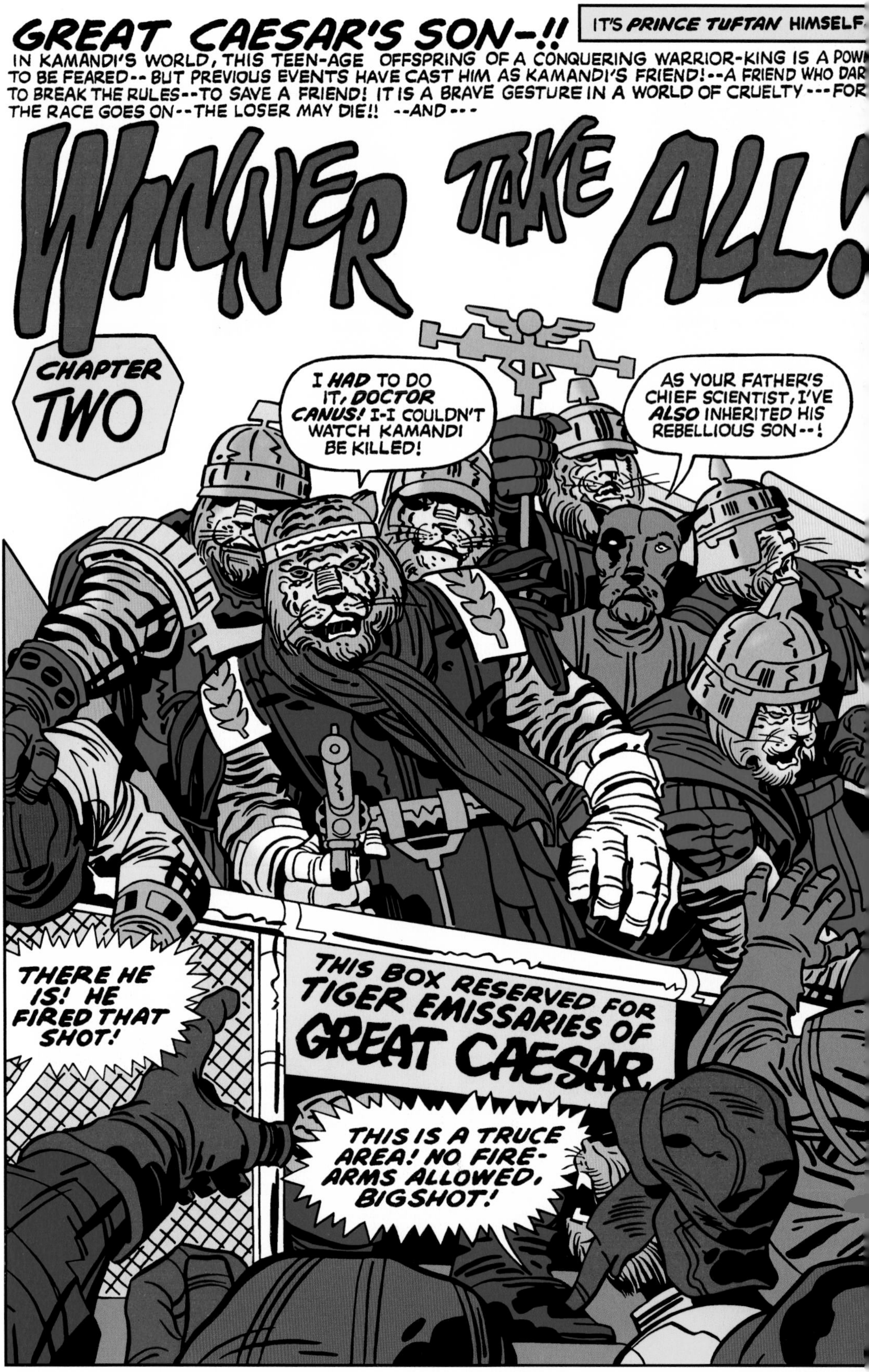
GREAT CAESAR'S SON-!!
IT'S PRINCE TUFTAN HIMSELF.
IN KAMANDI'S WORLD, THIS TEEN-AGE OFFSPRING OF A CONQUERING WARRIOR-KING IS A POW
TO BE FEARED--BUT PREVIOUS EVENTS HAVE CAST HIM AS KAMANDI'S FRIEND!--A FRIEND WHO DAR
TO BREAK THE RULES--TO SAVE A FRIEND! IT IS A BRAVE GESTURE IN A WORLD OF CRUELTY---FOR
THE RACE GOES ON--THE LOSER MAY DIE!! --AND---
WINNER TAKE ALL!
CHAPTER TWO
I HAD TO DO IT, DOCTOR CANUS! I-I COULDN'T WATCH KAMANDI BE KILLED!
AS YOUR FATHER'S CHIEF SCIENTIST, I'VE ALSO INHERITED HIS REBELLIOUS SON--!
THERE HE IS! HE FIRED THAT SHOT!
THIS BOX RESERVED FOR TIGER EMISSARIES OF GREAT CAESAR
THIS IS A TRUCE AREA! NO FIRE-ARMS ALLOWED, BIGSHOT!

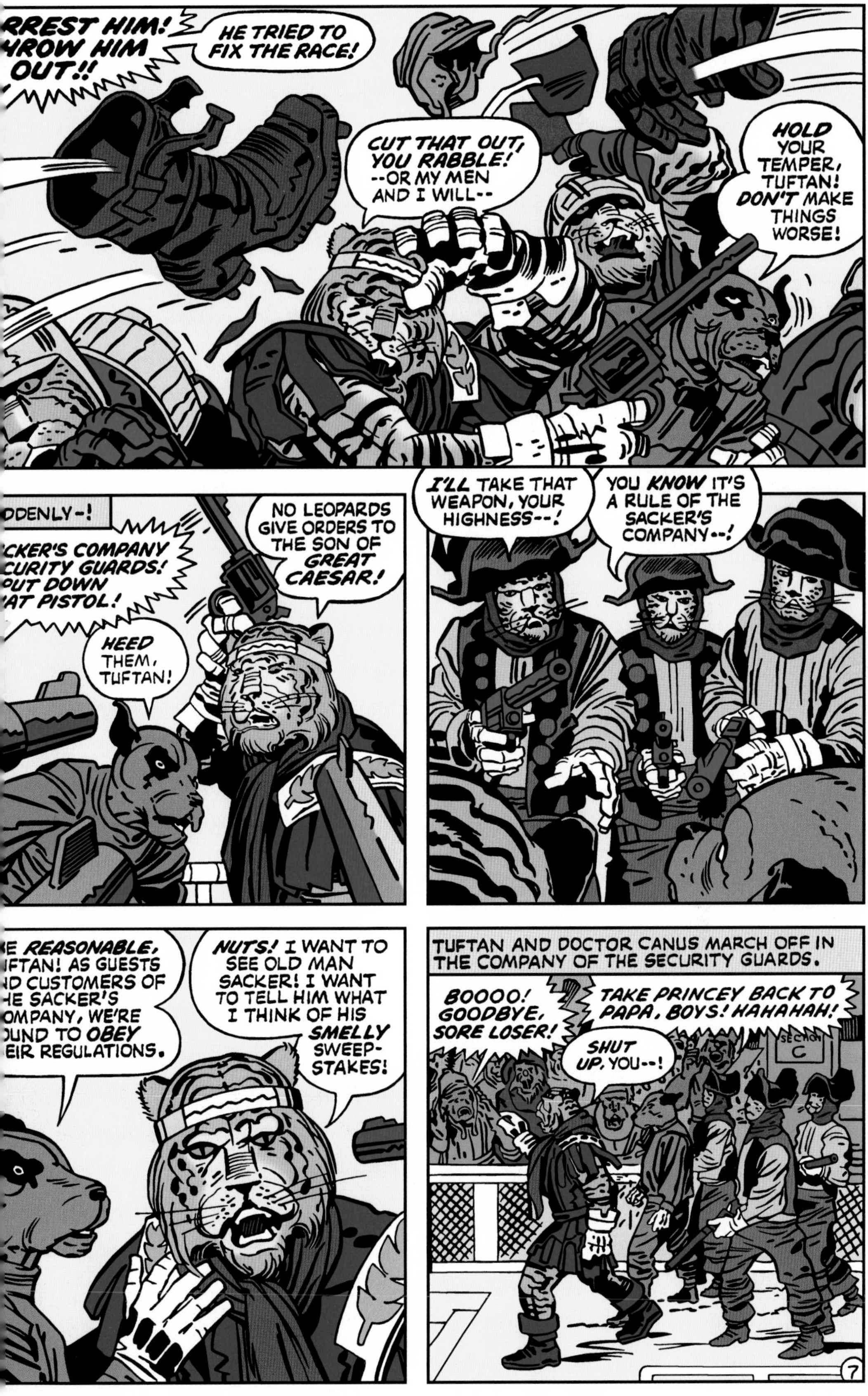
RREST HIM! HROW HIM OUT!!
HE TRIED TO FIX THE RACE!
CUT THAT OUT, YOU RABBLE! --OR MY MEN AND I WILL--
HOLD YOUR TEMPER, TUFTAN! DON'T MAKE THINGS WORSE!
DDENLY-!
CKER'S COMPANY CURITY GUARDS! PUT DOWN AT PISTOL!
NO LEOPARDS GIVE ORDERS TO THE SON OF GREAT CAESAR!
HEED THEM, TUFTAN!
I'LL TAKE THAT WEAPON, YOUR HIGHNESS--!
YOU KNOW IT'S A RULE OF THE SACKER'S COMPANY--!
E REASONABLE, FTAN! AS GUESTS D CUSTOMERS OF E SACKER'S OMPANY, WE'RE UND TO OBEY EIR REGULATIONS.
NUTS! I WANT TO SEE OLD MAN SACKER! I WANT TO TELL HIM WHAT I THINK OF HIS SMELLY SWEEP-STAKES!
TUFTAN AND DOCTOR CANUS MARCH OFF IN THE COMPANY OF THE SECURITY GUARDS.
BOOOO! GOODBYE, SORE LOSER!
TAKE PRINCEY BACK TO PAPA, BOYS! HAHAHAH!
SHUT UP, YOU--!
SECTION C
7

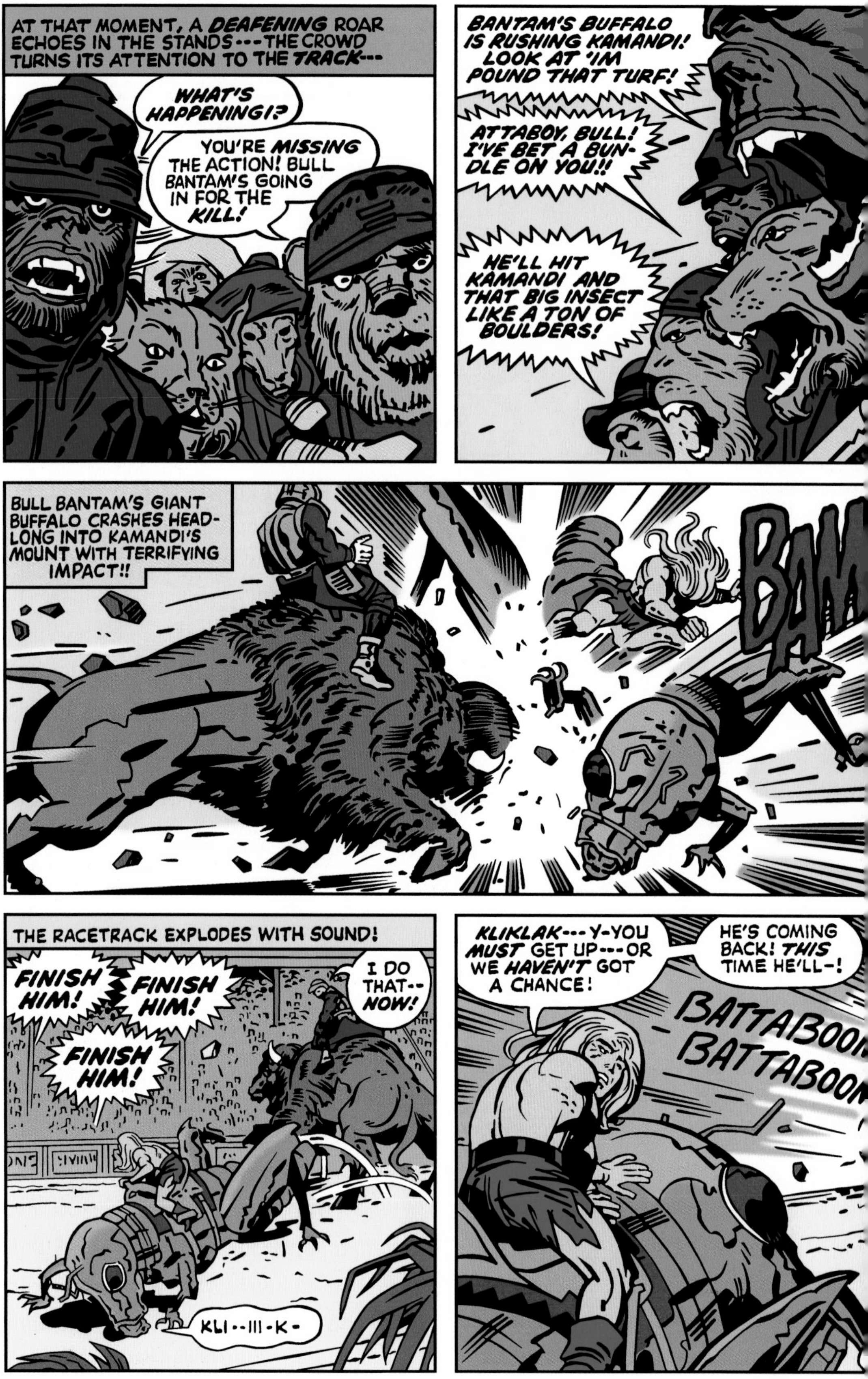
AT THAT MOMENT, A DEAFENING ROAR ECHOES IN THE STANDS---THE CROWD TURNS ITS ATTENTION TO THE TRACK--
WHAT'S HAPPENING!?
YOU'RE MISSING THE ACTION! BULL BANTAM'S GOING IN FOR THE KILL!
BANTAM'S BUFFALO IS RUSHING KAMANDI! LOOK AT 'IM POUND THAT TURF!
ATTABOY, BULL! I'VE BET A BUNDLE ON YOU!!
HE'LL HIT KAMANDI AND THAT BIG INSECT LIKE A TON OF BOULDERS!
BULL BANTAM'S GIANT BUFFALO CRASHES HEADLONG INTO KAMANDI'S MOUNT WITH TERRIFYING IMPACT!!
BAM
THE RACETRACK EXPLODES WITH SOUND!
FINISH HIM!
FINISH HIM!
FINISH HIM!
I DO THAT-- NOW!
KLI--III-K-
KLIKLAK--- Y-YOU MUST GET UP---OR WE HAVEN'T GOT A CHANCE!
HE'S COMING BACK! THIS TIME HE'LL-!
BATTABOOM BATTABOOM

LIKLAK, THE GIANT INSECT, IS EVERELY INJURED. ALTHOUGH EAK AND BATTERED, HE IANAGES TO RISE---
MOVE, LIKLAK!
KLIK--
BATTABOOM BATTABOOM
ASTRIDE HIS FIERCE BUFFALO, BULL BANTAM REACHES INTO A SADDLE POCKET AND DRAWS A GRENADE!
YOU DIE HARD NOW, KAMANDI!
S THE GRENADE STRIKES, THE GREAT NSECT LEAPS OUT OF RANGE.
WHAAM!
HEN, KLIKLAK ALTERS AND RASHES TO THE GROUND--
BOMP!
RELENTLESS AND EAGER, BULL BANTAM CHARGES FORWARD!
I-I'VE GOT TO STOP HIM-- SOMEHOW--
KLI--K--
9

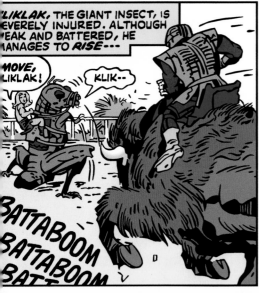

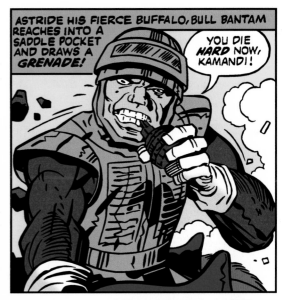

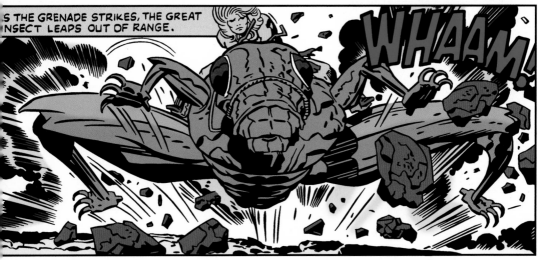

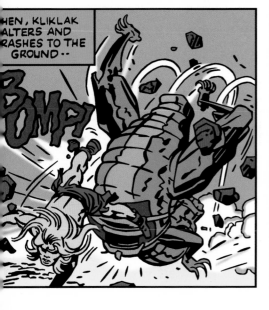

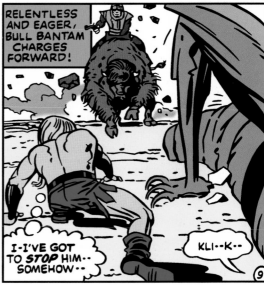

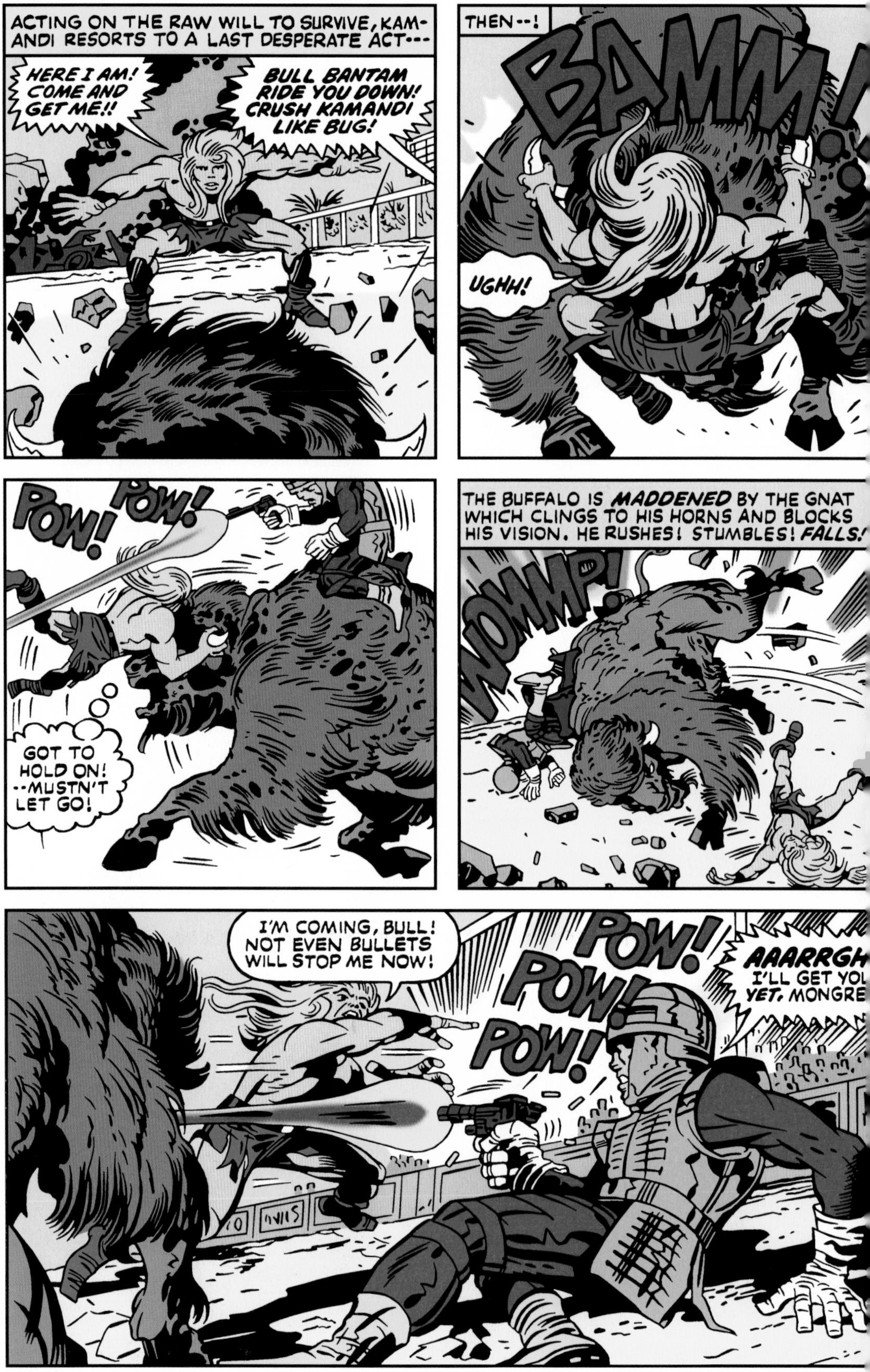
ACTING ON THE RAW WILL TO SURVIVE, KAMANDI RESORTS TO A LAST DESPERATE ACT---
HERE I AM! COME AND GET ME!!
BULL BANTAM RIDE YOU DOWN! CRUSH KAMANDI LIKE BUG!
THEN--!
BAMM!!
UGHH!
POW! POW!
GOT TO HOLD ON! --MUSTN'T LET GO!
THE BUFFALO IS MADDENED BY THE GNAT WHICH CLINGS TO HIS HORNS AND BLOCKS HIS VISION. HE RUSHES! STUMBLES! FALLS!
WOMMP!
I'M COMING, BULL! NOT EVEN BULLETS WILL STOP ME NOW!
POW! POW! POW!
AAARRGH
I'LL GET YO
YET, MONGRE

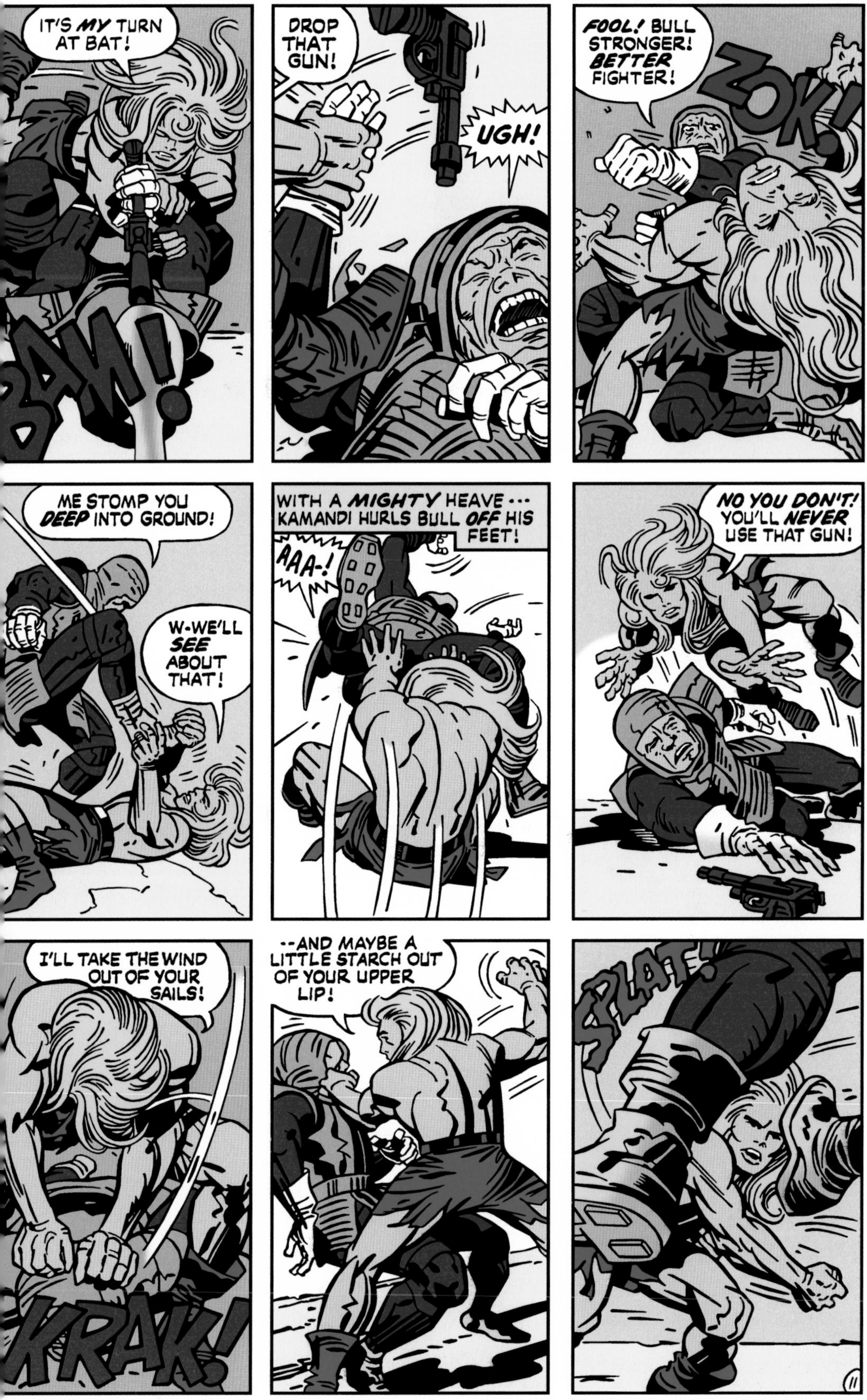
IT'S MY TURN AT BAT!
BAM!
DROP THAT GUN!
UGH!
FOOL! BULL STRONGER! BETTER FIGHTER!
ZOK!
ME STOMP YOU DEEP INTO GROUND!
W-WE'LL SEE ABOUT THAT!
WITH A MIGHTY HEAVE --- KAMANDI HURLS BULL OFF HIS FEET!
AAA-!
NO YOU DON'T! YOU'LL NEVER USE THAT GUN!
I'LL TAKE THE WIND OUT OF YOUR SAILS!
KRAK!
--AND MAYBE A LITTLE STARCH OUT OF YOUR UPPER LIP!
SPLAT!
11

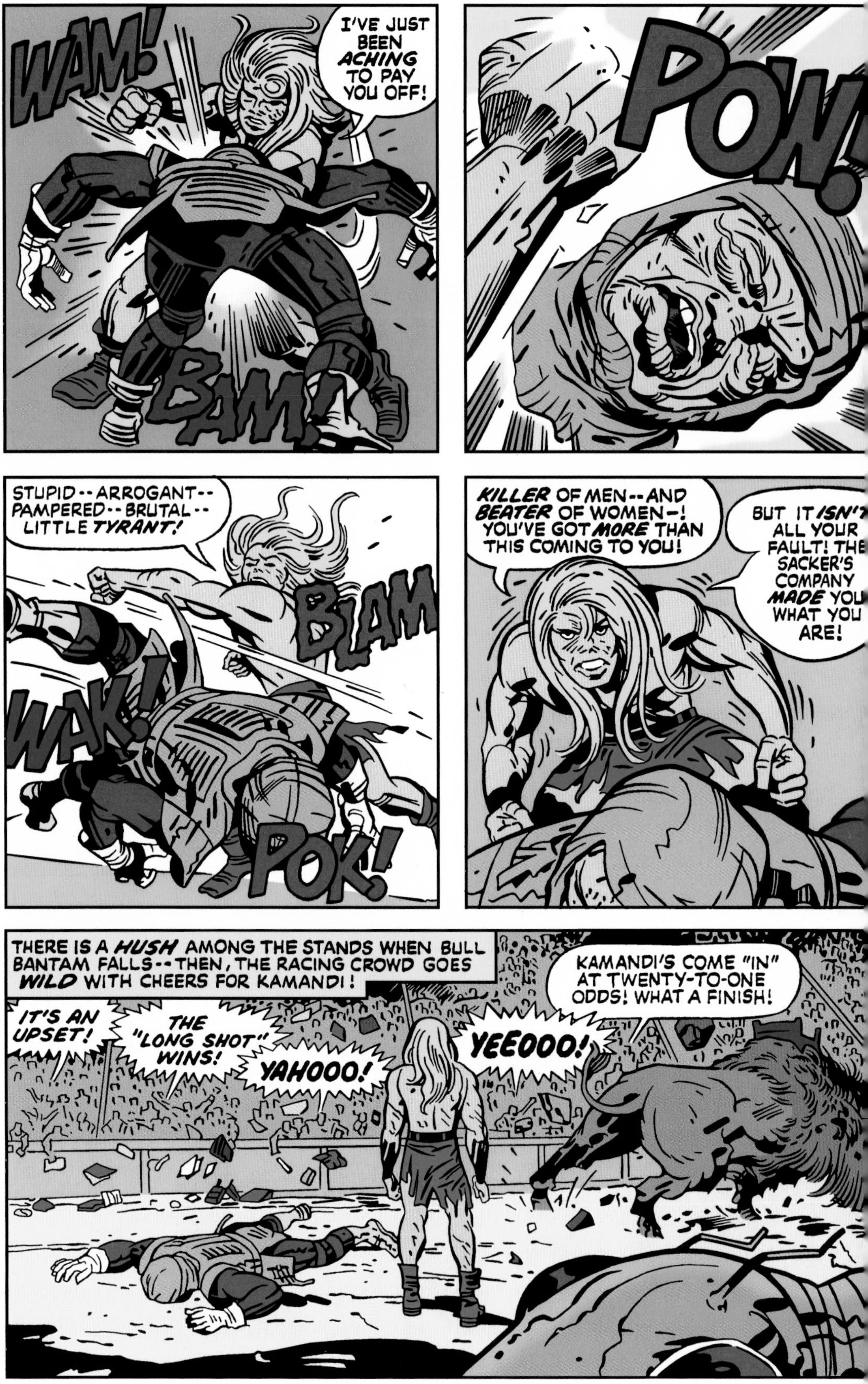
WAM!
I'VE JUST BEEN ACHING TO PAY YOU OFF!
BAM!
POW!
STUPID--ARROGANT--PAMPERED--BRUTAL--LITTLE TYRANT!
BLAM
WAK!
POK!
KILLER OF MEN--AND BEATER OF WOMEN--! YOU'VE GOT MORE THAN THIS COMING TO YOU!
BUT IT ISN'T ALL YOUR FAULT! THE SACKER'S COMPANY MADE YOU WHAT YOU ARE!
THERE IS A HUSH AMONG THE STANDS WHEN BULL BANTAM FALLS--THEN, THE RACING CROWD GOES WILD WITH CHEERS FOR KAMANDI!
KAMANDI'S COME "IN" AT TWENTY-TO-ONE ODDS! WHAT A FINISH!
IT'S AN UPSET!
THE "LONG SHOT" WINS!
YAHOOO!
YEEOOO!

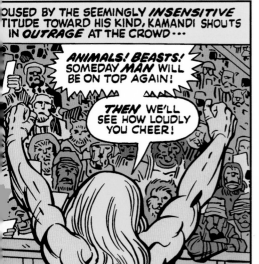

OUSED BY THE SEEMINGLY *INSENSITIVE* TITUDE TOWARD HIS KIND, KAMANDI SHOUTS IN *OUTRAGE* AT THE CROWD...

ANIMALS! BEASTS! SOMEDAY *MAN* WILL BE ON TOP AGAIN!

THEN WE'LL SEE HOW LOUDLY YOU CHEER!

WHAT'S THE USE--- TO *THEM* --*I* AM THE ANIMAL ---

KLIKLAK! YOU POOR CREATURE--- YOU'VE TAKEN SOME *MEAN* PUNISHMENT--

KLIK-- ----- KLAK--

ODENLY--!

OOD WORK, KAMANDI! E SACKER'S COMPANY *PROUD* F YOU!

WHAT DO I WIN? --A BOX OF *DOG BISCUITS?*

YOUR FRIEND KLIKLAK LOOKS LIKE HE'S *HAD* IT!

WELL, *DON'T* JUST STAND AND GAPE! HE *NEEDS* MEDICAL ATTENTION!

VETERINARY AN HELP HIM--- 'VE SEEN THIS PPEN *BEFORE!*

THAT THING IS *DYING,* KAMANDI. THERE'S ONLY *ONE* THING TO DO...

W-WHAT-?

IT'S *BEST* TO FINISH HIM OFF *QUICKLY.* ONE WELL-PLACED SHOT WILL DO THE JOB--

NO! NO! *WAIT-!*

13

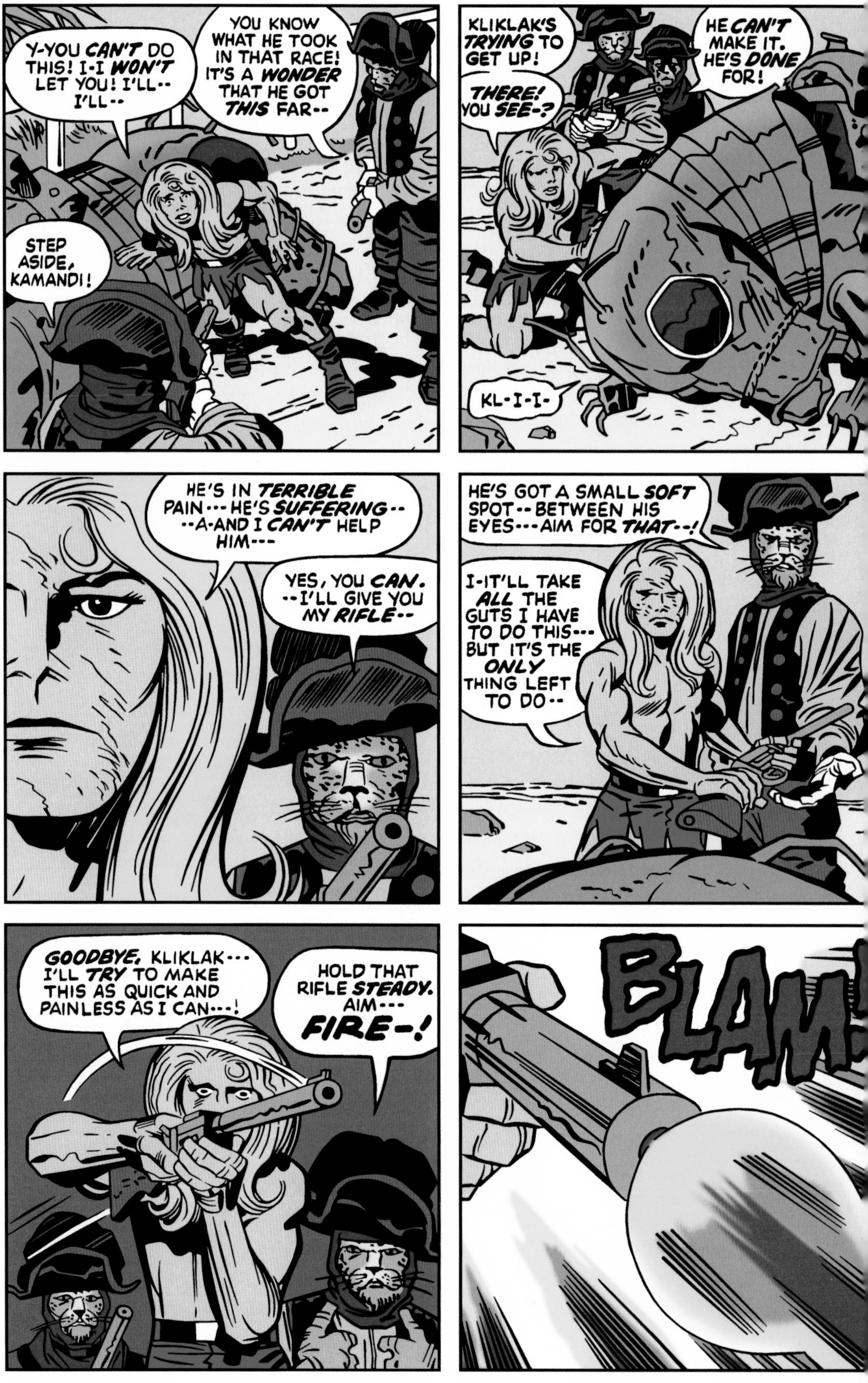
Y-YOU CAN'T DO THIS! I-I WON'T LET YOU! I'LL-- I'LL--
YOU KNOW WHAT HE TOOK IN THAT RACE! IT'S A WONDER THAT HE GOT THIS FAR--
STEP ASIDE, KAMANDI!
KLIKLAK'S TRYING TO GET UP!
HE CAN'T MAKE IT. HE'S DONE FOR!
THERE! YOU SEE-?
KL-I-I-
HE'S IN TERRIBLE PAIN--- HE'S SUFFERING-- --A-AND I CAN'T HELP HIM---
YES, YOU CAN. --I'LL GIVE YOU MY RIFLE--
HE'S GOT A SMALL SOFT SPOT-- BETWEEN HIS EYES--- AIM FOR THAT--!
I-IT'LL TAKE ALL THE GUTS I HAVE TO DO THIS--- BUT IT'S THE ONLY THING LEFT TO DO--
GOODBYE, KLIKLAK--- I'LL TRY TO MAKE THIS AS QUICK AND PAINLESS AS I CAN---!
HOLD THAT RIFLE STEADY. AIM--- FIRE-!
BLAM

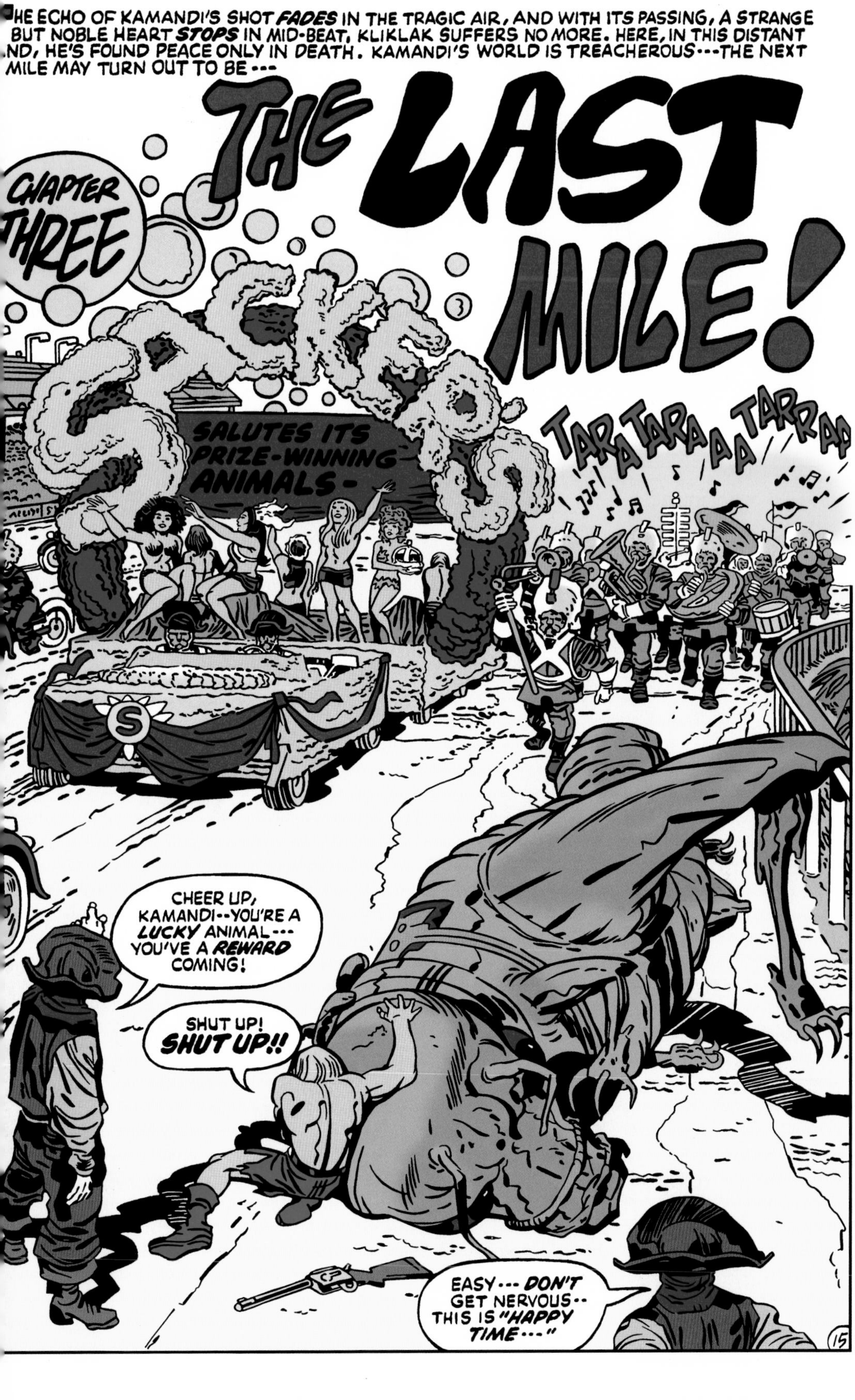
HE ECHO OF KAMANDI'S SHOT FADES IN THE TRAGIC AIR, AND WITH ITS PASSING, A STRANGE BUT NOBLE HEART STOPS IN MID-BEAT. KLIKLAK SUFFERS NO MORE. HERE, IN THIS DISTANT ND, HE'S FOUND PEACE ONLY IN DEATH. KAMANDI'S WORLD IS TREACHEROUS---THE NEXT MILE MAY TURN OUT TO BE---
THE LAST MILE!
CHAPTER THREE
SALUTES ITS PRIZE-WINNING ANIMALS-
TARA TARA A A A TARRAP
CHEER UP, KAMANDI--YOU'RE A LUCKY ANIMAL--- YOU'VE A REWARD COMING!
SHUT UP! SHUT UP!!
EASY--- DON'T GET NERVOUS-- THIS IS "HAPPY TIME---"
15

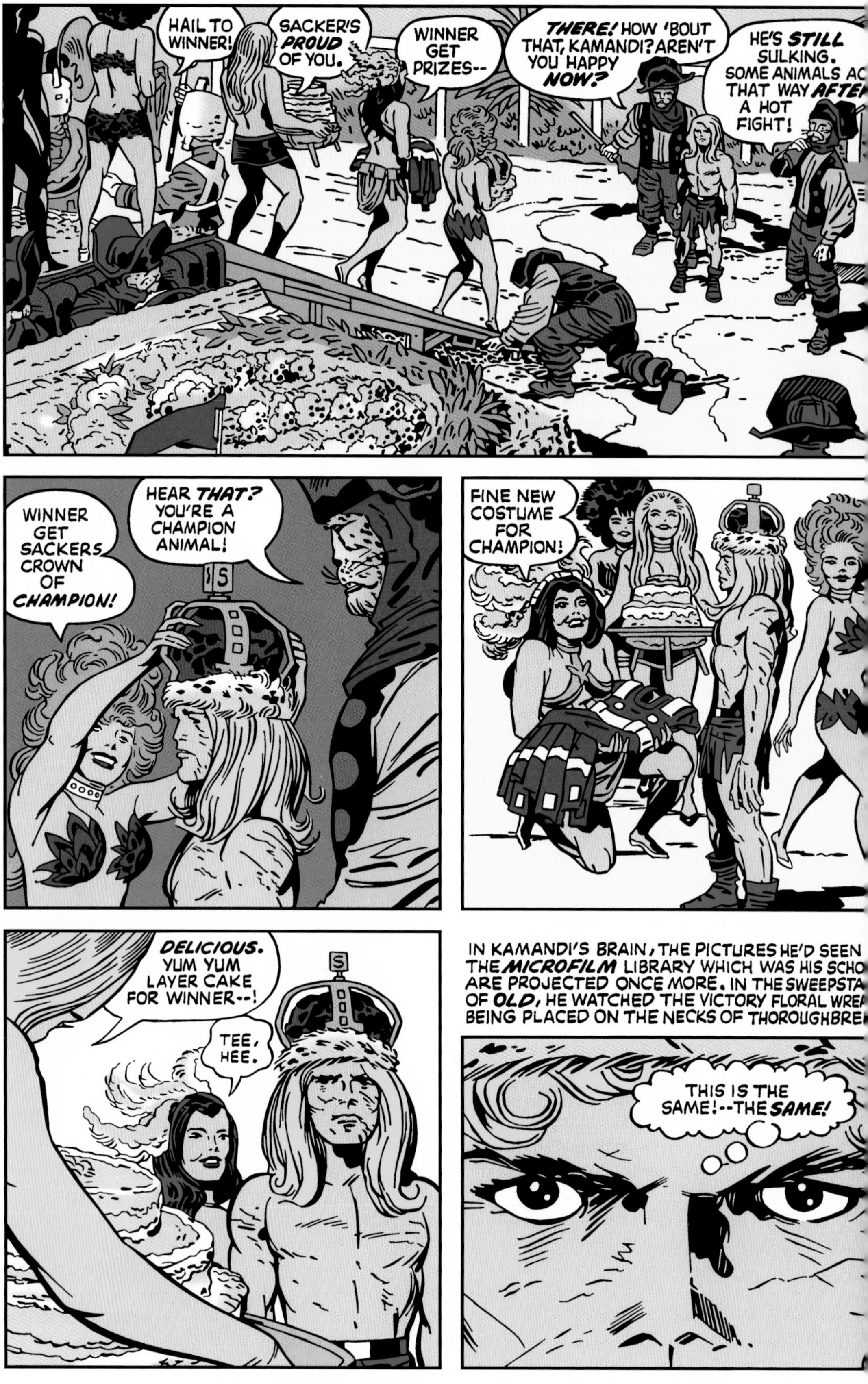
HAIL TO WINNER!
SACKER'S PROUD OF YOU.
WINNER GET PRIZES--
THERE! HOW 'BOUT THAT, KAMANDI? AREN'T YOU HAPPY NOW?
HE'S STILL SULKING. SOME ANIMALS AC THAT WAY AFTE A HOT FIGHT!
WINNER GET SACKERS CROWN OF CHAMPION!
HEAR THAT? YOU'RE A CHAMPION ANIMAL!
FINE NEW COSTUME FOR CHAMPION!
DELICIOUS. YUM YUM LAYER CAKE FOR WINNER--!
TEE, HEE.
IN KAMANDI'S BRAIN, THE PICTURES HE'D SEEN THE MICROFILM LIBRARY WHICH WAS HIS SCHO ARE PROJECTED ONCE MORE. IN THE SWEEPSTA OF OLD, HE WATCHED THE VICTORY FLORAL WRE BEING PLACED ON THE NECKS OF THOROUGHBRE
THIS IS THE SAME! --THE SAME!

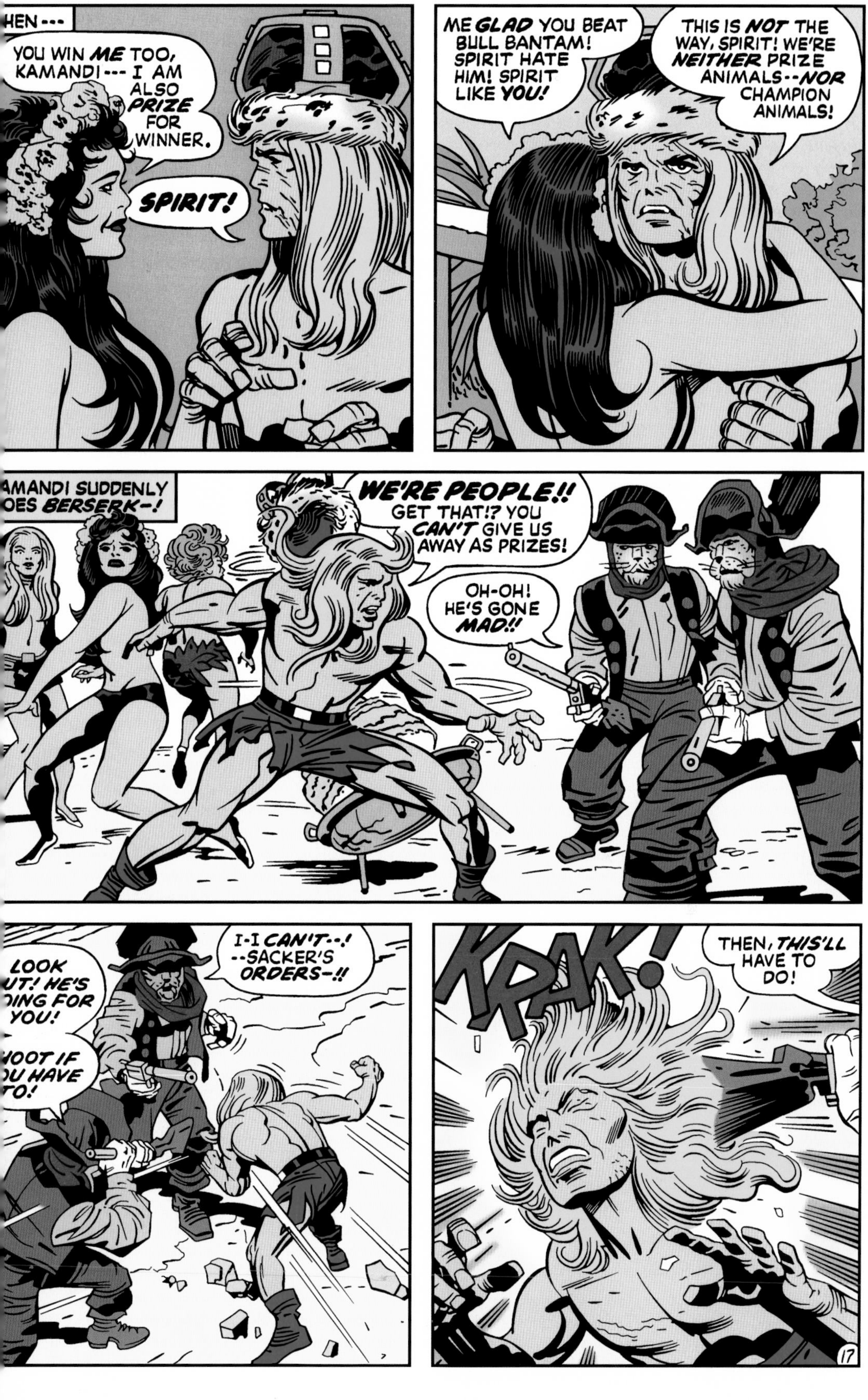
HEN ---
YOU WIN ME TOO, KAMANDI --- I AM ALSO PRIZE FOR WINNER.
SPIRIT!
ME GLAD YOU BEAT BULL BANTAM! SPIRIT HATE HIM! SPIRIT LIKE YOU!
THIS IS NOT THE WAY, SPIRIT! WE'RE NEITHER PRIZE ANIMALS--NOR CHAMPION ANIMALS!
AMANDI SUDDENLY OES BERSERK-!
WE'RE PEOPLE!! GET THAT!? YOU CAN'T GIVE US AWAY AS PRIZES!
OH-OH! HE'S GONE MAD!!
LOOK UT! HE'S OING FOR YOU!
HOOT IF OU HAVE TO!
I-I CAN'T--! --SACKER'S ORDERS-!!
KRAK!
THEN, THIS'LL HAVE TO DO!
17

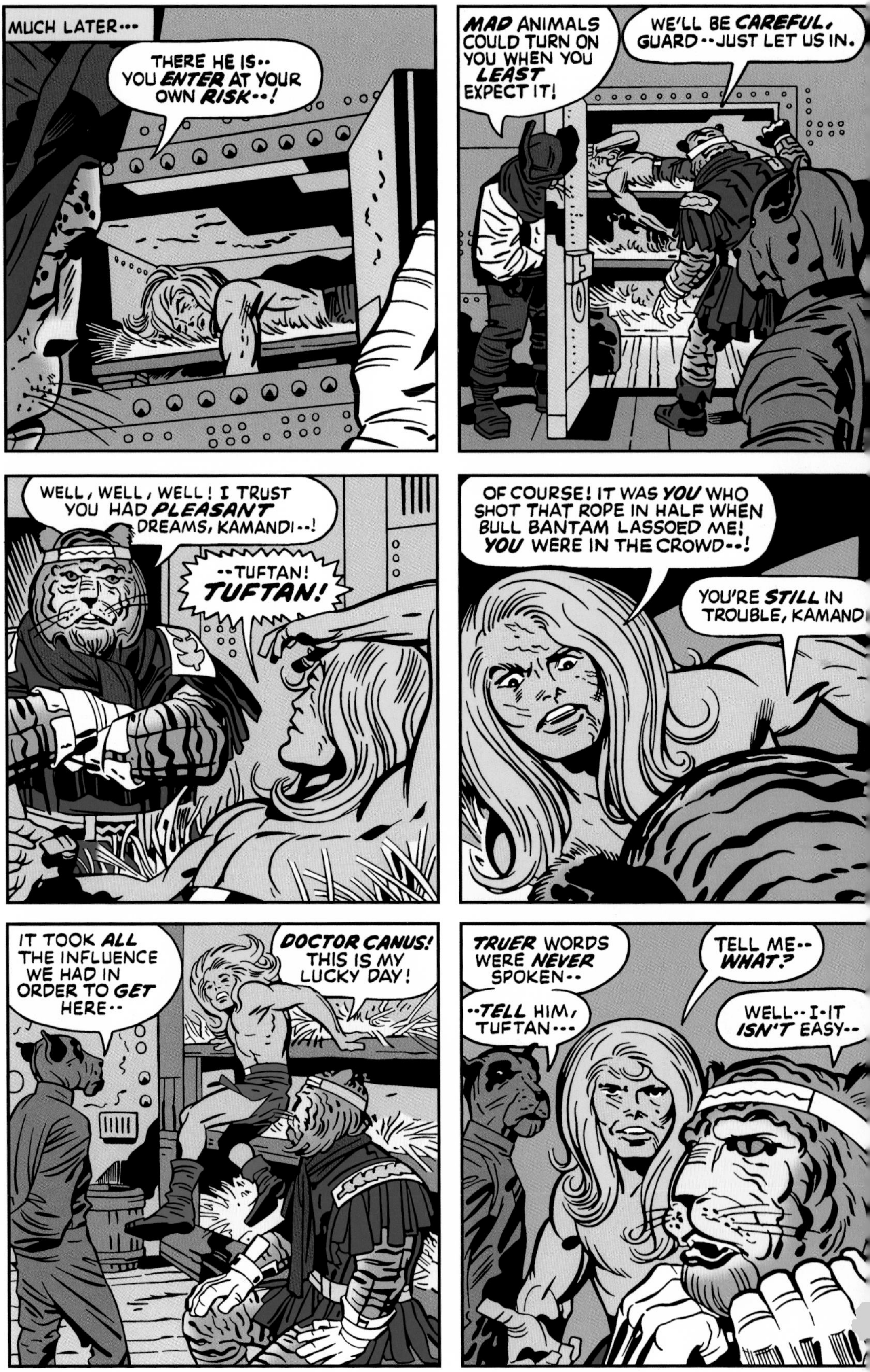
MUCH LATER...
THERE HE IS.. YOU ENTER AT YOUR OWN RISK--!
MAD ANIMALS COULD TURN ON YOU WHEN YOU LEAST EXPECT IT!
WE'LL BE CAREFUL, GUARD--JUST LET US IN.
WELL, WELL, WELL! I TRUST YOU HAD PLEASANT DREAMS, KAMANDI--!
--TUFTAN! TUFTAN!
OF COURSE! IT WAS YOU WHO SHOT THAT ROPE IN HALF WHEN BULL BANTAM LASSOED ME! YOU WERE IN THE CROWD--!
YOU'RE STILL IN TROUBLE, KAMANDI
IT TOOK ALL THE INFLUENCE WE HAD IN ORDER TO GET HERE--
DOCTOR CANUS! THIS IS MY LUCKY DAY!
TRUER WORDS WERE NEVER SPOKEN--
--TELL HIM, TUFTAN---
TELL ME-- WHAT?
WELL--I-IT ISN'T EASY--

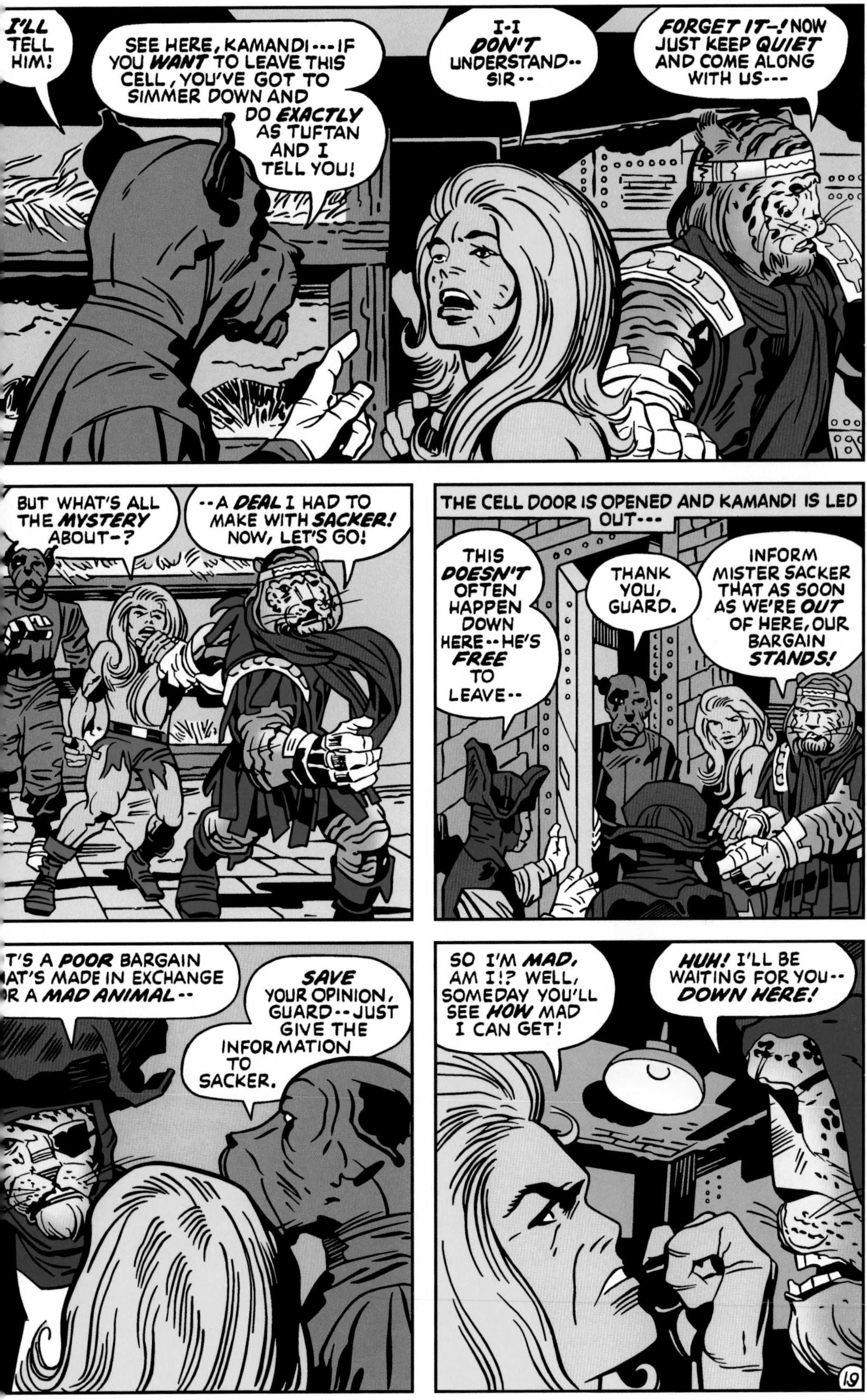
I'LL TELL HIM!
SEE HERE, KAMANDI --- IF YOU WANT TO LEAVE THIS CELL, YOU'VE GOT TO SIMMER DOWN AND DO EXACTLY AS TUFTAN AND I TELL YOU!
I-I DON'T UNDERSTAND-- SIR--
FORGET IT--! NOW JUST KEEP QUIET AND COME ALONG WITH US---
BUT WHAT'S ALL THE MYSTERY ABOUT--?
--A DEAL I HAD TO MAKE WITH SACKER! NOW, LET'S GO!
THE CELL DOOR IS OPENED AND KAMANDI IS LED OUT---
THIS DOESN'T OFTEN HAPPEN DOWN HERE--HE'S FREE TO LEAVE--
THANK YOU, GUARD.
INFORM MISTER SACKER THAT AS SOON AS WE'RE OUT OF HERE, OUR BARGAIN STANDS!
T'S A POOR BARGAIN AT'S MADE IN EXCHANGE R A MAD ANIMAL--
SAVE YOUR OPINION, GUARD--JUST GIVE THE INFORMATION TO SACKER.
SO I'M MAD, AM I!? WELL, SOMEDAY YOU'LL SEE HOW MAD I CAN GET!
HUH! I'LL BE WAITING FOR YOU-- DOWN HERE!
19

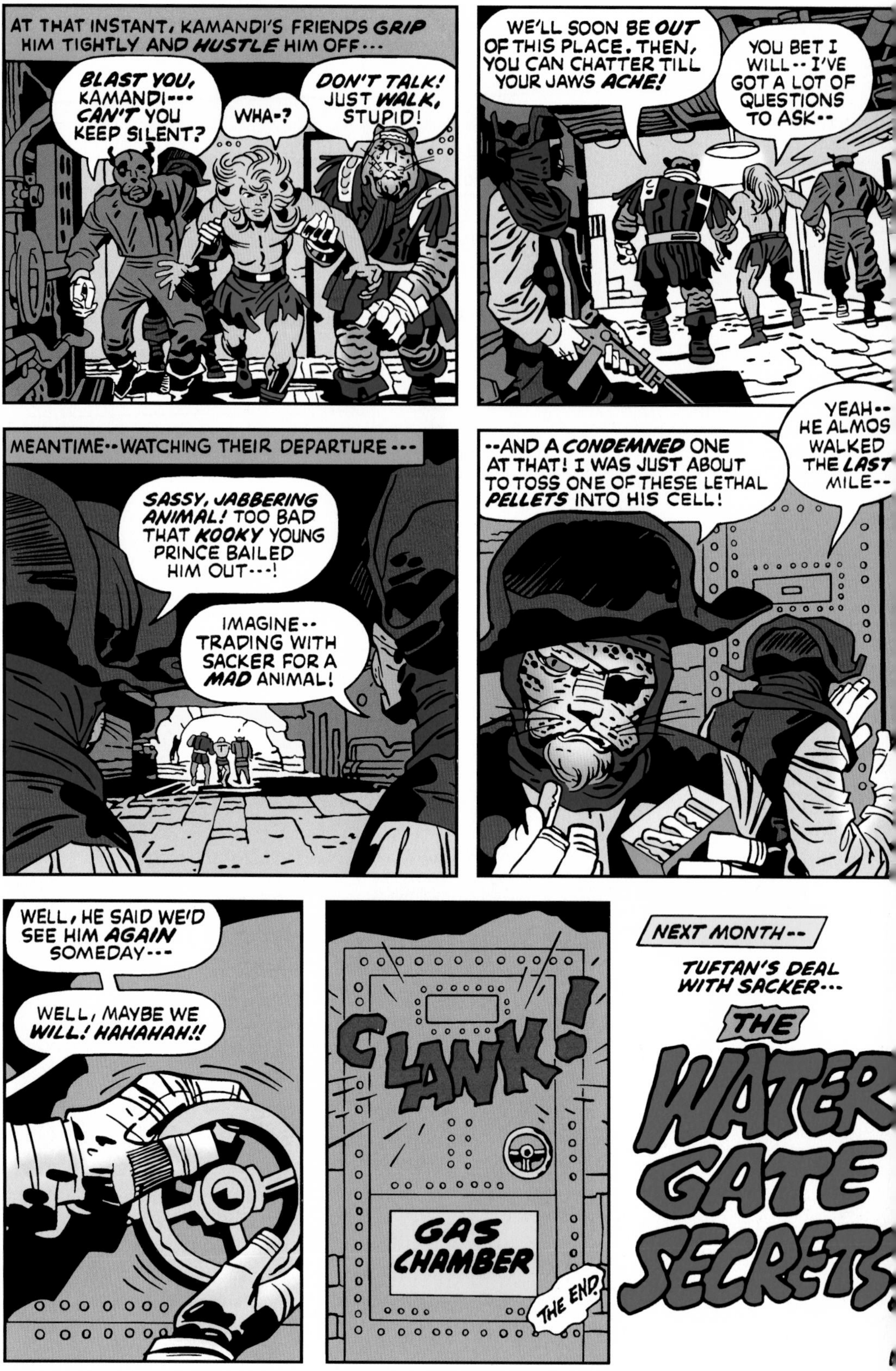
AT THAT INSTANT, KAMANDI'S FRIENDS GRIP HIM TIGHTLY AND HUSTLE HIM OFF---
BLAST YOU, KAMANDI--- CAN'T YOU KEEP SILENT?
WHA-?
DON'T TALK! JUST WALK, STUPID!
WE'LL SOON BE OUT OF THIS PLACE. THEN, YOU CAN CHATTER TILL YOUR JAWS ACHE!
YOU BET I WILL -- I'VE GOT A LOT OF QUESTIONS TO ASK--
MEANTIME--WATCHING THEIR DEPARTURE---
SASSY, JABBERING ANIMAL! TOO BAD THAT KOOKY YOUNG PRINCE BAILED HIM OUT---!
IMAGINE-- TRADING WITH SACKER FOR A MAD ANIMAL!
--AND A CONDEMNED ONE AT THAT! I WAS JUST ABOUT TO TOSS ONE OF THESE LETHAL PELLETS INTO HIS CELL!
YEAH-- HE ALMOS WALKED THE LAST MILE--
WELL, HE SAID WE'D SEE HIM AGAIN SOMEDAY---
WELL, MAYBE WE WILL! HAHAHAH!!
CLANK!
GAS CHAMBER
THE END
NEXT MONTH--
TUFTAN'S DEAL WITH SACKER---
THE WATER GATE SECRETS

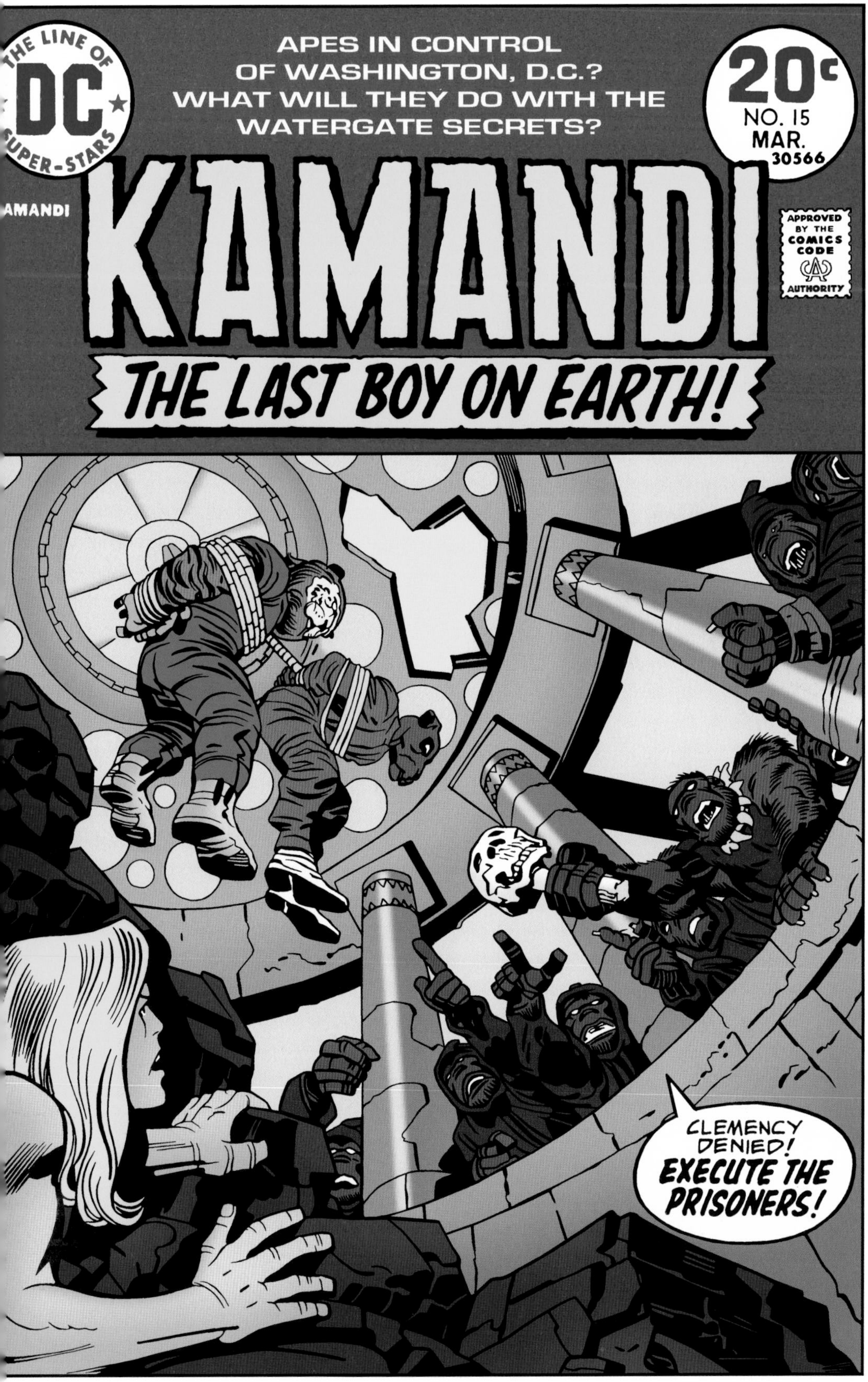
THE LINE OF DC SUPER-STARS
APES IN CONTROL OF WASHINGTON, D.C.? WHAT WILL THEY DO WITH THE WATERGATE SECRETS?
20¢
NO. 15
MAR.
30566
KAMANDI
APPROVED BY THE COMICS CODE AUTHORITY
KAMANDI
THE LAST BOY ON EARTH!
CLEMENCY DENIED! EXECUTE THE PRISONERS!

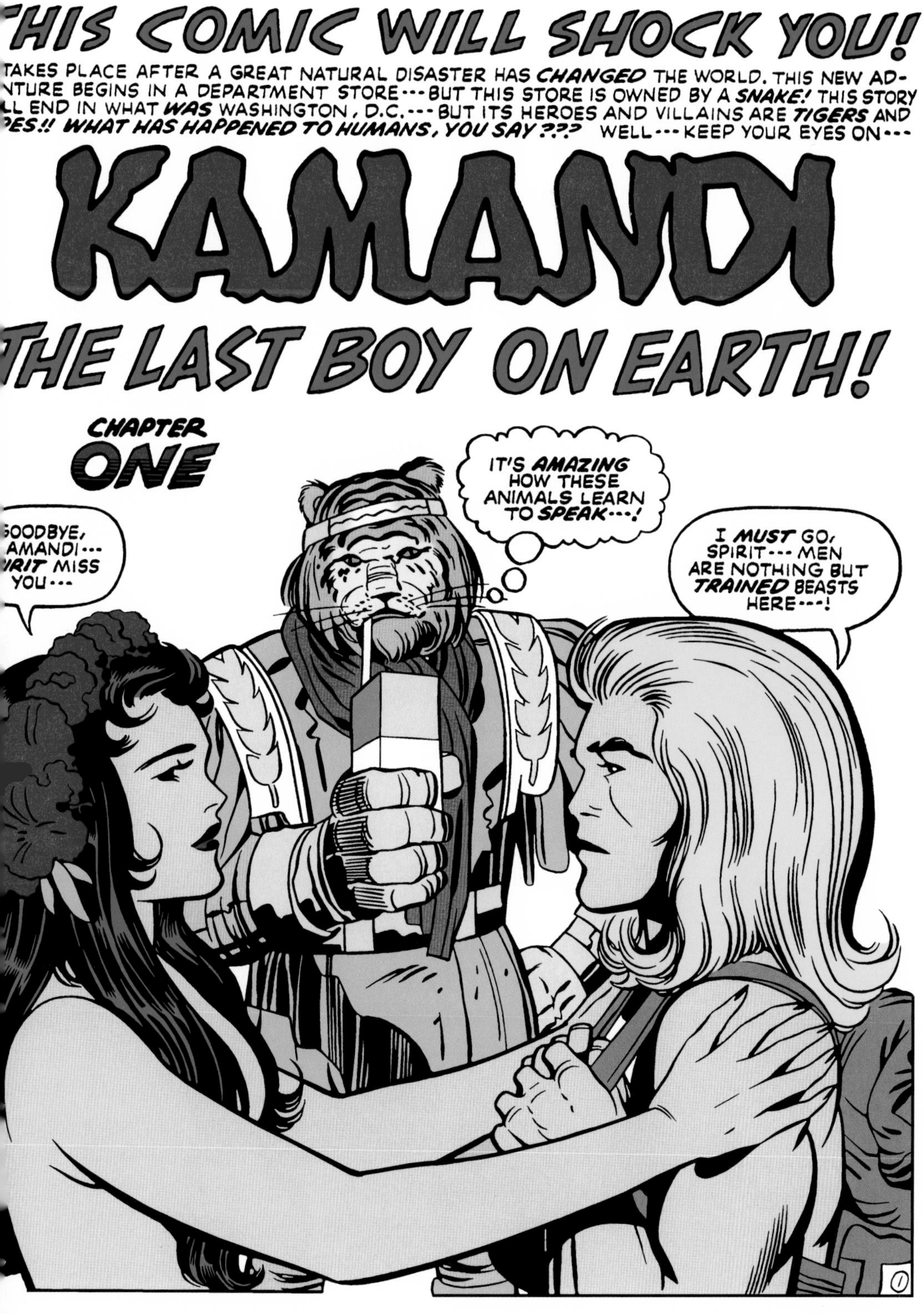
HIS COMIC WILL SHOCK YOU!
TAKES PLACE AFTER A GREAT NATURAL DISASTER HAS CHANGED THE WORLD. THIS NEW AD-
NTURE BEGINS IN A DEPARTMENT STORE--- BUT THIS STORE IS OWNED BY A SNAKE! THIS STORY
LL END IN WHAT WAS WASHINGTON, D.C.--- BUT ITS HEROES AND VILLAINS ARE TIGERS AND
ES!! WHAT HAS HAPPENED TO HUMANS, YOU SAY??? WELL--- KEEP YOUR EYES ON---
KAMANDI
THE LAST BOY ON EARTH!
CHAPTER ONE
OODBYE, AMANDI--- IRIT MISS YOU---
IT'S AMAZING HOW THESE ANIMALS LEARN TO SPEAK---!
I MUST GO, SPIRIT--- MEN ARE NOTHING BUT TRAINED BEASTS HERE---!
1

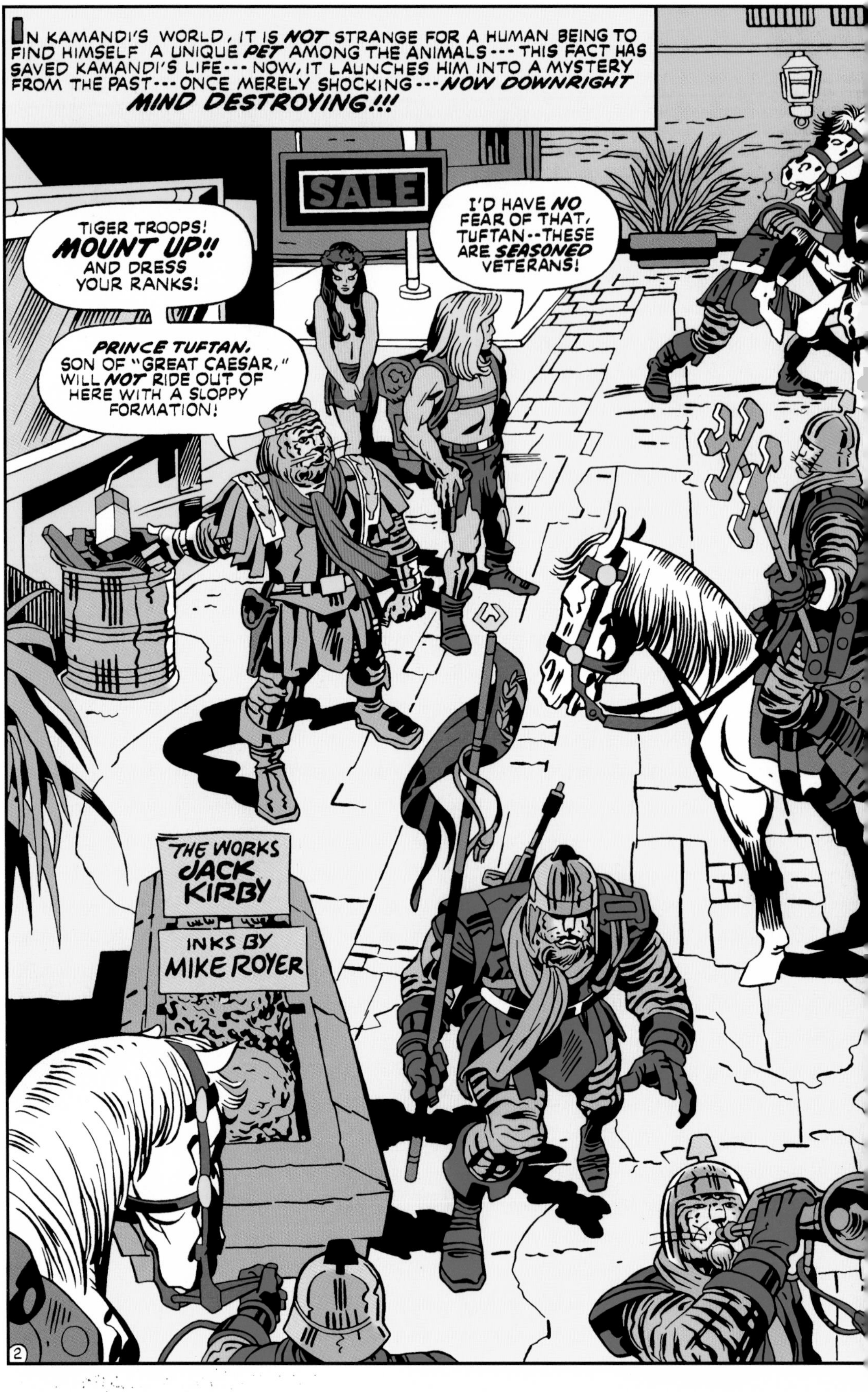
IN KAMANDI'S WORLD, IT IS NOT STRANGE FOR A HUMAN BEING TO FIND HIMSELF A UNIQUE PET AMONG THE ANIMALS--- THIS FACT HAS SAVED KAMANDI'S LIFE--- NOW, IT LAUNCHES HIM INTO A MYSTERY FROM THE PAST--- ONCE MERELY SHOCKING--- NOW DOWNRIGHT MIND DESTROYING!!!
SALE
TIGER TROOPS! MOUNT UP!! AND DRESS YOUR RANKS!
PRINCE TUFTAN, SON OF "GREAT CAESAR," WILL NOT RIDE OUT OF HERE WITH A SLOPPY FORMATION!
I'D HAVE NO FEAR OF THAT, TUFTAN--THESE ARE SEASONED VETERANS!
THE WORKS JACK KIRBY
INKS BY MIKE ROYER
2

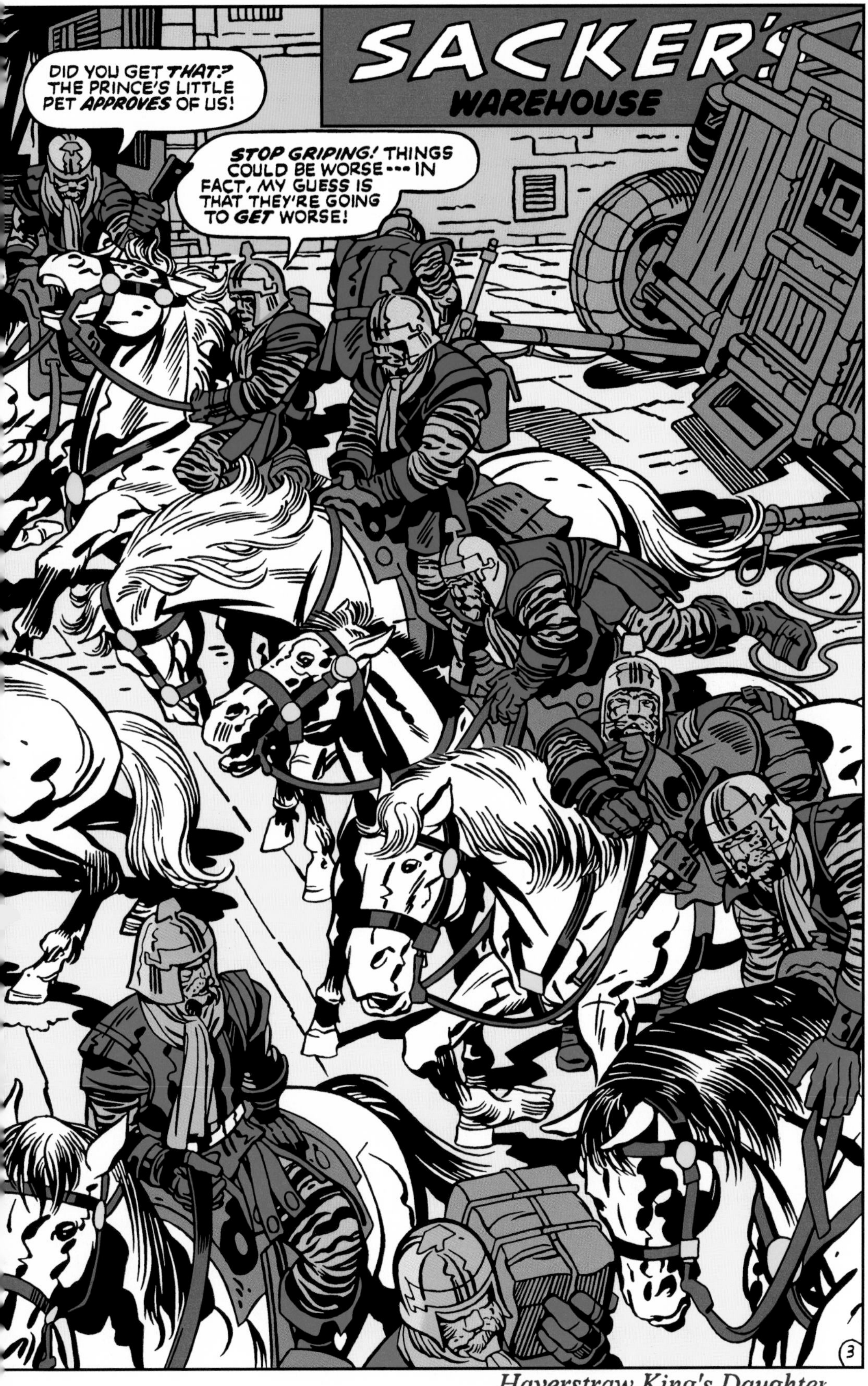
SACKER'S
WAREHOUSE
DID YOU GET *THAT?* THE PRINCE'S LITTLE PET *APPROVES* OF US!
STOP GRIPING! THINGS COULD BE WORSE--- IN FACT, MY GUESS IS THAT THEY'RE GOING TO *GET* WORSE!
3

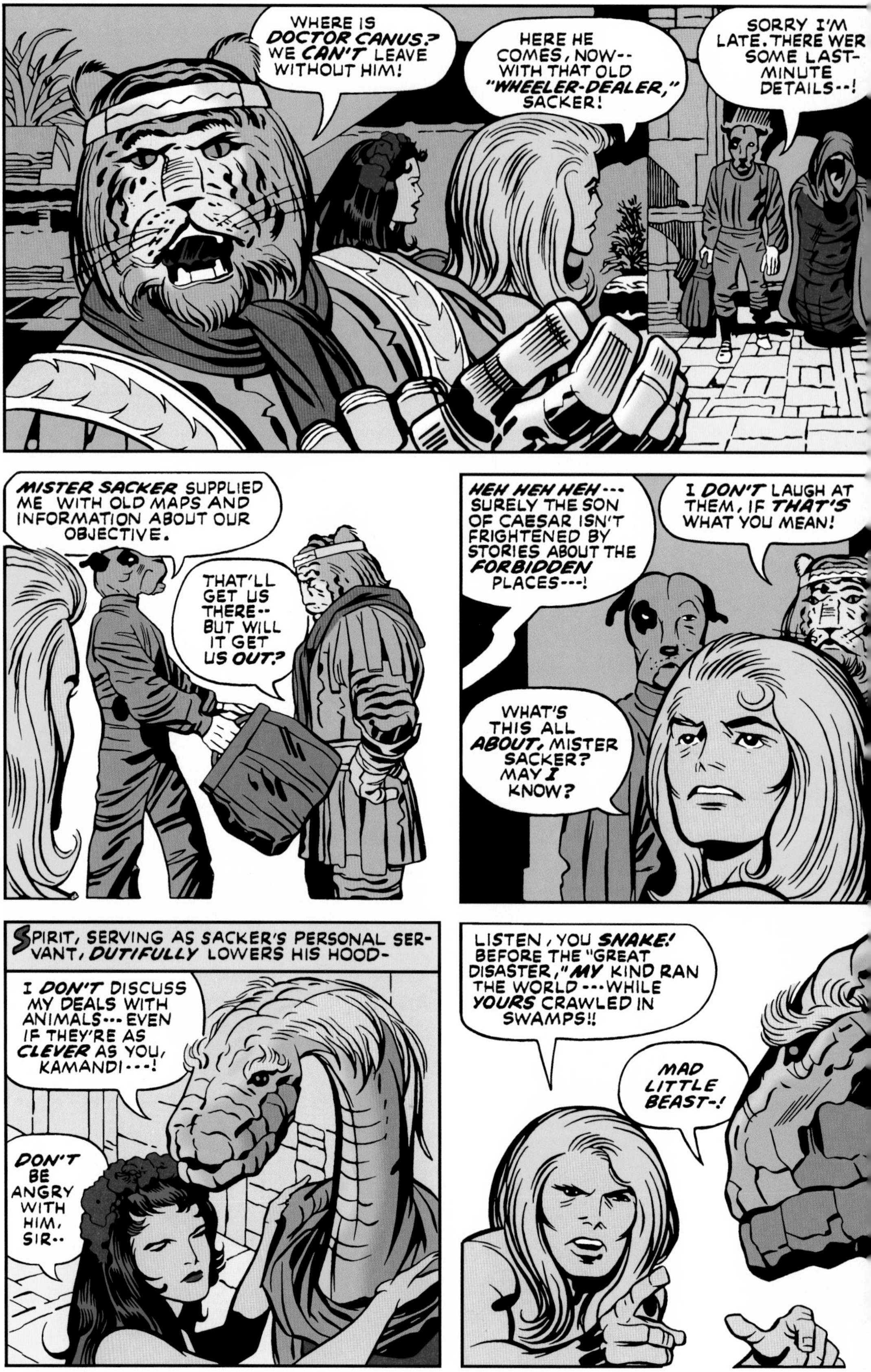
WHERE IS DOCTOR CANUS? WE CAN'T LEAVE WITHOUT HIM!
HERE HE COMES, NOW-- WITH THAT OLD "WHEELER-DEALER," SACKER!
SORRY I'M LATE. THERE WER SOME LAST-MINUTE DETAILS--!
MISTER SACKER SUPPLIED ME WITH OLD MAPS AND INFORMATION ABOUT OUR OBJECTIVE.
THAT'LL GET US THERE-- BUT WILL IT GET US OUT?
HEH HEH HEH--- SURELY THE SON OF CAESAR ISN'T FRIGHTENED BY STORIES ABOUT THE FORBIDDEN PLACES---!
I DON'T LAUGH AT THEM, IF THAT'S WHAT YOU MEAN!
WHAT'S THIS ALL ABOUT, MISTER SACKER? MAY I KNOW?
SPIRIT, SERVING AS SACKER'S PERSONAL SER-VANT, DUTIFULLY LOWERS HIS HOOD-
I DON'T DISCUSS MY DEALS WITH ANIMALS--- EVEN IF THEY'RE AS CLEVER AS YOU, KAMANDI---!
DON'T BE ANGRY WITH HIM, SIR--
LISTEN, YOU SNAKE! BEFORE THE "GREAT DISASTER," MY KIND RAN THE WORLD---WHILE YOURS CRAWLED IN SWAMPS!!
MAD LITTLE BEAST-!

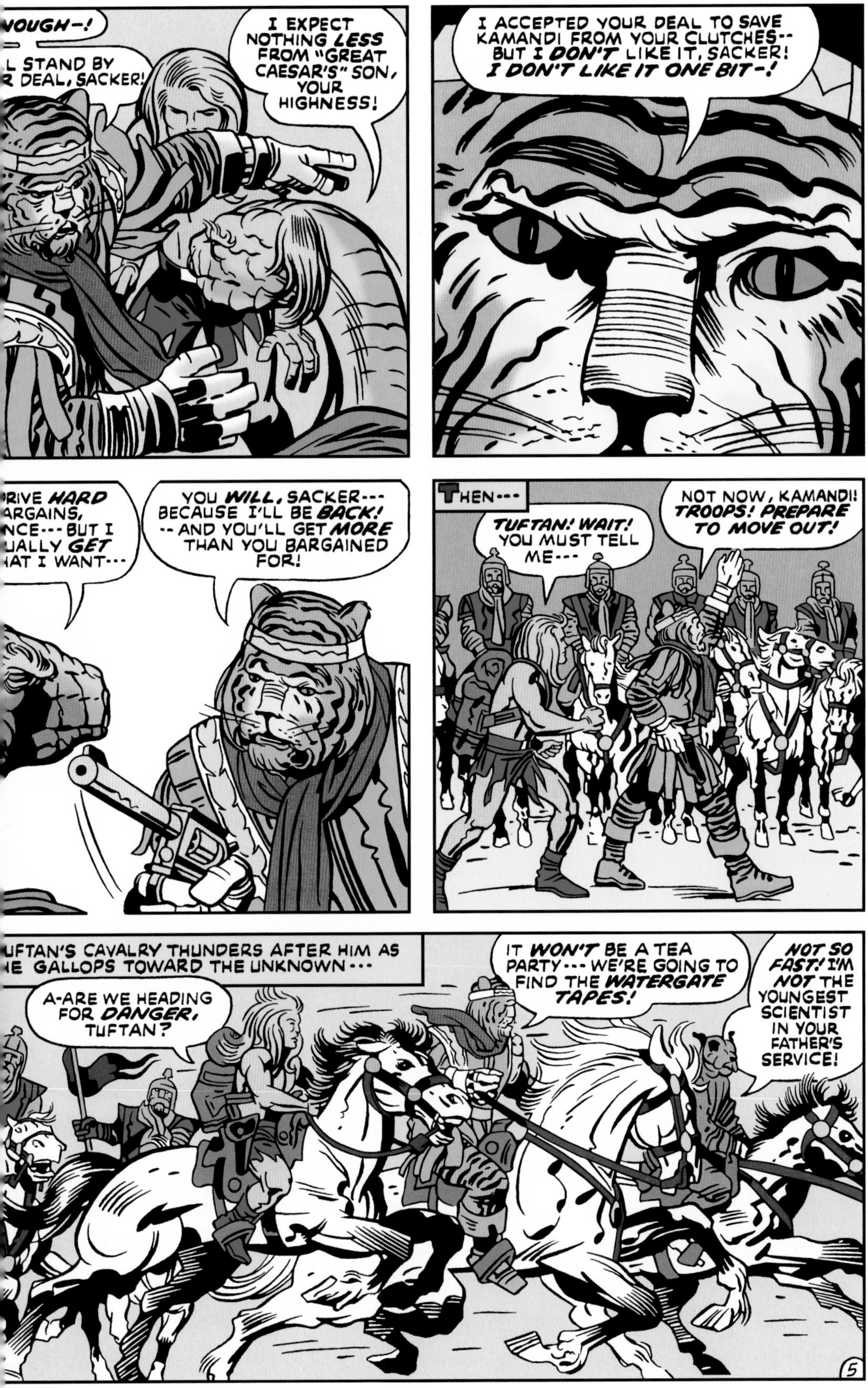
NOUGH-!
L STAND BY
R DEAL, SACKER!
I EXPECT NOTHING LESS FROM "GREAT CAESAR'S" SON, YOUR HIGHNESS!
I ACCEPTED YOUR DEAL TO SAVE KAMANDI FROM YOUR CLUTCHES-- BUT I DON'T LIKE IT, SACKER! I DON'T LIKE IT ONE BIT-!
RIVE HARD ARGAINS, NCE--- BUT I UALLY GET HAT I WANT---
YOU WILL, SACKER--- BECAUSE I'LL BE BACK! --AND YOU'LL GET MORE THAN YOU BARGAINED FOR!
THEN---
TUFTAN! WAIT! YOU MUST TELL ME---
NOT NOW, KAMANDI! TROOPS! PREPARE TO MOVE OUT!
UFTAN'S CAVALRY THUNDERS AFTER HIM AS E GALLOPS TOWARD THE UNKNOWN---
A-ARE WE HEADING FOR DANGER, TUFTAN?
IT WON'T BE A TEA PARTY--- WE'RE GOING TO FIND THE WATERGATE TAPES!
NOT SO FAST! I'M NOT THE YOUNGEST SCIENTIST IN YOUR FATHER'S SERVICE!
5

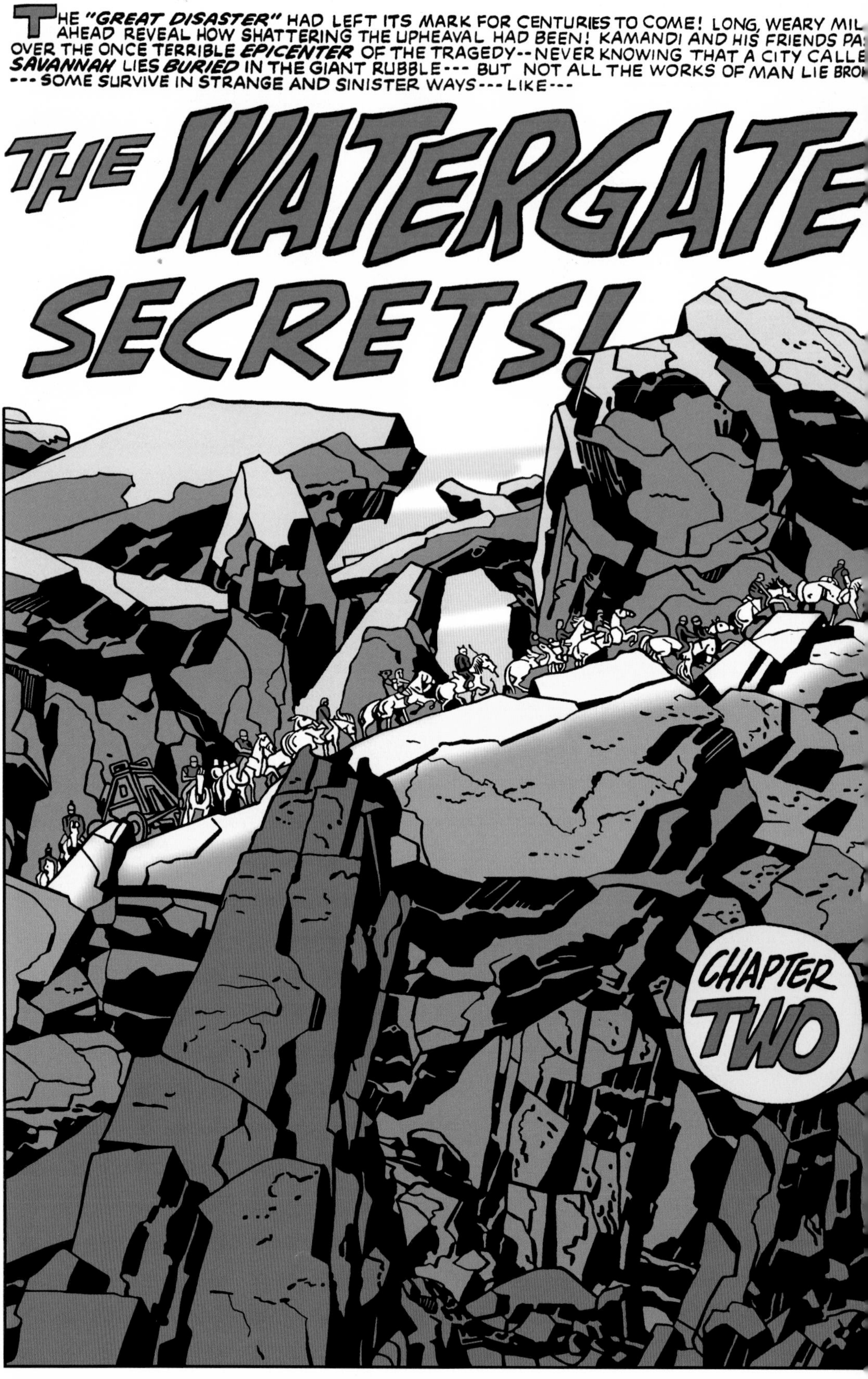
THE "GREAT DISASTER" HAD LEFT ITS MARK FOR CENTURIES TO COME! LONG, WEARY MIL
AHEAD REVEAL HOW SHATTERING THE UPHEAVAL HAD BEEN! KAMANDI AND HIS FRIENDS PA
OVER THE ONCE TERRIBLE EPICENTER OF THE TRAGEDY--NEVER KNOWING THAT A CITY CALLE
SAVANNAH LIES BURIED IN THE GIANT RUBBLE--- BUT NOT ALL THE WORKS OF MAN LIE BRO
--- SOME SURVIVE IN STRANGE AND SINISTER WAYS---LIKE---
THE WATERGATE SECRETS!
CHAPTER TWO

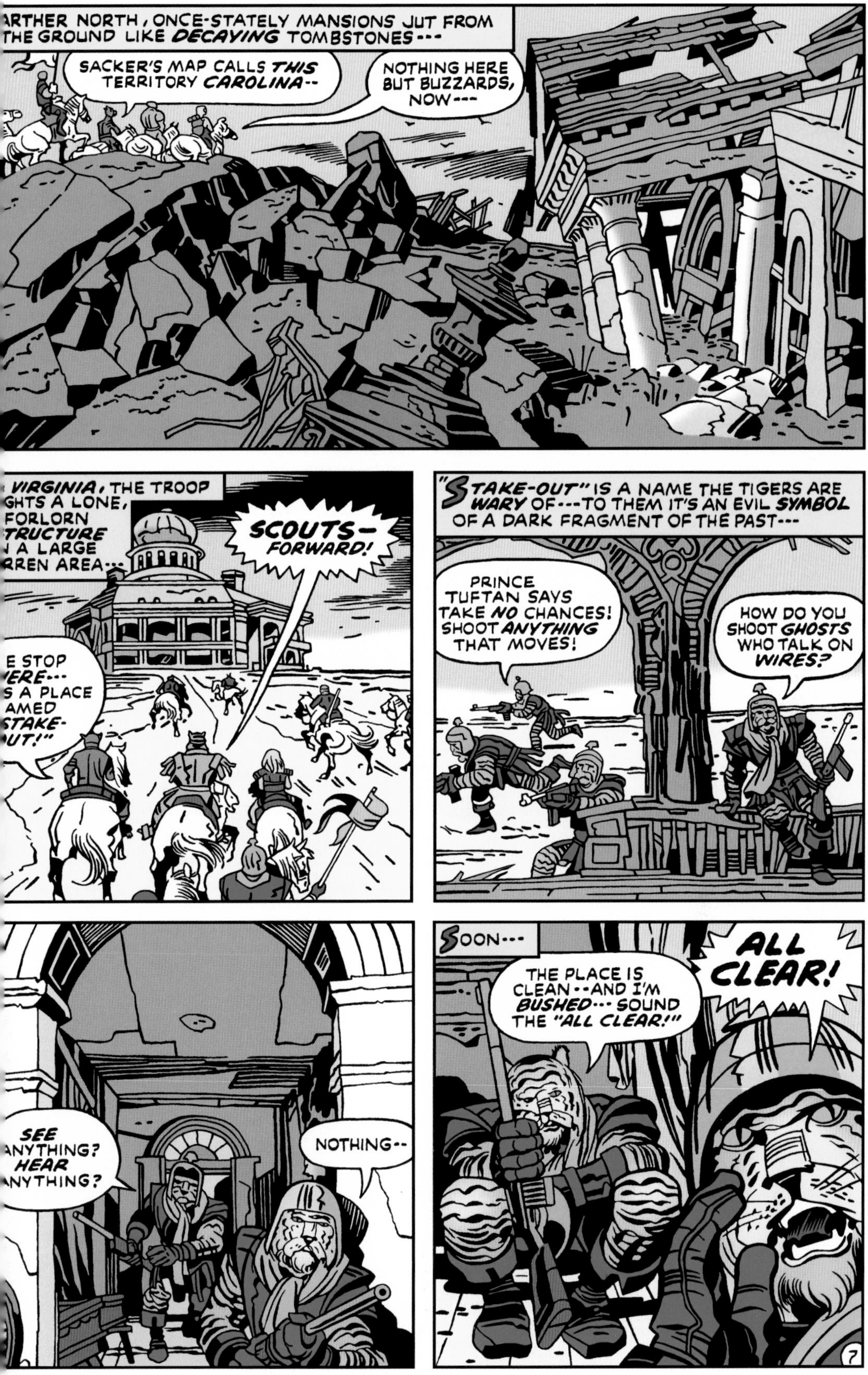
ARTHER NORTH, ONCE-STATELY MANSIONS JUT FROM THE GROUND LIKE DECAYING TOMBSTONES---
SACKER'S MAP CALLS THIS TERRITORY CAROLINA--
NOTHING HERE BUT BUZZARDS, NOW---
VIRGINIA, THE TROOP GHTS A LONE, FORLORN TRUCTURE N A LARGE RREN AREA---
SCOUTS--FORWARD!
E STOP ERE--- S A PLACE AMED STAKE-UT!"
"STAKE-OUT" IS A NAME THE TIGERS ARE WARY OF---TO THEM IT'S AN EVIL SYMBOL OF A DARK FRAGMENT OF THE PAST---
PRINCE TUFTAN SAYS TAKE NO CHANCES! SHOOT ANYTHING THAT MOVES!
HOW DO YOU SHOOT GHOSTS WHO TALK ON WIRES?
SEE NYTHING? HEAR NYTHING?
NOTHING--
SOON---
THE PLACE IS CLEAN--AND I'M BUSHED--- SOUND THE "ALL CLEAR!"
ALL CLEAR!
7

THE TROOP THEN ENTERS AND RESTS---

♪ WE ALL LIVE IN A YELLOW SUB-MARINE····A ♪ YELLOW ♪ SUBMARINE···

QUIET, KAMANDI!

RELAX, TUFTAN!

I *LIKE* THAT SONG -- MY GREAT-GRANDFATHER CLAIMED IT WAS WRITTEN BY *BEETLES*---!

THAT'S *NOT* FUNNY--- I'M EXPECTING LOTS OF TROUBLE FROM *BUGS!*

WHAT ABOUT IT, DOCTOR CANUS--- WHAT ABOUT THESE--- *BUGS?*

THIS OLD DATA SEEMS TO INDICATE THAT THEY'RE IMPORTANT--- A DEFINITE *LEAD* TO THE WATERGATE TAPES---

--WHATEVER *THEY* ARE---!

I KNOW ABOUT THEM--

THE TAPES WERE PART OF A POLITICAL PROBLEM *BEFORE* THE GREAT DISASTER---

I LEARNED OF IT FROM A *MICRO-FILM* LIBRARY.

NO, KAMANDI-- *OUR* BUGS ARE PART OF A SECRET AND POWERFUL RELIGIOUS CULT!

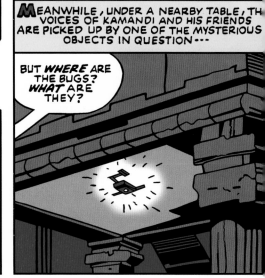

MEANWHILE, UNDER A NEARBY TABLE, THE VOICES OF KAMANDI AND HIS FRIENDS ARE PICKED UP BY ONE OF THE MYSTERIOUS OBJECTS IN QUESTION---

BUT *WHERE* ARE THE BUGS? *WHAT* ARE THEY?

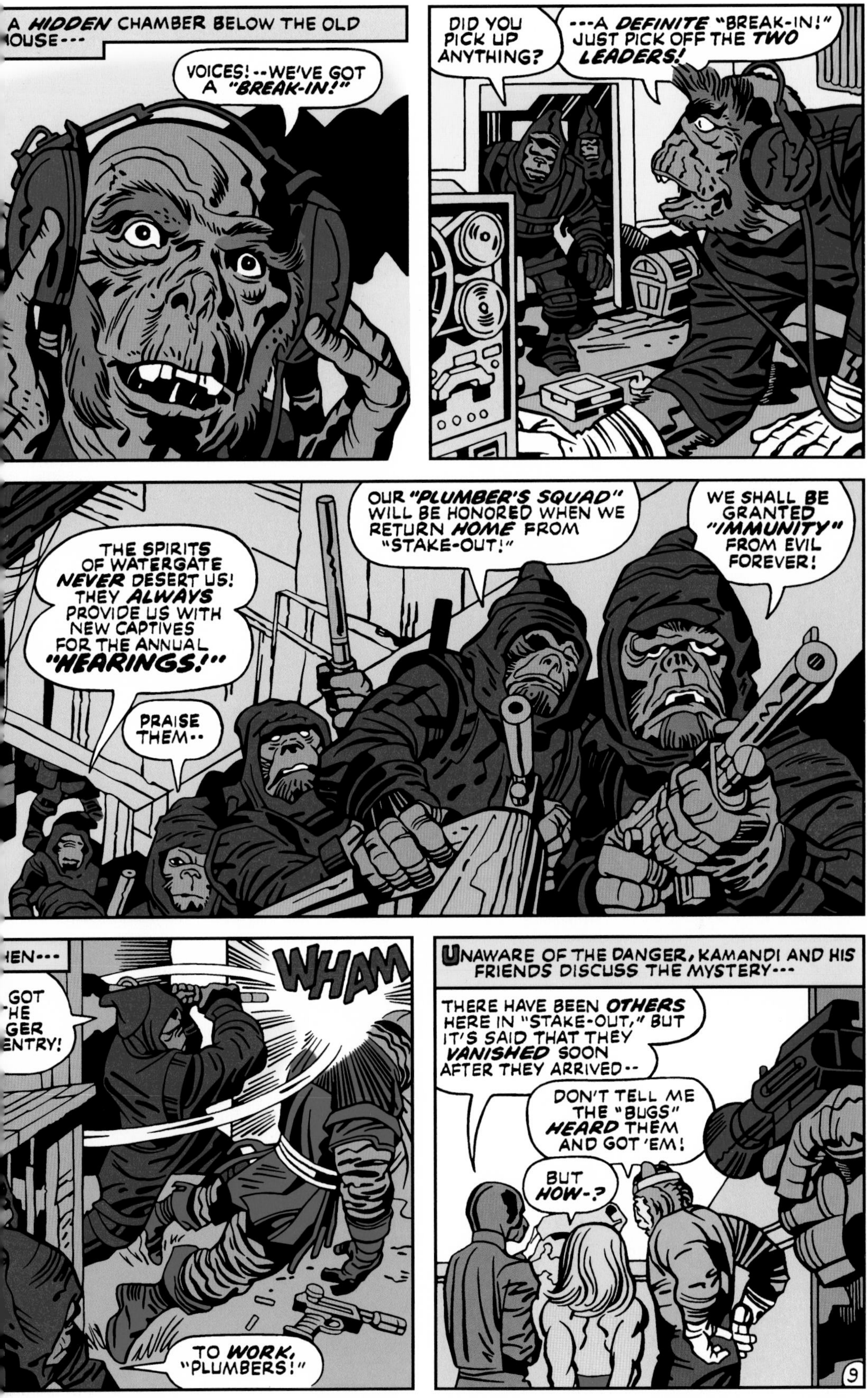
A HIDDEN CHAMBER BELOW THE OLD OUSE---
VOICES! --WE'VE GOT A "BREAK-IN!"
DID YOU PICK UP ANYTHING?
---A DEFINITE "BREAK-IN!" JUST PICK OFF THE TWO LEADERS!
THE SPIRITS OF WATERGATE NEVER DESERT US! THEY ALWAYS PROVIDE US WITH NEW CAPTIVES FOR THE ANNUAL "HEARINGS!"
PRAISE THEM--
OUR "PLUMBER'S SQUAD" WILL BE HONORED WHEN WE RETURN HOME FROM "STAKE-OUT!"
WE SHALL BE GRANTED "IMMUNITY" FROM EVIL FOREVER!
HEN---
GOT HE GER ENTRY!
WHAM
TO WORK, "PLUMBERS!"
UNAWARE OF THE DANGER, KAMANDI AND HIS FRIENDS DISCUSS THE MYSTERY---
THERE HAVE BEEN OTHERS HERE IN "STAKE-OUT," BUT IT'S SAID THAT THEY VANISHED SOON AFTER THEY ARRIVED--
DON'T TELL ME THE "BUGS" HEARD THEM AND GOT 'EM!
BUT HOW-?
9

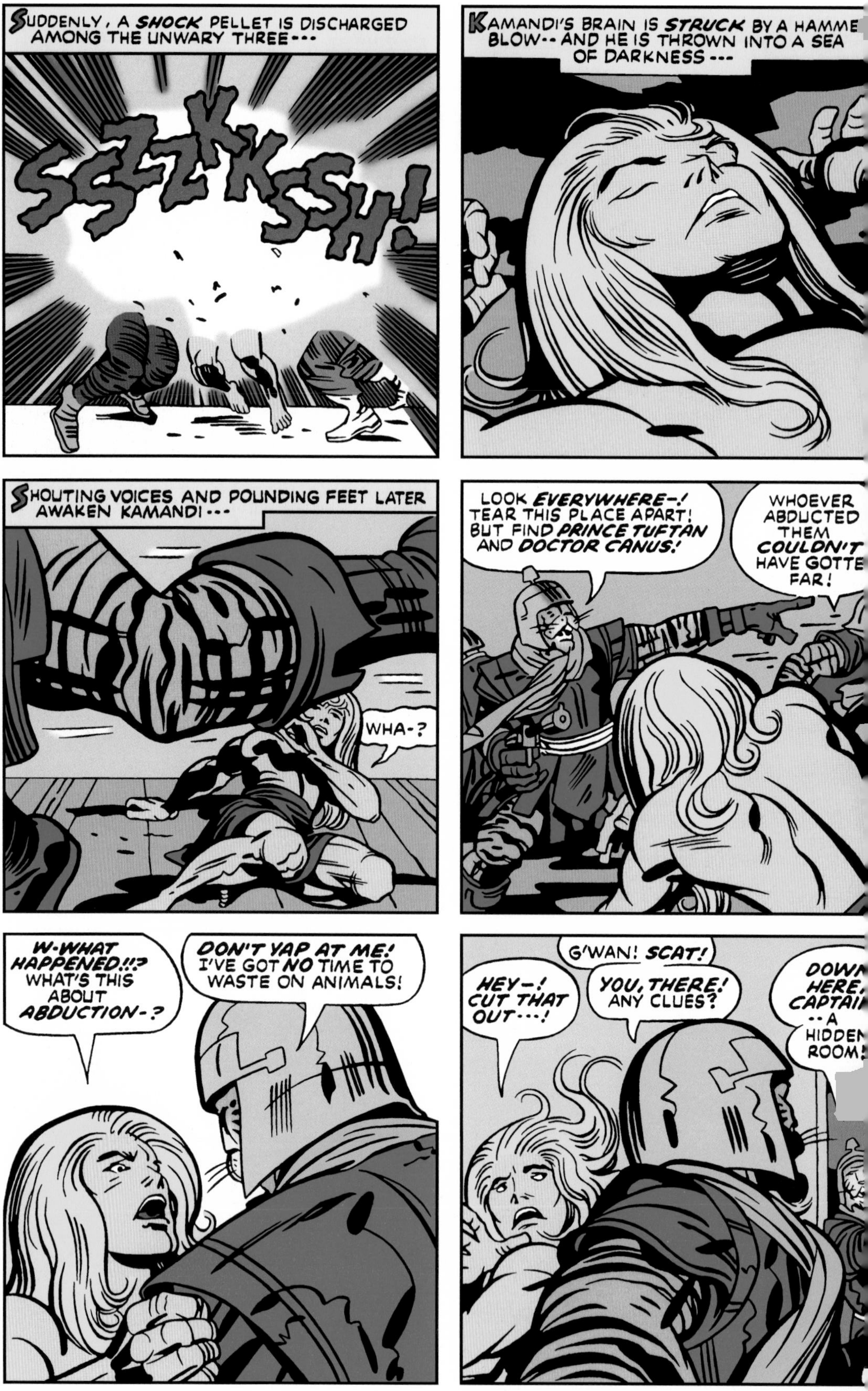
SUDDENLY, A SHOCK PELLET IS DISCHARGED AMONG THE UNWARY THREE---
SSZZKKSSH!
KAMANDI'S BRAIN IS STRUCK BY A HAMME
BLOW-- AND HE IS THROWN INTO A SEA OF DARKNESS---
SHOUTING VOICES AND POUNDING FEET LATER AWAKEN KAMANDI---
WHA-?
LOOK EVERYWHERE-! TEAR THIS PLACE APART! BUT FIND PRINCE TUFTAN AND DOCTOR CANUS!
WHOEVER ABDUCTED THEM COULDN'T HAVE GOTTE FAR!
W-WHAT HAPPENED!!? WHAT'S THIS ABOUT ABDUCTION-?
DON'T YAP AT ME! I'VE GOT NO TIME TO WASTE ON ANIMALS!
G'WAN! SCAT!
HEY-! CUT THAT OUT---!
YOU, THERE! ANY CLUES?
DOWN HERE, CAPTAI --A HIDDEN ROOM!

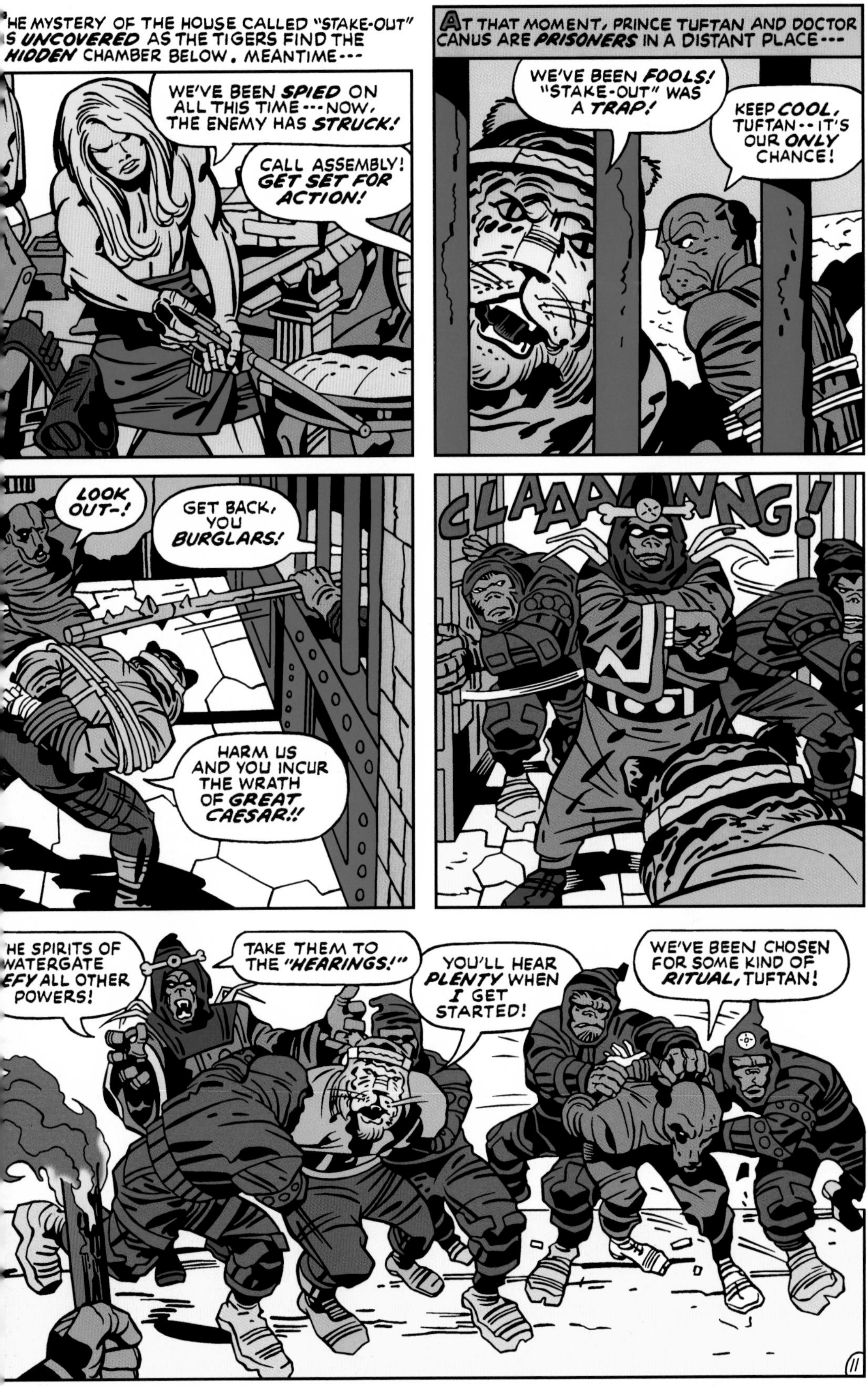
HE MYSTERY OF THE HOUSE CALLED "STAKE-OUT" S UNCOVERED AS THE TIGERS FIND THE HIDDEN CHAMBER BELOW. MEANTIME---
WE'VE BEEN SPIED ON ALL THIS TIME---NOW, THE ENEMY HAS STRUCK!
CALL ASSEMBLY! GET SET FOR ACTION!
AT THAT MOMENT, PRINCE TUFTAN AND DOCTOR CANUS ARE PRISONERS IN A DISTANT PLACE---
WE'VE BEEN FOOLS! "STAKE-OUT" WAS A TRAP!
KEEP COOL, TUFTAN--IT'S OUR ONLY CHANCE!
LOOK OUT-!
GET BACK, YOU BURGLARS!
HARM US AND YOU INCUR THE WRATH OF GREAT CAESAR!!
CLAAANNG!
HE SPIRITS OF WATERGATE EFY ALL OTHER POWERS!
TAKE THEM TO THE "HEARINGS!"
YOU'LL HEAR PLENTY WHEN I GET STARTED!
WE'VE BEEN CHOSEN FOR SOME KIND OF RITUAL, TUFTAN!
11

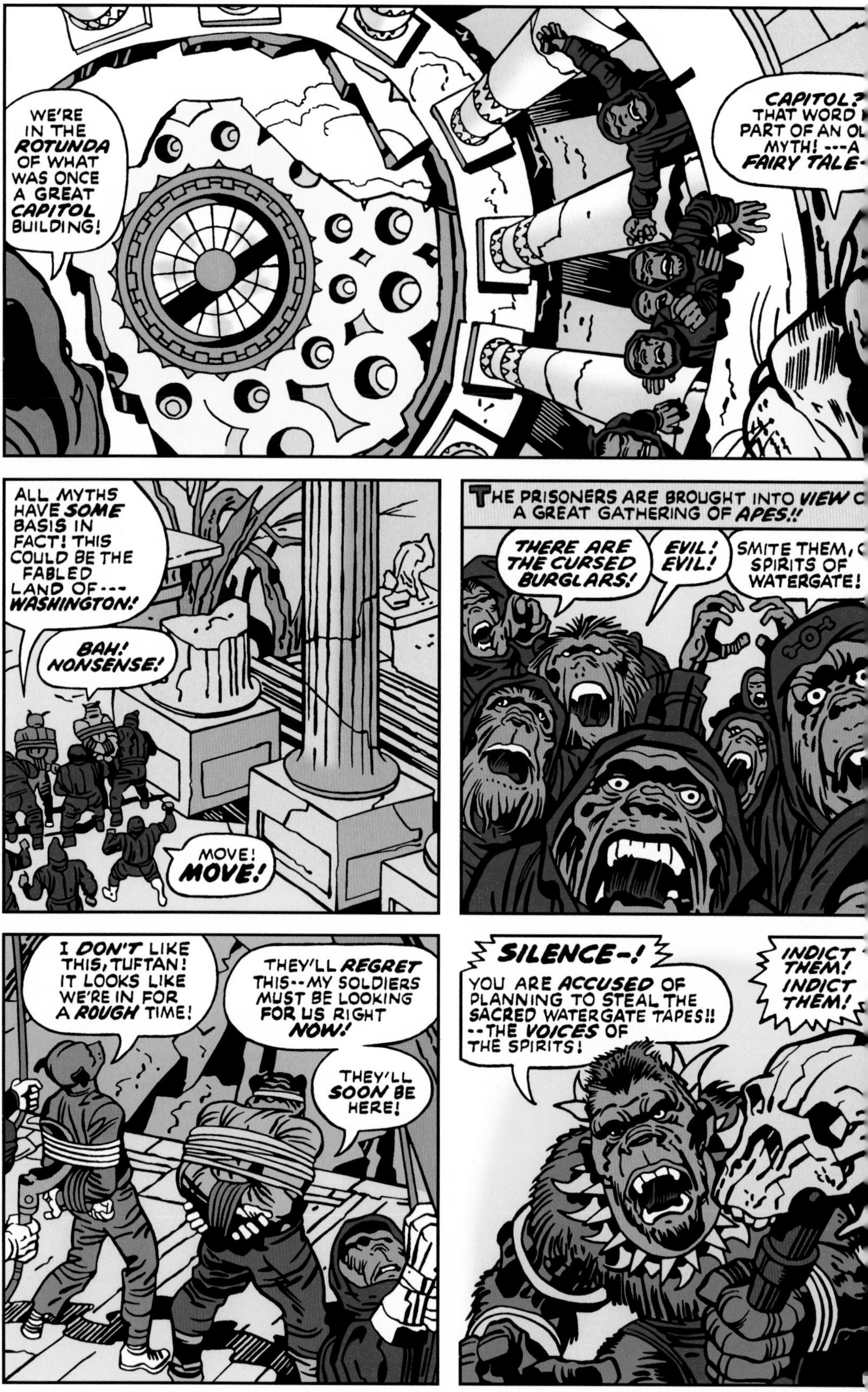
WE'RE IN THE ROTUNDA OF WHAT WAS ONCE A GREAT CAPITOL BUILDING!
CAPITOL? THAT WORD PART OF AN OL MYTH! ---A FAIRY TALE-
ALL MYTHS HAVE SOME BASIS IN FACT! THIS COULD BE THE FABLED LAND OF--- WASHINGTON!
BAH! NONSENSE!
MOVE! MOVE!
THE PRISONERS ARE BROUGHT INTO VIEW O A GREAT GATHERING OF APES!!
THERE ARE THE CURSED BURGLARS!
EVIL! EVIL!
SMITE THEM, SPIRITS OF WATERGATE!
I DON'T LIKE THIS, TUFTAN! IT LOOKS LIKE WE'RE IN FOR A ROUGH TIME!
THEY'LL REGRET THIS--MY SOLDIERS MUST BE LOOKING FOR US RIGHT NOW!
THEY'LL SOON BE HERE!
SILENCE-!
YOU ARE ACCUSED OF PLANNING TO STEAL THE SACRED WATERGATE TAPES!! --THE VOICES OF THE SPIRITS!
INDICT THEM! INDICT THEM!

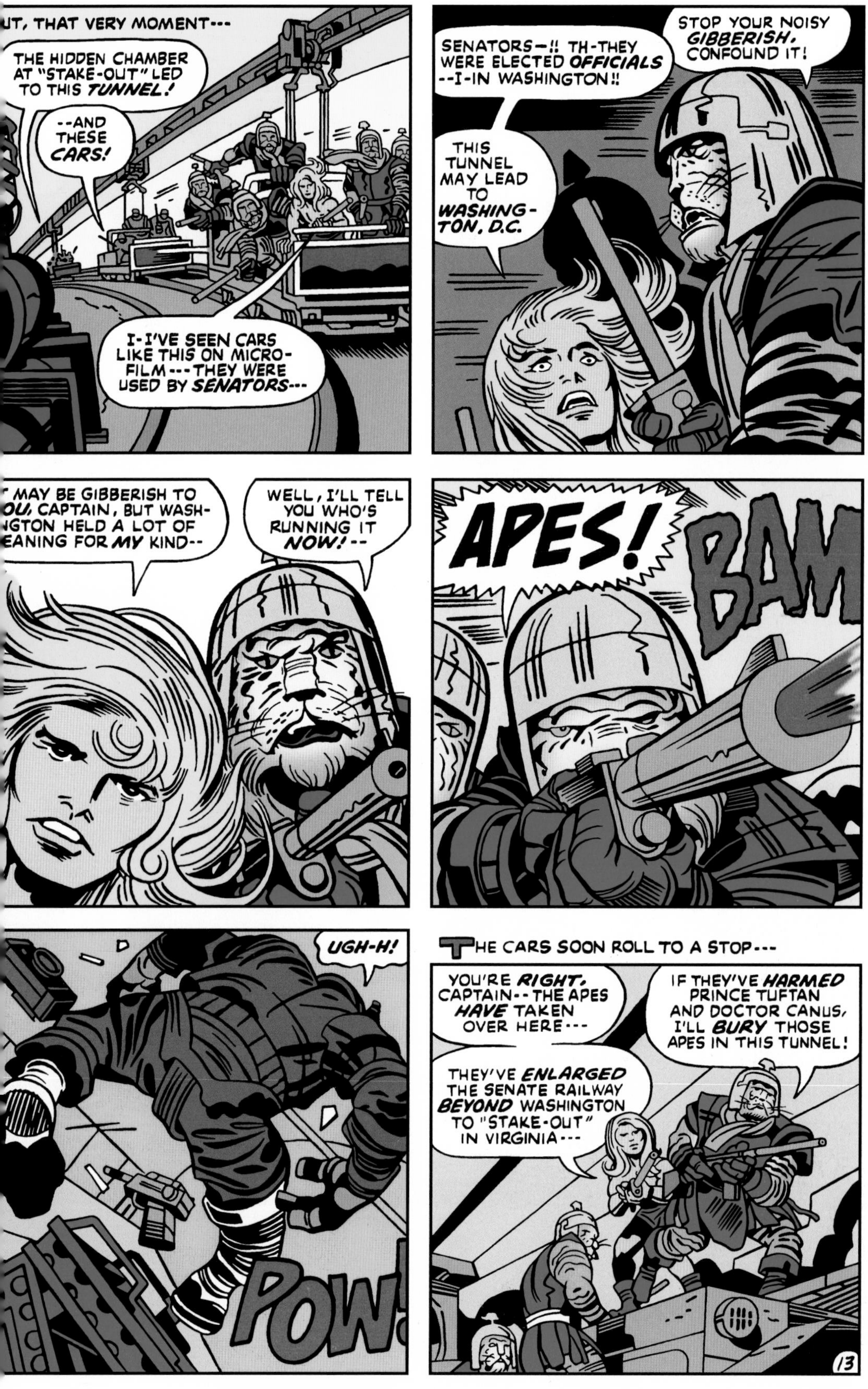
UT, THAT VERY MOMENT---
THE HIDDEN CHAMBER AT "STAKE-OUT" LED TO THIS TUNNEL!
--AND THESE CARS!
I-I'VE SEEN CARS LIKE THIS ON MICRO-FILM---THEY WERE USED BY SENATORS---
SENATORS--!! TH-THEY WERE ELECTED OFFICIALS --I-IN WASHINGTON!!
STOP YOUR NOISY GIBBERISH, CONFOUND IT!
THIS TUNNEL MAY LEAD TO WASHING-TON, D.C.
T MAY BE GIBBERISH TO OU, CAPTAIN, BUT WASH-NGTON HELD A LOT OF EANING FOR MY KIND--
WELL, I'LL TELL YOU WHO'S RUNNING IT NOW!--
APES!
BAM
UGH-H!
POW
THE CARS SOON ROLL TO A STOP---
YOU'RE RIGHT, CAPTAIN--THE APES HAVE TAKEN OVER HERE---
IF THEY'VE HARMED PRINCE TUFTAN AND DOCTOR CANUS, I'LL BURY THOSE APES IN THIS TUNNEL!
THEY'VE ENLARGED THE SENATE RAILWAY BEYOND WASHINGTON TO "STAKE-OUT" IN VIRGINIA---
13

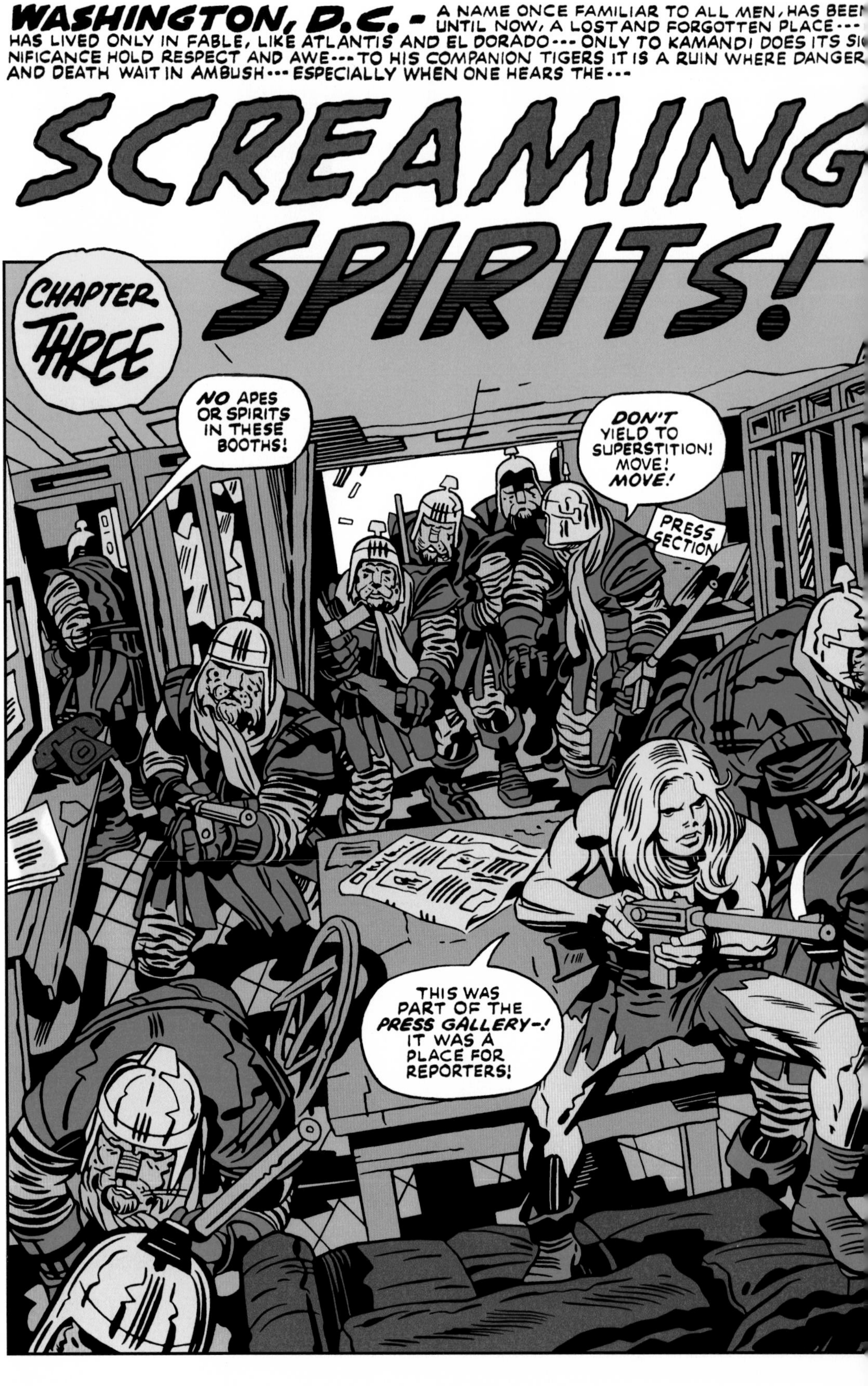
WASHINGTON, D.C. - A NAME ONCE FAMILIAR TO ALL MEN, HAS BEEN UNTIL NOW, A LOST AND FORGOTTEN PLACE --- HAS LIVED ONLY IN FABLE, LIKE ATLANTIS AND EL DORADO --- ONLY TO KAMANDI DOES ITS SIG NIFICANCE HOLD RESPECT AND AWE --- TO HIS COMPANION TIGERS IT IS A RUIN WHERE DANGER AND DEATH WAIT IN AMBUSH --- ESPECIALLY WHEN ONE HEARS THE ---
SCREAMING SPIRITS!
CHAPTER THREE
NO APES OR SPIRITS IN THESE BOOTHS!
DON'T YIELD TO SUPERSTITION! MOVE! MOVE!
PRESS SECTION
THIS WAS PART OF THE PRESS GALLERY-! IT WAS A PLACE FOR REPORTERS!

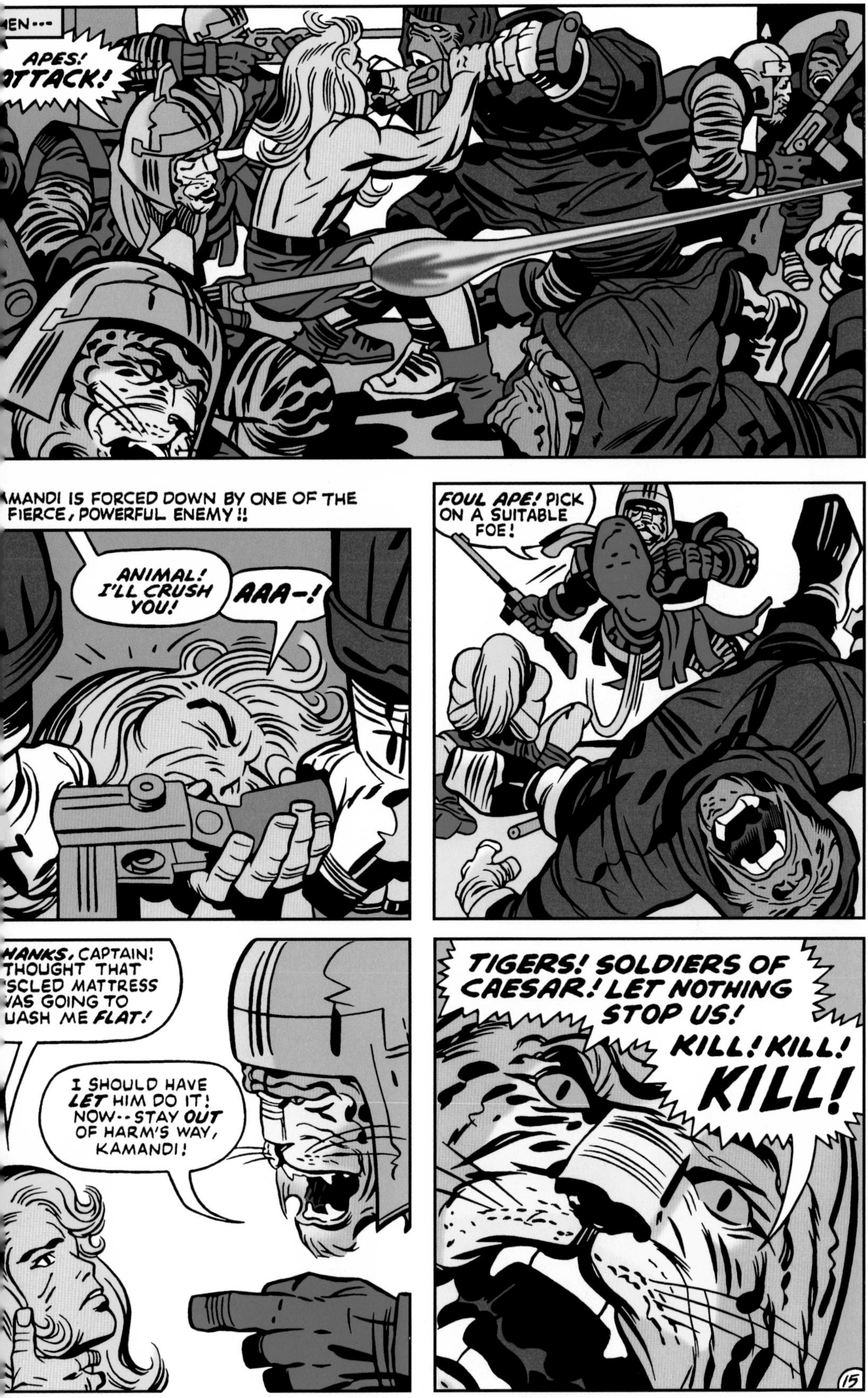
EN---
APES! TTACK!
MANDI IS FORCED DOWN BY ONE OF THE FIERCE, POWERFUL ENEMY!!
ANIMAL! I'LL CRUSH YOU!
AAA-!
FOUL APE! PICK ON A SUITABLE FOE!
HANKS, CAPTAIN! THOUGHT THAT SCLED MATTRESS VAS GOING TO UASH ME FLAT!
I SHOULD HAVE LET HIM DO IT! NOW--STAY OUT OF HARM'S WAY, KAMANDI!
TIGERS! SOLDIERS OF CAESAR! LET NOTHING STOP US!
KILL! KILL! KILL!
15

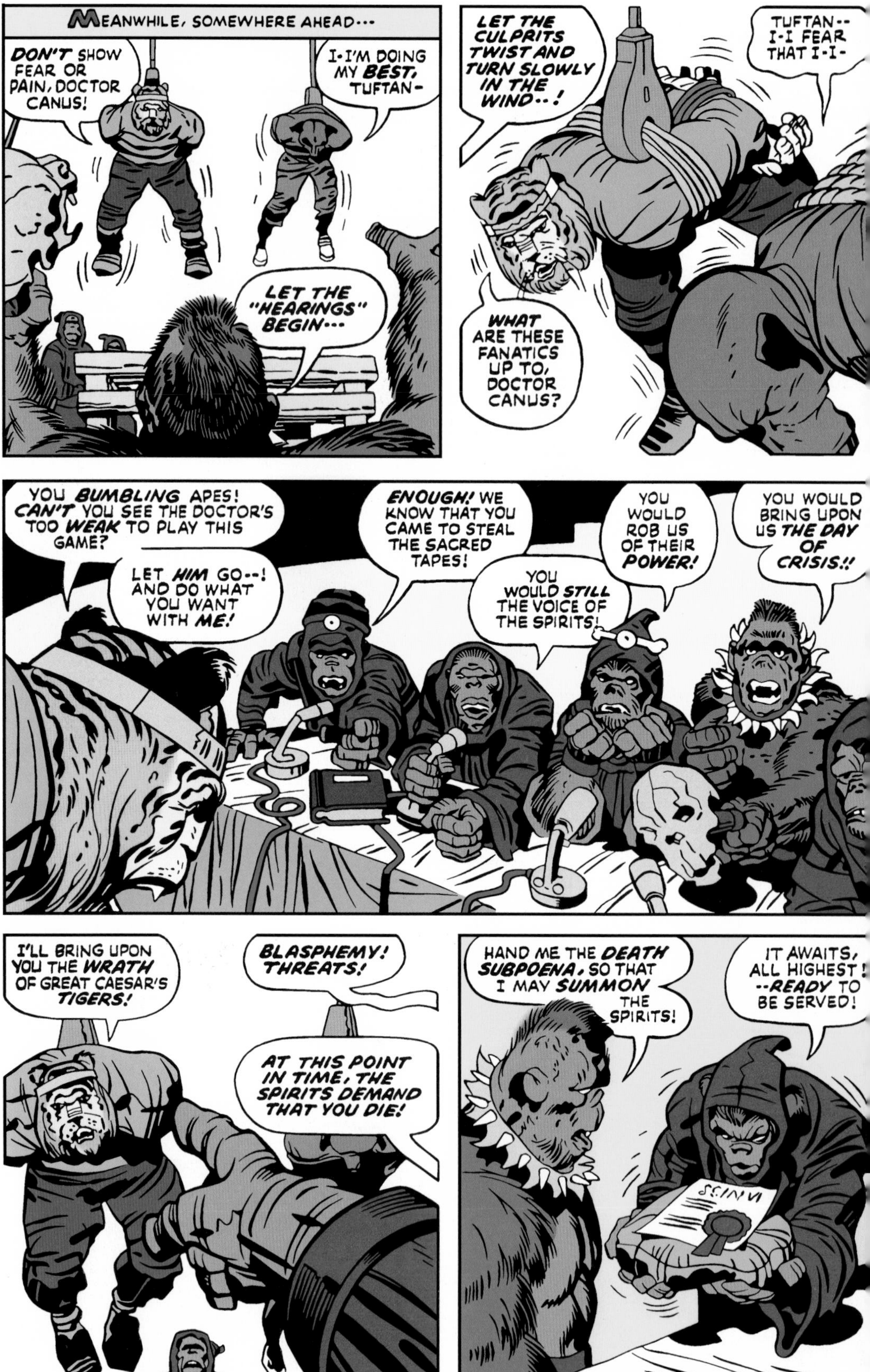
MEANWHILE, SOMEWHERE AHEAD...
DON'T SHOW FEAR OR PAIN, DOCTOR CANUS!
I-I'M DOING MY BEST, TUFTAN-
LET THE "HEARINGS" BEGIN...
LET THE CULPRITS TWIST AND TURN SLOWLY IN THE WIND..!
TUFTAN-- I-I FEAR THAT I-I-
WHAT ARE THESE FANATICS UP TO, DOCTOR CANUS?
YOU BUMBLING APES! CAN'T YOU SEE THE DOCTOR'S TOO WEAK TO PLAY THIS GAME?
LET HIM GO--! AND DO WHAT YOU WANT WITH ME!
ENOUGH! WE KNOW THAT YOU CAME TO STEAL THE SACRED TAPES!
YOU WOULD STILL THE VOICE OF THE SPIRITS!
YOU WOULD ROB US OF THEIR POWER!
YOU WOULD BRING UPON US THE DAY OF CRISIS!!
I'LL BRING UPON YOU THE WRATH OF GREAT CAESAR'S TIGERS!
BLASPHEMY! THREATS!
AT THIS POINT IN TIME, THE SPIRITS DEMAND THAT YOU DIE!
HAND ME THE DEATH SUBPOENA, SO THAT I MAY SUMMON THE SPIRITS!
IT AWAITS, ALL HIGHEST! --READY TO BE SERVED!

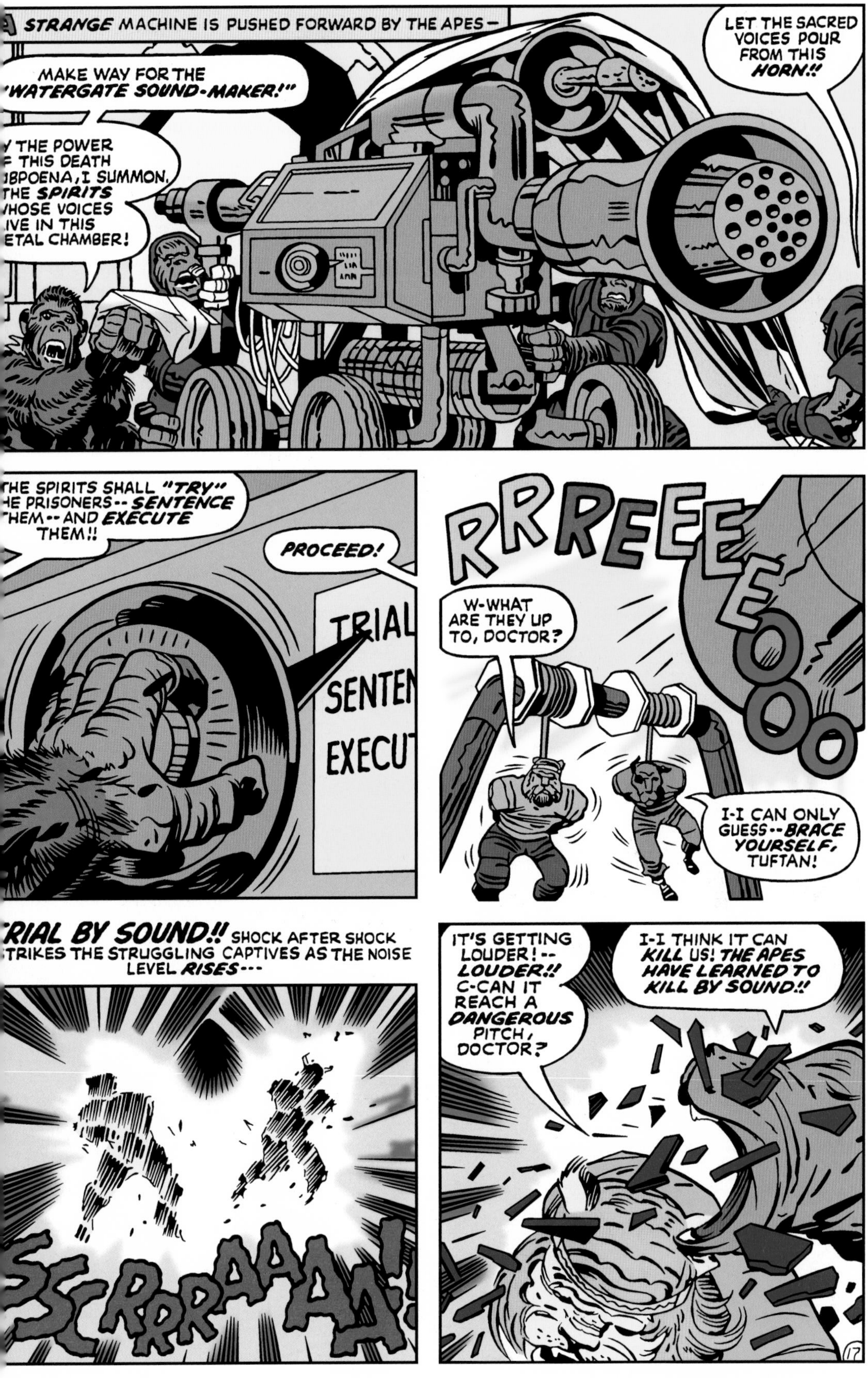
A STRANGE MACHINE IS PUSHED FORWARD BY THE APES—
MAKE WAY FOR THE "WATERGATE SOUND-MAKER!"
Y THE POWER F THIS DEATH JBPOENA, I SUMMON, THE SPIRITS WHOSE VOICES IVE IN THIS ETAL CHAMBER!
LET THE SACRED VOICES POUR FROM THIS HORN!!
THE SPIRITS SHALL "TRY" HE PRISONERS-- SENTENCE THEM-- AND EXECUTE THEM!!
PROCEED!
TRIAL
SENTEN
EXECUT
RRREEEEEOOOO
W-WHAT ARE THEY UP TO, DOCTOR?
I-I CAN ONLY GUESS-- BRACE YOURSELF, TUFTAN!
RIAL BY SOUND!! SHOCK AFTER SHOCK TRIKES THE STRUGGLING CAPTIVES AS THE NOISE LEVEL RISES---
SCRRRAAAA!
IT'S GETTING LOUDER! -- LOUDER!! C-CAN IT REACH A DANGEROUS PITCH, DOCTOR?
I-I THINK IT CAN KILL US! THE APES HAVE LEARNED TO KILL BY SOUND!!
17

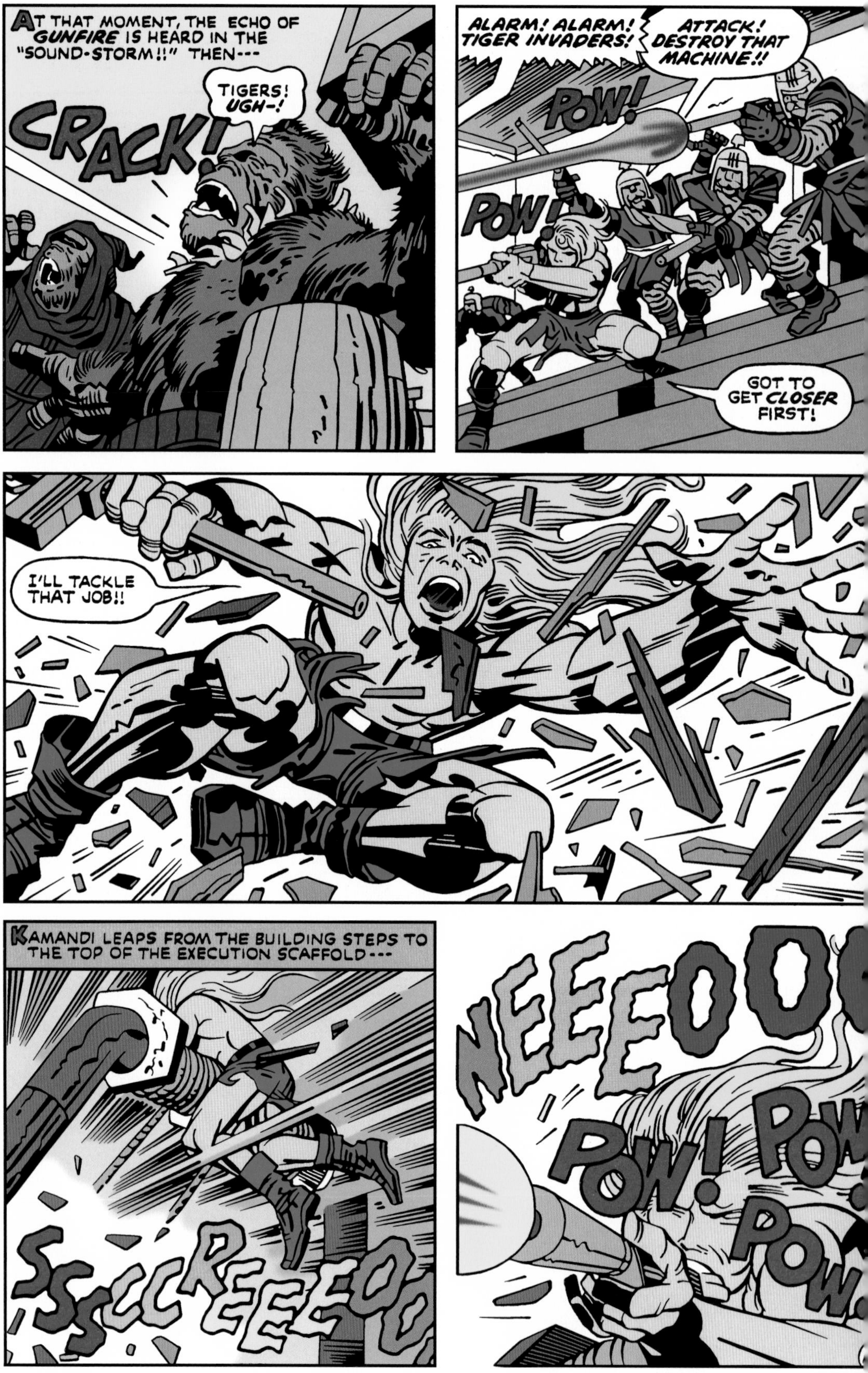
AT THAT MOMENT, THE ECHO OF GUNFIRE IS HEARD IN THE "SOUND-STORM!!" THEN---
CRACK!
TIGERS! UGH-!
ALARM! ALARM! TIGER INVADERS!
ATTACK! DESTROY THAT MACHINE!!
POW!
POW!
GOT TO GET CLOSER FIRST!
I'LL TACKLE THAT JOB!!
KAMANDI LEAPS FROM THE BUILDING STEPS TO THE TOP OF THE EXECUTION SCAFFOLD---
SSSCCREEEEOO
NEEEOO
POW!
POW!
POW!

A QUICK SUCCESSION OF *WELL-AIMED* SHOTS WRECKS THE HORN OF THE SOUND-MACHINE!

DID IT! THE SOUND HAS STOPPED!

KAMANDI! Y-YOU SAVED US!

CUT US DOWN!

WE'LL TAKE CARE OF THAT, SIR!

KEEP GOING, TIGERS! DRIVE THOSE FANATIC APES *BACK* INTO THEIR HOLES!!

THE TIGER SOLDIERS MOUNT A SAVAGE ATTACK WHICH SENDS THE APES REELING ---

BLAST THE APES!!

BREAK THEIR RANKS!

STOP THE TIGERS!

THE BATTLE RAGES ON UNTIL THE RUINS OF WASHINGTON, D.C. ARE ABLAZE WITH FIRES. THE OLD JEFFERSON MEMORIAL LOOKS UPON CATASTROPHE ONCE MORE ---

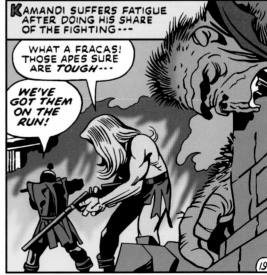

KAMANDI SUFFERS FATIGUE AFTER DOING HIS SHARE OF THE FIGHTING ---

WHAT A FRACAS! THOSE APES SURE ARE *TOUGH* ---

WE'VE GOT THEM ON THE RUN!

19

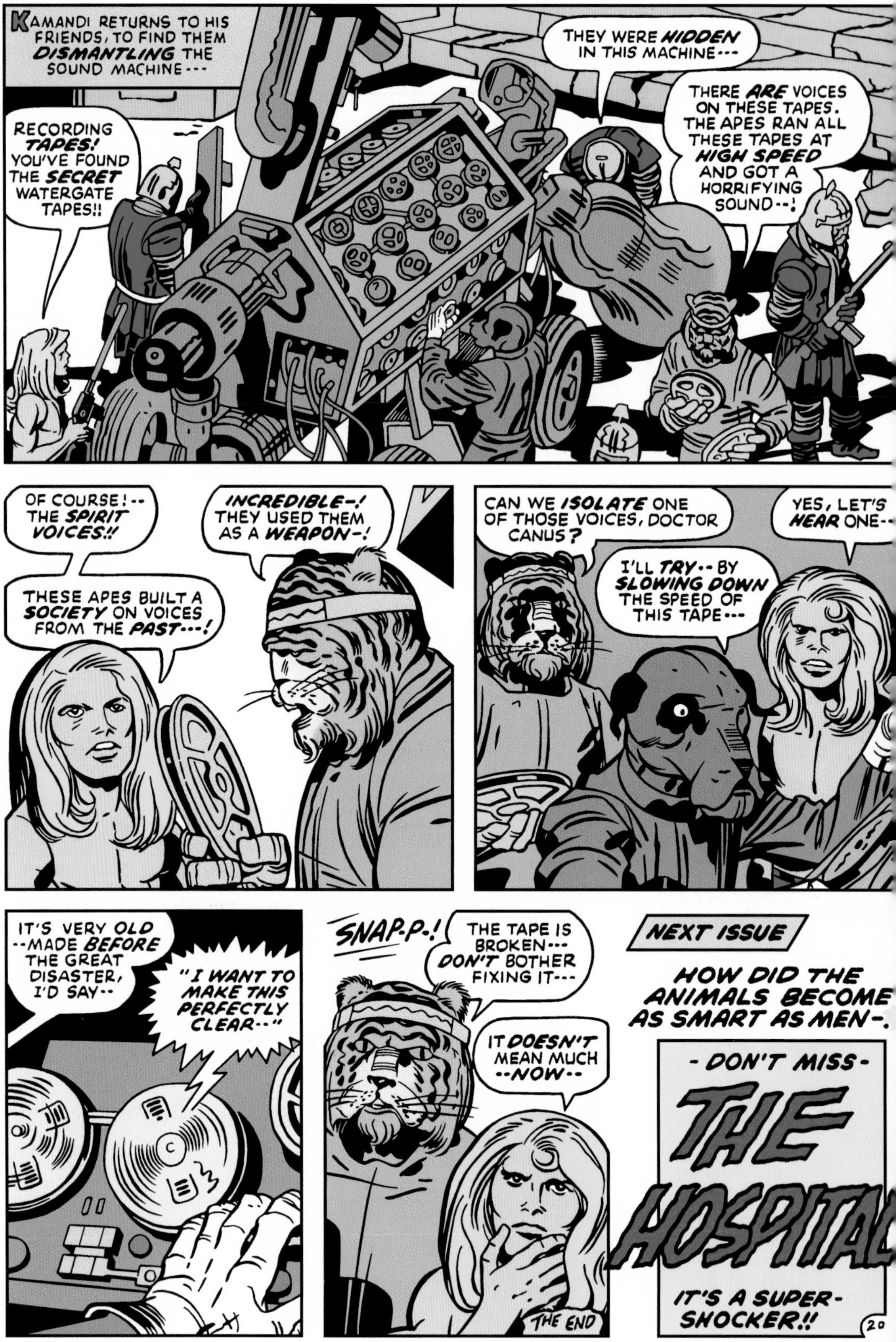
KAMANDI RETURNS TO HIS FRIENDS, TO FIND THEM DISMANTLING THE SOUND MACHINE---
THEY WERE HIDDEN IN THIS MACHINE---
RECORDING TAPES! YOU'VE FOUND THE SECRET WATERGATE TAPES!!
THERE ARE VOICES ON THESE TAPES. THE APES RAN ALL THESE TAPES AT HIGH SPEED AND GOT A HORRIFYING SOUND--!
OF COURSE!-- THE SPIRIT VOICES!!
THESE APES BUILT A SOCIETY ON VOICES FROM THE PAST---!
INCREDIBLE-! THEY USED THEM AS A WEAPON-!
CAN WE ISOLATE ONE OF THOSE VOICES, DOCTOR CANUS?
YES, LET'S HEAR ONE--
I'LL TRY-- BY SLOWING DOWN THE SPEED OF THIS TAPE---
IT'S VERY OLD --MADE BEFORE THE GREAT DISASTER, I'D SAY--
"I WANT TO MAKE THIS PERFECTLY CLEAR--"
SNAP-P-!
THE TAPE IS BROKEN--- DON'T BOTHER FIXING IT---
IT DOESN'T MEAN MUCH --NOW--
THE END
NEXT ISSUE
HOW DID THE ANIMALS BECOME AS SMART AS MEN-.
- DON'T MISS -
THE HOSPITAL
IT'S A SUPER-SHOCKER!!
20

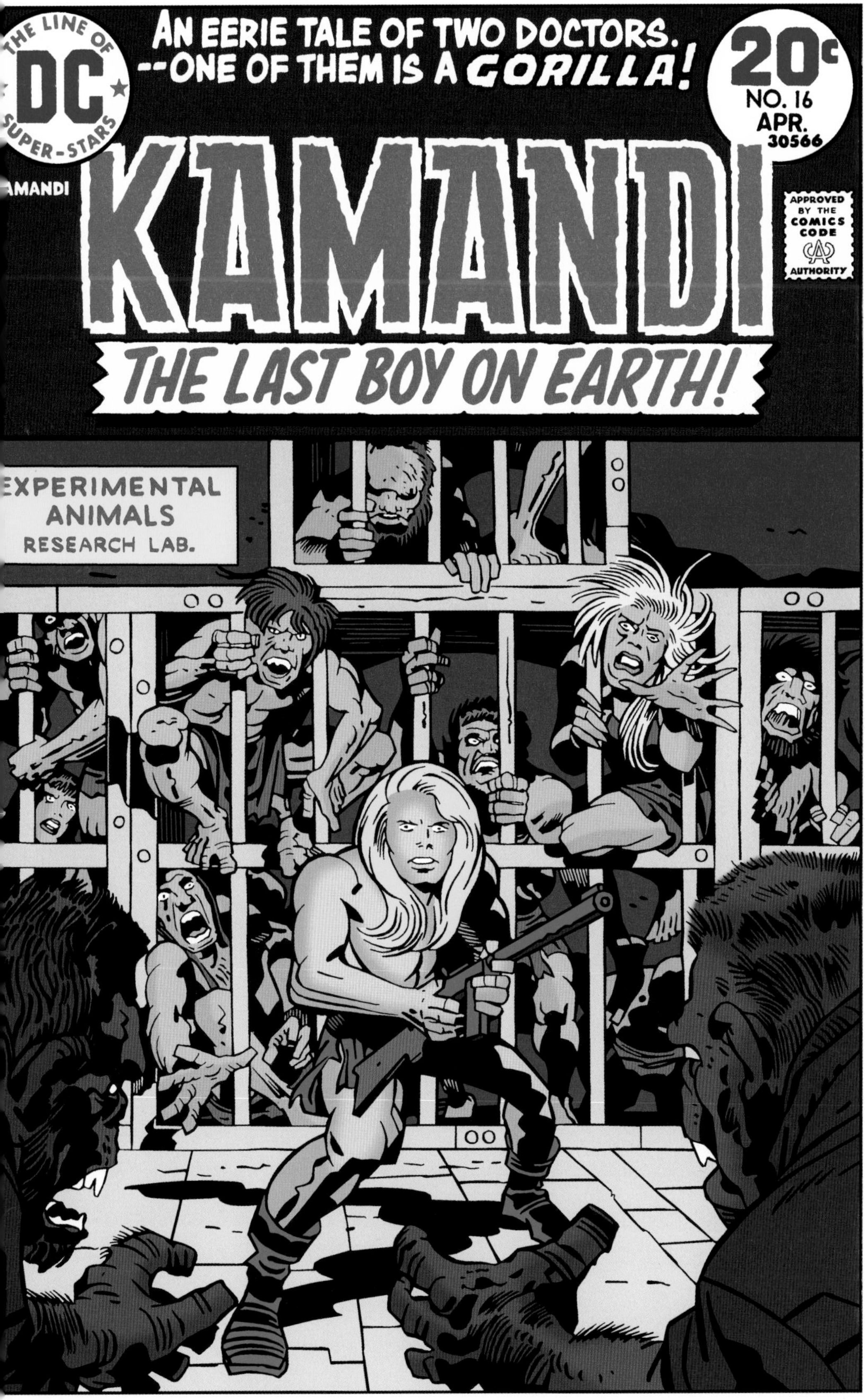
THE LINE OF DC SUPER-STARS
AN EERIE TALE OF TWO DOCTORS. --ONE OF THEM IS A GORILLA!
20¢
NO. 16
APR.
30566
KAMANDI
APPROVED BY THE COMICS CODE AUTHORITY
KAMANDI
THE LAST BOY ON EARTH!
EXPERIMENTAL ANIMALS RESEARCH LAB.

THE ANIMALS HAVE TAKEN OVER THE WORLD!

IN THIS MAGAZINE IT HAS HAPPENED!!! AT SOME UNKNOWN DATE, A GREAT NATURAL DISASTER HAS PULLED A FANTASTIC SWITCH!! MEN ROAM IN HERDS! THEY ARE HUNTED-CAPTURED AND USED LIKE BEASTS---! *THIS IS HOW IT MAY HAVE HAPPENED -- IN THE WORLD OF --*

KAMANDI

THE LAST BOY ON EARTH!

CHAPTER ONE

ANCIENT WASHINGTON, D.C. IS *NO* PLACE TO WANDER OFF FROM FRIENDS--

WHAT KIND OF PLACE IS THIS?

EDITED, WRITTEN AND DRAWN BY SEDENTARY JACK KIRBY

INKED BY MOUNTAIN-CLIMBING MIKE ROYER

WITH A HELPING HAND FROM D. BRUCE BERRY

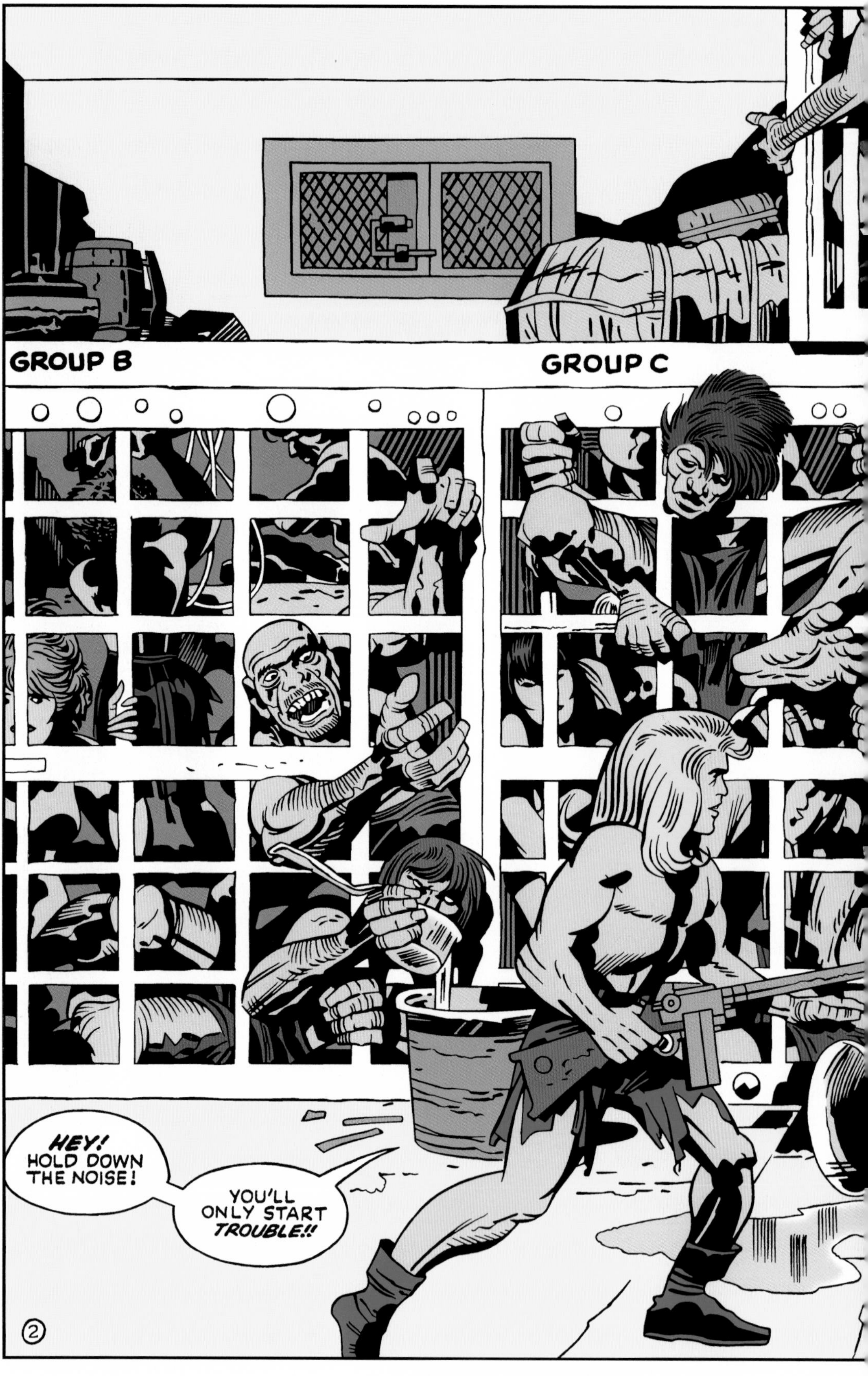
GROUP B
GROUP C
HEY! HOLD DOWN THE NOISE!
YOU'LL ONLY START TROUBLE!!
2

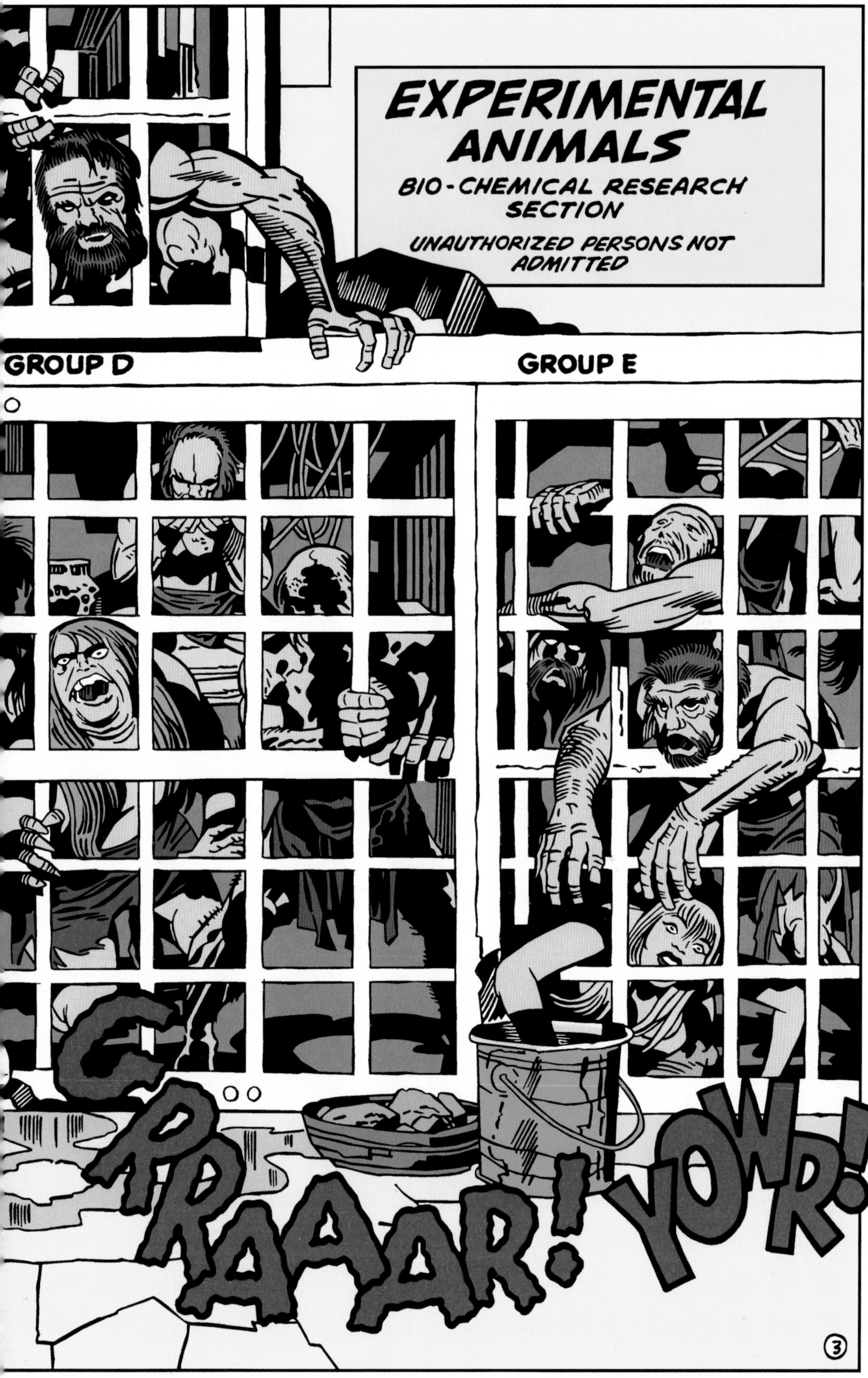
EXPERIMENTAL ANIMALS
BIO-CHEMICAL RESEARCH SECTION
UNAUTHORIZED PERSONS NOT ADMITTED
GROUP D
GROUP E
GRRAAAR!
YOWR!
3

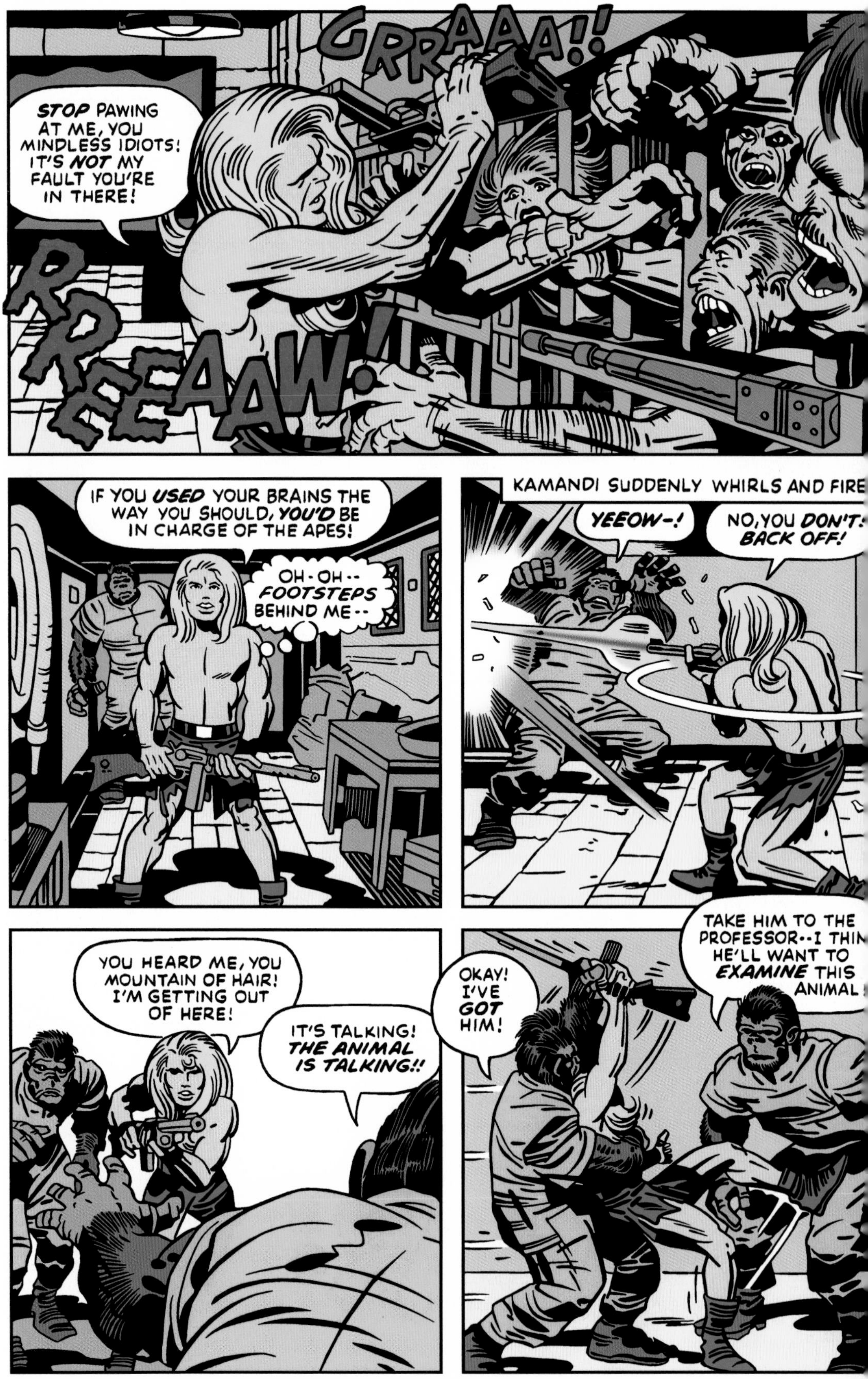
GRRAAAA!!
STOP PAWING AT ME, YOU MINDLESS IDIOTS! IT'S NOT MY FAULT YOU'RE IN THERE!
RREEAAW!
IF YOU USED YOUR BRAINS THE WAY YOU SHOULD, YOU'D BE IN CHARGE OF THE APES!
OH-OH-- FOOTSTEPS BEHIND ME--
KAMANDI SUDDENLY WHIRLS AND FIRE
YEEOW-!
NO, YOU DON'T! BACK OFF!
YOU HEARD ME, YOU MOUNTAIN OF HAIR! I'M GETTING OUT OF HERE!
IT'S TALKING! THE ANIMAL IS TALKING!!
OKAY! I'VE GOT HIM!
TAKE HIM TO THE PROFESSOR--I THIN HE'LL WANT TO EXAMINE THIS ANIMAL

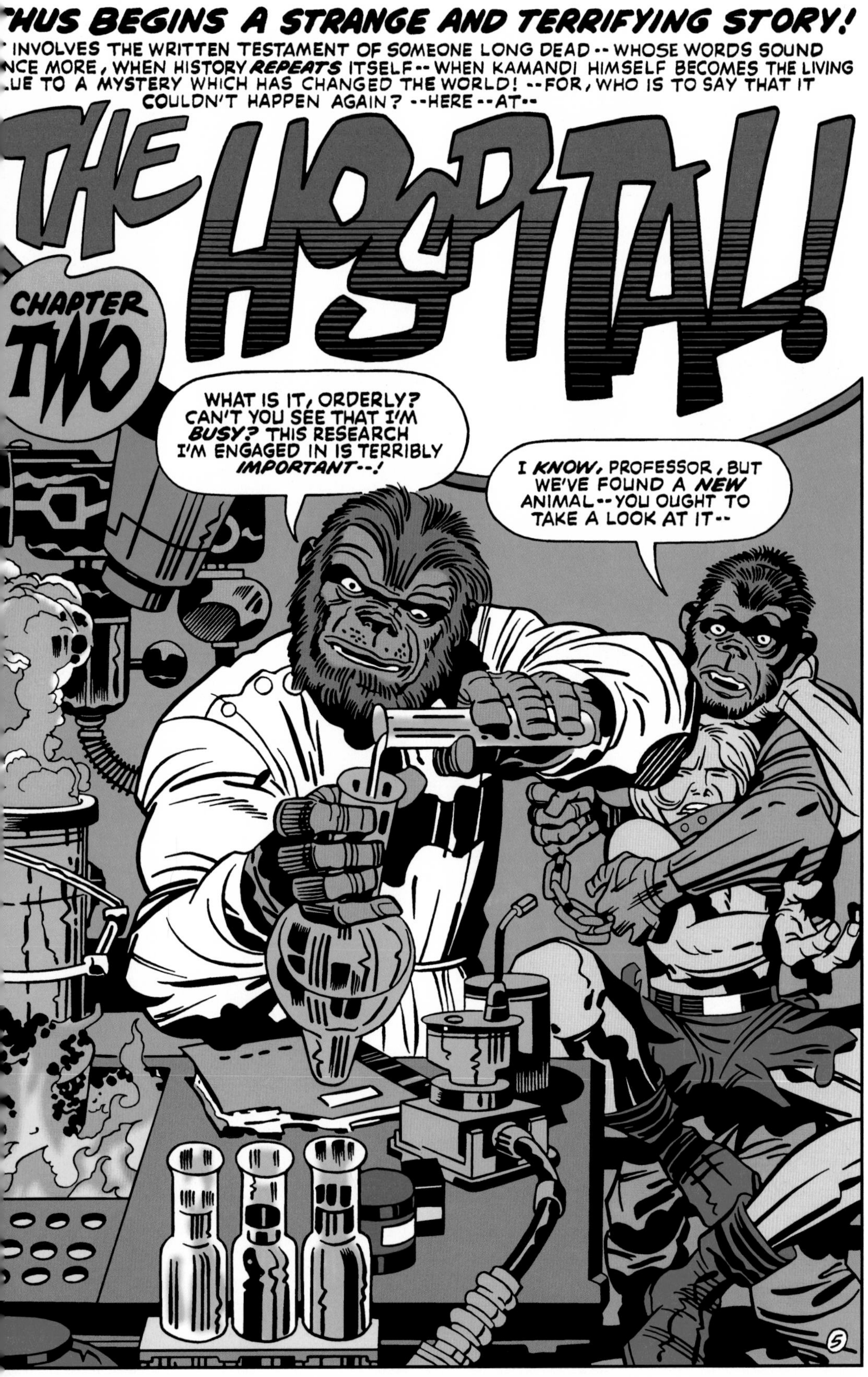
HUS BEGINS A STRANGE AND TERRIFYING STORY!
INVOLVES THE WRITTEN TESTAMENT OF SOMEONE LONG DEAD -- WHOSE WORDS SOUND
NCE MORE, WHEN HISTORY REPEATS ITSELF -- WHEN KAMANDI HIMSELF BECOMES THE LIVING
UE TO A MYSTERY WHICH HAS CHANGED THE WORLD! --FOR, WHO IS TO SAY THAT IT
COULDN'T HAPPEN AGAIN? --HERE--AT--
THE HOSPITAL!
CHAPTER TWO
WHAT IS IT, ORDERLY? CAN'T YOU SEE THAT I'M BUSY? THIS RESEARCH I'M ENGAGED IN IS TERRIBLY IMPORTANT--!
I KNOW, PROFESSOR, BUT WE'VE FOUND A NEW ANIMAL--YOU OUGHT TO TAKE A LOOK AT IT--
5

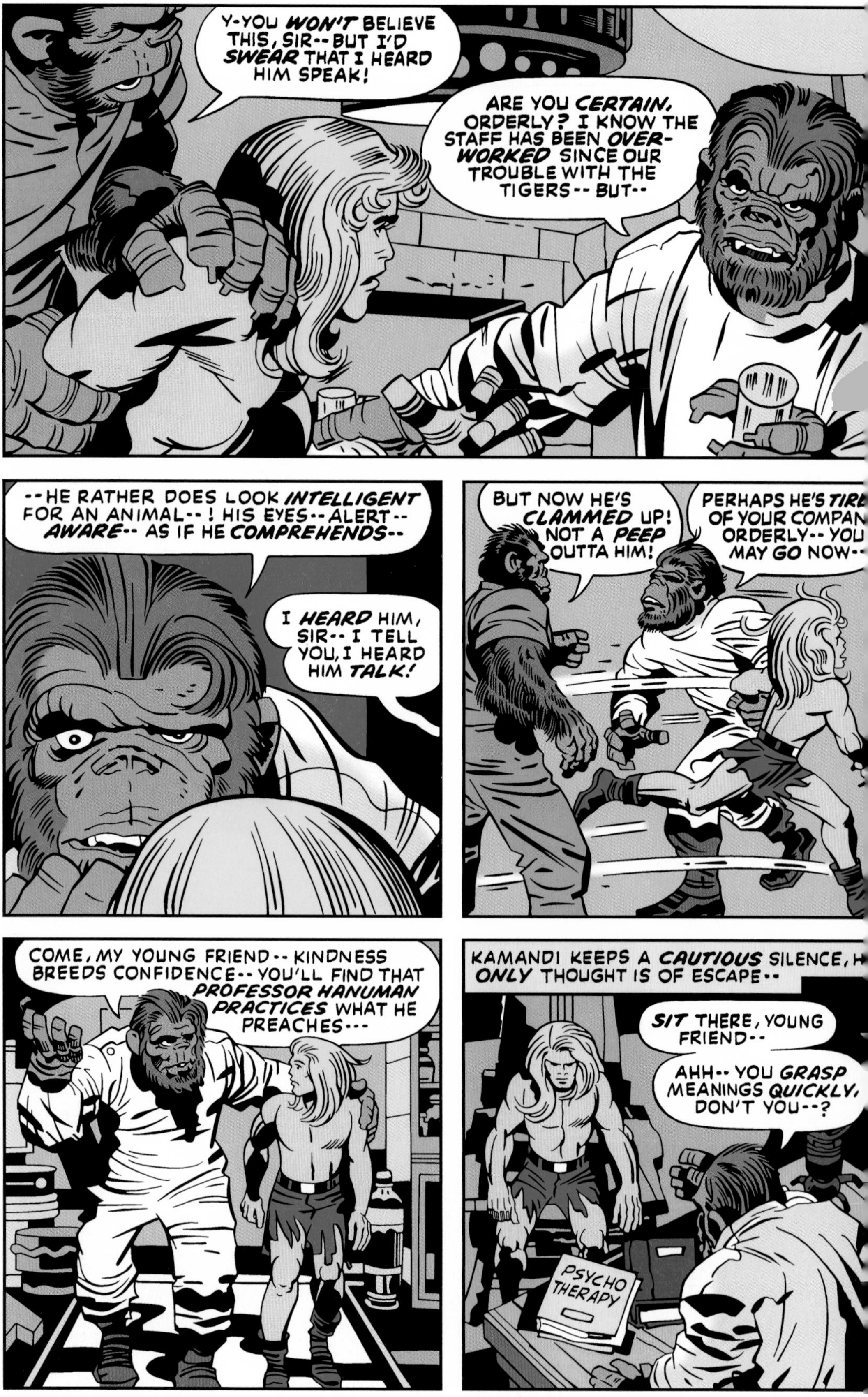
Y-YOU WON'T BELIEVE THIS, SIR-- BUT I'D SWEAR THAT I HEARD HIM SPEAK!
ARE YOU CERTAIN, ORDERLY? I KNOW THE STAFF HAS BEEN OVER-WORKED SINCE OUR TROUBLE WITH THE TIGERS-- BUT--
--HE RATHER DOES LOOK INTELLIGENT FOR AN ANIMAL--! HIS EYES--ALERT-- AWARE-- AS IF HE COMPREHENDS--
I HEARD HIM, SIR-- I TELL YOU, I HEARD HIM TALK!
BUT NOW HE'S CLAMMED UP! NOT A PEEP OUTTA HIM!
PERHAPS HE'S TIRE
OF YOUR COMPAN
ORDERLY-- YOU MAY GO NOW--
COME, MY YOUNG FRIEND-- KINDNESS BREEDS CONFIDENCE-- YOU'LL FIND THAT PROFESSOR HANUMAN PRACTICES WHAT HE PREACHES---
KAMANDI KEEPS A CAUTIOUS SILENCE,
ONLY THOUGHT IS OF ESCAPE--
SIT THERE, YOUNG FRIEND--
AHH-- YOU GRASP MEANINGS QUICKLY, DON'T YOU--?
PSYCHO THERAPY

EANWHILE, OUTSIDE, 'IGER PATROLS COMB THE RUINS OR KAMANDI--

I SURE DON'T LIKE THIS PLACE!

THE APES CAN *HAVE* IT! IT GIVES ME THE *CREEPS!*

I WISH THAT KAMANDI ANIMAL WOULD SHOW UP--SO WE COULD ALL *PULL OUT!*

OUR *PRINCE TUFTAN* SEEMS *OBSESSED* BY HIS CONCERN FOR THIS PET!

'ASHINGTON, D.C.-- ONCE A 'ENTER OF WORLD POWER, IS OW A PLACE OF *FOREBODING* -- FROM WHICH DARK MYTHS SPRING--

RUINS-- NOTHING BUT *RUINS* HERE--THIS STONE MASS IS A *MILE* LONG--

THAT TALKING ANIMAL, KAMANDI, CALLED IT *CLEOPATRA'S NEEDLE--*

SUDDENLY--FROM AMBUSH--!

FOREIGN *PIGS!*

WAZOM!

GRENADE! HIT THE DIRT!

ACTION AT LAST!

7

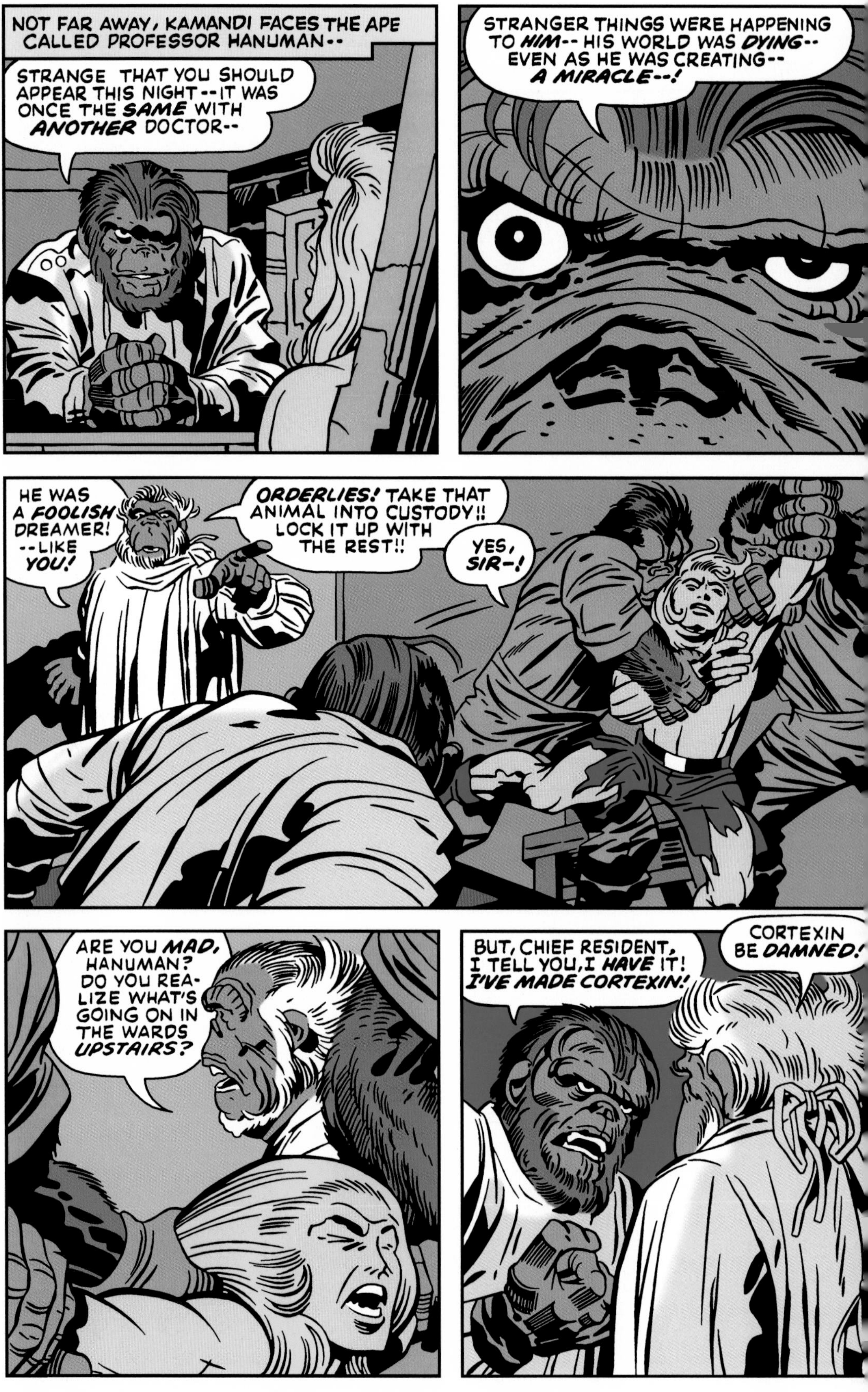
NOT FAR AWAY, KAMANDI FACES THE APE CALLED PROFESSOR HANUMAN--
STRANGE THAT YOU SHOULD APPEAR THIS NIGHT--IT WAS ONCE THE SAME WITH ANOTHER DOCTOR--
STRANGER THINGS WERE HAPPENING TO HIM-- HIS WORLD WAS DYING-- EVEN AS HE WAS CREATING-- A MIRACLE--!
HE WAS A FOOLISH DREAMER! --LIKE YOU!
ORDERLIES! TAKE THAT ANIMAL INTO CUSTODY!! LOCK IT UP WITH THE REST!!
YES, SIR-!
ARE YOU MAD, HANUMAN? DO YOU REALIZE WHAT'S GOING ON IN THE WARDS UPSTAIRS?
BUT, CHIEF RESIDENT, I TELL YOU, I HAVE IT! I'VE MADE CORTEXIN!
CORTEXIN BE DAMNED!

WITH THIS *NEW* ANIMAL, I COULD TEST IT WITH *GOOD* CHANCES OF SUCCESS--

A *BRAIN* STIMULANT! --LIQUID *SHOCK THERAPY!* BAH--!

IT COULD BE A *GREAT* STEP FORWARD IN MEDICINE--

THERE IS A *BATTLE* GOING ON--

WE'RE TAKING CASUALTIES. I'LL *EXPECT* YOU UPSTAIRS!

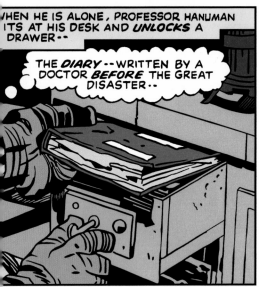

WHEN HE IS ALONE, PROFESSOR HANUMAN SITS AT HIS DESK AND *UNLOCKS* A DRAWER--

THE *DIARY* --WRITTEN BY A DOCTOR *BEFORE* THE GREAT DISASTER--

HE WAS THE *TRUE* FATHER OF CORTEXIN --*HE* PRODUCED IT, EVEN AS I HAVE --- HE, *TOO*, FOUGHT WITH HIS SUPERIOR ON THE *VERY* EVE OF DESTRUCTION!

--- PERSONAL NOTES ---
DR. MICHAEL GRANT

APR. 7. 19

Tonight, another hassle with my superior... It concerned the new animal ...

UNCANNY--! IS IT POSSIBLE THAT EVENTS CAN *REPEAT* THEMSELVES TO FINE DETAIL?

CAN WHAT HAPPENED LONG AGO TO *MICHAEL GRANT* -- HAPPEN TONIGHT -- TO *HANUMAN?*

CONDITIONS SEEM ALMOST THE SAME -- DESTRUCTION APPROACHES *NOW*, AS IT DID *THEN*--!!

BOOMM!
BAROOMM!

9

IN THE FACE OF DOOM, HANUMAN PONDERS UPON THE CONTENTS OF THE ANCIENT NOTES--
I FEAR THIS NIGHT-- BECAUSE--I FEAR THIS BOOK!
IT IMPLIES THAT GORILLAS WERE KEPT IN CAGES--JUST LIKE OUR EXPERIMENTAL ANIMALS--I-IT'S A MIND-BOGGLING, DEMEANING CONCEPT--
IN HIS NOTES, THIS DEAD DOCTOR GRANT CLAIMS THAT WE GORILLAS GAINED MAN-LIKE INTELLIGENCE BY ACCIDENT--
YOU'RE NEEDED UPSTAIRS IN SURGERY, PROFESSOR--IT'S GETTING PRETTY ROUGH--
TELL THEM I'M ON MY WAY, ORDERLY!
IT'S INCREDIBLE HOW THIS NIGHT DUPLICATES THE NOTES IN THIS DIARY--!
IF THERE IS TRUTH IN THE DIARY, I'VE BROUGHT INTO BEING THE ELEMENTS WHICH CAN TRULY TEST IT--EXPERIMENTAL ANIMALS, AND--CORTEXIN--
NOW--I FEAR THE TEST IS INDEFINITELY POSTPONED--
TONIGHT
DR.-MICHAEL GRANT
I've been called to operate..
BUT, AS IT IS WRITTEN IN THE DIARY, FATE CAN MAKE ITS OWN TESTS--
PERSONAL NOTES
DR. MICHAEL GRANT...
I believe Cortexin to be as revolutionary as the wheel...
If I live through this night, I can prove it...

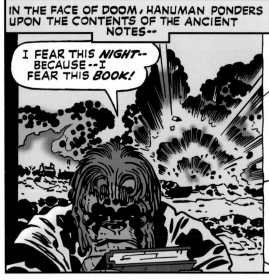

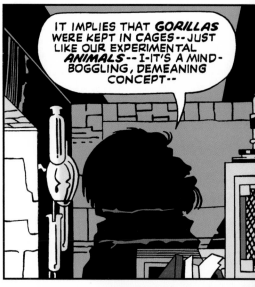

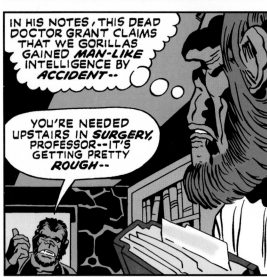

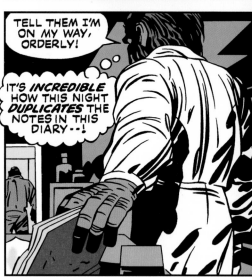

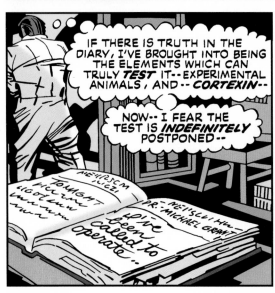

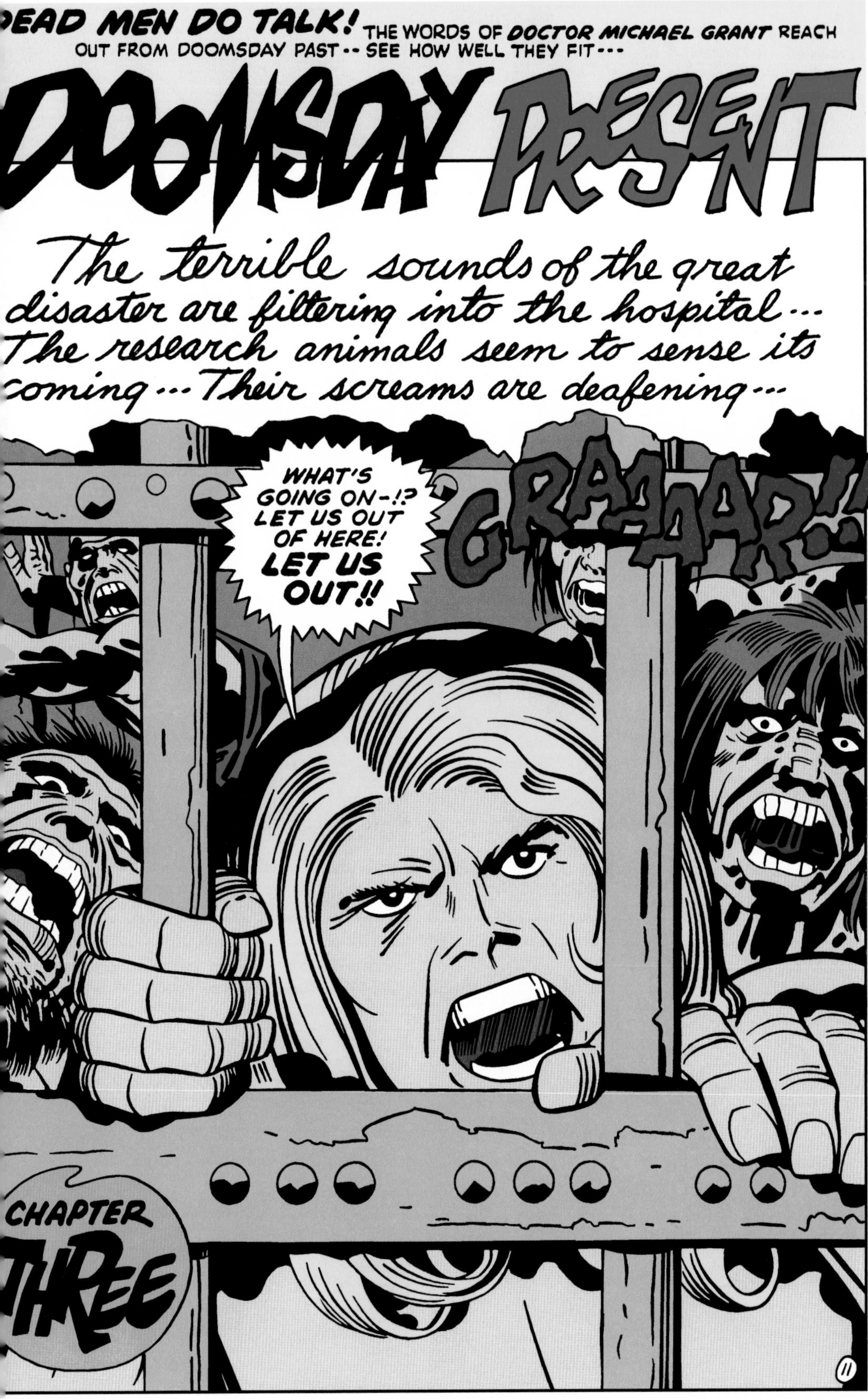
DEAD MEN DO TALK! THE WORDS OF DOCTOR MICHAEL GRANT REACH OUT FROM DOOMSDAY PAST -- SEE HOW WELL THEY FIT ---
DOOMSDAY PRESENT
The terrible sounds of the great disaster are filtering into the hospital... The research animals seem to sense its coming... Their screams are deafening...
WHAT'S GOING ON-!? LET US OUT OF HERE! LET US OUT!!
GRAAAAR!!
CHAPTER THREE
11

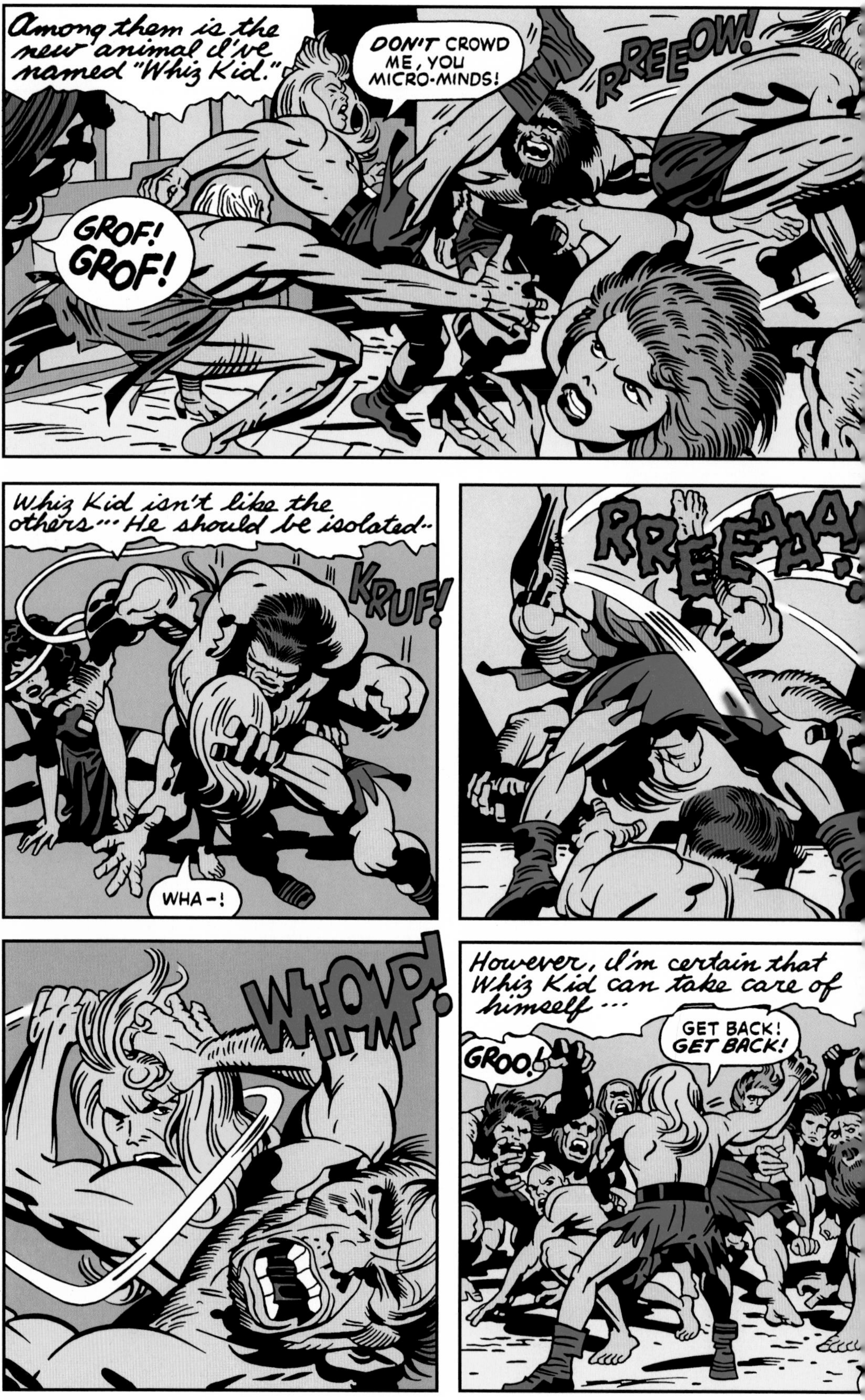
Among them is the new animal I've named "Whiz Kid."
DON'T CROWD ME, YOU MICRO-MINDS!
RREEOW!
GROF! GROF!
Whiz Kid isn't like the others... He should be isolated..
KRUF!
WHA-!
RREEAA
WHOMP!
However, I'm certain that Whiz Kid can take care of himself...
GET BACK! GET BACK!
GROO!

Poor Whiz Kid ··· poor animals. I shall try to release them when the disaster draws near ···

THAT NOISE IN THE DISTANCE IT'S THE SOUND OF BATTLE--

But I am needed in the wards ··· Casualties are pouring in ···

I-IT MUST BE TUFTAN AND HIS TIGERS-- *THEY'LL* GET ME OUT--!

Outside there is chaos! Panic! ···I can hear the cries of the wounded and the dying ···

FIGHT, TIGERS, FIGHT! BREAK THROUGH THOSE APES!

BLASTED, BOW-LEGGED TREE-CLIMBING *FREAKS!* THEY'RE *HOLDING* FAST!

THIS WAY, PRINCE TUFTAN! WE'VE *TAKEN* A WEAPON THAT CAN *ROUT* THEM!

A *CANNON!*

GOOD WORK, MEN! TURN IT ON THEIR LINES! PUT SOME *MUSCLE* IN IT!

13

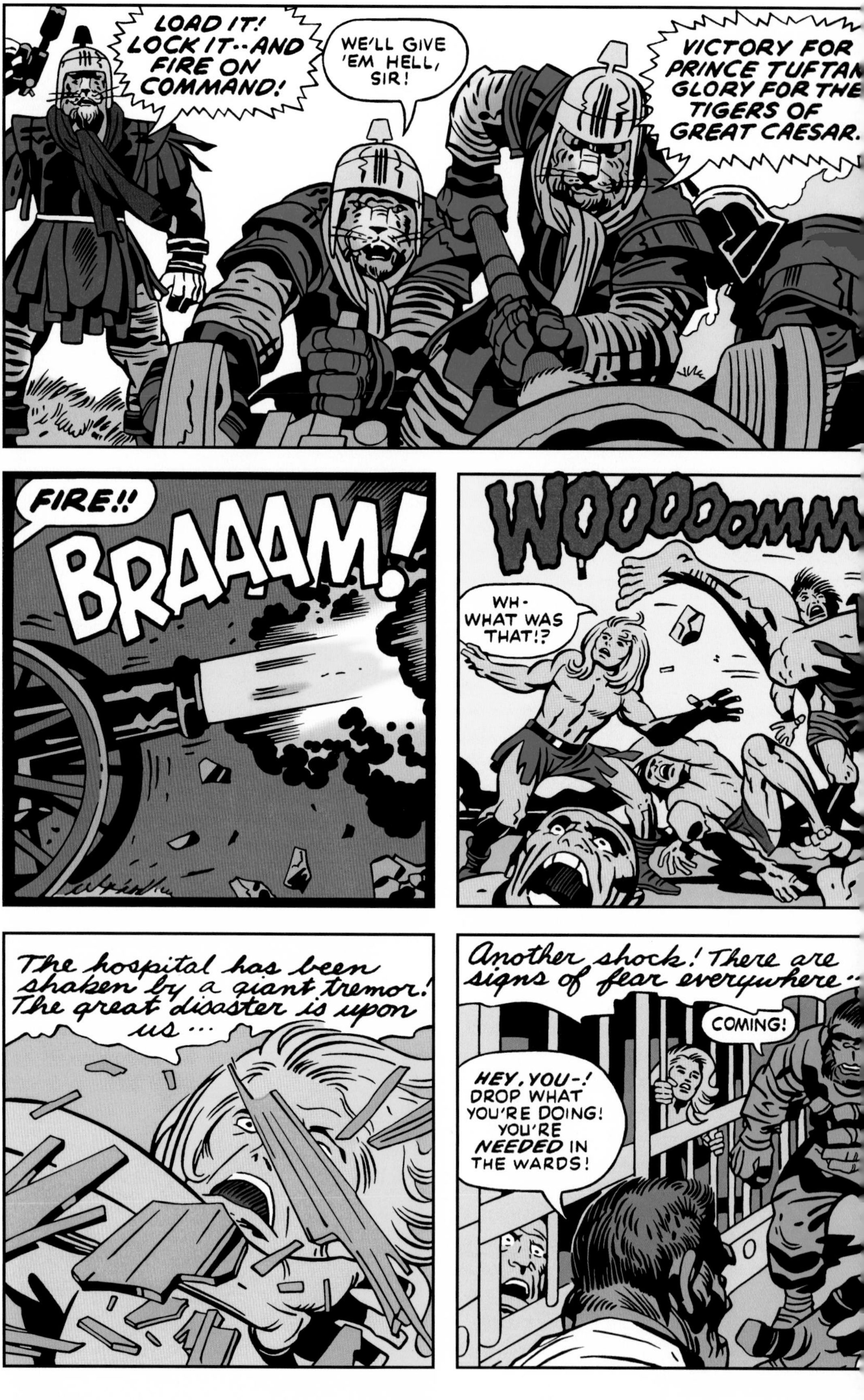
LOAD IT! LOCK IT--AND FIRE ON COMMAND!
WE'LL GIVE 'EM HELL, SIR!
VICTORY FOR PRINCE TUFTAN GLORY FOR THE TIGERS OF GREAT CAESAR.
FIRE!!
BRAAAM!
WOOOOOMM
WH- WHAT WAS THAT!?
The hospital has been shaken by a giant tremor! The great disaster is upon us...
Another shock! There are signs of fear everywhere...
COMING!
HEY, YOU-! DROP WHAT YOU'RE DOING! YOU'RE NEEDED IN THE WARDS!

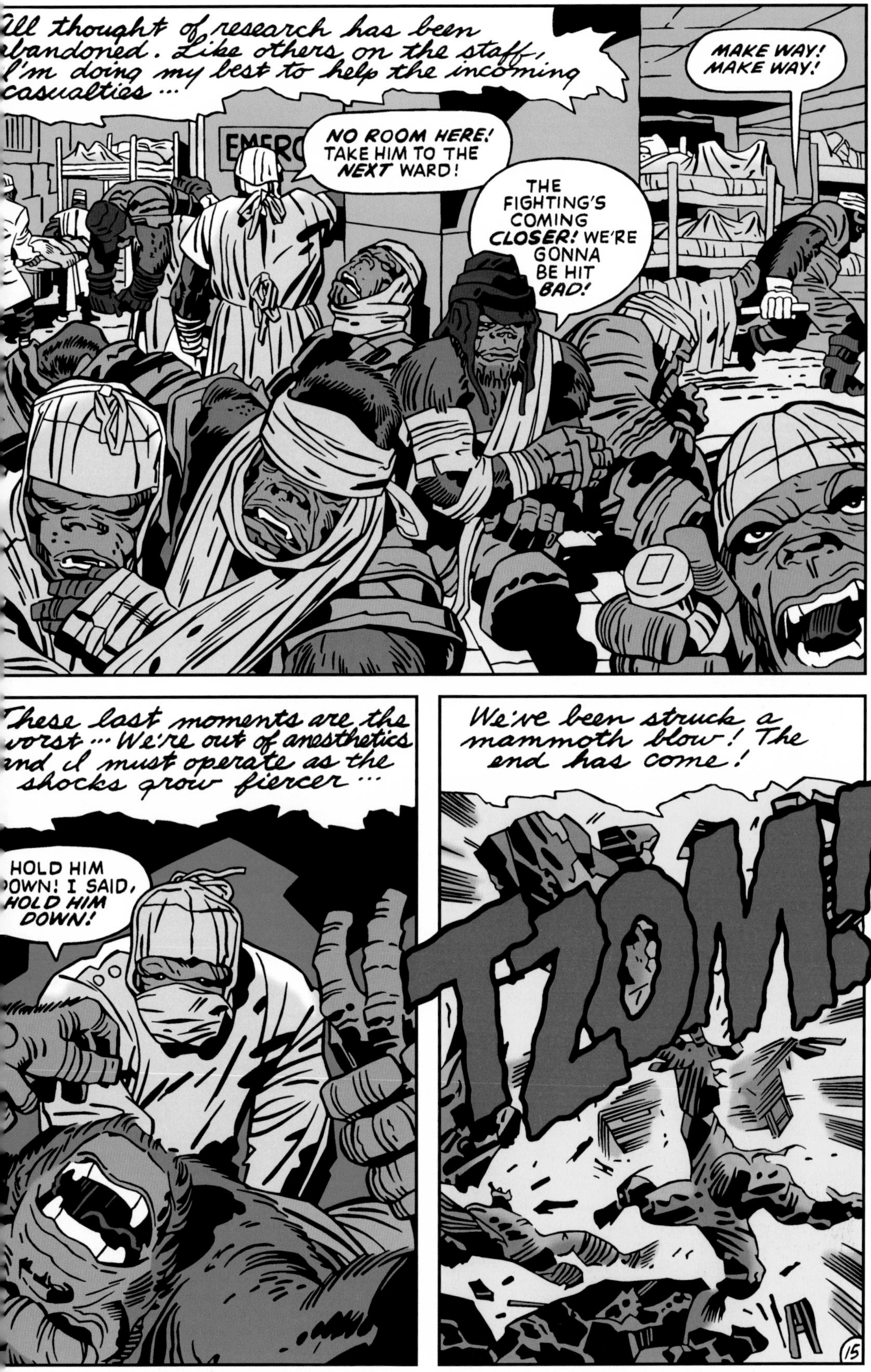
All thought of research has been abandoned. Like others on the staff, I'm doing my best to help the incoming casualties...
EMERG
NO ROOM HERE! TAKE HIM TO THE NEXT WARD!
THE FIGHTING'S COMING CLOSER! WE'RE GONNA BE HIT BAD!
MAKE WAY! MAKE WAY!
These last moments are the worst... We're out of anesthetics and I must operate as the shocks grow fiercer...
HOLD HIM DOWN! I SAID, HOLD HIM DOWN!
We've been struck a mammoth blow! The end has come!
TZOM!
15

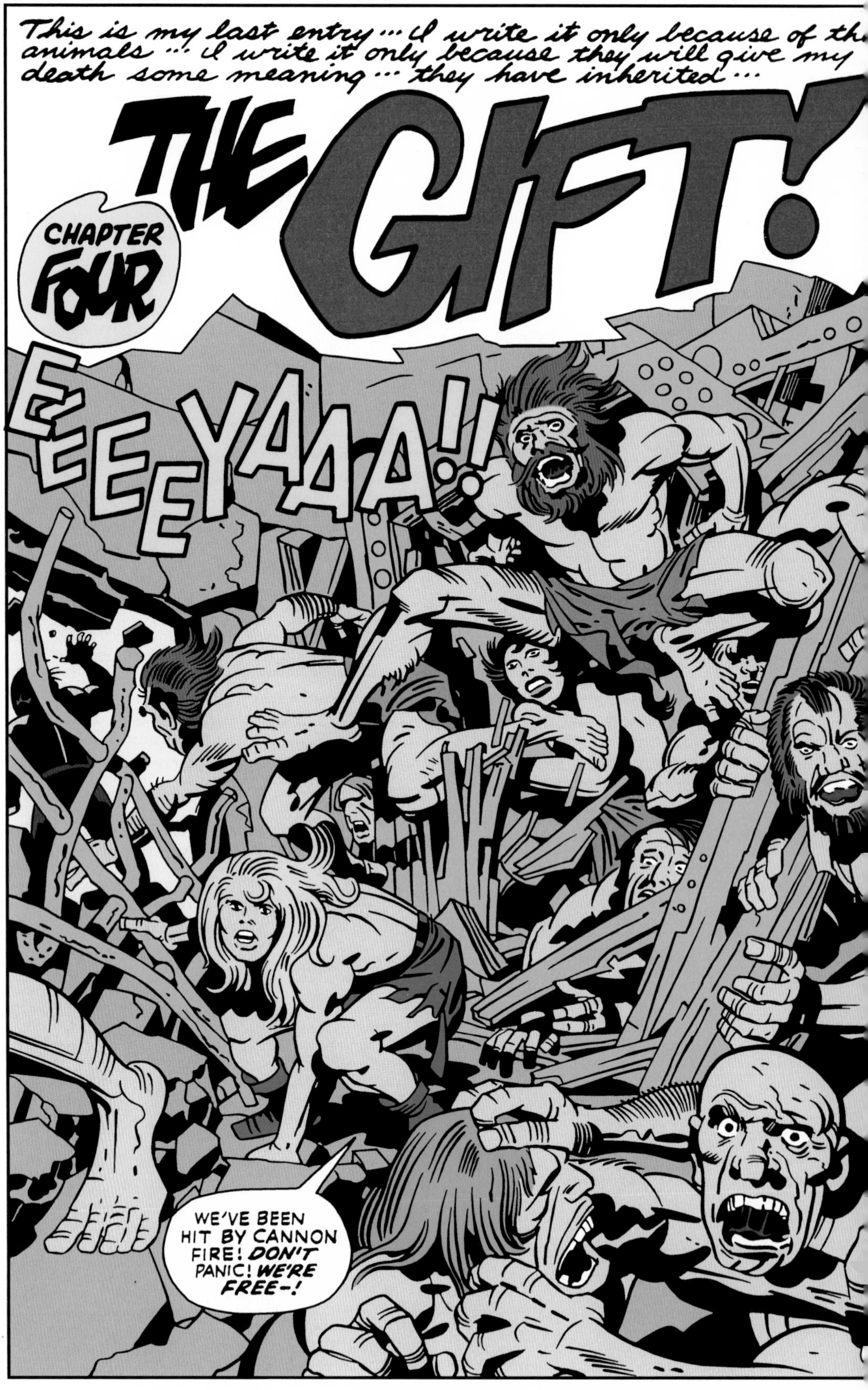
This is my last entry... I write it only because of the animals... I write it only because they will give my death some meaning... they have inherited...
THE GIFT!
CHAPTER FOUR
EEEEYAAA!!
WE'VE BEEN HIT BY CANNON FIRE! DON'T PANIC! WE'RE FREE-!

I know I wasn't there to see what happened ··· But I think I can make an accurate guess ···

The last great tremor freed the animals ··· Still, it blocked every passage of escape ···

I can imagine the blind fear that overtook the poor trapped beasts ···

··· But not Whiz Kid! I'll bet on that! My guess is that he was thinking quickly and clearly ···

THERE *MUST* BE A WAY OUT--!

I'll bet it was Whiz Kid who found the only exit ···

THE FLOOR'S CRACKED! THERE'S AN OPENING BELOW!

He must have discovered the storage basement. It's the only answer ···

THERE'S *NOTHING* TO LOSE--! I'M GOING DOWN!

17

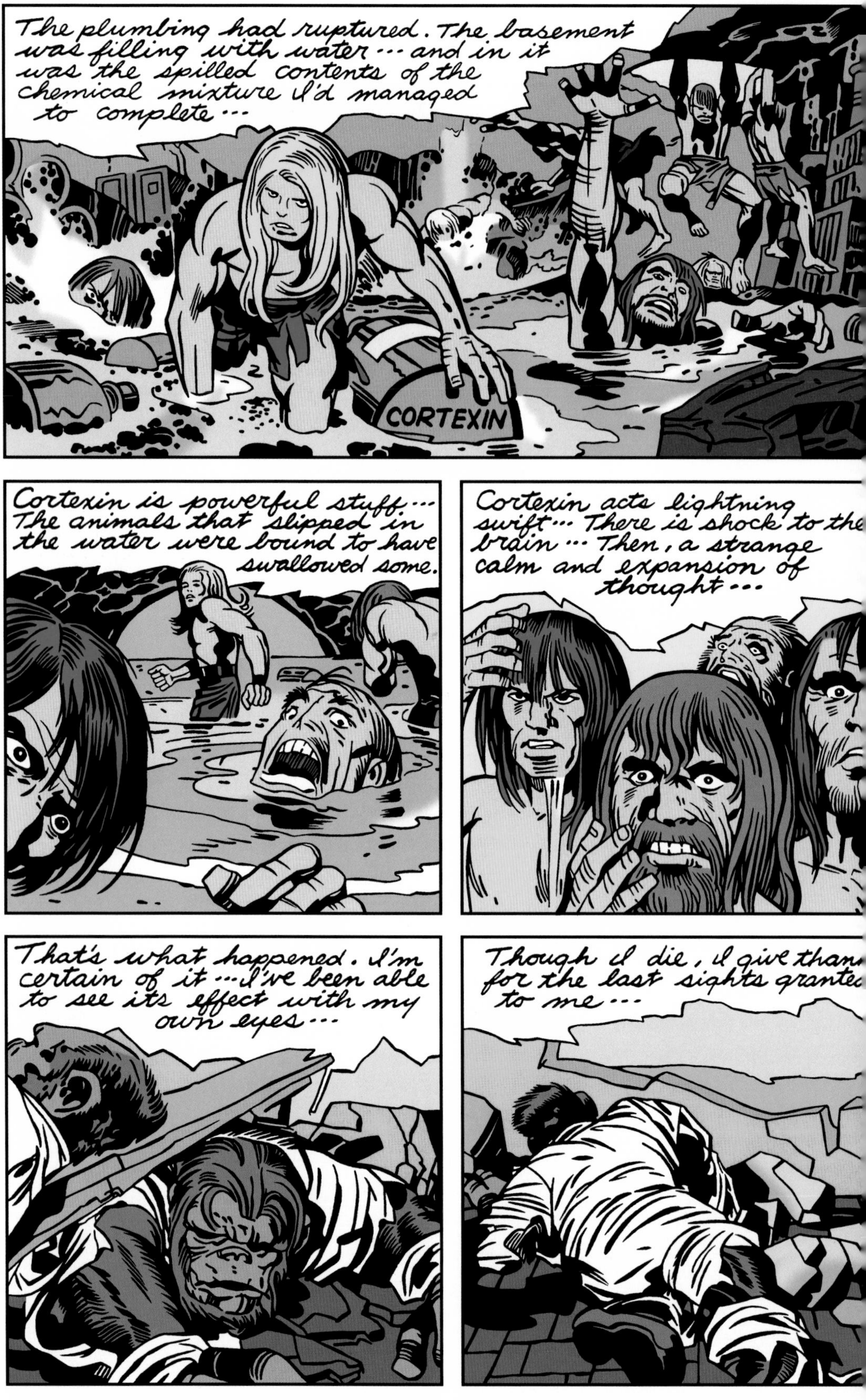
The plumbing had ruptured. The basement was filling with water... and in it was the spilled contents of the chemical mixture I'd managed to complete...
CORTEXIN
Cortexin is powerful stuff... The animals that slipped in the water were bound to have swallowed some.
Cortexin acts lightning swift... There is shock to the brain... Then, a strange calm and expansion of thought...
That's what happened. I'm certain of it... I've been able to see its effect with my own eyes...
Though I die, I give than
for the last sights grante
to me...

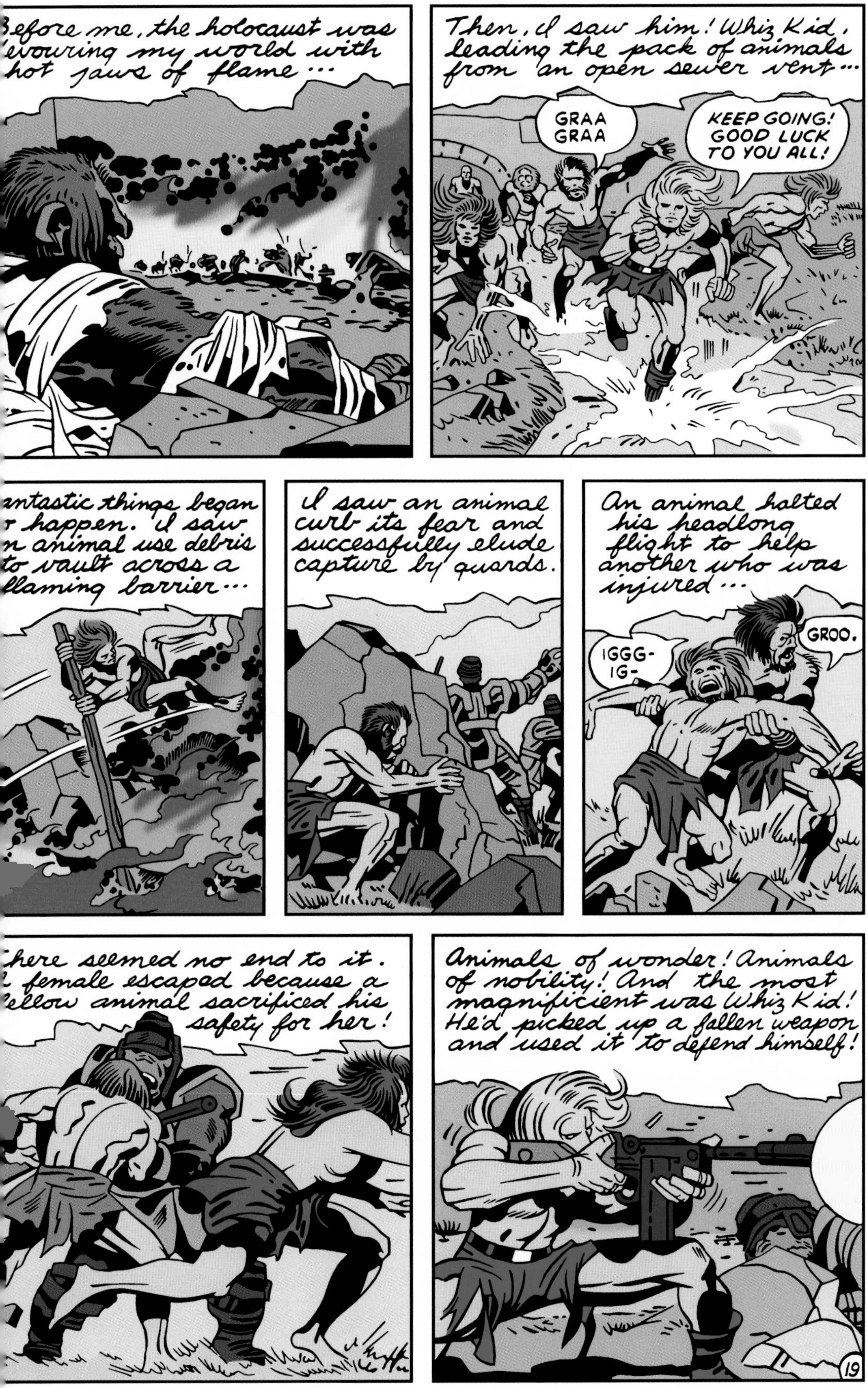
efore me, the holocaust was
evouring my world with
hot jaws of flame...
Then, I saw him! Whiz Kid,
leading the pack of animals
from an open sewer vent...
GRAA GRAA
KEEP GOING! GOOD LUCK TO YOU ALL!
ntastic things began
happen. I saw
n animal use debris
to vault across a
laming barrier...
I saw an animal
curb its fear and
successfully elude
capture by guards.
An animal halted
his headlong
flight to help
another who was
injured...
IGGG-IG-
GROO.
here seemed no end to it.
female escaped because a
ellow animal sacrificed his
safety for her!
Animals of wonder! Animals
of nobility! And the most
magnificient was Whiz Kid!
He'd picked up a fallen weapon
and used it to defend himself!
19

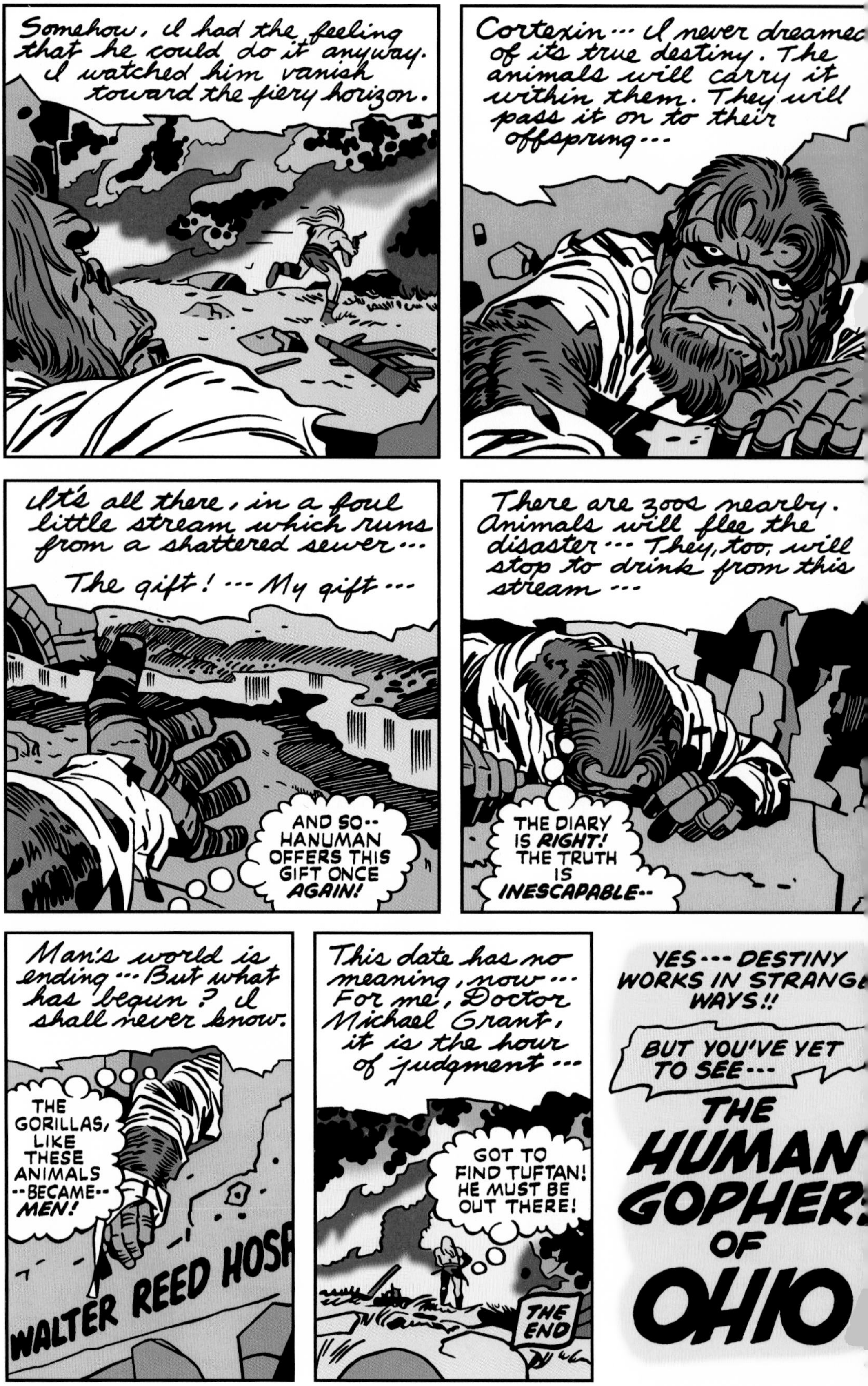

Somehow, I had the feeling that he could do it anyway. I watched him vanish toward the fiery horizon.
Cortexin... I never dreamed of its true destiny. The animals will carry it within them. They will pass it on to their offspring...
It's all there, in a foul little stream which runs from a shattered sewer...
The gift! ... My gift...
AND SO-- HANUMAN OFFERS THIS GIFT ONCE AGAIN!
There are zoos nearby. Animals will flee the disaster... They, too, will stop to drink from this stream...
THE DIARY IS RIGHT! THE TRUTH IS INESCAPABLE--
Man's world is ending... But what has begun? I shall never know.
THE GORILLAS, LIKE THESE ANIMALS --BECAME-- MEN!
WALTER REED HOS
This date has no meaning, now... For me, Doctor Michael Grant, it is the hour of judgment...
GOT TO FIND TUFTAN! HE MUST BE OUT THERE!
THE END
YES--- DESTINY WORKS IN STRANGE WAYS!!
BUT YOU'VE YET TO SEE---
THE HUMAN GOPHERS OF OHIO

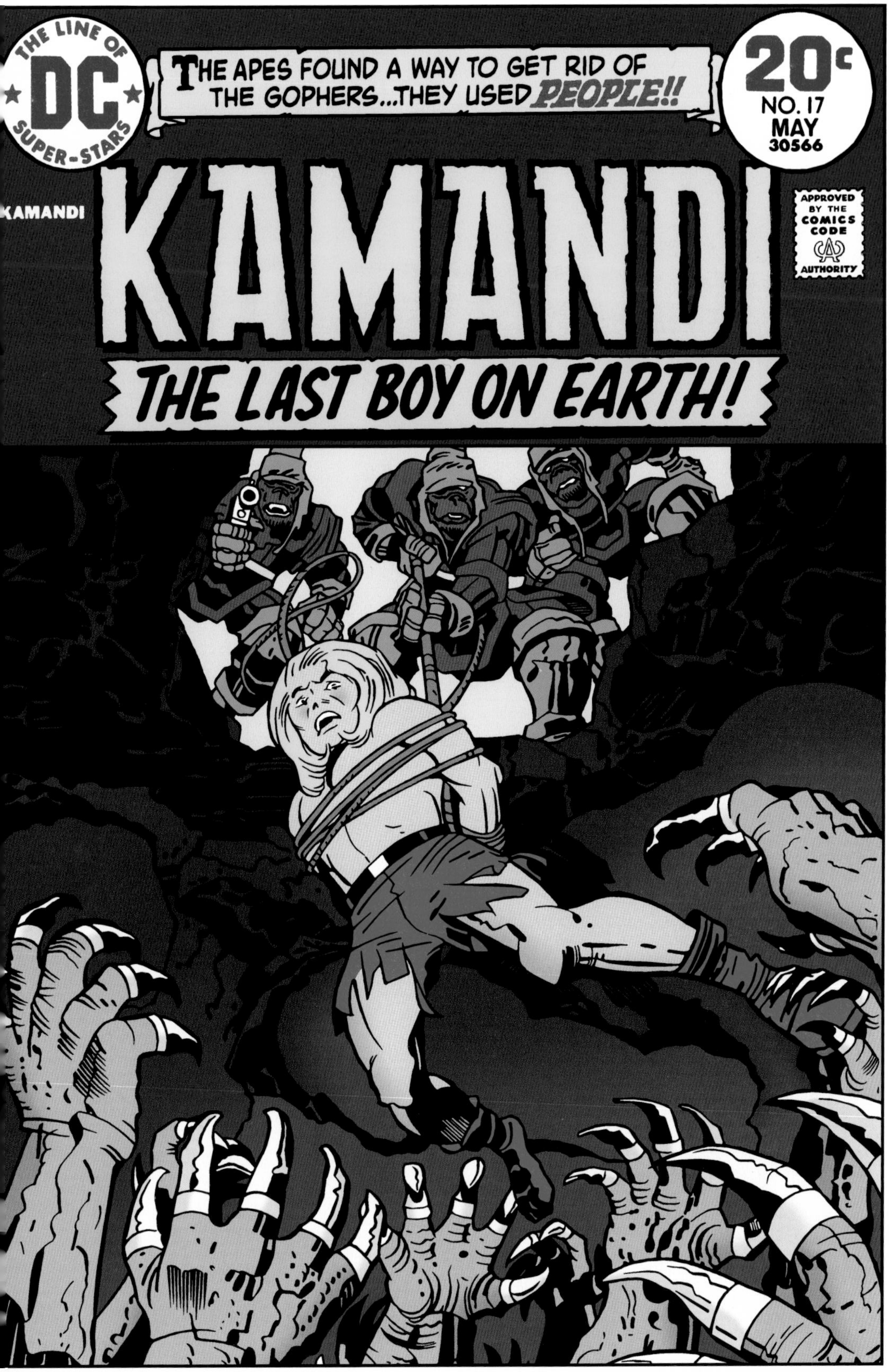
THE LINE OF
DC
SUPER-STARS
THE APES FOUND A WAY TO GET RID OF THE GOPHERS...THEY USED PEOPLE!!
20¢
NO. 17
MAY
30566
KAMANDI
KAMANDI
APPROVED BY THE COMICS CODE AUTHORITY
THE LAST BOY ON EARTH!

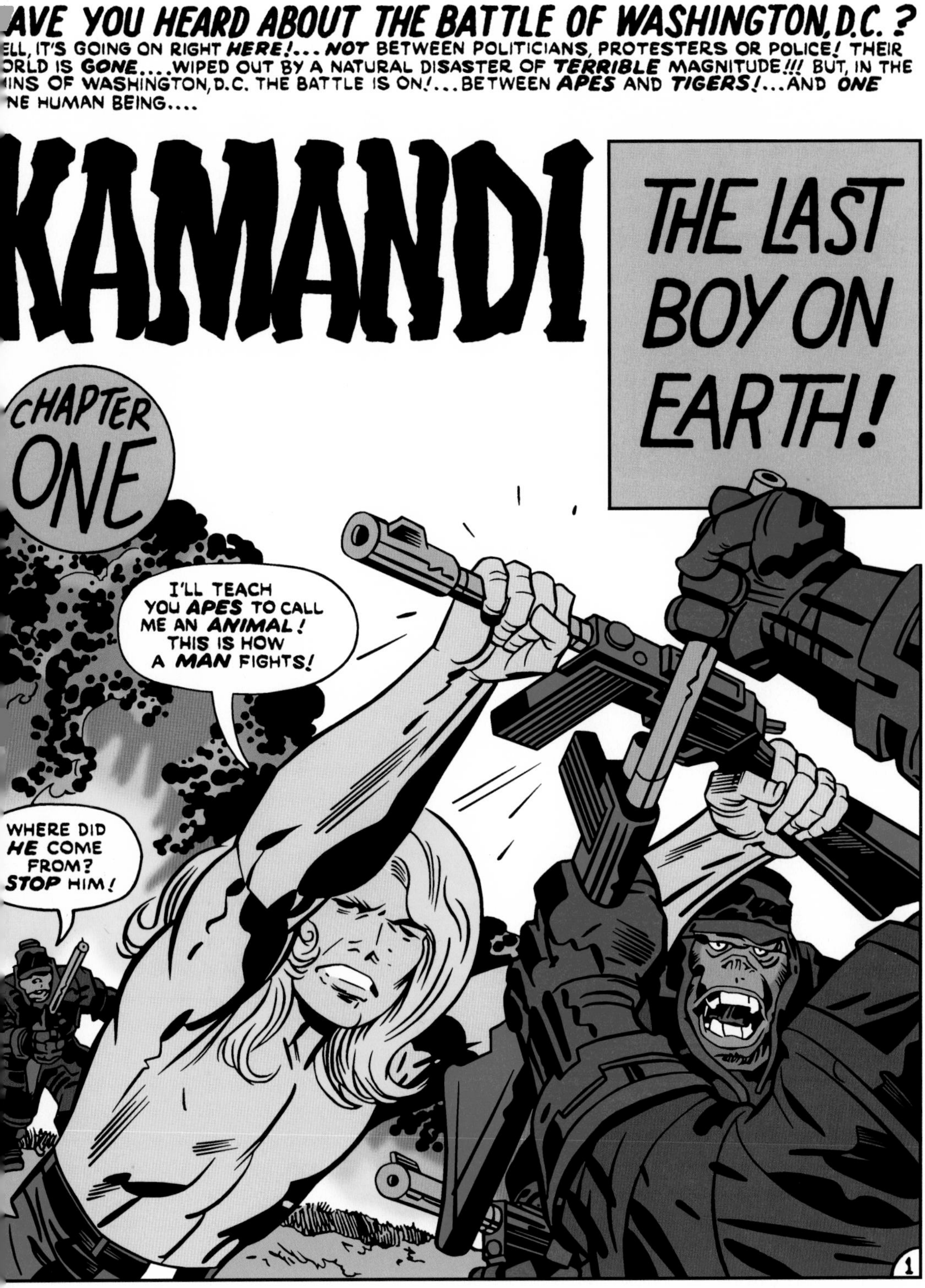
AVE YOU HEARD ABOUT THE BATTLE OF WASHINGTON, D.C. ?
ELL, IT'S GOING ON RIGHT HERE!... NOT BETWEEN POLITICIANS, PROTESTERS OR POLICE! THEIR ORLD IS GONE....WIPED OUT BY A NATURAL DISASTER OF TERRIBLE MAGNITUDE!!! BUT, IN THE INS OF WASHINGTON, D.C. THE BATTLE IS ON!... BETWEEN APES AND TIGERS!...AND ONE NE HUMAN BEING....
KAMANDI
THE LAST BOY ON EARTH!
CHAPTER ONE
I'LL TEACH YOU APES TO CALL ME AN ANIMAL! THIS IS HOW A MAN FIGHTS!
WHERE DID HE COME FROM? STOP HIM!
1

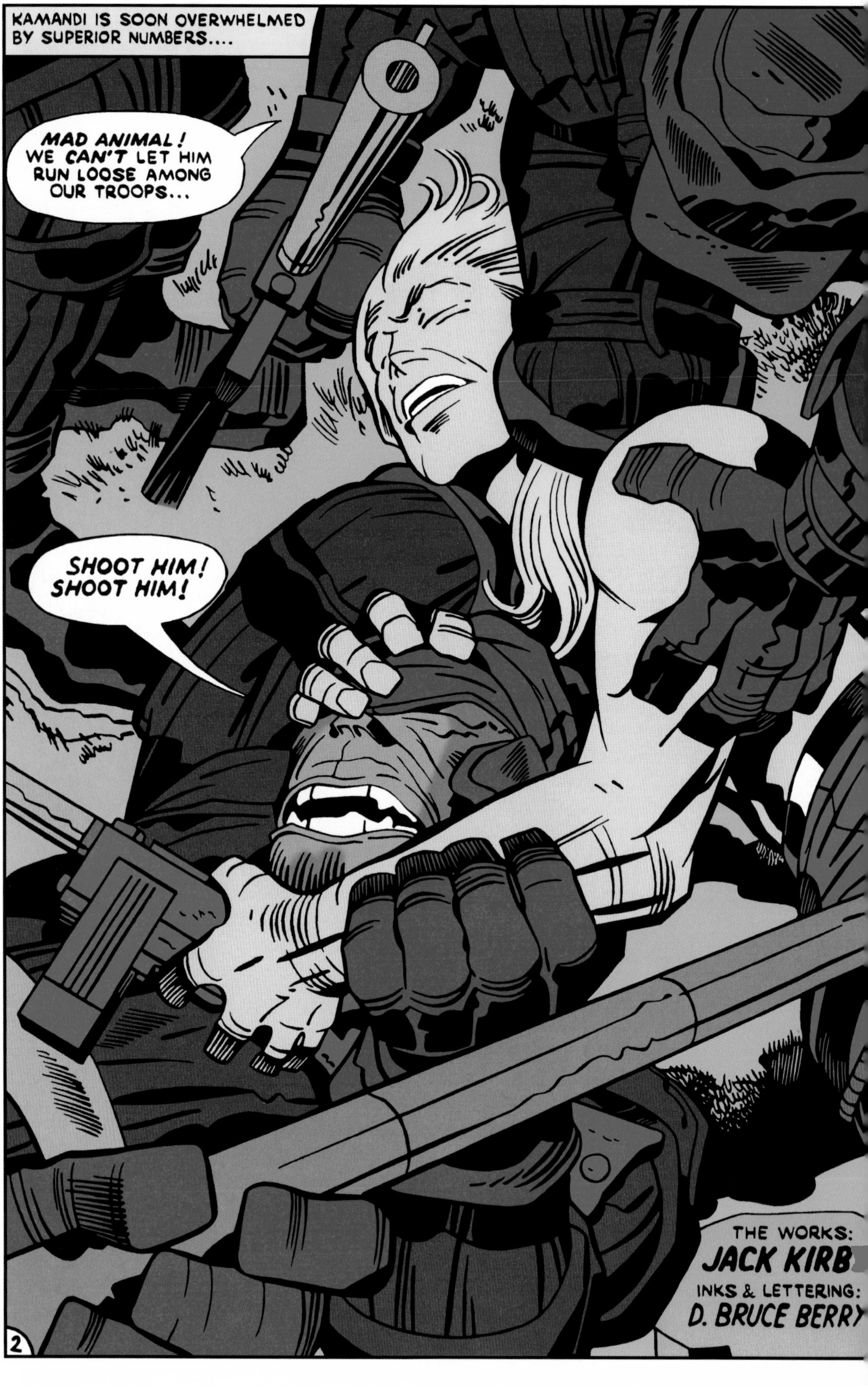
KAMANDI IS SOON OVERWHELMED BY SUPERIOR NUMBERS....
MAD ANIMAL! WE CAN'T LET HIM RUN LOOSE AMONG OUR TROOPS...
SHOOT HIM! SHOOT HIM!
THE WORKS: JACK KIRB
INKS & LETTERING: D. BRUCE BERRY
2

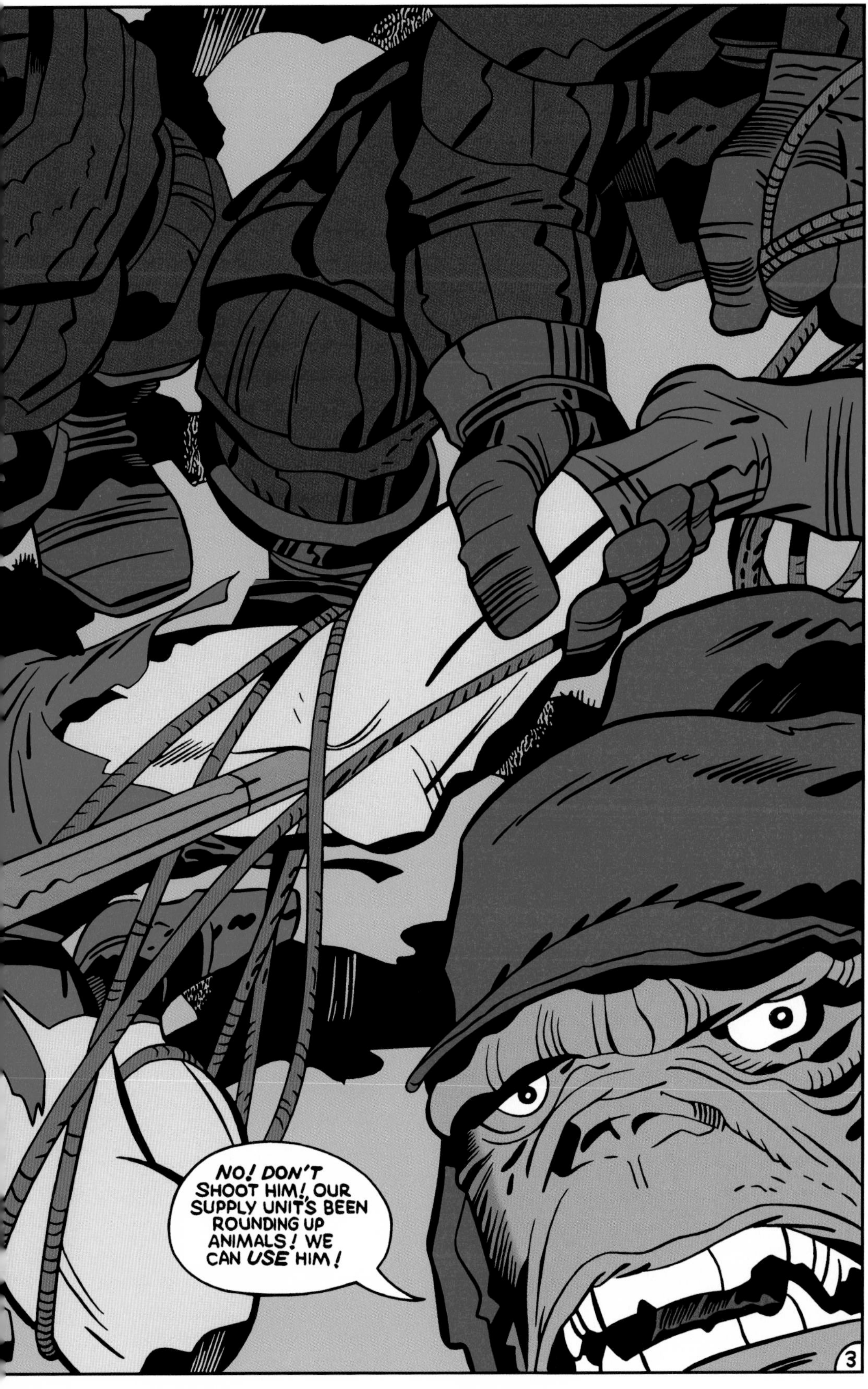
NO! DON'T SHOOT HIM! OUR SUPPLY UNIT'S BEEN ROUNDING UP ANIMALS! WE CAN USE HIM!
3

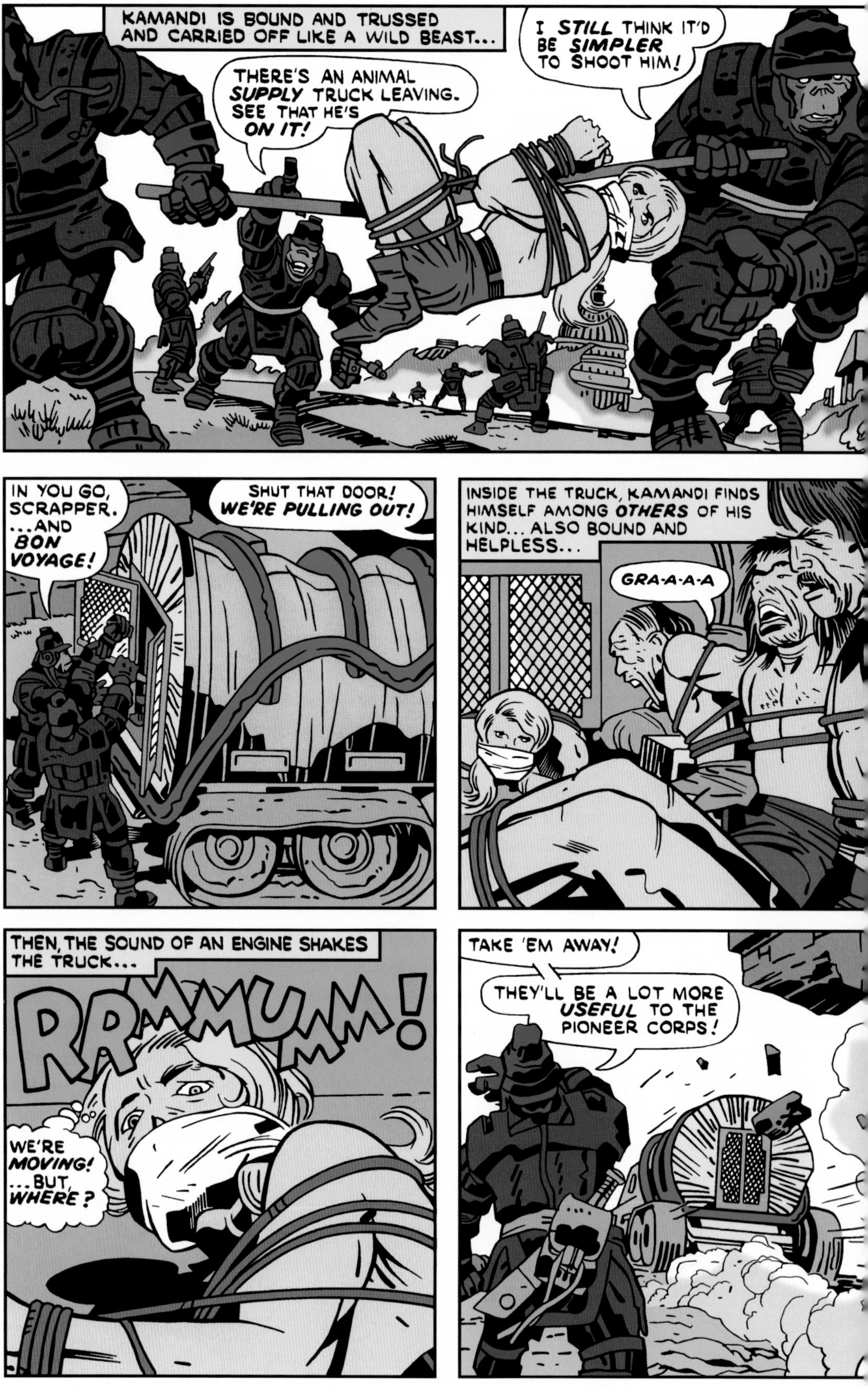
KAMANDI IS BOUND AND TRUSSED AND CARRIED OFF LIKE A WILD BEAST...
I STILL THINK IT'D BE SIMPLER TO SHOOT HIM!
THERE'S AN ANIMAL SUPPLY TRUCK LEAVING. SEE THAT HE'S ON IT!
IN YOU GO, SCRAPPER. ...AND BON VOYAGE!
SHUT THAT DOOR! WE'RE PULLING OUT!
INSIDE THE TRUCK, KAMANDI FINDS HIMSELF AMONG OTHERS OF HIS KIND... ALSO BOUND AND HELPLESS...
GRA-A-A-A
THEN, THE SOUND OF AN ENGINE SHAKES THE TRUCK...
RRMMUMM!
WE'RE MOVING! ...BUT, WHERE?
TAKE 'EM AWAY!
THEY'LL BE A LOT MORE USEFUL TO THE PIONEER CORPS!

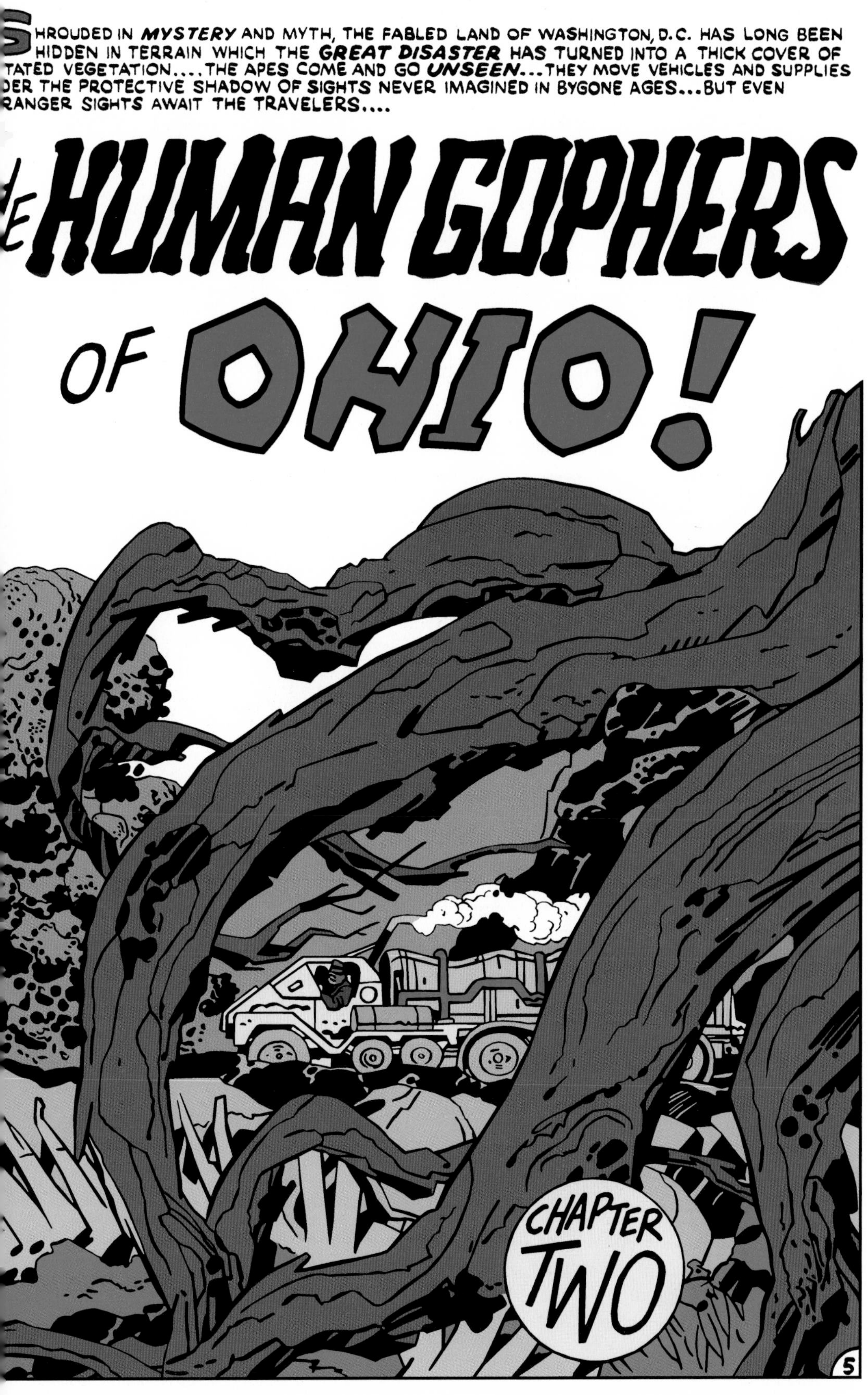
HROUDED IN MYSTERY AND MYTH, THE FABLED LAND OF WASHINGTON, D.C. HAS LONG BEEN HIDDEN IN TERRAIN WHICH THE GREAT DISASTER HAS TURNED INTO A THICK COVER OF TATED VEGETATION....THE APES COME AND GO UNSEEN...THEY MOVE VEHICLES AND SUPPLIES DER THE PROTECTIVE SHADOW OF SIGHTS NEVER IMAGINED IN BYGONE AGES...BUT EVEN RANGER SIGHTS AWAIT THE TRAVELERS....
HUMAN GOPHERS
OF OHIO!
CHAPTER TWO
5

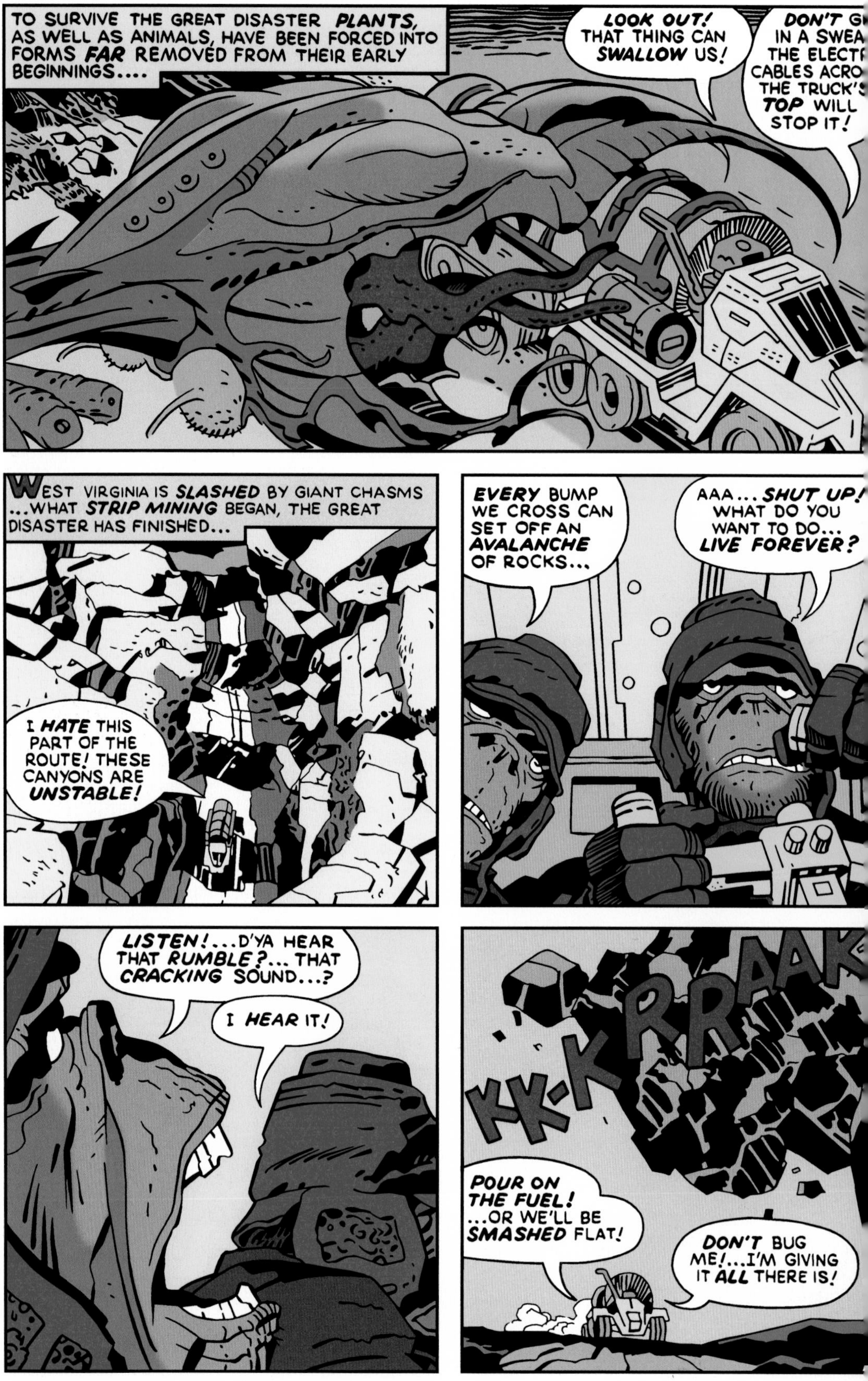
TO SURVIVE THE GREAT DISASTER PLANTS, AS WELL AS ANIMALS, HAVE BEEN FORCED INTO FORMS FAR REMOVED FROM THEIR EARLY BEGINNINGS....
LOOK OUT! THAT THING CAN SWALLOW US!
DON'T G IN A SWEA THE ELECT CABLES ACRO THE TRUCK'S TOP WILL STOP IT!
WEST VIRGINIA IS SLASHED BY GIANT CHASMS ...WHAT STRIP MINING BEGAN, THE GREAT DISASTER HAS FINISHED...
I HATE THIS PART OF THE ROUTE! THESE CANYONS ARE UNSTABLE!
EVERY BUMP WE CROSS CAN SET OFF AN AVALANCHE OF ROCKS...
AAA... SHUT UP! WHAT DO YOU WANT TO DO... LIVE FOREVER?
LISTEN!...D'YA HEAR THAT RUMBLE?... THAT CRACKING SOUND...?
I HEAR IT!
KK-KRRAAK
POUR ON THE FUEL! ...OR WE'LL BE SMASHED FLAT!
DON'T BUG ME!...I'M GIVING IT ALL THERE IS!

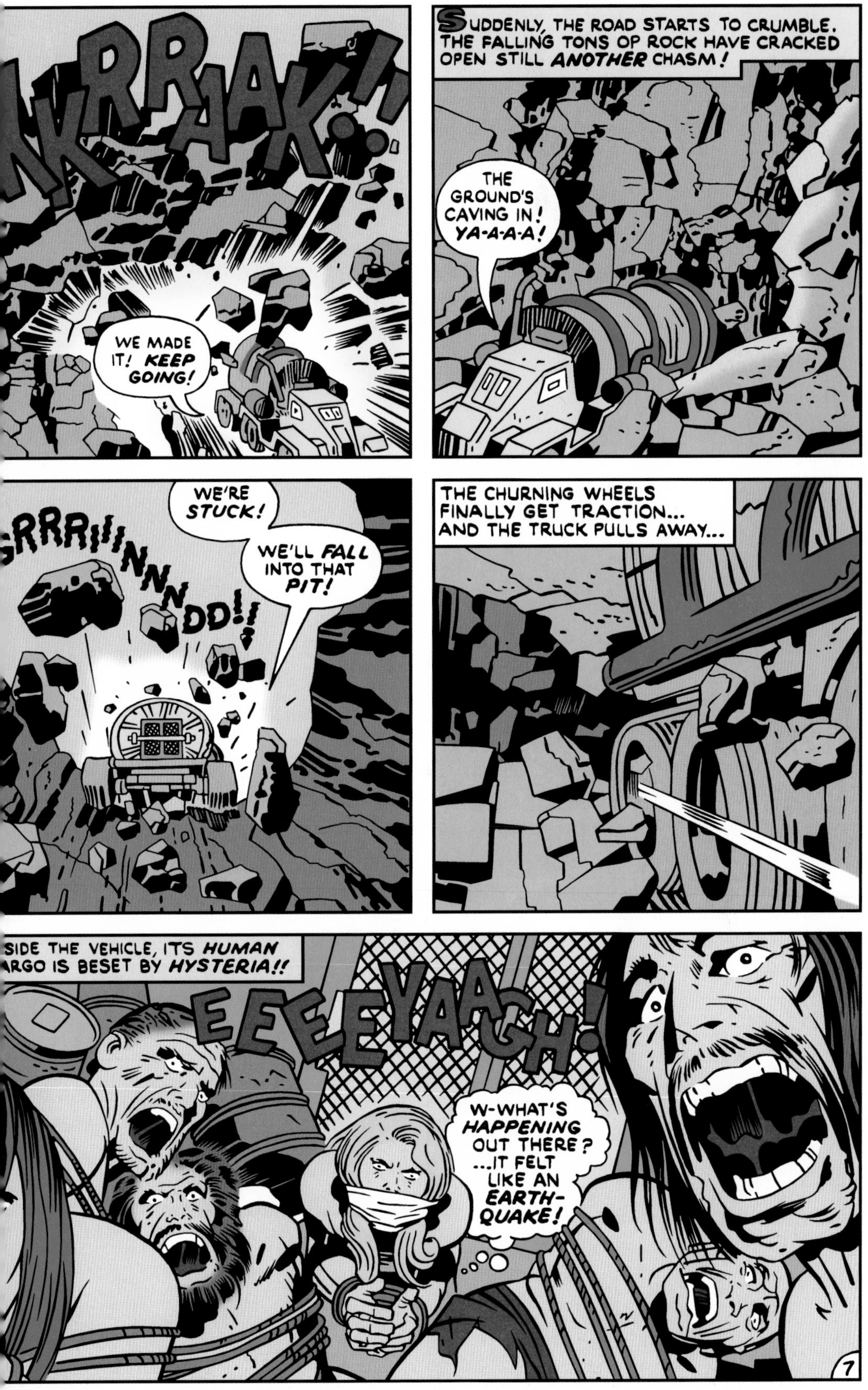
KRRAAK!!
WE MADE IT! KEEP GOING!
SUDDENLY, THE ROAD STARTS TO CRUMBLE. THE FALLING TONS OF ROCK HAVE CRACKED OPEN STILL ANOTHER CHASM!
THE GROUND'S CAVING IN! YA-A-A-A!
GRRRIIINNNDD!!
WE'RE STUCK!
WE'LL FALL INTO THAT PIT!
THE CHURNING WHEELS FINALLY GET TRACTION... AND THE TRUCK PULLS AWAY...
SIDE THE VEHICLE, ITS HUMAN ARGO IS BESET BY HYSTERIA!!
EEEEYAAGH!
W-WHAT'S HAPPENING OUT THERE? ...IT FELT LIKE AN EARTH-QUAKE!
7

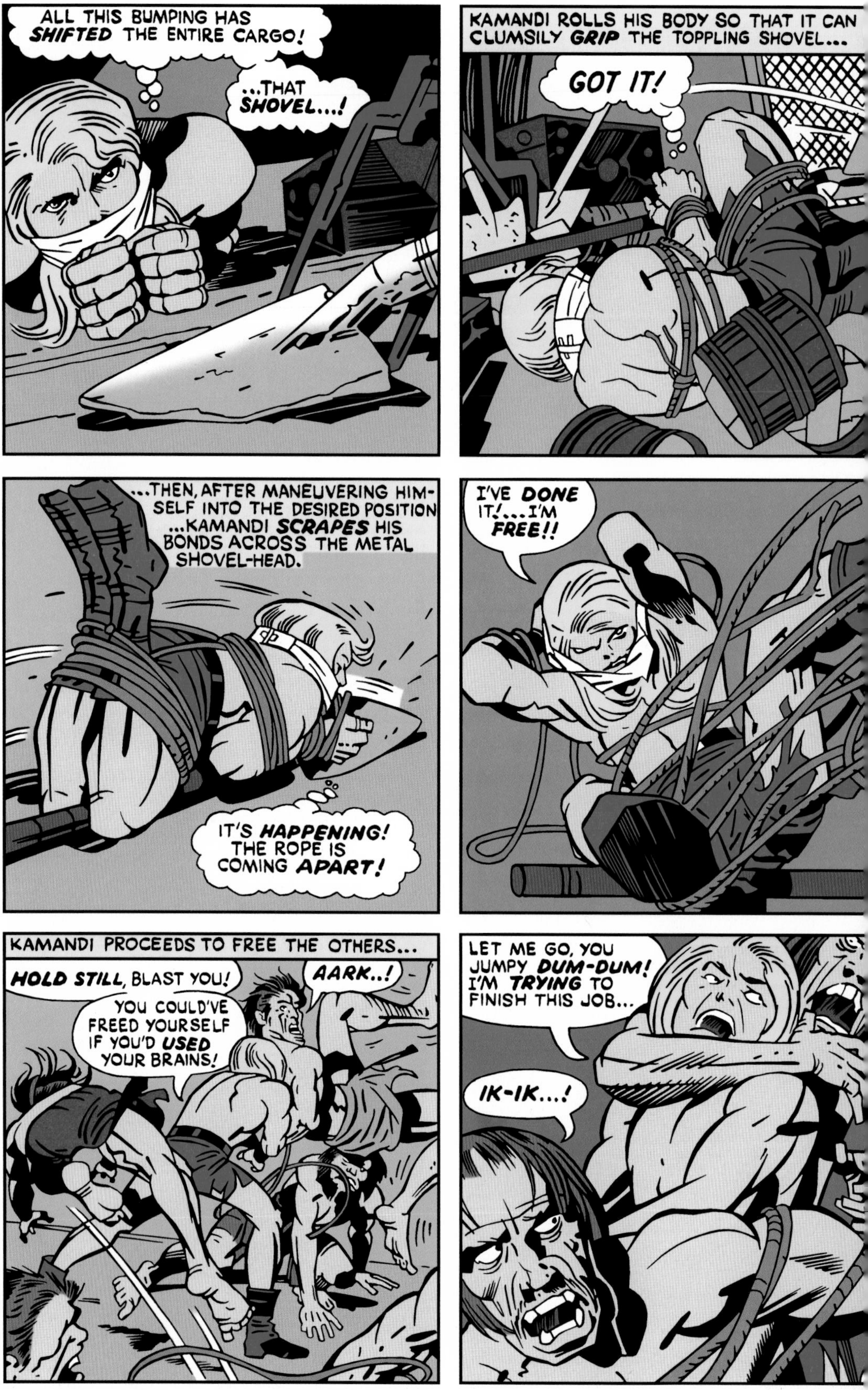
ALL THIS BUMPING HAS SHIFTED THE ENTIRE CARGO!
...THAT SHOVEL...!
KAMANDI ROLLS HIS BODY SO THAT IT CAN CLUMSILY GRIP THE TOPPLING SHOVEL...
GOT IT!
...THEN, AFTER MANEUVERING HIMSELF INTO THE DESIRED POSITION ...KAMANDI SCRAPES HIS BONDS ACROSS THE METAL SHOVEL-HEAD.
IT'S HAPPENING! THE ROPE IS COMING APART!
I'VE DONE IT!...I'M FREE!!
KAMANDI PROCEEDS TO FREE THE OTHERS...
HOLD STILL, BLAST YOU!
AARK..!
YOU COULD'VE FREED YOURSELF IF YOU'D USED YOUR BRAINS!
LET ME GO, YOU JUMPY DUM-DUM! I'M TRYING TO FINISH THIS JOB...
IK-IK...!

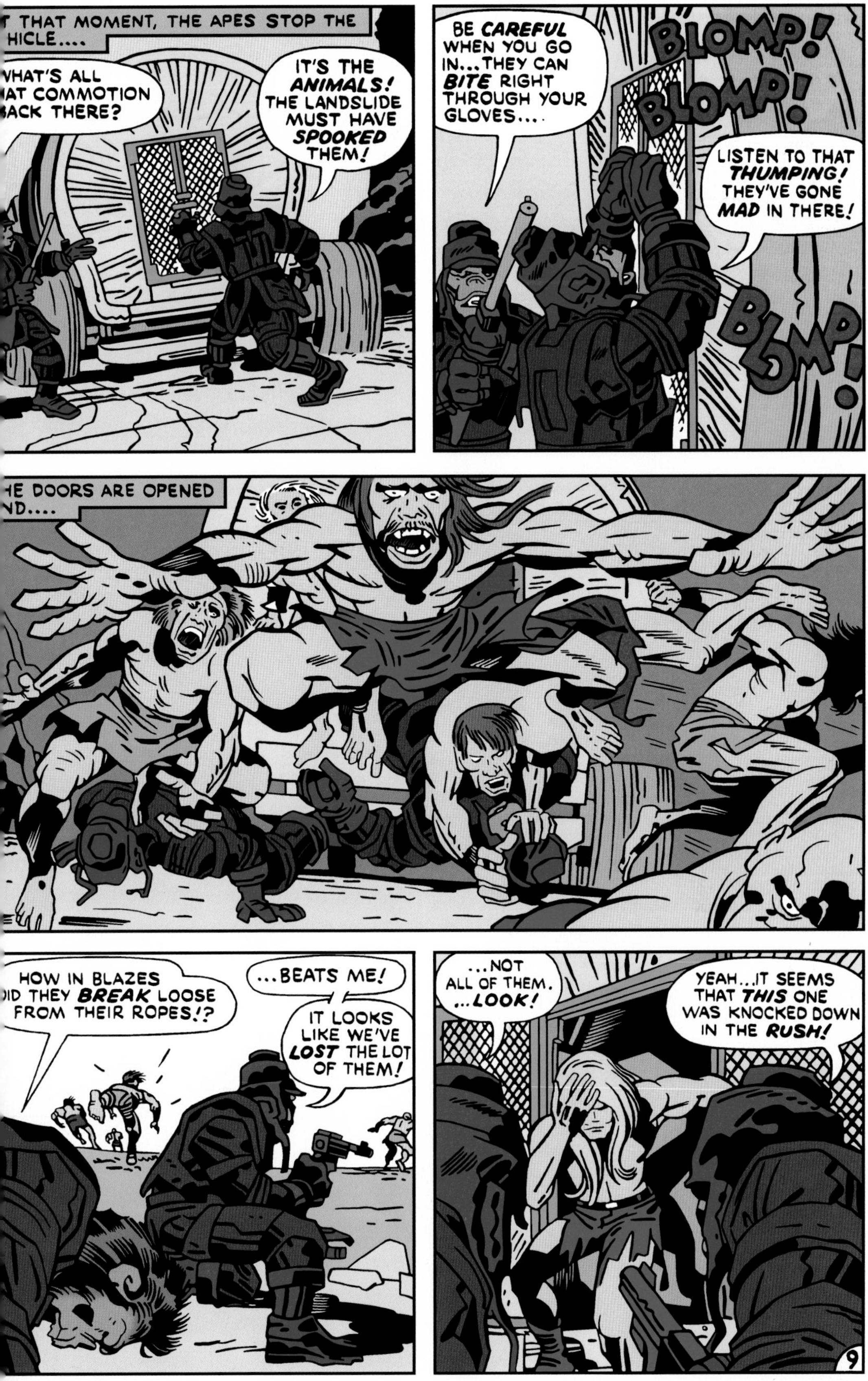
T THAT MOMENT, THE APES STOP THE HICLE....
WHAT'S ALL AT COMMOTION BACK THERE?
IT'S THE ANIMALS! THE LANDSLIDE MUST HAVE SPOOKED THEM!
BE CAREFUL WHEN YOU GO IN...THEY CAN BITE RIGHT THROUGH YOUR GLOVES....
BLOMP! BLOMP!
LISTEN TO THAT THUMPING! THEY'VE GONE MAD IN THERE!
BLOMP!
HE DOORS ARE OPENED ND....
HOW IN BLAZES DID THEY BREAK LOOSE FROM THEIR ROPES!?
...BEATS ME!
IT LOOKS LIKE WE'VE LOST THE LOT OF THEM!
...NOT ALL OF THEM. ...LOOK!
YEAH...IT SEEMS THAT THIS ONE WAS KNOCKED DOWN IN THE RUSH!
9

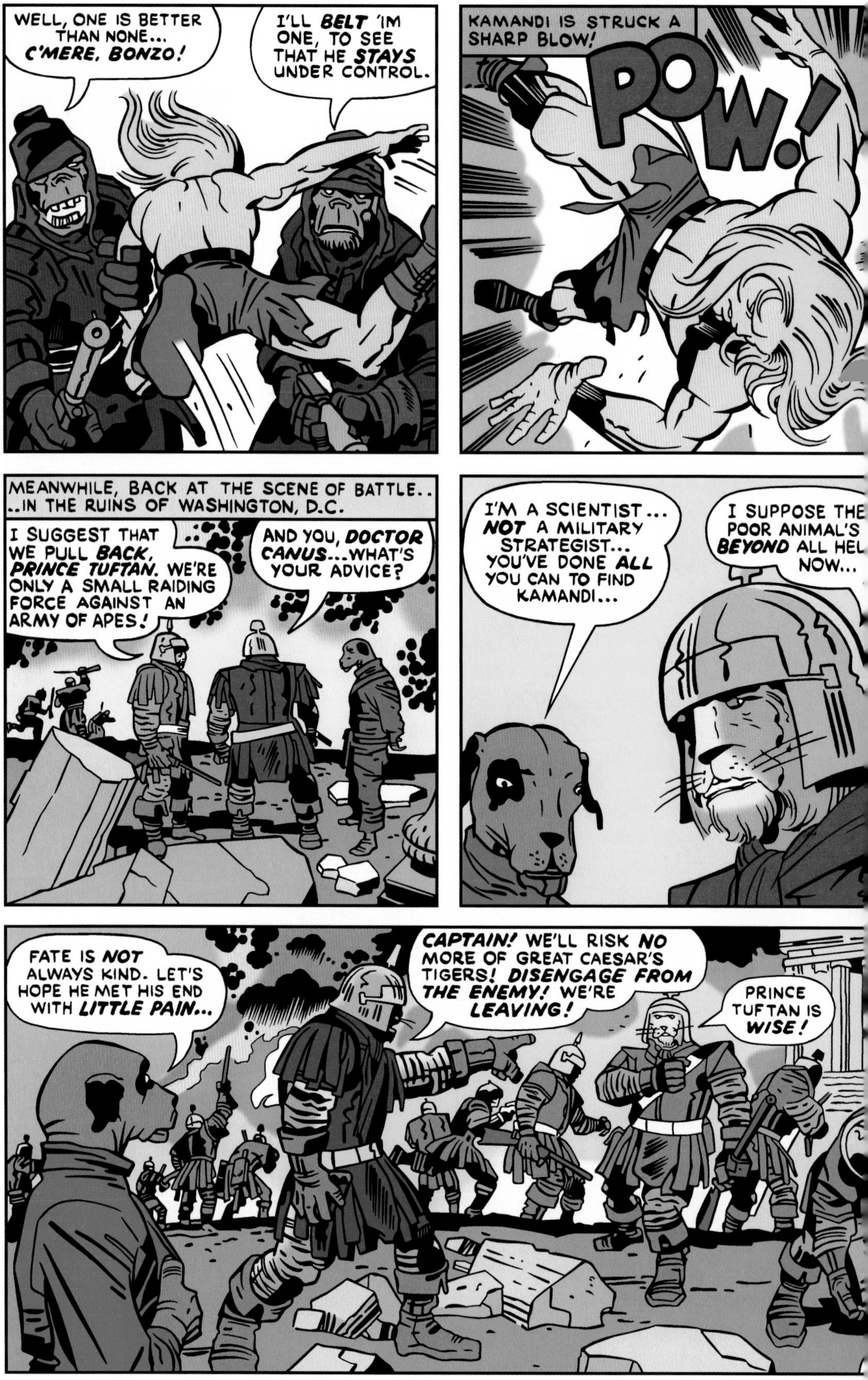
WELL, ONE IS BETTER THAN NONE... C'MERE, BONZO!
I'LL BELT 'IM ONE, TO SEE THAT HE STAYS UNDER CONTROL.
KAMANDI IS STRUCK A SHARP BLOW!
POW!
MEANWHILE, BACK AT THE SCENE OF BATTLE.. ..IN THE RUINS OF WASHINGTON, D.C.
I SUGGEST THAT WE PULL BACK, PRINCE TUFTAN. WE'RE ONLY A SMALL RAIDING FORCE AGAINST AN ARMY OF APES!
AND YOU, DOCTOR CANUS...WHAT'S YOUR ADVICE?
I'M A SCIENTIST... NOT A MILITARY STRATEGIST... YOU'VE DONE ALL YOU CAN TO FIND KAMANDI...
FATE IS NOT ALWAYS KIND. LET'S HOPE HE MET HIS END WITH LITTLE PAIN...
CAPTAIN! WE'LL RISK NO MORE OF GREAT CAESAR'S TIGERS! DISENGAGE FROM THE ENEMY! WE'RE LEAVING!
PRINCE TUFTAN IS WISE!

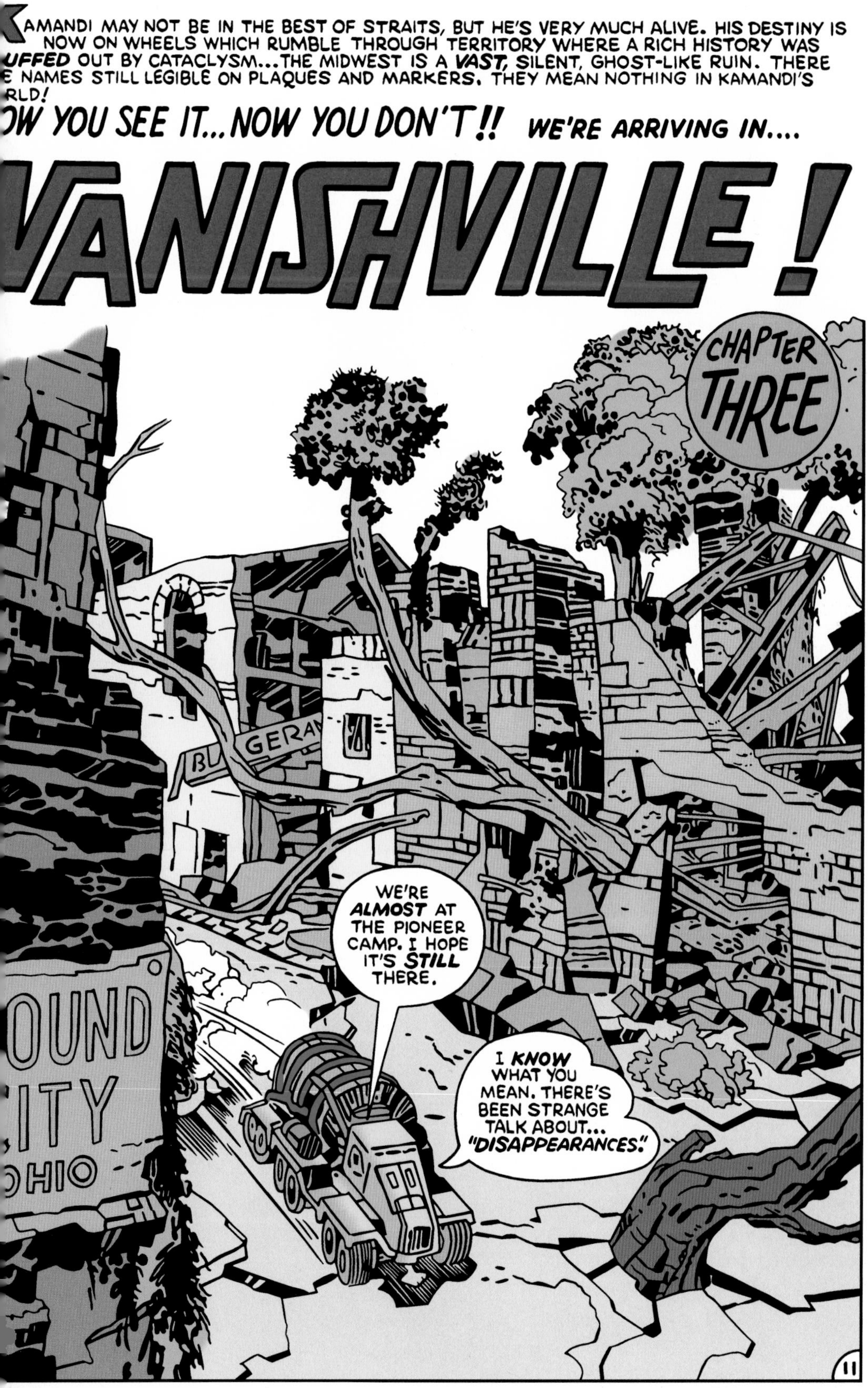
KAMANDI MAY NOT BE IN THE BEST OF STRAITS, BUT HE'S VERY MUCH ALIVE. HIS DESTINY IS NOW ON WHEELS WHICH RUMBLE THROUGH TERRITORY WHERE A RICH HISTORY WAS UFFED OUT BY CATACLYSM...THE MIDWEST IS A VAST, SILENT, GHOST-LIKE RUIN. THERE E NAMES STILL LEGIBLE ON PLAQUES AND MARKERS. THEY MEAN NOTHING IN KAMANDI'S RLD!
OW YOU SEE IT...NOW YOU DON'T!! WE'RE ARRIVING IN....
VANISHVILLE!
CHAPTER THREE
BU GERA
OUND ITY OHIO
WE'RE ALMOST AT THE PIONEER CAMP. I HOPE IT'S STILL THERE.
I KNOW WHAT YOU MEAN. THERE'S BEEN STRANGE TALK ABOUT... "DISAPPEARANCES."
11

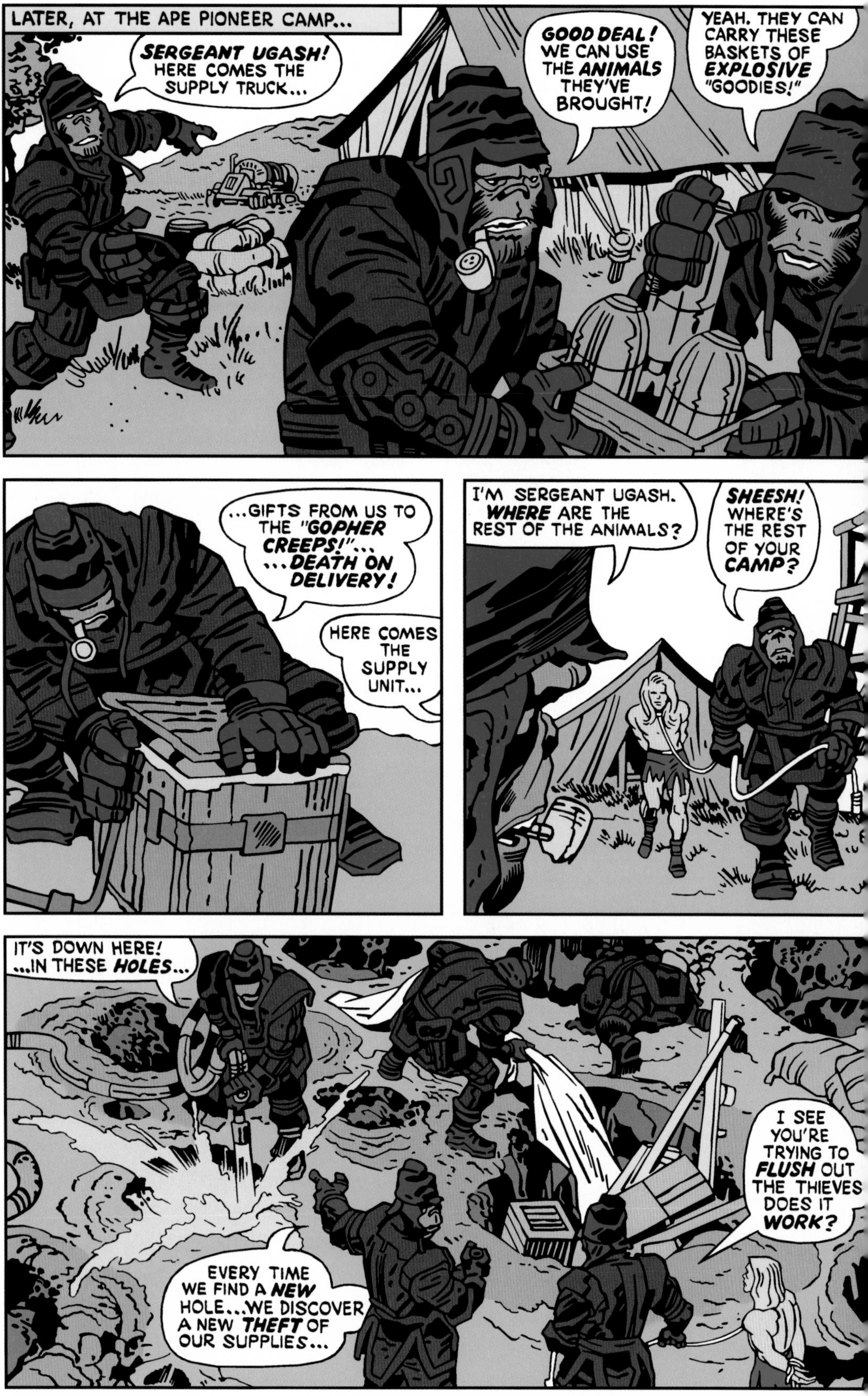
LATER, AT THE APE PIONEER CAMP...
SERGEANT UGASH! HERE COMES THE SUPPLY TRUCK...
GOOD DEAL! WE CAN USE THE ANIMALS THEY'VE BROUGHT!
YEAH. THEY CAN CARRY THESE BASKETS OF EXPLOSIVE "GOODIES!"
...GIFTS FROM US TO THE "GOPHER CREEPS!"... ...DEATH ON DELIVERY!
HERE COMES THE SUPPLY UNIT...
I'M SERGEANT UGASH. WHERE ARE THE REST OF THE ANIMALS?
SHEESH! WHERE'S THE REST OF YOUR CAMP?
IT'S DOWN HERE! ...IN THESE HOLES...
I SEE YOU'RE TRYING TO FLUSH OUT THE THIEVES DOES IT WORK?
EVERY TIME WE FIND A NEW HOLE...WE DISCOVER A NEW THEFT OF OUR SUPPLIES...

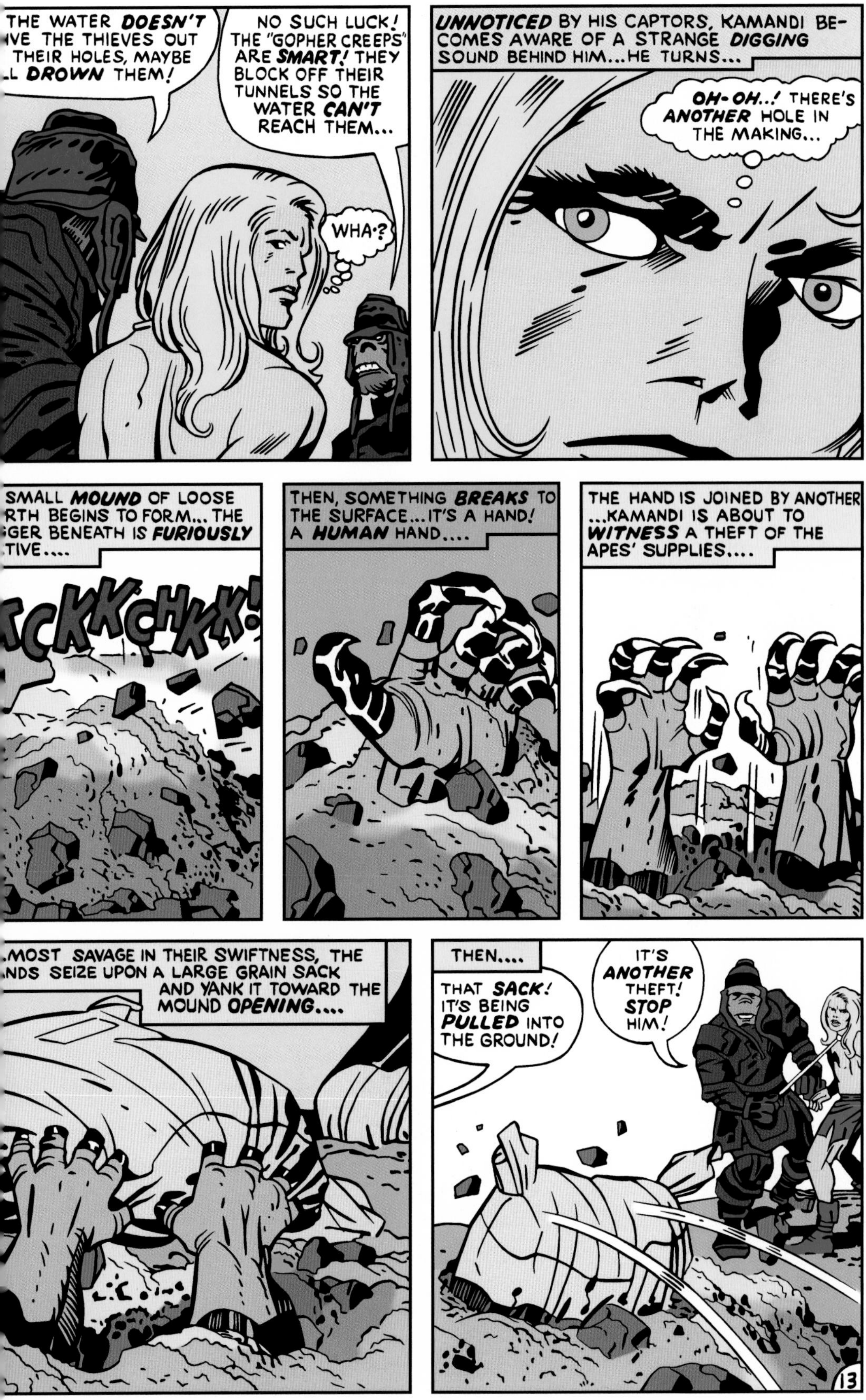
THE WATER DOESN'T
IVE THE THIEVES OUT
THEIR HOLES, MAYBE
L DROWN THEM!
NO SUCH LUCK! THE "GOPHER CREEPS" ARE SMART! THEY BLOCK OFF THEIR TUNNELS SO THE WATER CAN'T REACH THEM...
WHA-?
UNNOTICED BY HIS CAPTORS, KAMANDI BECOMES AWARE OF A STRANGE DIGGING SOUND BEHIND HIM...HE TURNS...
OH-OH..! THERE'S ANOTHER HOLE IN THE MAKING...
SMALL MOUND OF LOOSE
RTH BEGINS TO FORM... THE
GER BENEATH IS FURIOUSLY
TIVE....
CKKCHKK!
THEN, SOMETHING BREAKS TO THE SURFACE...IT'S A HAND! A HUMAN HAND....
THE HAND IS JOINED BY ANOTHER ...KAMANDI IS ABOUT TO WITNESS A THEFT OF THE APES' SUPPLIES....
MOST SAVAGE IN THEIR SWIFTNESS, THE
NDS SEIZE UPON A LARGE GRAIN SACK
AND YANK IT TOWARD THE MOUND OPENING....
THEN....
THAT SACK! IT'S BEING PULLED INTO THE GROUND!
IT'S ANOTHER THEFT! STOP HIM!
13

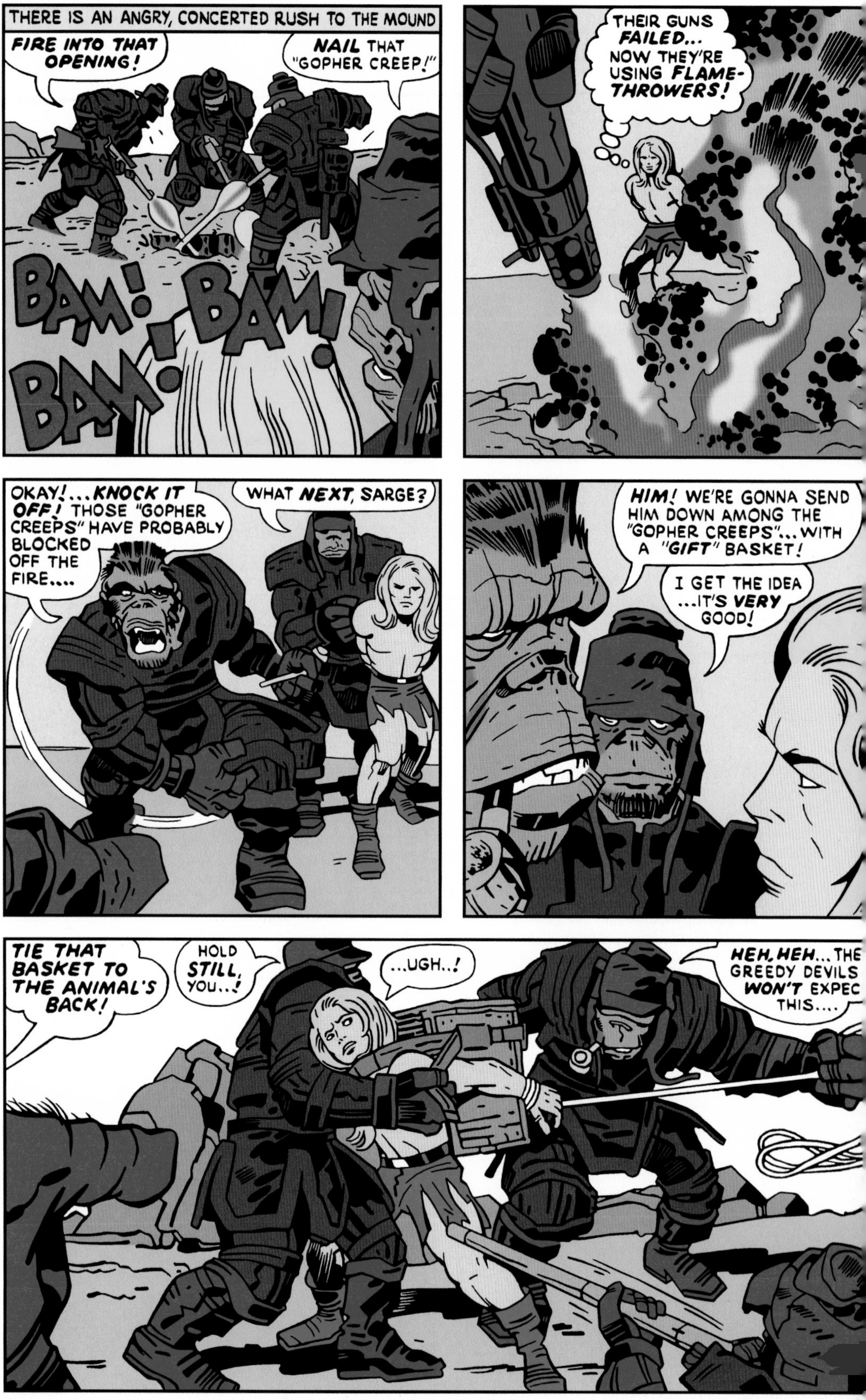
THERE IS AN ANGRY, CONCERTED RUSH TO THE MOUND
FIRE INTO THAT OPENING!
NAIL THAT "GOPHER CREEP!"
BAM! BAM! BAM!
THEIR GUNS FAILED... NOW THEY'RE USING FLAME-THROWERS!
OKAY!...KNOCK IT OFF! THOSE "GOPHER CREEPS" HAVE PROBABLY BLOCKED OFF THE FIRE....
WHAT NEXT, SARGE?
HIM! WE'RE GONNA SEND HIM DOWN AMONG THE "GOPHER CREEPS"...WITH A "GIFT" BASKET!
I GET THE IDEA ...IT'S VERY GOOD!
TIE THAT BASKET TO THE ANIMAL'S BACK!
HOLD STILL, YOU..!
...UGH..!
HEH, HEH... THE GREEDY DEVILS WON'T EXPEC THIS....

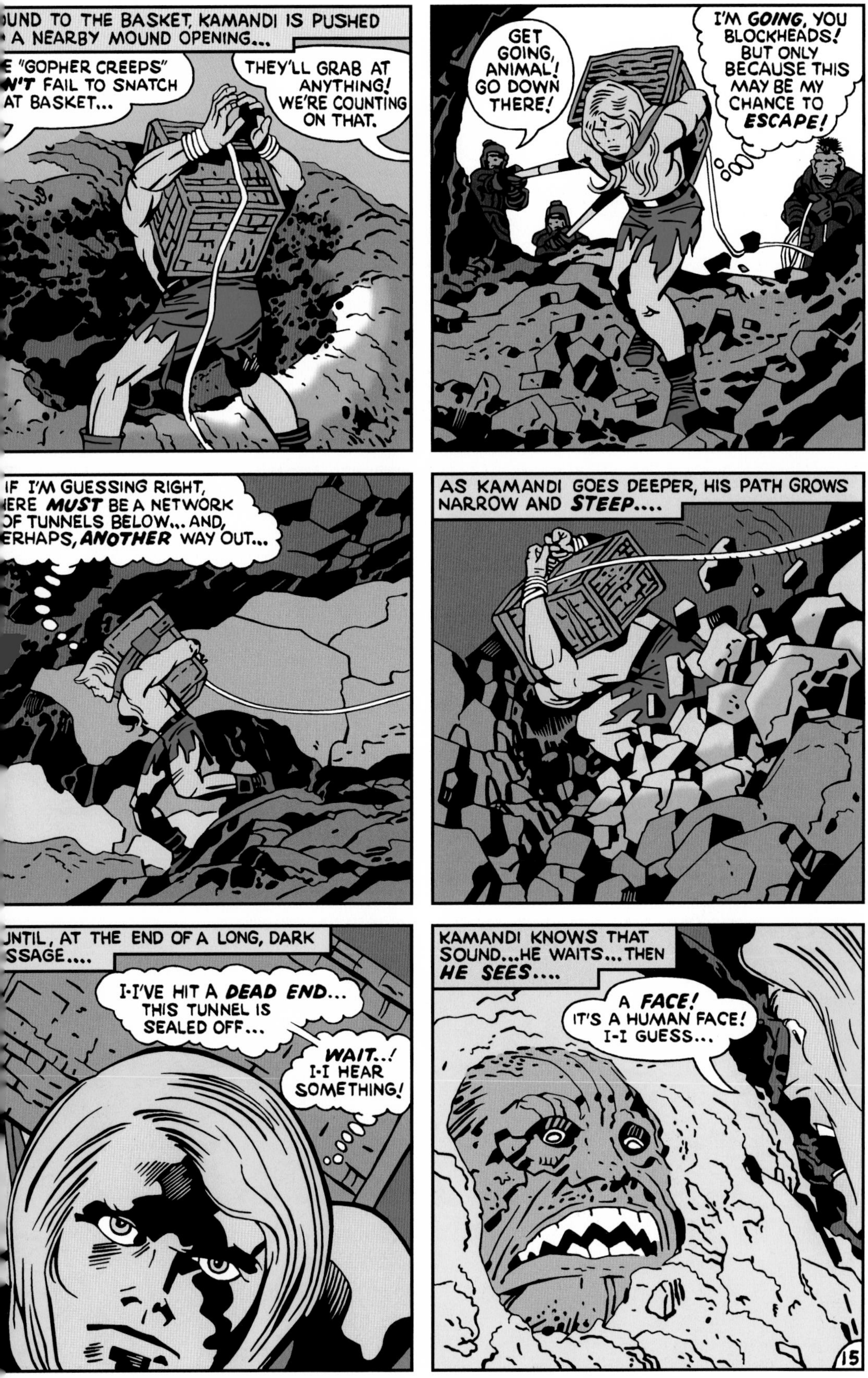

…UND TO THE BASKET, KAMANDI IS PUSHED … A NEARBY MOUND OPENING...
…E "GOPHER CREEPS" …N'T FAIL TO SNATCH …AT BASKET...
THEY'LL GRAB AT ANYTHING! WE'RE COUNTING ON THAT.
GET GOING, ANIMAL! GO DOWN THERE!
I'M GOING, YOU BLOCKHEADS! BUT ONLY BECAUSE THIS MAY BE MY CHANCE TO ESCAPE!
IF I'M GUESSING RIGHT, …ERE MUST BE A NETWORK …OF TUNNELS BELOW... AND, …ERHAPS, ANOTHER WAY OUT...
AS KAMANDI GOES DEEPER, HIS PATH GROWS NARROW AND STEEP....
…UNTIL, AT THE END OF A LONG, DARK …SSAGE....
I-I'VE HIT A DEAD END... THIS TUNNEL IS SEALED OFF...
WAIT..! I-I HEAR SOMETHING!
KAMANDI KNOWS THAT SOUND...HE WAITS...THEN HE SEES....
A FACE! IT'S A HUMAN FACE! I-I GUESS...
15

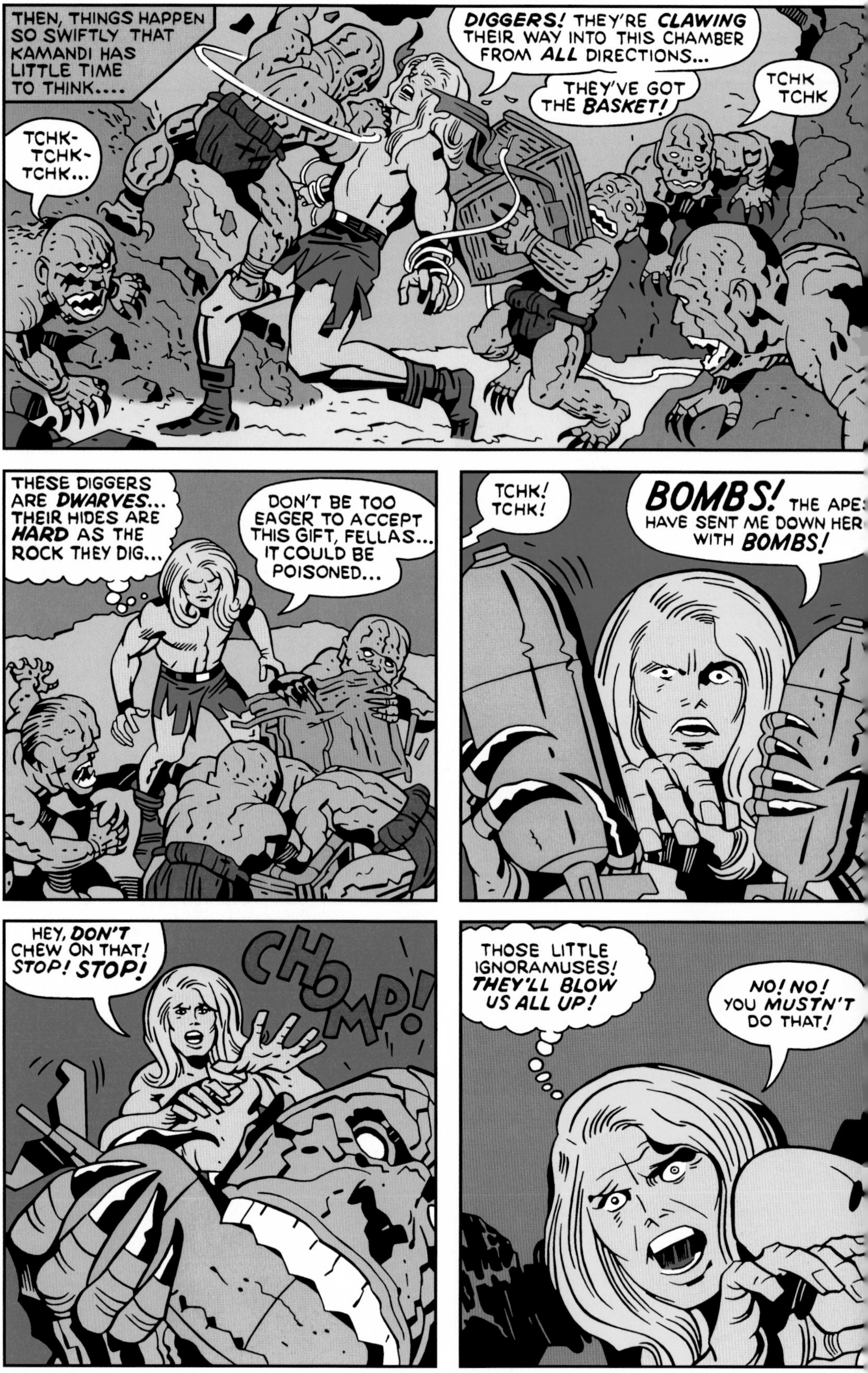
THEN, THINGS HAPPEN SO SWIFTLY THAT KAMANDI HAS LITTLE TIME TO THINK....
DIGGERS! THEY'RE CLAWING THEIR WAY INTO THIS CHAMBER FROM ALL DIRECTIONS...
THEY'VE GOT THE BASKET!
TCHK TCHK
TCHK-TCHK-TCHK...
THESE DIGGERS ARE DWARVES... THEIR HIDES ARE HARD AS THE ROCK THEY DIG...
DON'T BE TOO EAGER TO ACCEPT THIS GIFT, FELLAS... IT COULD BE POISONED...
TCHK! TCHK!
BOMBS! THE APES HAVE SENT ME DOWN HERE WITH BOMBS!
HEY, DON'T CHEW ON THAT! STOP! STOP!
CHOMP!
THOSE LITTLE IGNORAMUSES! THEY'LL BLOW US ALL UP!
NO! NO! YOU MUSTN'T DO THAT!

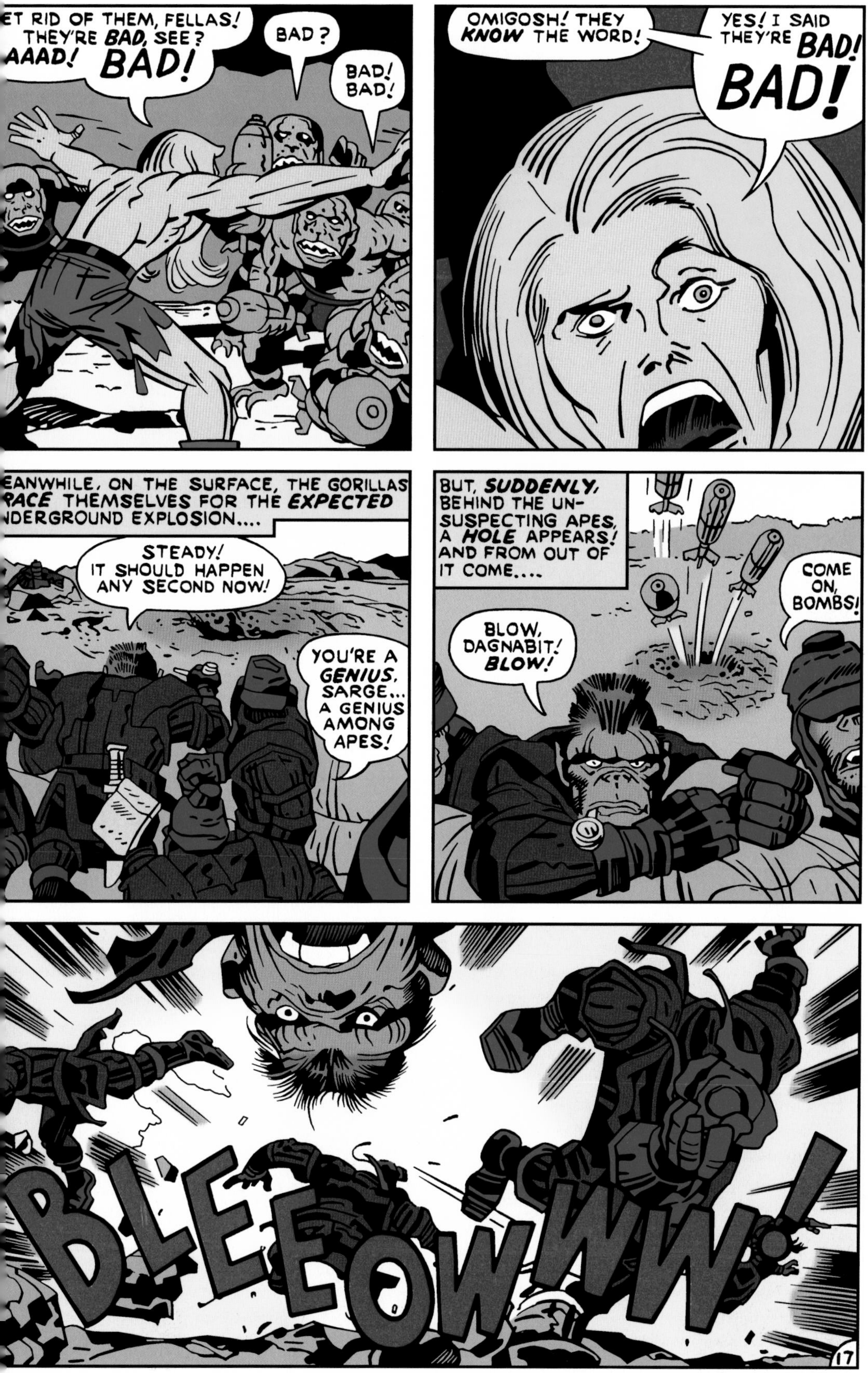
ET RID OF THEM, FELLAS! THEY'RE BAD, SEE? AAAD! BAD!
BAD?
BAD! BAD!
OMIGOSH! THEY KNOW THE WORD!
YES! I SAID THEY'RE BAD! BAD!
EANWHILE, ON THE SURFACE, THE GORILLAS RACE THEMSELVES FOR THE EXPECTED NDERGROUND EXPLOSION....
STEADY! IT SHOULD HAPPEN ANY SECOND NOW!
YOU'RE A GENIUS, SARGE... A GENIUS AMONG APES!
BUT, SUDDENLY, BEHIND THE UN-SUSPECTING APES, A HOLE APPEARS! AND FROM OUT OF IT COME....
COME ON, BOMBS!
BLOW, DAGNABIT! BLOW!
BLEEOWWW!
17

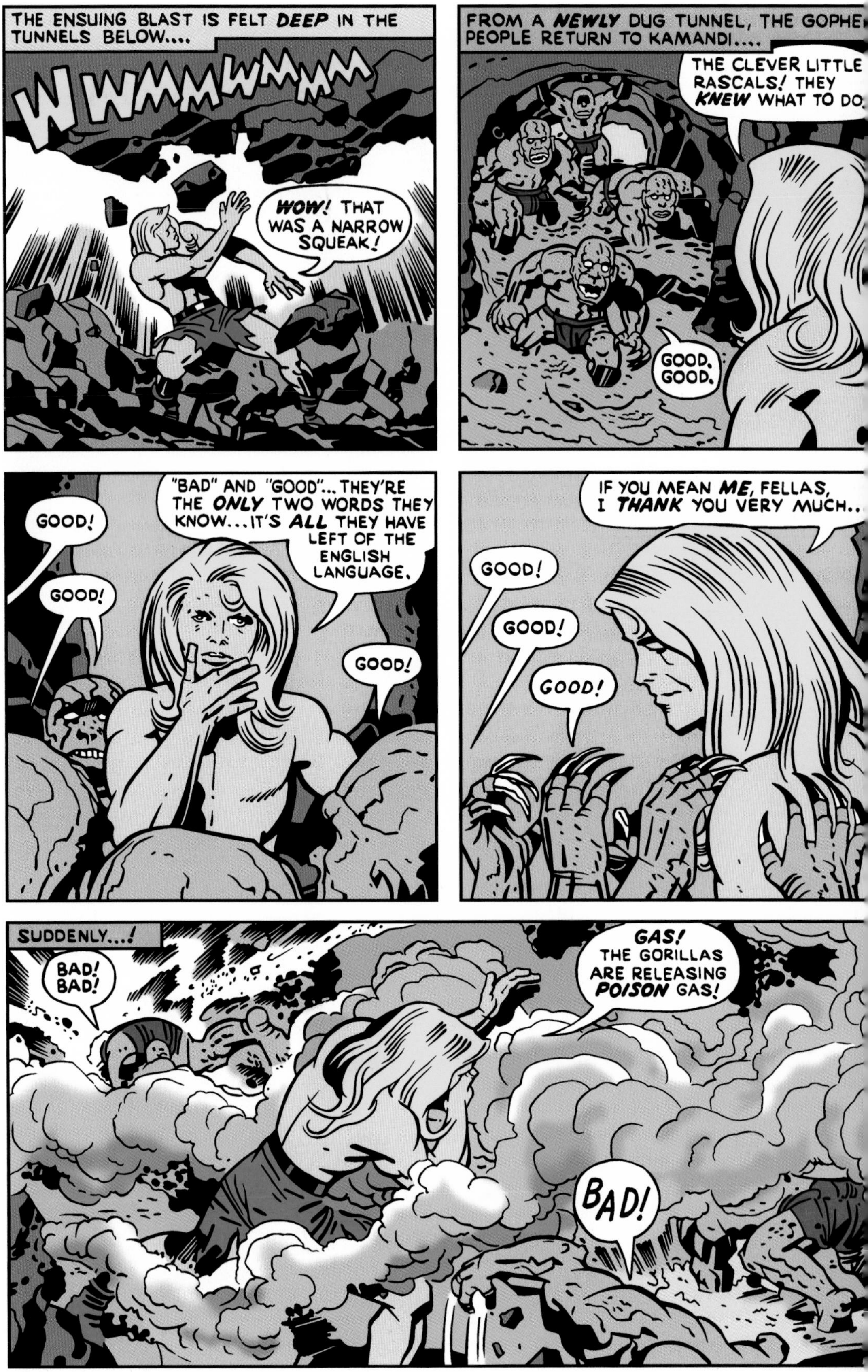
THE ENSUING BLAST IS FELT DEEP IN THE TUNNELS BELOW....
WWMMWMMM
WOW! THAT WAS A NARROW SQUEAK!
FROM A NEWLY DUG TUNNEL, THE GOPHE PEOPLE RETURN TO KAMANDI....
THE CLEVER LITTLE RASCALS! THEY KNEW WHAT TO DO
GOOD, GOOD.
GOOD!
GOOD!
"BAD" AND "GOOD"... THEY'RE THE ONLY TWO WORDS THEY KNOW... IT'S ALL THEY HAVE LEFT OF THE ENGLISH LANGUAGE.
GOOD!
IF YOU MEAN ME, FELLAS, I THANK YOU VERY MUCH..
GOOD!
GOOD!
GOOD!
SUDDENLY...!
BAD! BAD!
GAS! THE GORILLAS ARE RELEASING POISON GAS!
BAD!

FORE KAMANDI CAN ACT, HE IS *PULLED* INTO BANK OF LOOSENED EARTH....

WHA..?

THEN, HE FINDS HIMSELF IN AN ADJOINING CHAMBER....

HE WALL OF EARTH IS QUICKLY HORED UP TO KEEP THE GAS OUT KAMANDI IS USTLED AWAY O SAFETY.

GOOD.

GOOD! GOOD!

EASY, FELLAS... *DON'T* PUSH SO HARD...I'LL GO ALONG..

AMANDI IS TAKEN *DEEP* INTO HE TUNNELS OF HIS CAPTORS...

THEN....

THE RUINS OF AN OLD FACTORY....BURIED BY THE GREAT DISASTER...

FACTORY

19

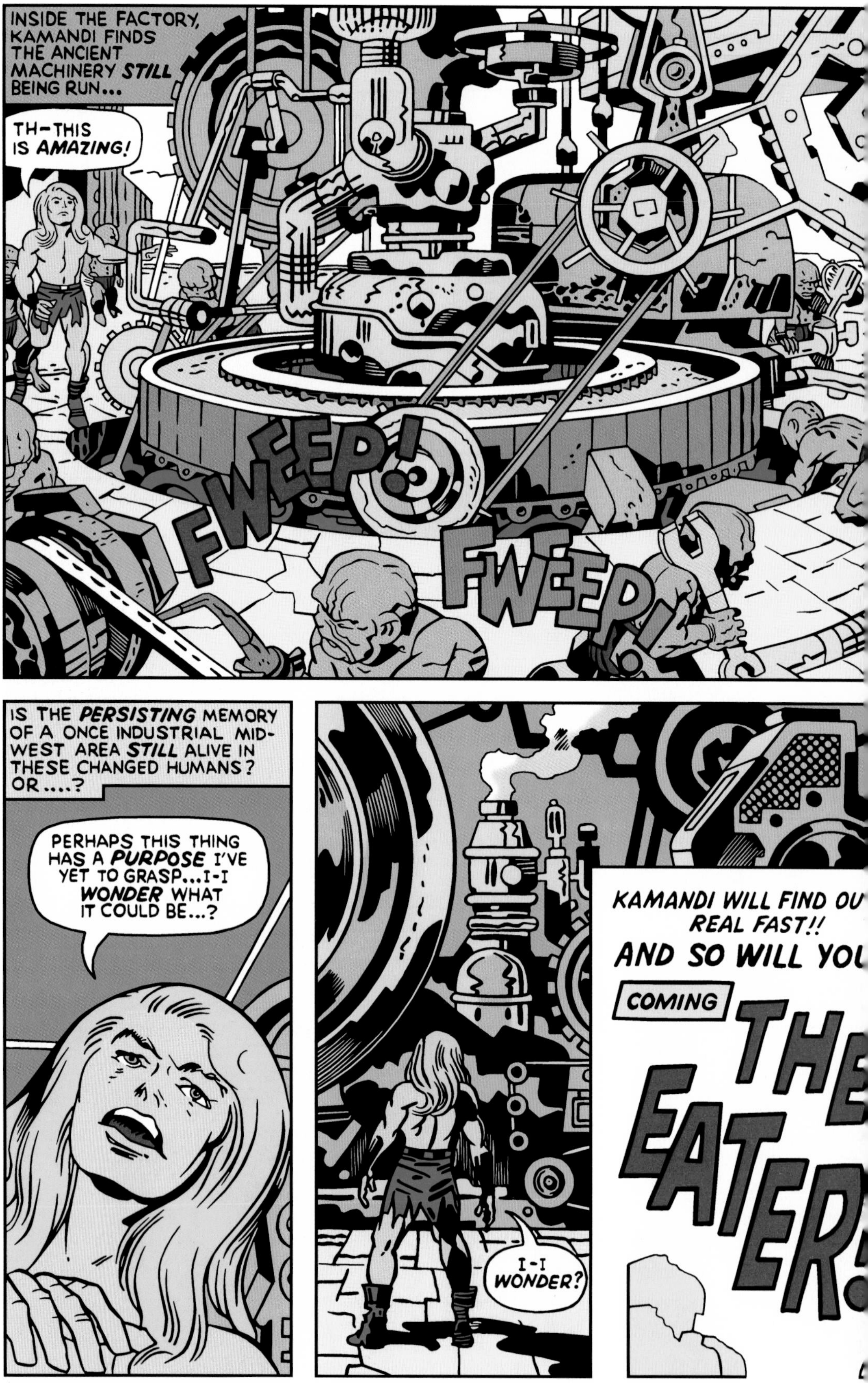
INSIDE THE FACTORY, KAMANDI FINDS THE ANCIENT MACHINERY STILL BEING RUN...
TH-THIS IS AMAZING!
FWEEP!
FWEEP!
IS THE PERSISTING MEMORY OF A ONCE INDUSTRIAL MID-WEST AREA STILL ALIVE IN THESE CHANGED HUMANS? OR....?
PERHAPS THIS THING HAS A PURPOSE I'VE YET TO GRASP...I-I WONDER WHAT IT COULD BE...?
I-I WONDER?
KAMANDI WILL FIND OU
REAL FAST!!
AND SO WILL YOU
COMING
THE
EATER

SUBJECT; ANIMALS THAT STAND ERECT ...
USURPER-IN-RESIDENCE: JACK KIRBY
REASON: CONTINUOUS DRUMBEATING BY
MAUDLIN PARTISANS OF SPECIFIC
SPECIES, SUCH AS HORSES, COWS,
CHICKENS AND WOMBATS ...

Yes, dear readers, I do peruse the letters we receive. And I must say that between the comments and brickbats there runs an insidious and recurrent allusion to my faulty views on the duality of animals. I find this shocking, of course, considering my unabashed surrender to my daughter's concern for all organic life and ecological balance. Believe me when I say that this kind of icky reformation is a bitter pill for one who must now politely doff his hat to a passing scorpion or run to the aid of an ant who is stupidly en route to drowning.

Then why, in the World of Kamandi, do I discriminate among the animals, giving some the intelligence of Man and others less sentient awareness? Why must the stately horse still serve as transportation for a smelly old gorilla? Why must the bird remain a beautiful dum-dum? And, my answer must be that they don't have to. My personal theory is that all animals have a common link. Thus, if given time and proper circumstance, it's possible for all species to achieve the status or similar status of Man.

However, that's a sweeping generalization and I can easily be assailed from any quarter by equal counter-logic.

Still, I base my Kamandi premise on a variety of authoritative articles written by qualified men who have speculated on the form life must take in order to acquire intelligence as we know it. Their conclusions are that skeletal structure dictates this phenomenon, and the ability to stand erect is a sort of first rung on the I.Q. ladder.

I bought that. I ruminated on its possibilities and strung it all out in the World of Kamandi. It's my job. And it's fascinating to work out this logic in graphic terms.

Think of all the animals that can stand erect and walk like a man and you'll come up with the same characters I have. Think of time and mutational changes that can further enhance the ghastly foot and spine so that adaptation to erectness becomes permanent. Who but the lowly ape, the dog, the cat, the rat and its cousins are more likely candidates for making an effortless transition? There is left field, of course. There's something always going on out there. Destiny holds continual surprises. And, to be frank, I'm eagerly awaiting any.

To my mind, the hoofed animals and our feathered friends would have to undergo changes too extreme in nature in order to reach a civilized statehood. It would pain me to know that a wonderful animal like the horse had endured a millennium of backaches in order to sit in a chair and drink his coffee at the television set. I would kick up and roll on the floor if a sincere and intelligent turkey were to run for Congress. This action would occur despite the fact that he'd

probably get my vote.

No, dear friends, I'm attempting to portray my animal-people as logically and objectively as I can. In a few instances, I will dabble with variations such as Kliklak, the giant insect who has broken the biological size-barrier. With that premise in mind, I visualized him with less legs and a more herd-like instinct, like the horse.

As for old man Sacker, the Snake, he was part possibility and part satire. He will be followed by new variations. The aim is to maintain your interest and to slug it out with your pugnacious combativeness. Keep reading. Keep writing. Keep nit-picking. There's no harm in proving that the human brain works.

Jack Kirby

P.S. This is just a passing thought on the meaning of Kamandi's World. In developing my animal characters, I find myself relating to them with astonishing ease. Once they have acquired human qualities and names, they become real people, friends and enemies, some to be scorned and others to be respected. It seems to me that all of us have been doing this for centuries, forgetting that these creatures are merely animals. From the largest to the smallest, they seek only to survive as best they can. In the scale of things, they are as important to our well-being as we can be to theirs. Let's not make them the Kamandis of our world. If you feel like arguing this point, my address is Box 336, Newbury Park, Calif. 91320.

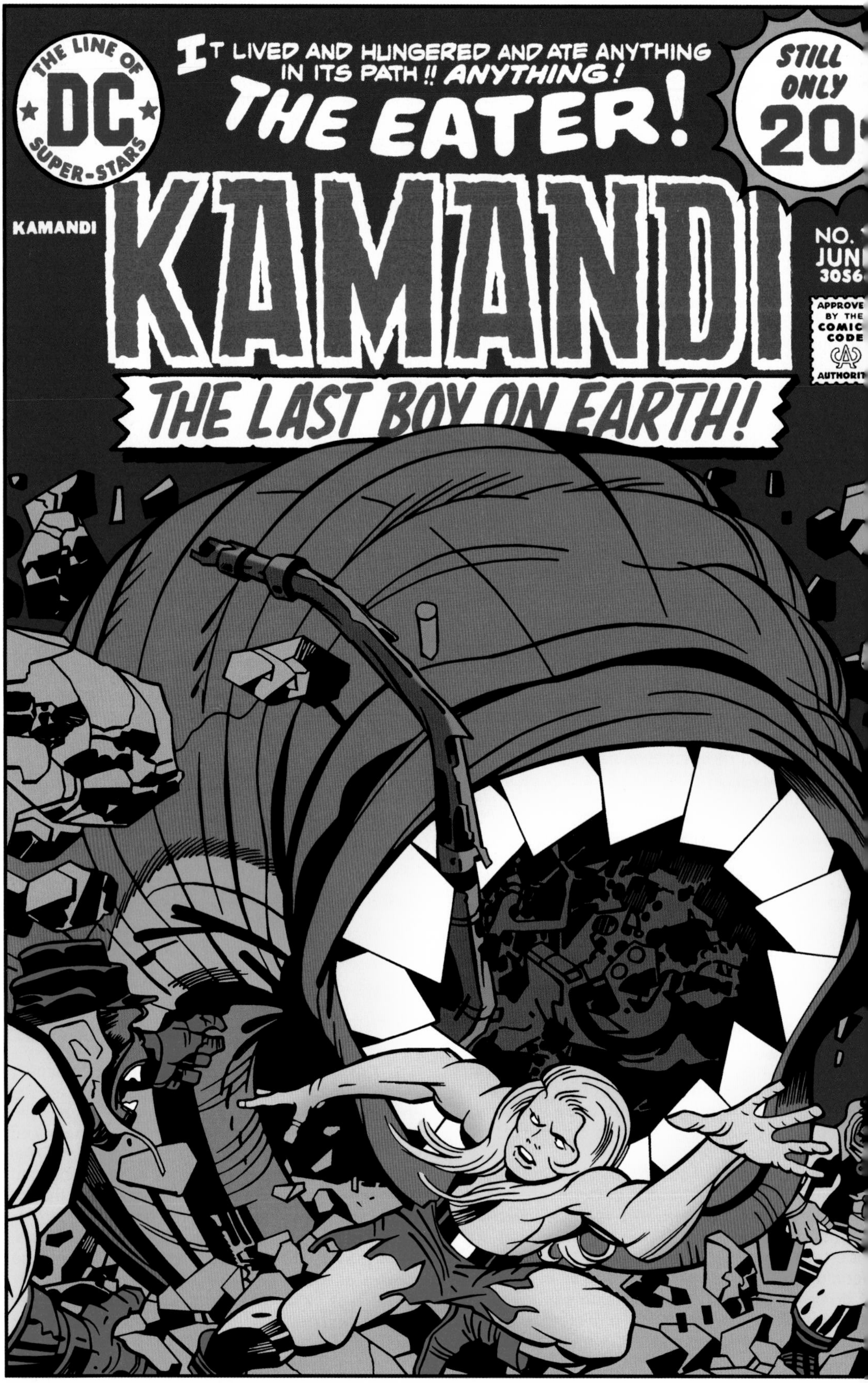
THE LINE OF DC SUPER-STARS
IT LIVED AND HUNGERED AND ATE ANYTHING IN ITS PATH !! ANYTHING!
THE EATER!
STILL ONLY 20
KAMANDI
KAMANDI
NO.
JUN
3056
APPROVE BY THE COMIC CODE AUTHORIT
THE LAST BOY ON EARTH!

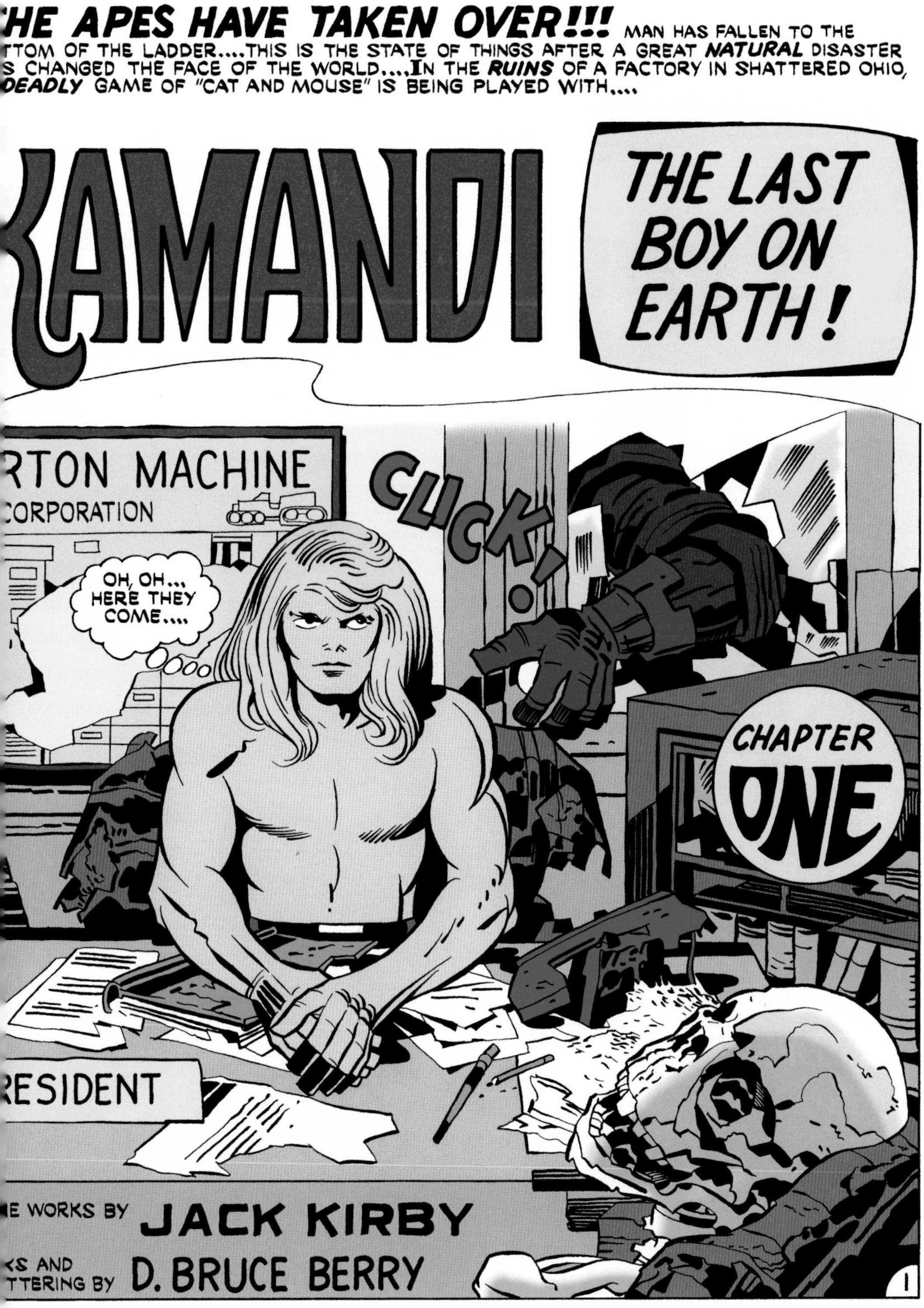
HE APES HAVE TAKEN OVER!!! MAN HAS FALLEN TO THE
TTOM OF THE LADDER....THIS IS THE STATE OF THINGS AFTER A GREAT NATURAL DISASTER
S CHANGED THE FACE OF THE WORLD....IN THE RUINS OF A FACTORY IN SHATTERED OHIO,
DEADLY GAME OF "CAT AND MOUSE" IS BEING PLAYED WITH....
AMANDI
THE LAST BOY ON EARTH!
RTON MACHINE
CORPORATION
CLICK!
OH, OH... HERE THEY COME....
CHAPTER ONE
RESIDENT
E WORKS BY JACK KIRBY
KS AND
TTERING BY D. BRUCE BERRY
1

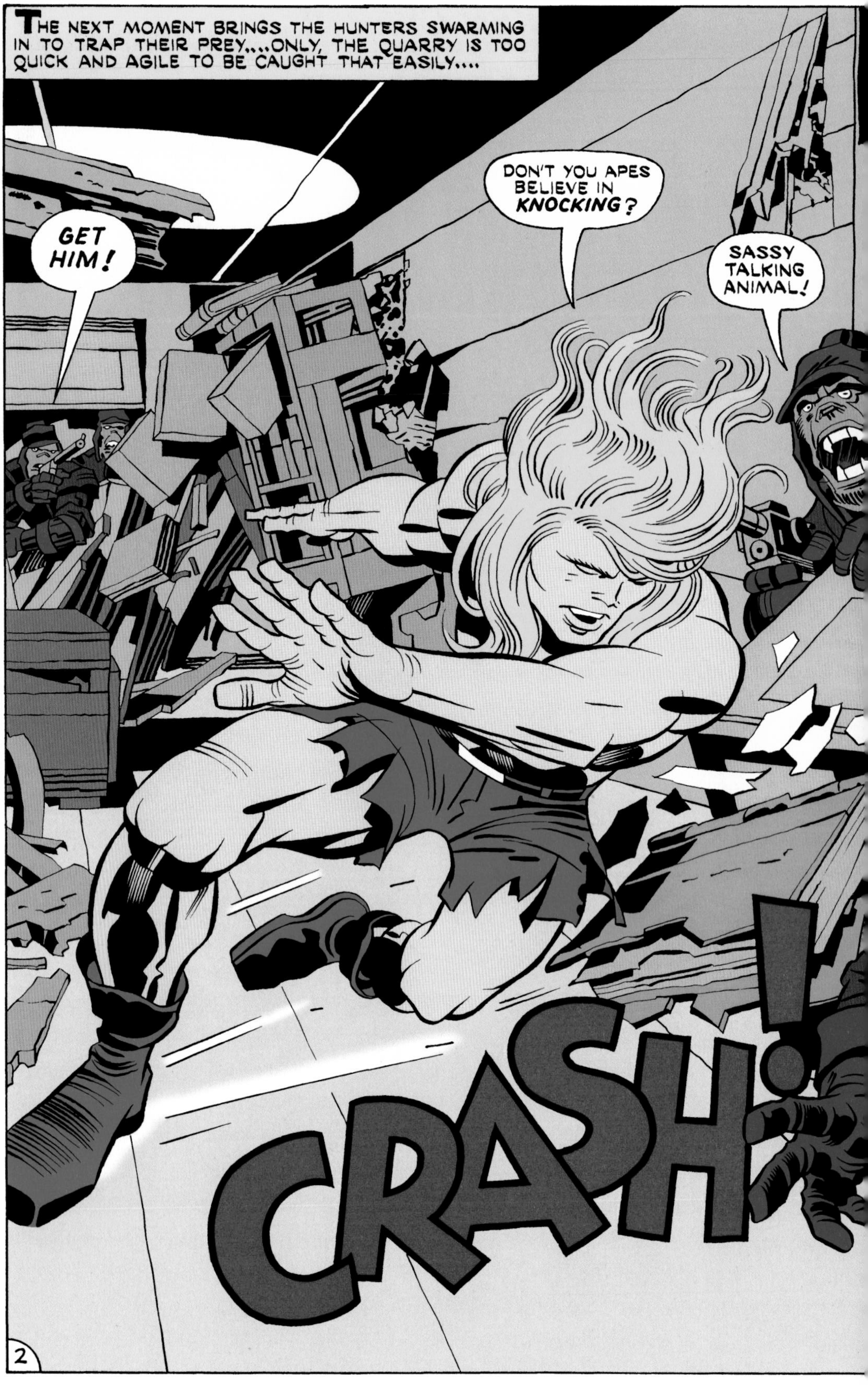
THE NEXT MOMENT BRINGS THE HUNTERS SWARMING IN TO TRAP THEIR PREY....ONLY, THE QUARRY IS TOO QUICK AND AGILE TO BE CAUGHT THAT EASILY....
GET HIM!
DON'T YOU APES BELIEVE IN KNOCKING?
SASSY TALKING ANIMAL!
CRASH!
2

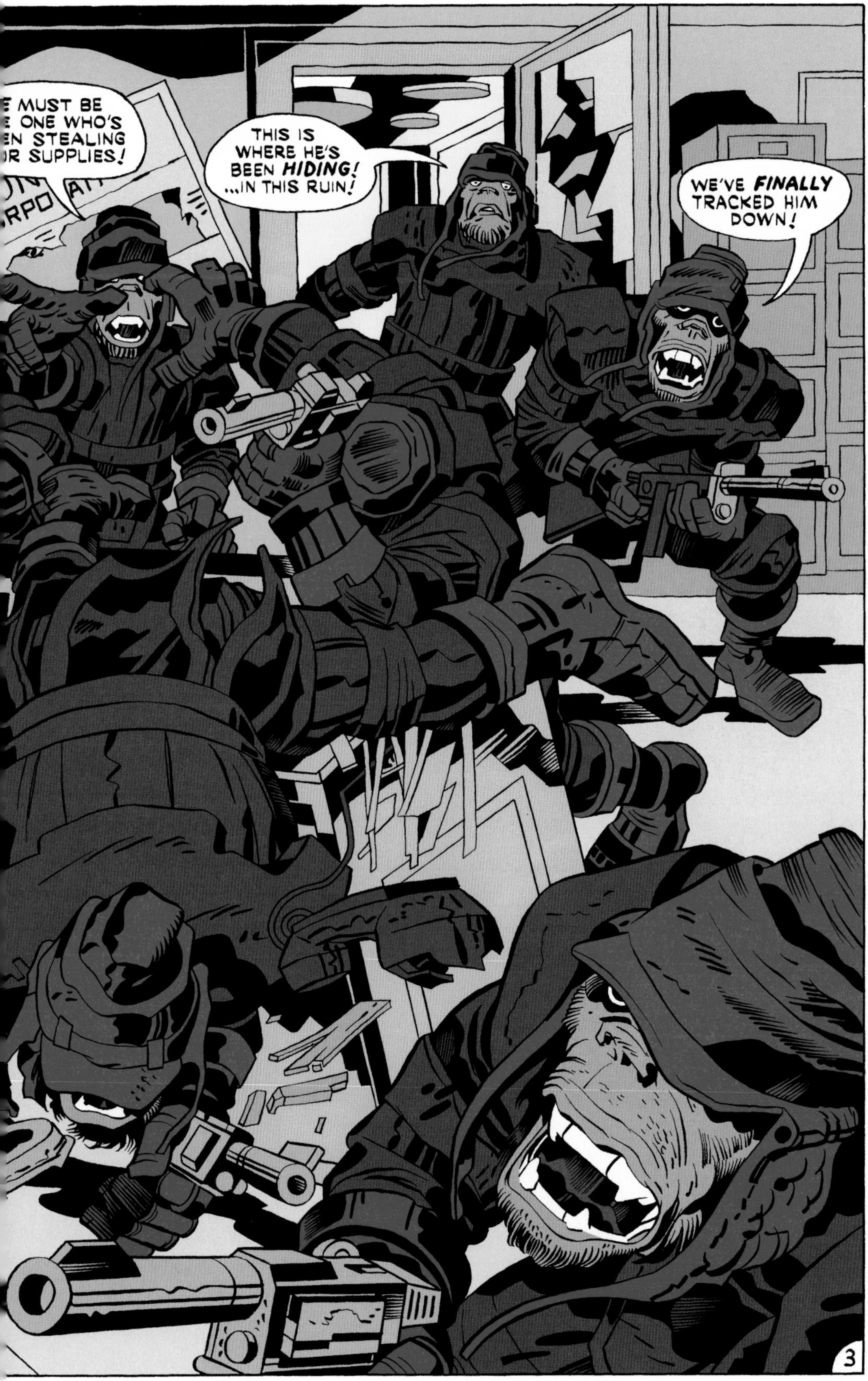
E MUST BE
E ONE WHO'S
EN STEALING
R SUPPLIES!
THIS IS
WHERE HE'S
BEEN HIDING!
...IN THIS RUIN!
WE'VE FINALLY
TRACKED HIM
DOWN!
3

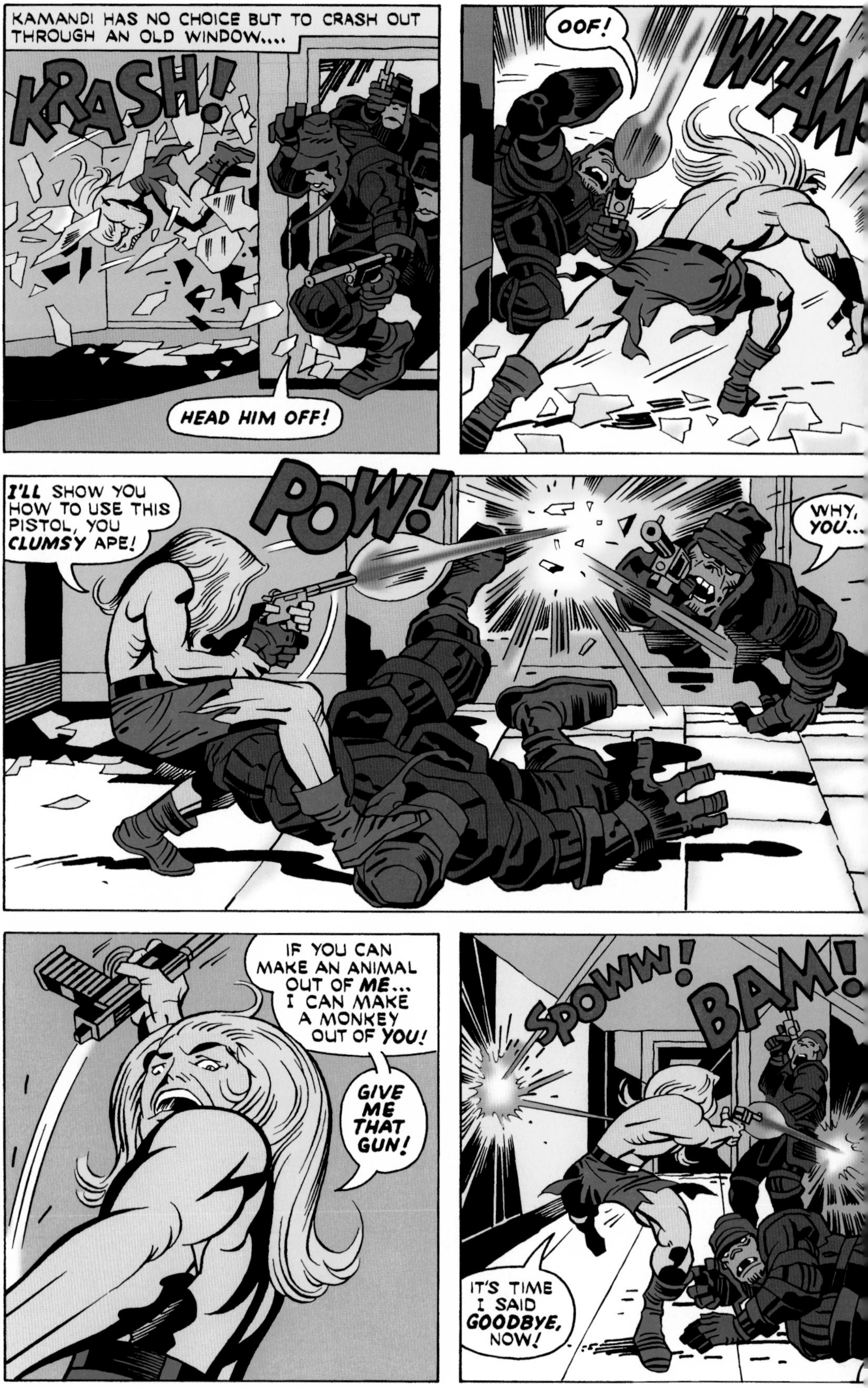
KAMANDI HAS NO CHOICE BUT TO CRASH OUT THROUGH AN OLD WINDOW....
KRASH!
HEAD HIM OFF!
OOF!
WHAM!
I'LL SHOW YOU HOW TO USE THIS PISTOL, YOU CLUMSY APE!
POW!
WHY, YOU...
IF YOU CAN MAKE AN ANIMAL OUT OF ME... I CAN MAKE A MONKEY OUT OF YOU!
GIVE ME THAT GUN!
SPOWW!
BAM!
IT'S TIME I SAID GOODBYE, NOW!

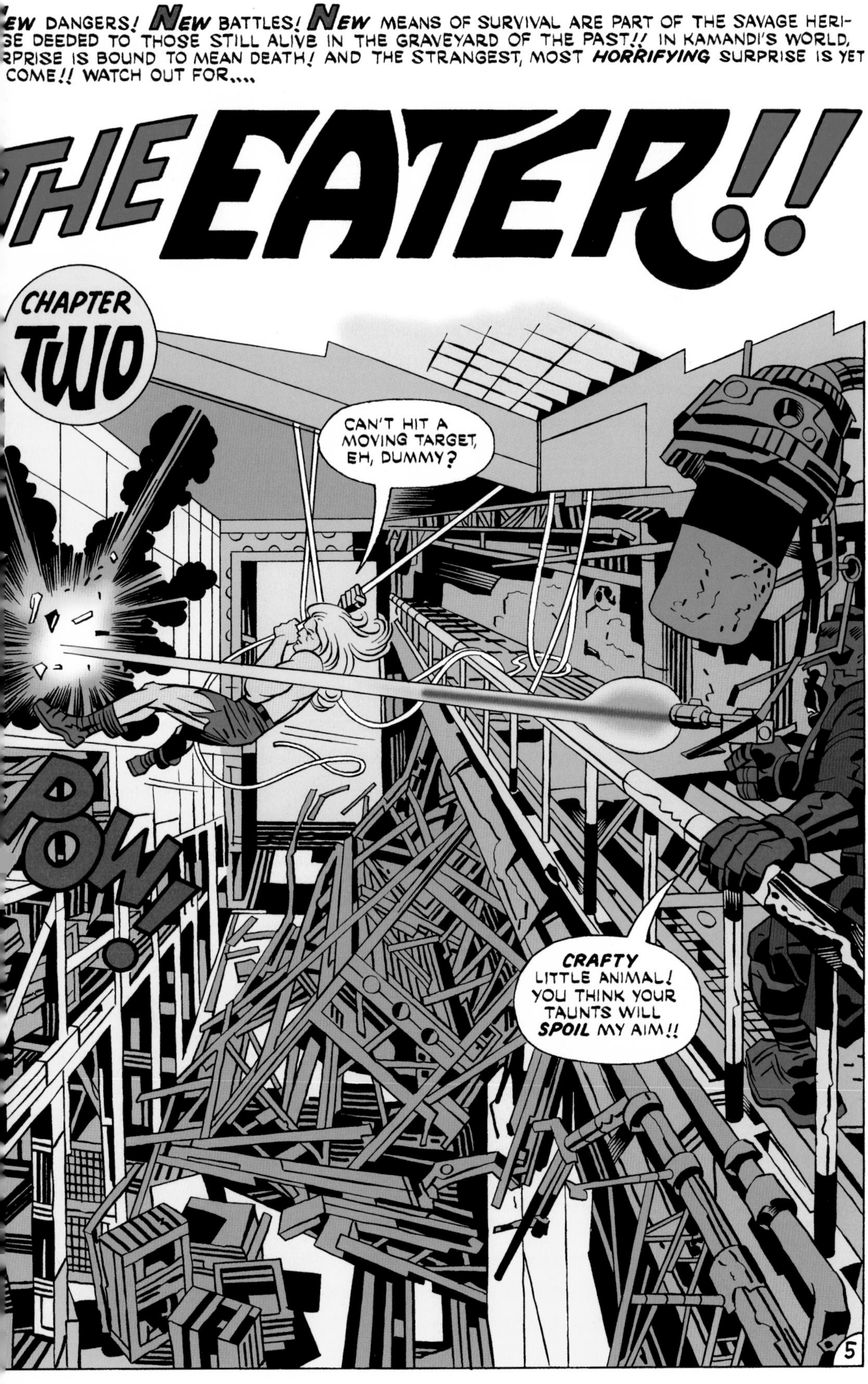
EW DANGERS! NEW BATTLES! NEW MEANS OF SURVIVAL ARE PART OF THE SAVAGE HERI-
GE DEEDED TO THOSE STILL ALIVE IN THE GRAVEYARD OF THE PAST!! IN KAMANDI'S WORLD,
RPRISE IS BOUND TO MEAN DEATH! AND THE STRANGEST, MOST HORRIFYING SURPRISE IS YET
COME!! WATCH OUT FOR....
THE EATER!!
CHAPTER TWO
CAN'T HIT A MOVING TARGET, EH, DUMMY?
POW!
CRAFTY LITTLE ANIMAL! YOU THINK YOUR TAUNTS WILL SPOIL MY AIM!!
5

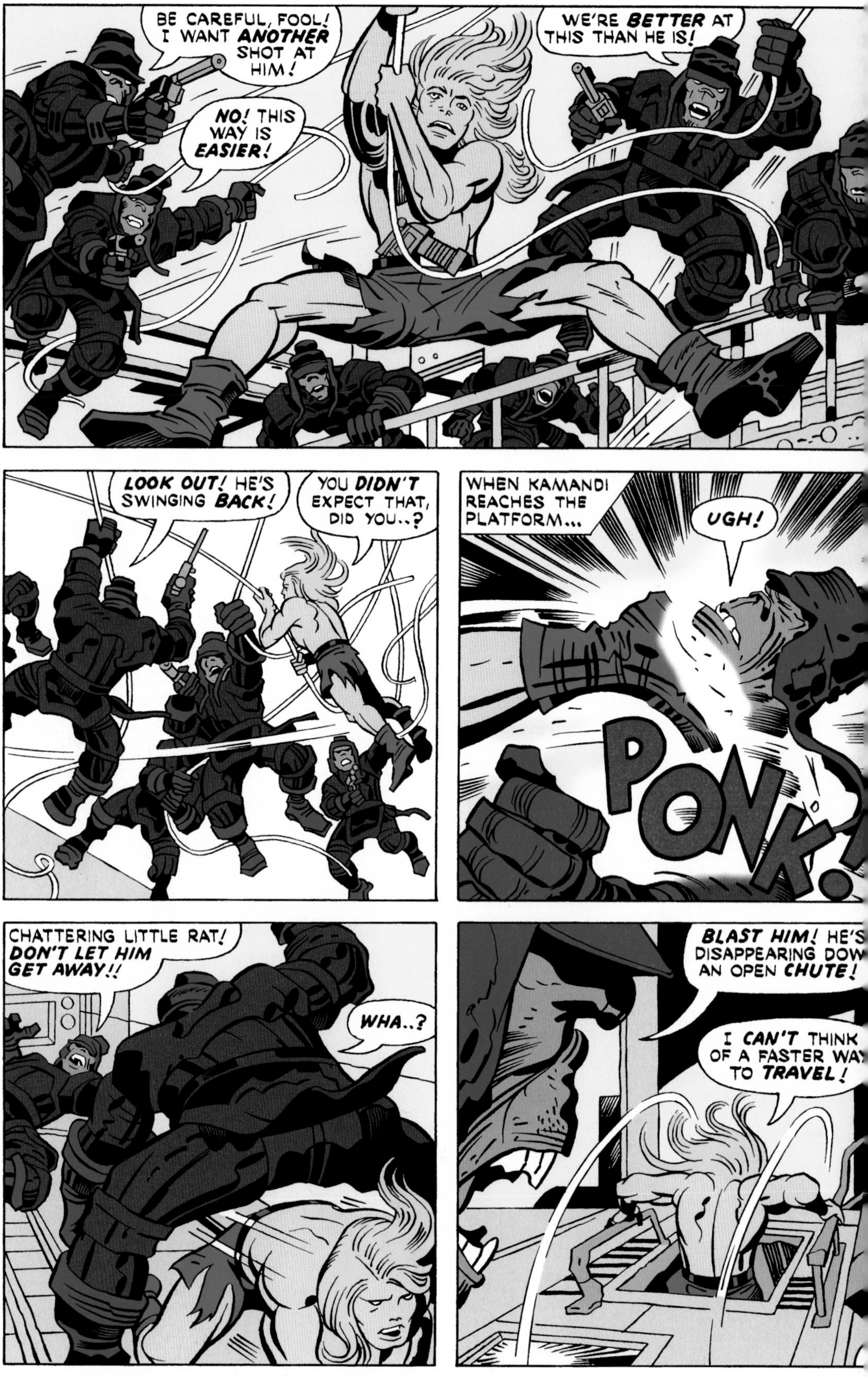
BE CAREFUL, FOOL! I WANT ANOTHER SHOT AT HIM!
NO! THIS WAY IS EASIER!
WE'RE BETTER AT THIS THAN HE IS!
LOOK OUT! HE'S SWINGING BACK!
YOU DIDN'T EXPECT THAT, DID YOU..?
WHEN KAMANDI REACHES THE PLATFORM...
UGH!
PONK!
CHATTERING LITTLE RAT! DON'T LET HIM GET AWAY!!
WHA..?
BLAST HIM! HE'S DISAPPEARING DOW AN OPEN CHUTE!
I CAN'T THINK OF A FASTER WAY TO TRAVEL!

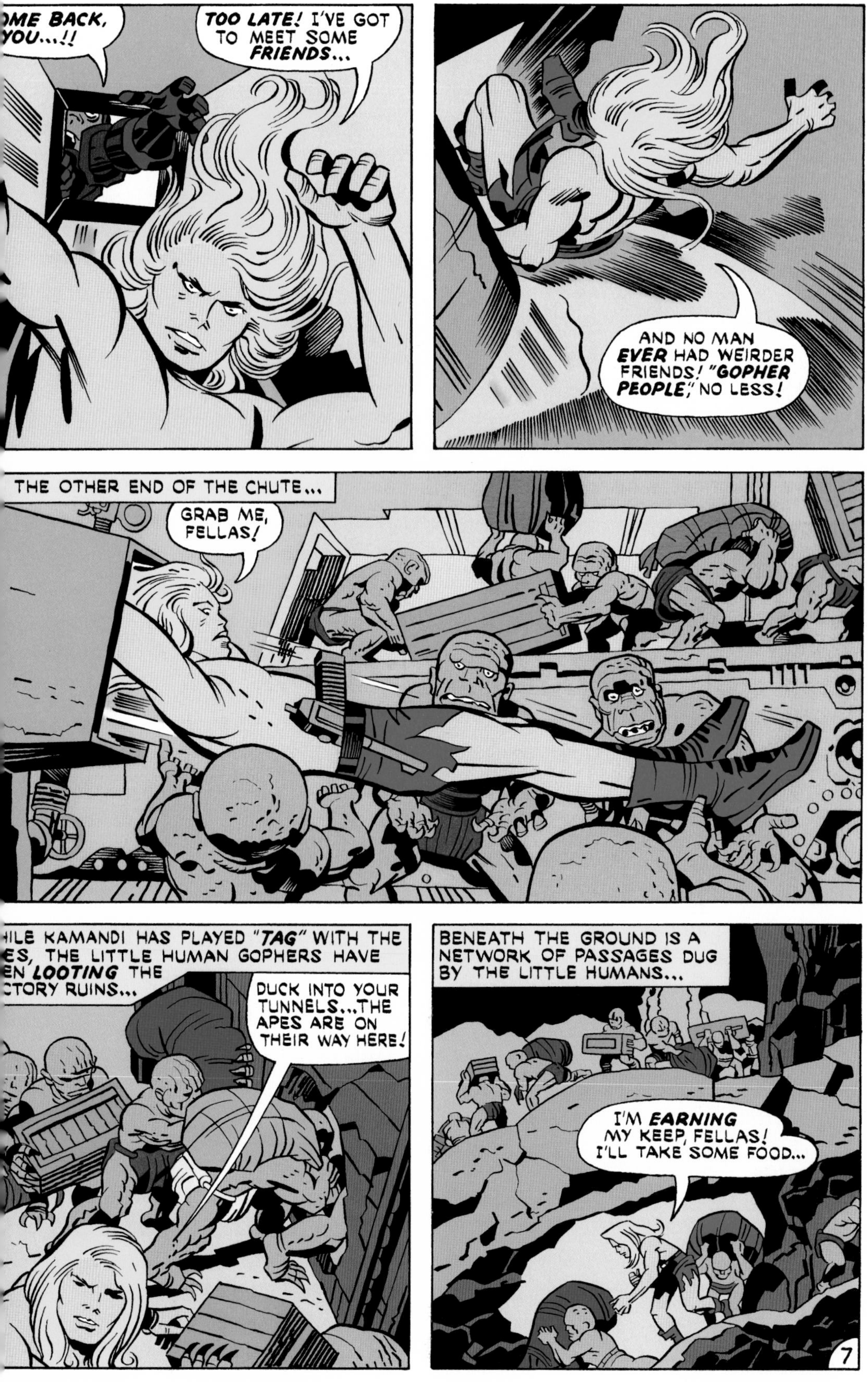
OME BACK, YOU...!!
TOO LATE! I'VE GOT TO MEET SOME FRIENDS...
AND NO MAN EVER HAD WEIRDER FRIENDS! "GOPHER PEOPLE," NO LESS!
THE OTHER END OF THE CHUTE...
GRAB ME, FELLAS!
HILE KAMANDI HAS PLAYED "TAG" WITH THE ES, THE LITTLE HUMAN GOPHERS HAVE EN LOOTING THE CTORY RUINS...
DUCK INTO YOUR TUNNELS...THE APES ARE ON THEIR WAY HERE!
BENEATH THE GROUND IS A NETWORK OF PASSAGES DUG BY THE LITTLE HUMANS...
I'M EARNING MY KEEP, FELLAS! I'LL TAKE SOME FOOD...
7

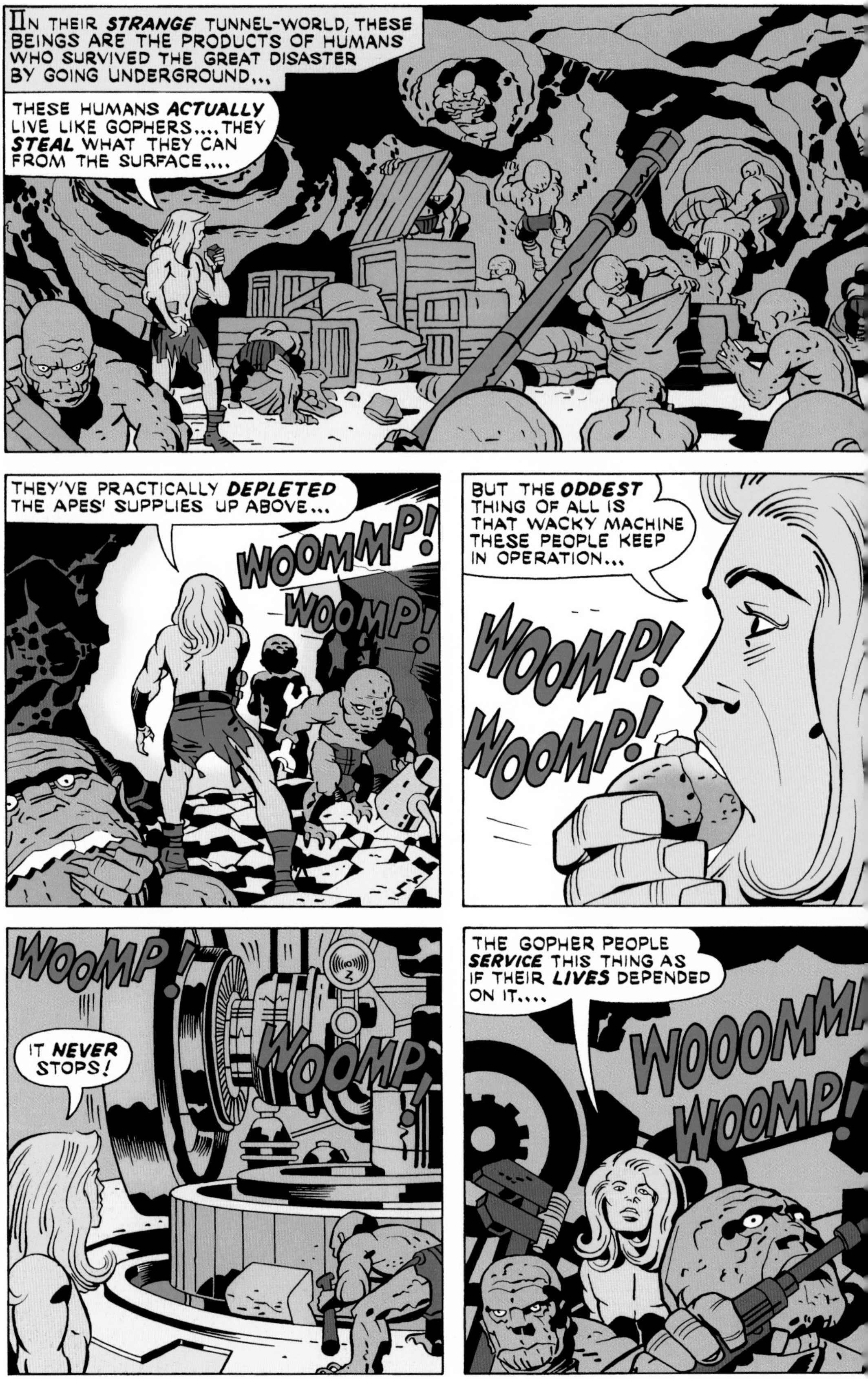
IN THEIR STRANGE TUNNEL-WORLD, THESE BEINGS ARE THE PRODUCTS OF HUMANS WHO SURVIVED THE GREAT DISASTER BY GOING UNDERGROUND,..
THESE HUMANS ACTUALLY LIVE LIKE GOPHERS.... THEY STEAL WHAT THEY CAN FROM THE SURFACE,...
THEY'VE PRACTICALLY DEPLETED THE APES' SUPPLIES UP ABOVE...
WOOMMP!
WOOMP!
BUT THE ODDEST THING OF ALL IS THAT WACKY MACHINE THESE PEOPLE KEEP IN OPERATION...
WOOMP!
WOOMP!
WOOMP!
IT NEVER STOPS!
WOOMP!
THE GOPHER PEOPLE SERVICE THIS THING AS IF THEIR LIVES DEPENDED ON IT....
WOOOMM
WOOMP!

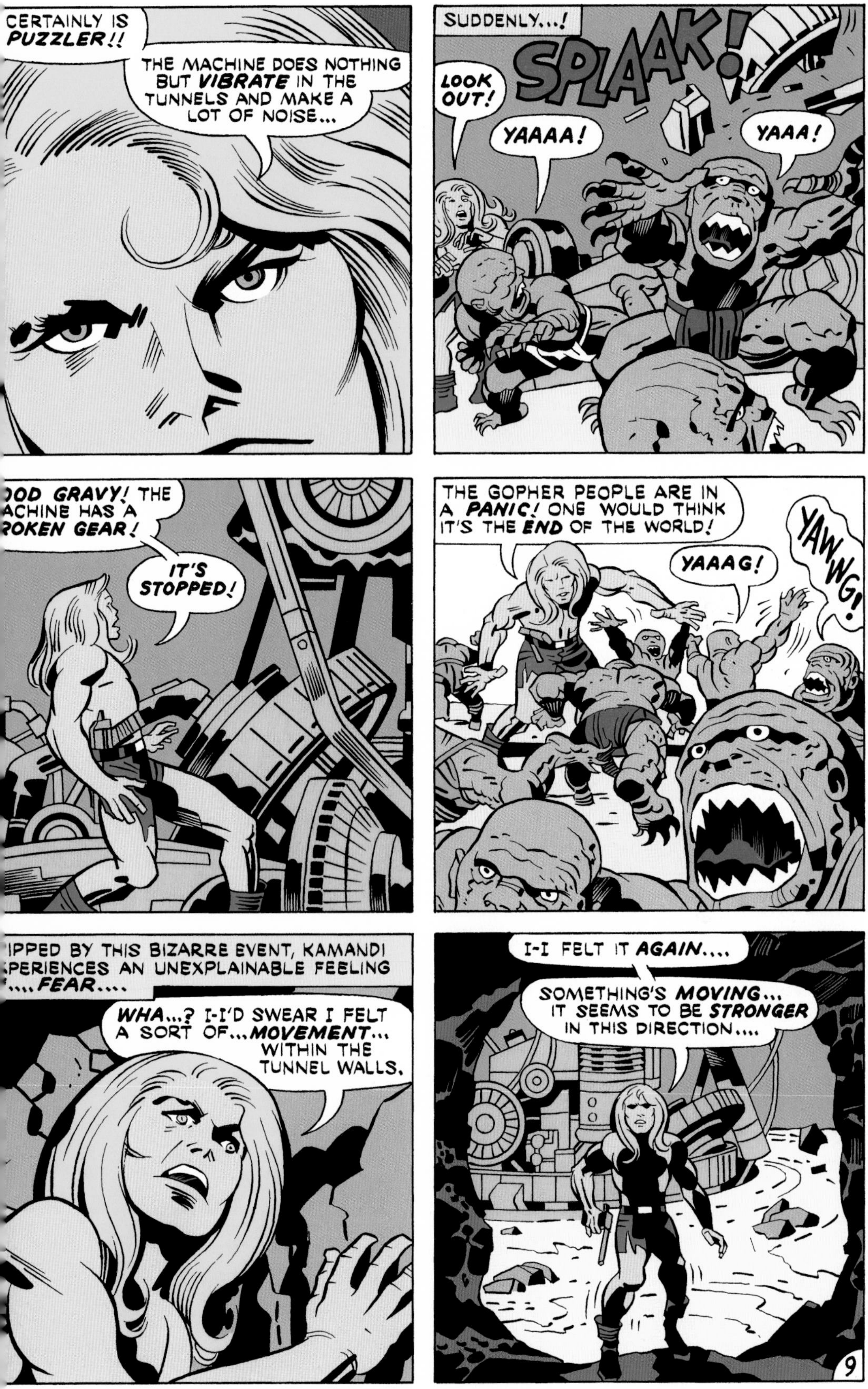
CERTAINLY IS PUZZLER!!
THE MACHINE DOES NOTHING BUT VIBRATE IN THE TUNNELS AND MAKE A LOT OF NOISE...
SUDDENLY...!
SPLAAK!
LOOK OUT!
YAAAA!
YAAA!
OOD GRAVY! THE ACHINE HAS A ROKEN GEAR!
IT'S STOPPED!
THE GOPHER PEOPLE ARE IN A PANIC! ONE WOULD THINK IT'S THE END OF THE WORLD!
YAAAG!
YAWWG!
IPPED BY THIS BIZARRE EVENT, KAMANDI PERIENCES AN UNEXPLAINABLE FEELING ....FEAR....
WHA...? I-I'D SWEAR I FELT A SORT OF...MOVEMENT... WITHIN THE TUNNEL WALLS.
I-I FELT IT AGAIN....
SOMETHING'S MOVING... IT SEEMS TO BE STRONGER IN THIS DIRECTION....
9

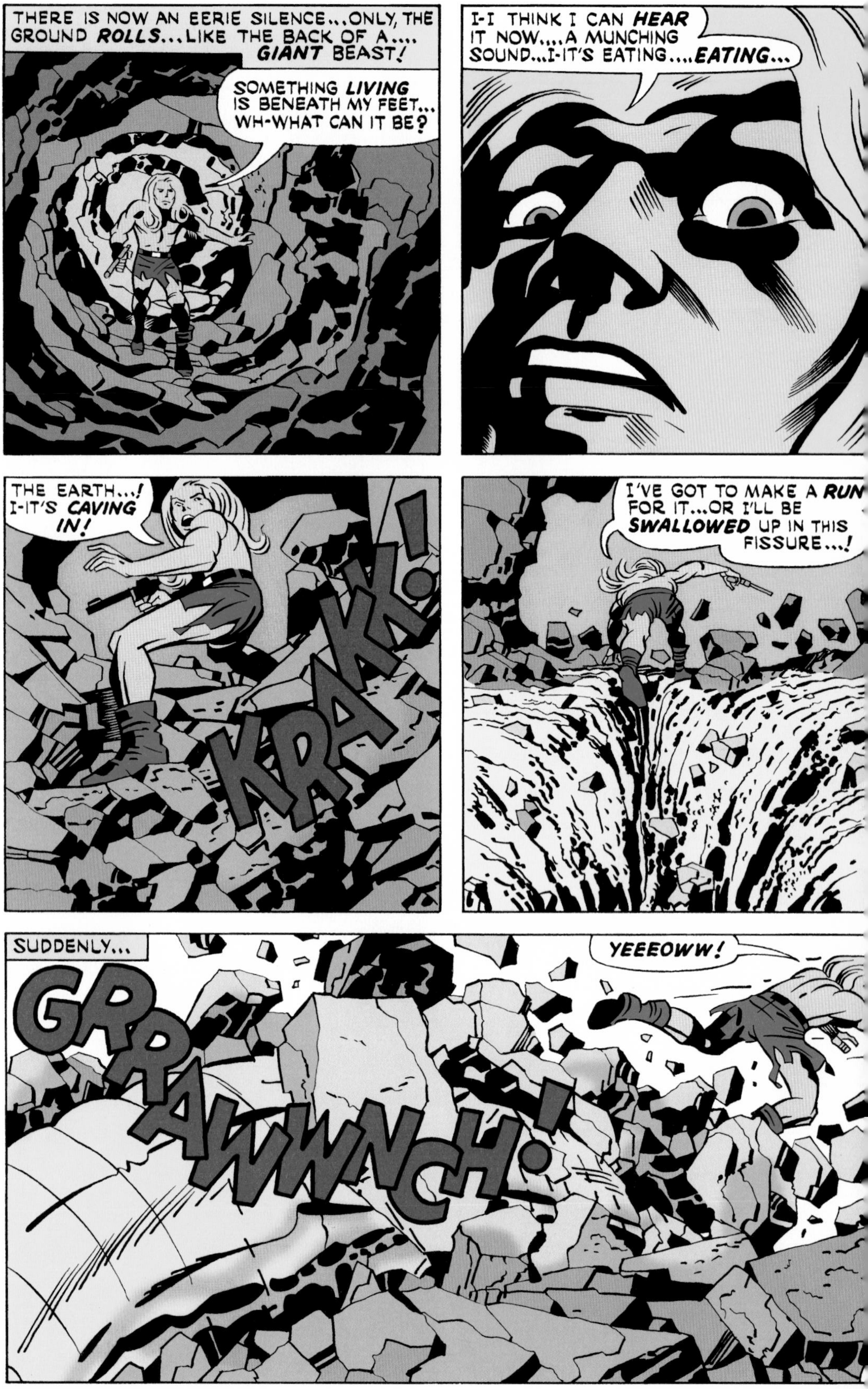
THERE IS NOW AN EERIE SILENCE...ONLY, THE GROUND ROLLS...LIKE THE BACK OF A.... GIANT BEAST!
SOMETHING LIVING IS BENEATH MY FEET... WH-WHAT CAN IT BE?
I-I THINK I CAN HEAR IT NOW....A MUNCHING SOUND...I-IT'S EATING....EATING...
THE EARTH...! I-IT'S CAVING IN!
KRAKK!
I'VE GOT TO MAKE A RUN FOR IT...OR I'LL BE SWALLOWED UP IN THIS FISSURE...!
SUDDENLY...
YEEEOWW!
GRRAWWNCH!

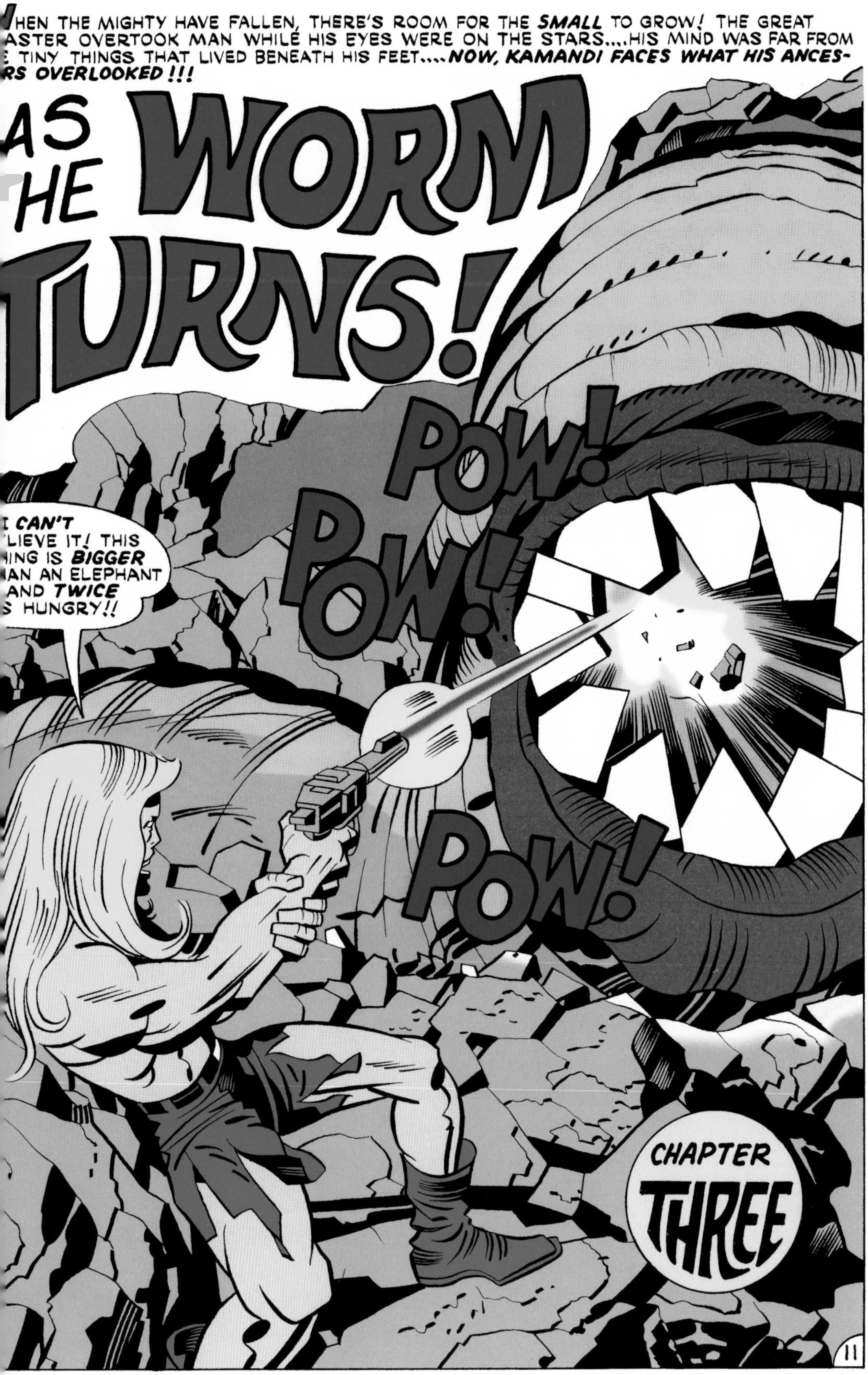
HEN THE MIGHTY HAVE FALLEN, THERE'S ROOM FOR THE SMALL TO GROW! THE GREAT
ASTER OVERTOOK MAN WHILE HIS EYES WERE ON THE STARS....HIS MIND WAS FAR FROM
TINY THINGS THAT LIVED BENEATH HIS FEET....NOW, KAMANDI FACES WHAT HIS ANCES-
RS OVERLOOKED!!!
AS HE WORM TURNS!
POW!
POW!
I CAN'T LIEVE IT! THIS IING IS BIGGER IAN AN ELEPHANT AND TWICE S HUNGRY!!
POW!
CHAPTER THREE
11

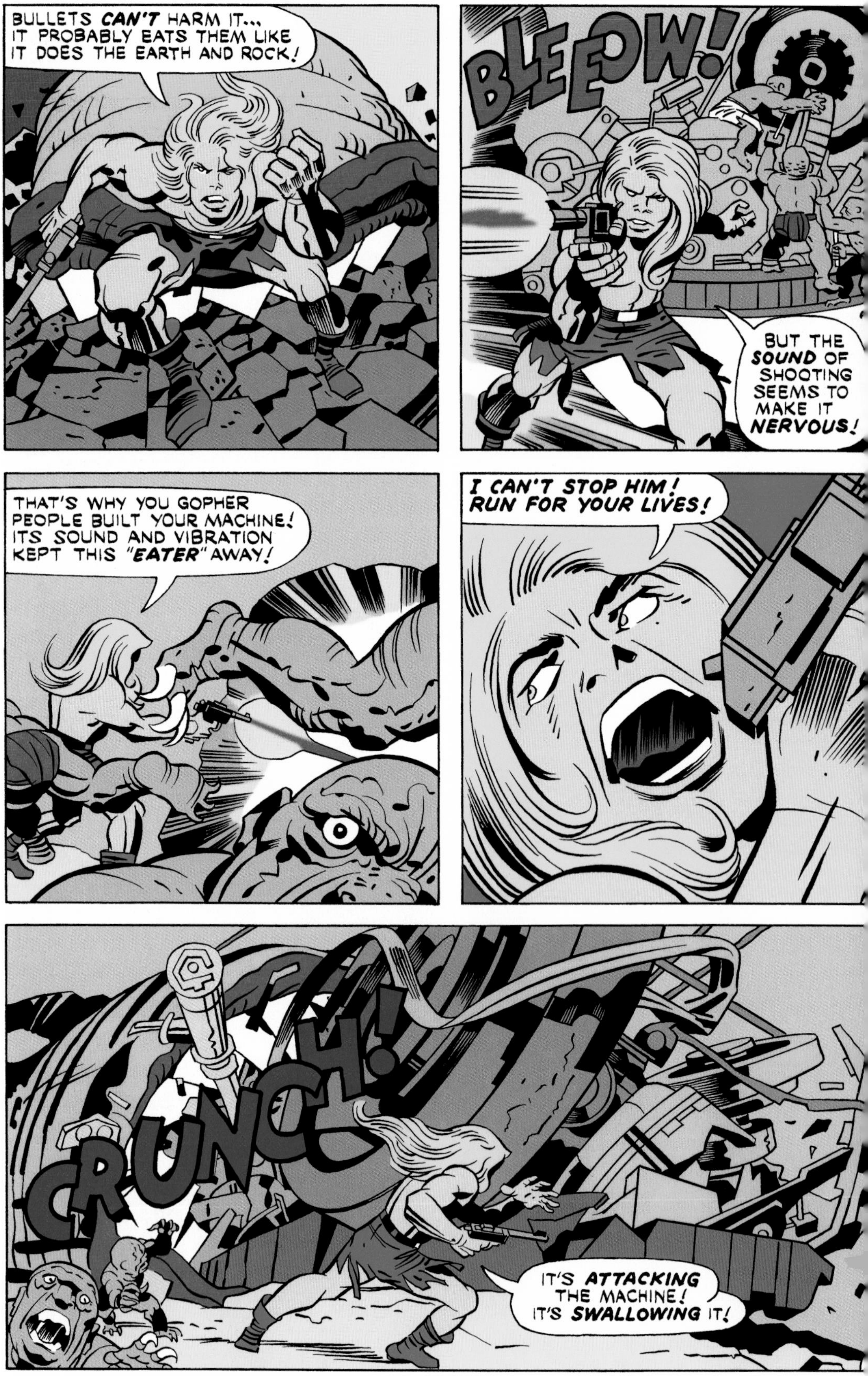
BULLETS CAN'T HARM IT... IT PROBABLY EATS THEM LIKE IT DOES THE EARTH AND ROCK!
BLEEOW!
BUT THE SOUND OF SHOOTING SEEMS TO MAKE IT NERVOUS!
THAT'S WHY YOU GOPHER PEOPLE BUILT YOUR MACHINE! ITS SOUND AND VIBRATION KEPT THIS "EATER" AWAY!
I CAN'T STOP HIM! RUN FOR YOUR LIVES!
CRUNCH!
IT'S ATTACKING THE MACHINE! IT'S SWALLOWING IT!

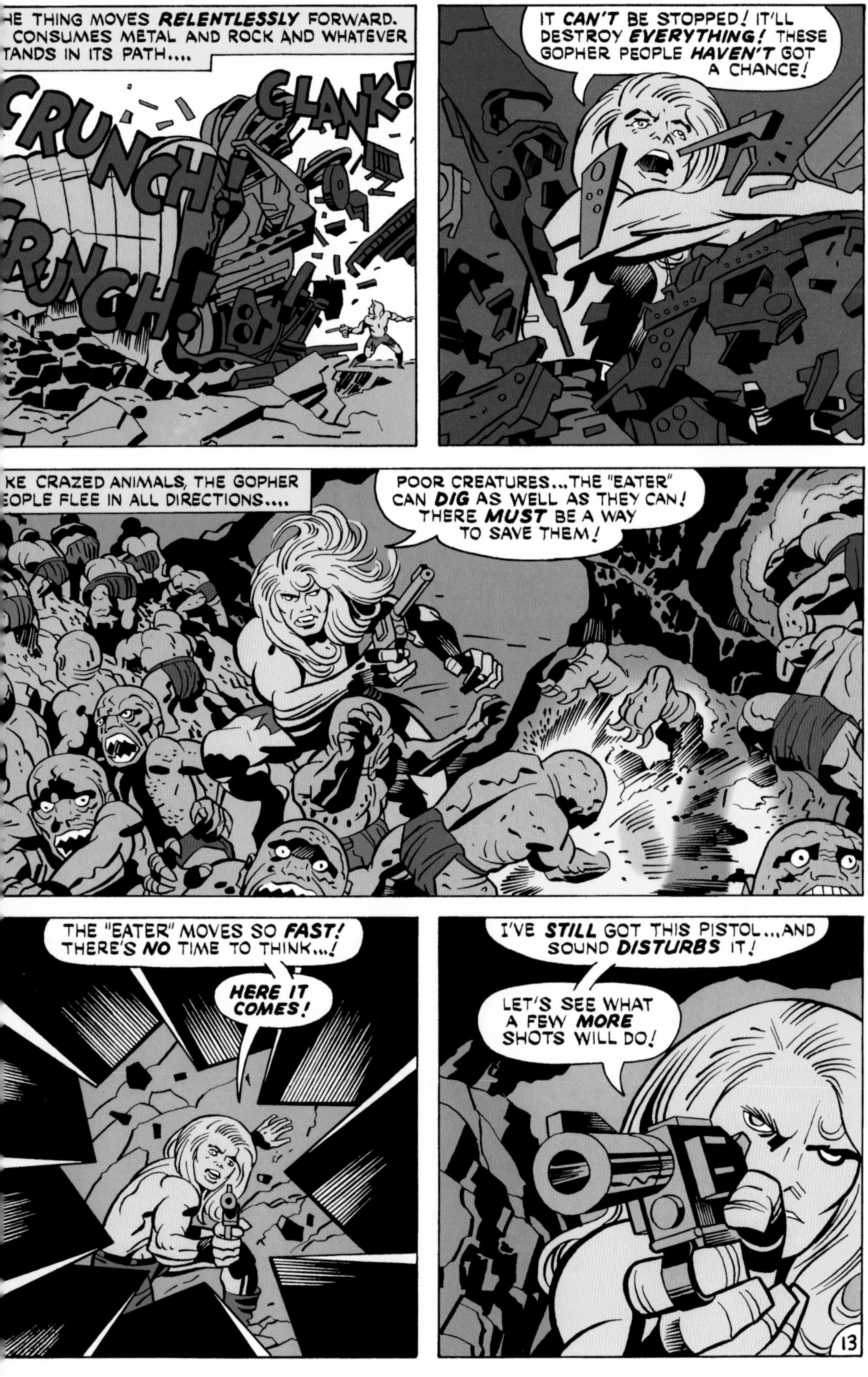
HE THING MOVES RELENTLESSLY FORWARD. CONSUMES METAL AND ROCK AND WHATEVER TANDS IN ITS PATH....
CRUNCH!
CLANK!
CRUNCH!
IT CAN'T BE STOPPED! IT'LL DESTROY EVERYTHING! THESE GOPHER PEOPLE HAVEN'T GOT A CHANCE!
KE CRAZED ANIMALS, THE GOPHER EOPLE FLEE IN ALL DIRECTIONS....
POOR CREATURES...THE "EATER" CAN DIG AS WELL AS THEY CAN! THERE MUST BE A WAY TO SAVE THEM!
THE "EATER" MOVES SO FAST! THERE'S NO TIME TO THINK...!
HERE IT COMES!
I'VE STILL GOT THIS PISTOL...AND SOUND DISTURBS IT!
LET'S SEE WHAT A FEW MORE SHOTS WILL DO!
13

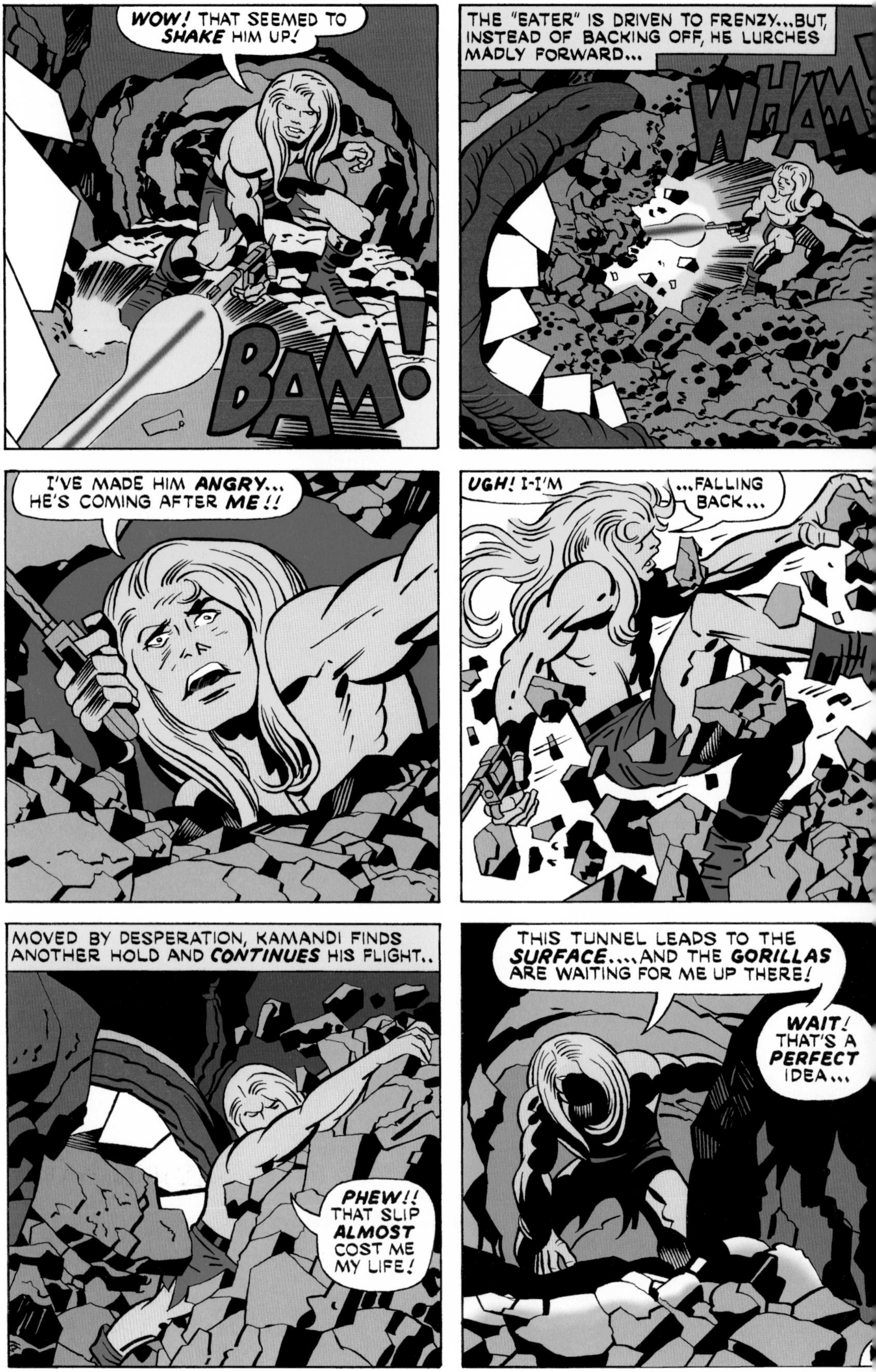
WOW! THAT SEEMED TO SHAKE HIM UP!
BAM!
THE "EATER" IS DRIVEN TO FRENZY...BUT, INSTEAD OF BACKING OFF, HE LURCHES MADLY FORWARD...
WHAM!
I'VE MADE HIM ANGRY... HE'S COMING AFTER ME!!
UGH! I-I'M
...FALLING BACK...
MOVED BY DESPERATION, KAMANDI FINDS ANOTHER HOLD AND CONTINUES HIS FLIGHT..
PHEW!! THAT SLIP ALMOST COST ME MY LIFE!
THIS TUNNEL LEADS TO THE SURFACE....AND THE GORILLAS ARE WAITING FOR ME UP THERE!
WAIT! THAT'S A PERFECT IDEA...

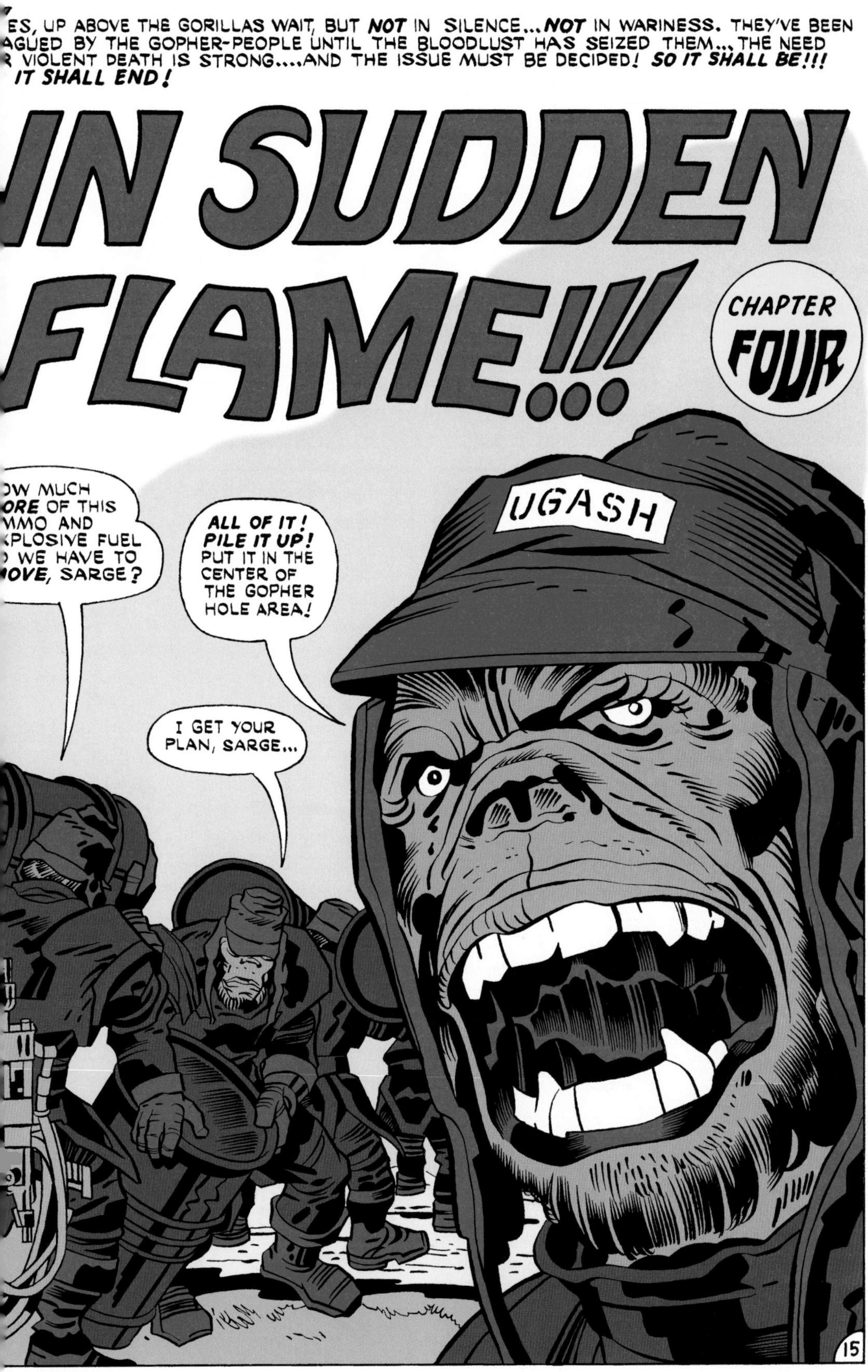
ES, UP ABOVE THE GORILLAS WAIT, BUT NOT IN SILENCE...NOT IN WARINESS. THEY'VE BEEN
AGUED BY THE GOPHER-PEOPLE UNTIL THE BLOODLUST HAS SEIZED THEM...THE NEED
R VIOLENT DEATH IS STRONG....AND THE ISSUE MUST BE DECIDED! SO IT SHALL BE!!!
IT SHALL END!
IN SUDDEN FLAME!!!...
CHAPTER FOUR
UGASH
OW MUCH ORE OF THIS MMO AND XPLOSIVE FUEL O WE HAVE TO MOVE, SARGE?
ALL OF IT! PILE IT UP! PUT IT IN THE CENTER OF THE GOPHER HOLE AREA!
I GET YOUR PLAN, SARGE...
15

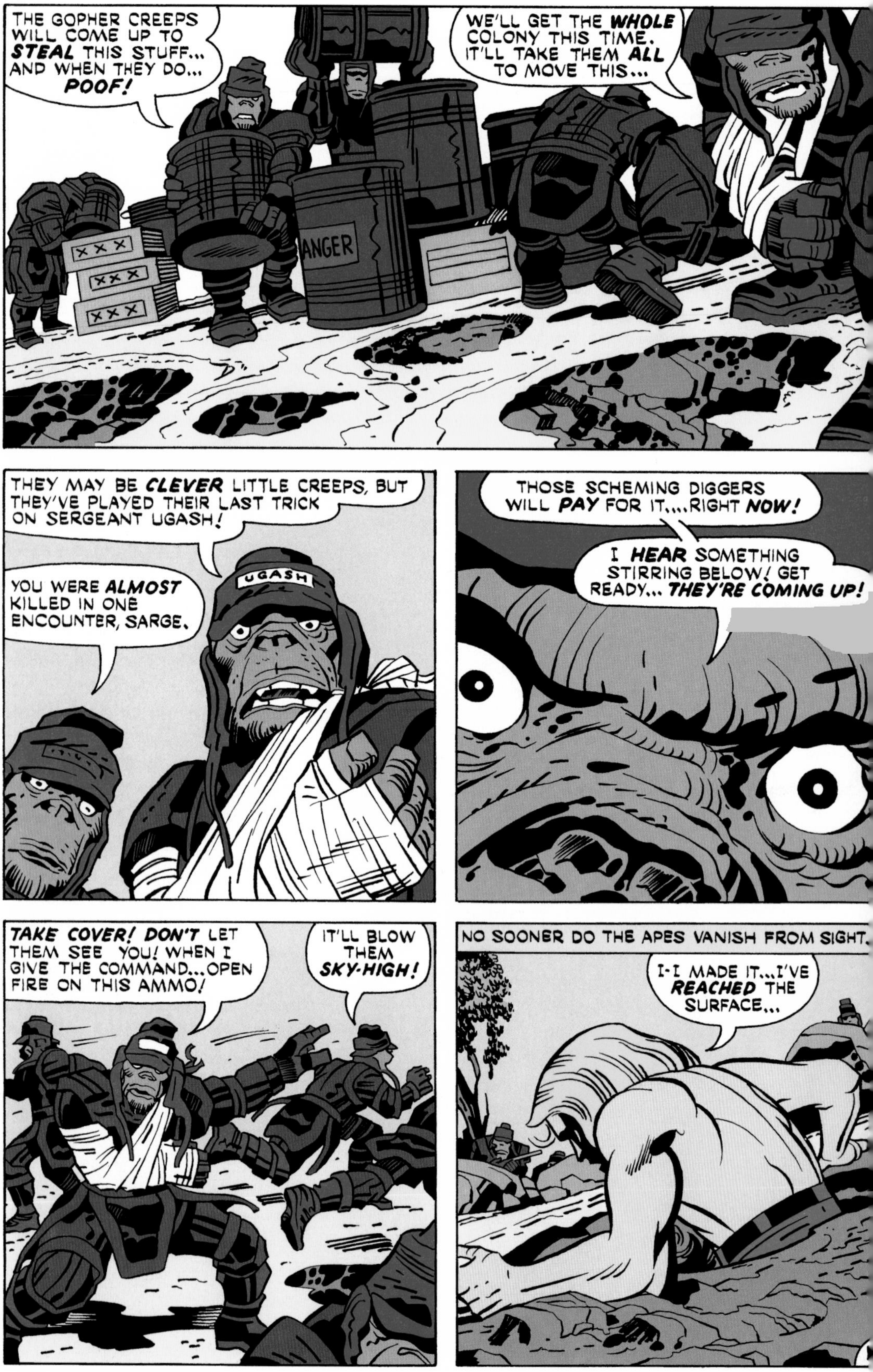
THE GOPHER CREEPS WILL COME UP TO STEAL THIS STUFF... AND WHEN THEY DO... POOF!
WE'LL GET THE WHOLE COLONY THIS TIME. IT'LL TAKE THEM ALL TO MOVE THIS...
ANGER
THEY MAY BE CLEVER LITTLE CREEPS, BUT THEY'VE PLAYED THEIR LAST TRICK ON SERGEANT UGASH!
YOU WERE ALMOST KILLED IN ONE ENCOUNTER, SARGE.
UGASH
THOSE SCHEMING DIGGERS WILL PAY FOR IT....RIGHT NOW!
I HEAR SOMETHING STIRRING BELOW! GET READY... THEY'RE COMING UP!
TAKE COVER! DON'T LET THEM SEE YOU! WHEN I GIVE THE COMMAND...OPEN FIRE ON THIS AMMO!
IT'LL BLOW THEM SKY-HIGH!
NO SOONER DO THE APES VANISH FROM SIGHT,
I-I MADE IT...I'VE REACHED THE SURFACE...

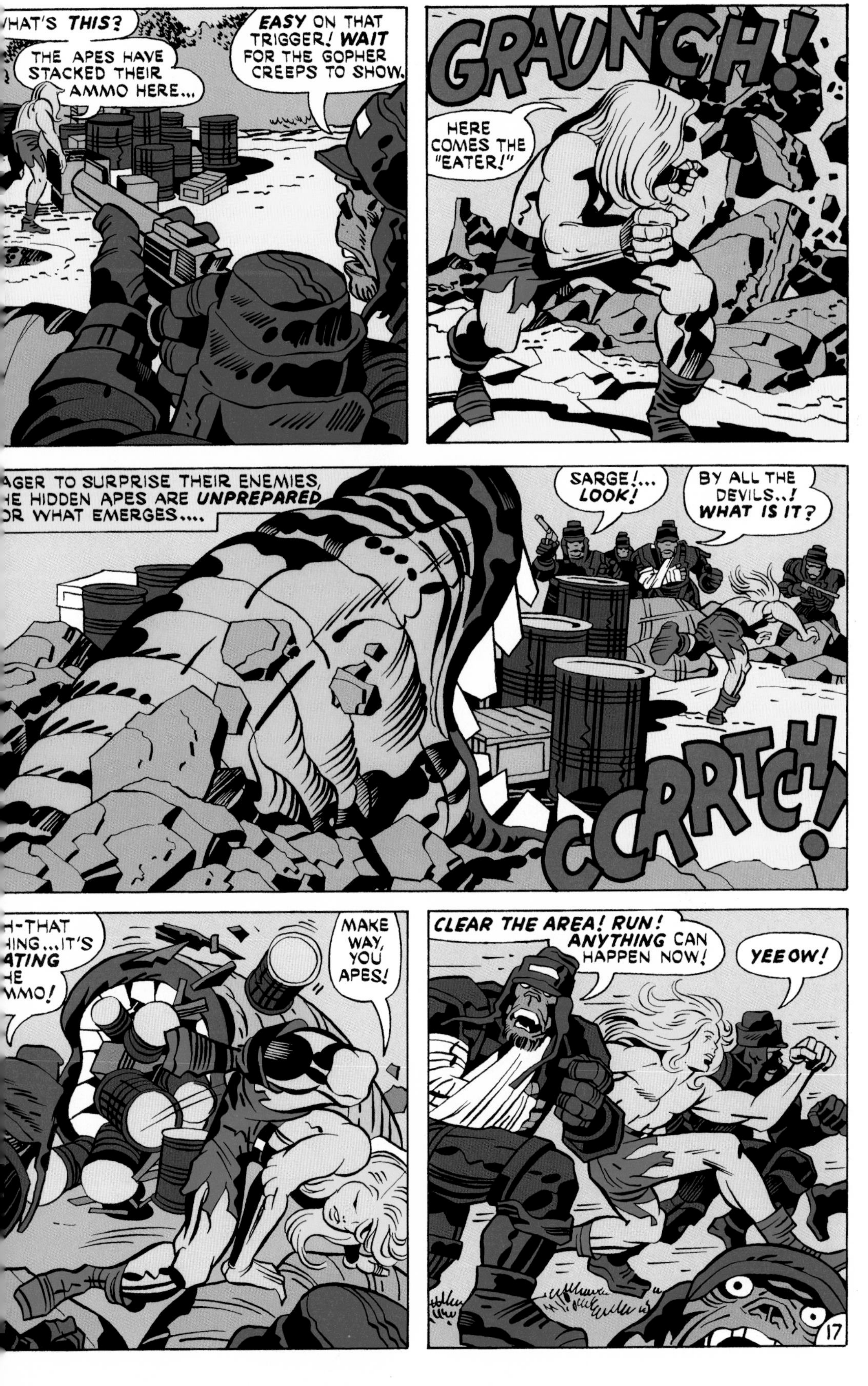
HAT'S THIS?
THE APES HAVE STACKED THEIR AMMO HERE...
EASY ON THAT TRIGGER! WAIT FOR THE GOPHER CREEPS TO SHOW.
GRAUNCH!
HERE COMES THE "EATER!"
AGER TO SURPRISE THEIR ENEMIES, HE HIDDEN APES ARE UNPREPARED OR WHAT EMERGES....
SARGE!... LOOK!
BY ALL THE DEVILS..! WHAT IS IT?
CCRRTCH!
H-THAT HING...IT'S ATING HE MMO!
MAKE WAY, YOU APES!
CLEAR THE AREA! RUN! ANYTHING CAN HAPPEN NOW!
YEEOW!
17

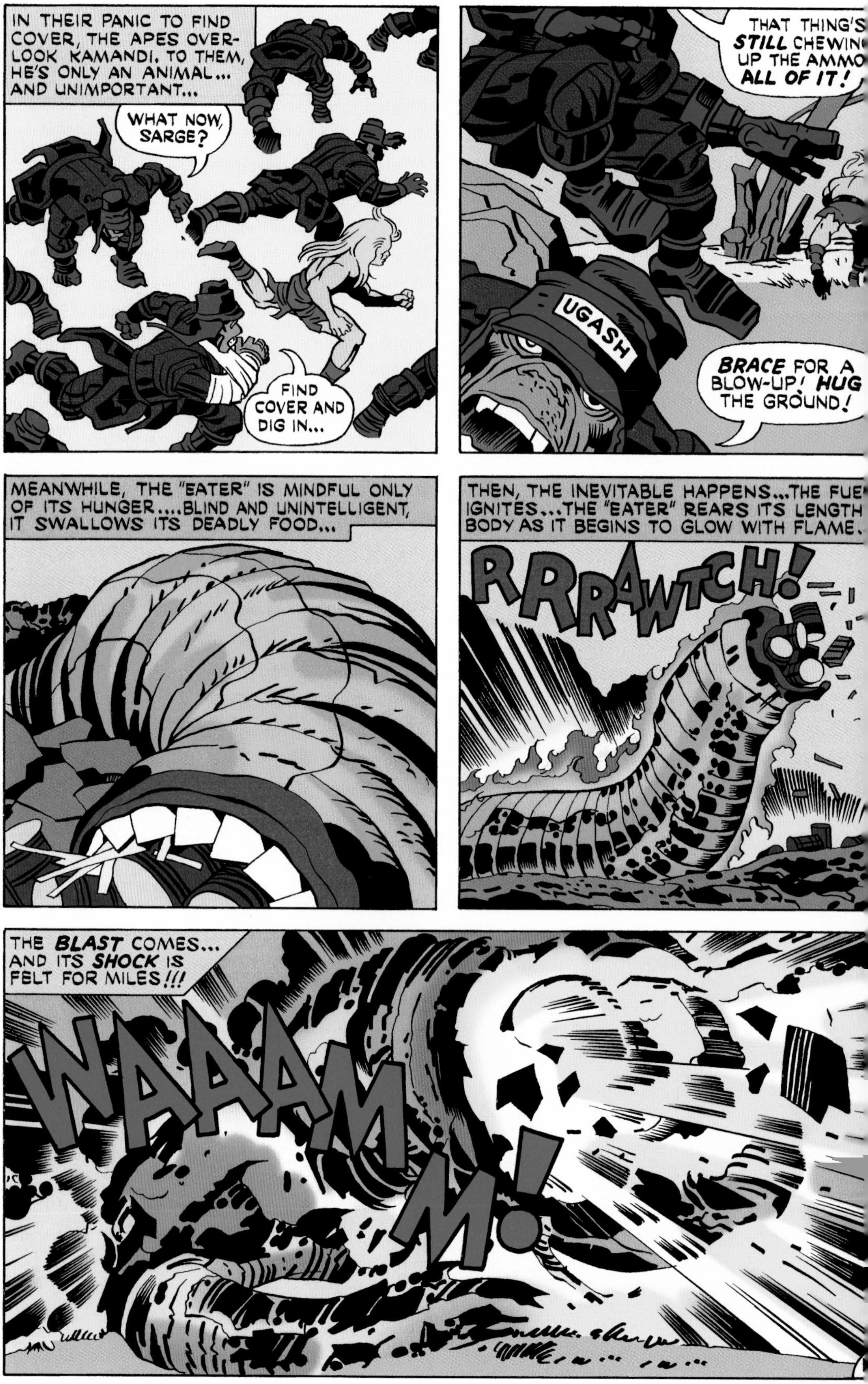
IN THEIR PANIC TO FIND COVER, THE APES OVERLOOK KAMANDI. TO THEM, HE'S ONLY AN ANIMAL... AND UNIMPORTANT...
WHAT NOW, SARGE?
FIND COVER AND DIG IN...
THAT THING'S STILL CHEWIN UP THE AMMO ALL OF IT!
UGASH
BRACE FOR A BLOW-UP! HUG THE GROUND!
MEANWHILE, THE "EATER" IS MINDFUL ONLY OF ITS HUNGER....BLIND AND UNINTELLIGENT, IT SWALLOWS ITS DEADLY FOOD...
THEN, THE INEVITABLE HAPPENS...THE FUE IGNITES...THE "EATER" REARS ITS LENGTH BODY AS IT BEGINS TO GLOW WITH FLAME.
RRRAWTCH!
THE BLAST COMES... AND ITS SHOCK IS FELT FOR MILES!!!
WAAAMM!

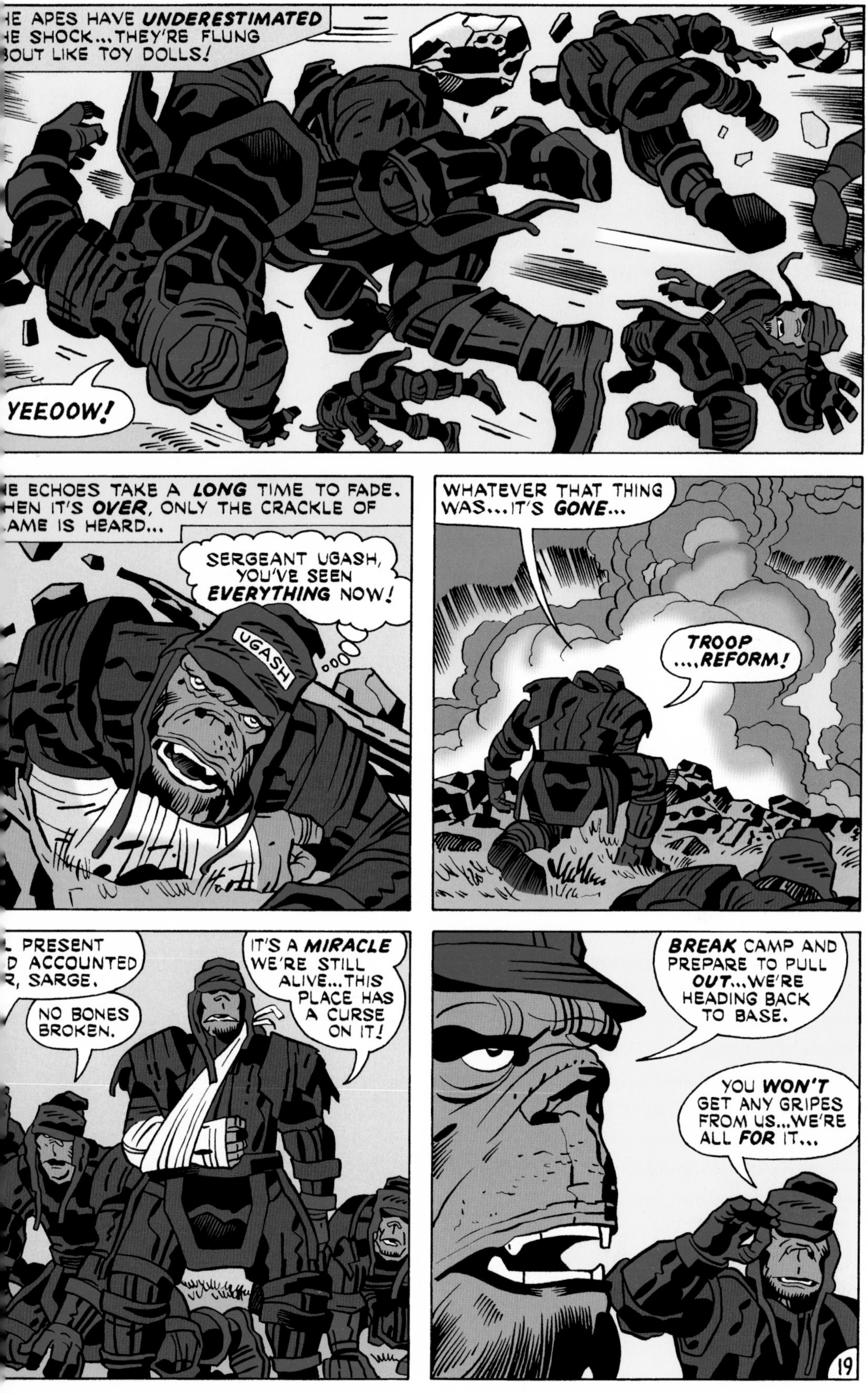
IE APES HAVE UNDERESTIMATED
IE SHOCK...THEY'RE FLUNG
BOUT LIKE TOY DOLLS!
YEEOOW!
IE ECHOES TAKE A LONG TIME TO FADE.
HEN IT'S OVER, ONLY THE CRACKLE OF
AME IS HEARD...
SERGEANT UGASH, YOU'VE SEEN EVERYTHING NOW!
UGASH
WHATEVER THAT THING WAS...IT'S GONE...
TROOP ...,REFORM!
L PRESENT
D ACCOUNTED
R, SARGE.
NO BONES BROKEN.
IT'S A MIRACLE WE'RE STILL ALIVE...THIS PLACE HAS A CURSE ON IT!
BREAK CAMP AND PREPARE TO PULL OUT...WE'RE HEADING BACK TO BASE.
YOU WON'T GET ANY GRIPES FROM US...WE'RE ALL FOR IT...
19

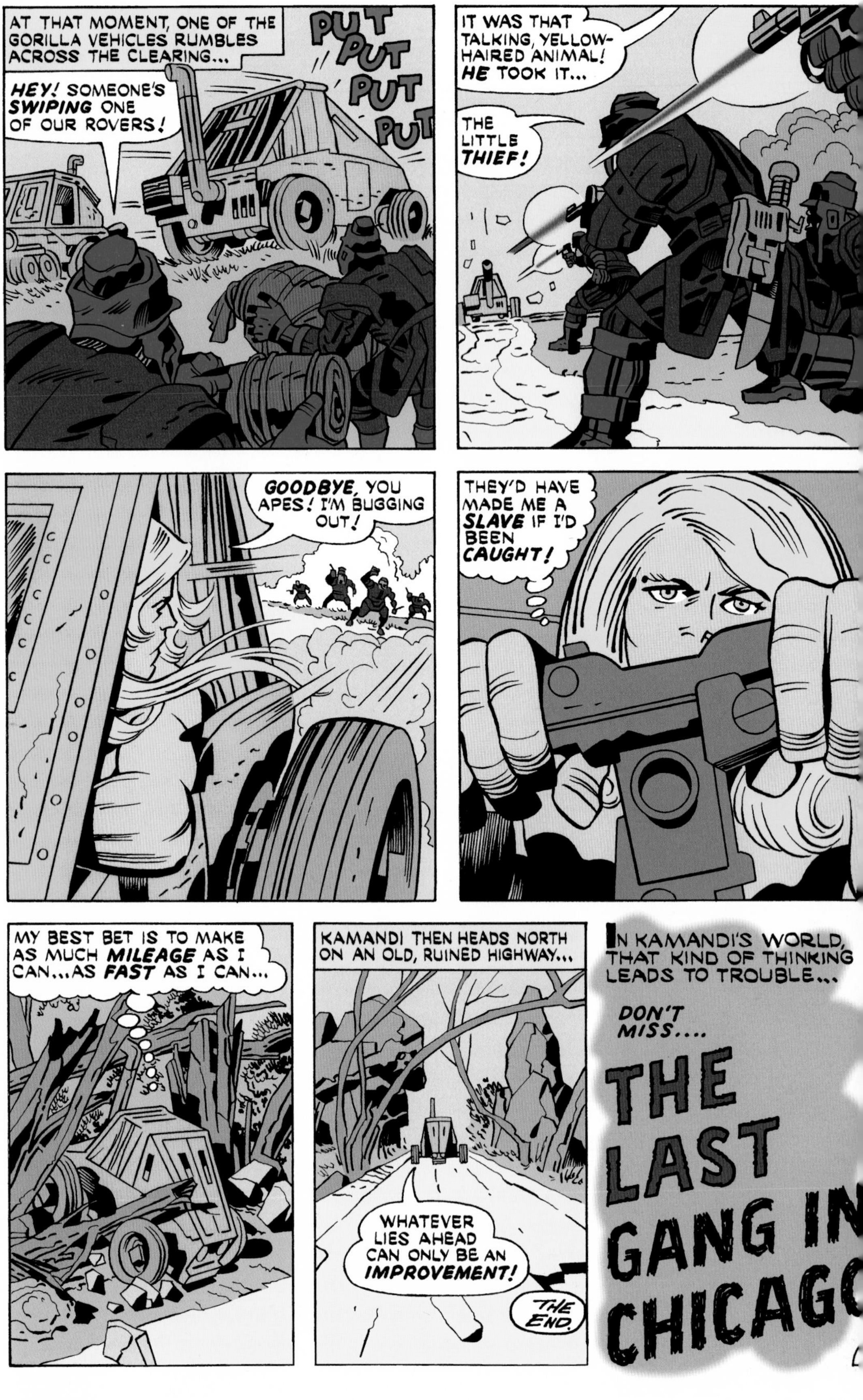
AT THAT MOMENT, ONE OF THE GORILLA VEHICLES RUMBLES ACROSS THE CLEARING...
PUT PUT PUT PUT
HEY! SOMEONE'S SWIPING ONE OF OUR ROVERS!
IT WAS THAT TALKING, YELLOW-HAIRED ANIMAL! HE TOOK IT...
THE LITTLE THIEF!
GOODBYE, YOU APES! I'M BUGGING OUT!
THEY'D HAVE MADE ME A SLAVE IF I'D BEEN CAUGHT!
MY BEST BET IS TO MAKE AS MUCH MILEAGE AS I CAN...AS FAST AS I CAN...
KAMANDI THEN HEADS NORTH ON AN OLD, RUINED HIGHWAY...
WHATEVER LIES AHEAD CAN ONLY BE AN IMPROVEMENT!
THE END.
IN KAMANDI'S WORLD, THAT KIND OF THINKING LEADS TO TROUBLE...
DON'T MISS....
THE LAST GANG IN CHICAGO

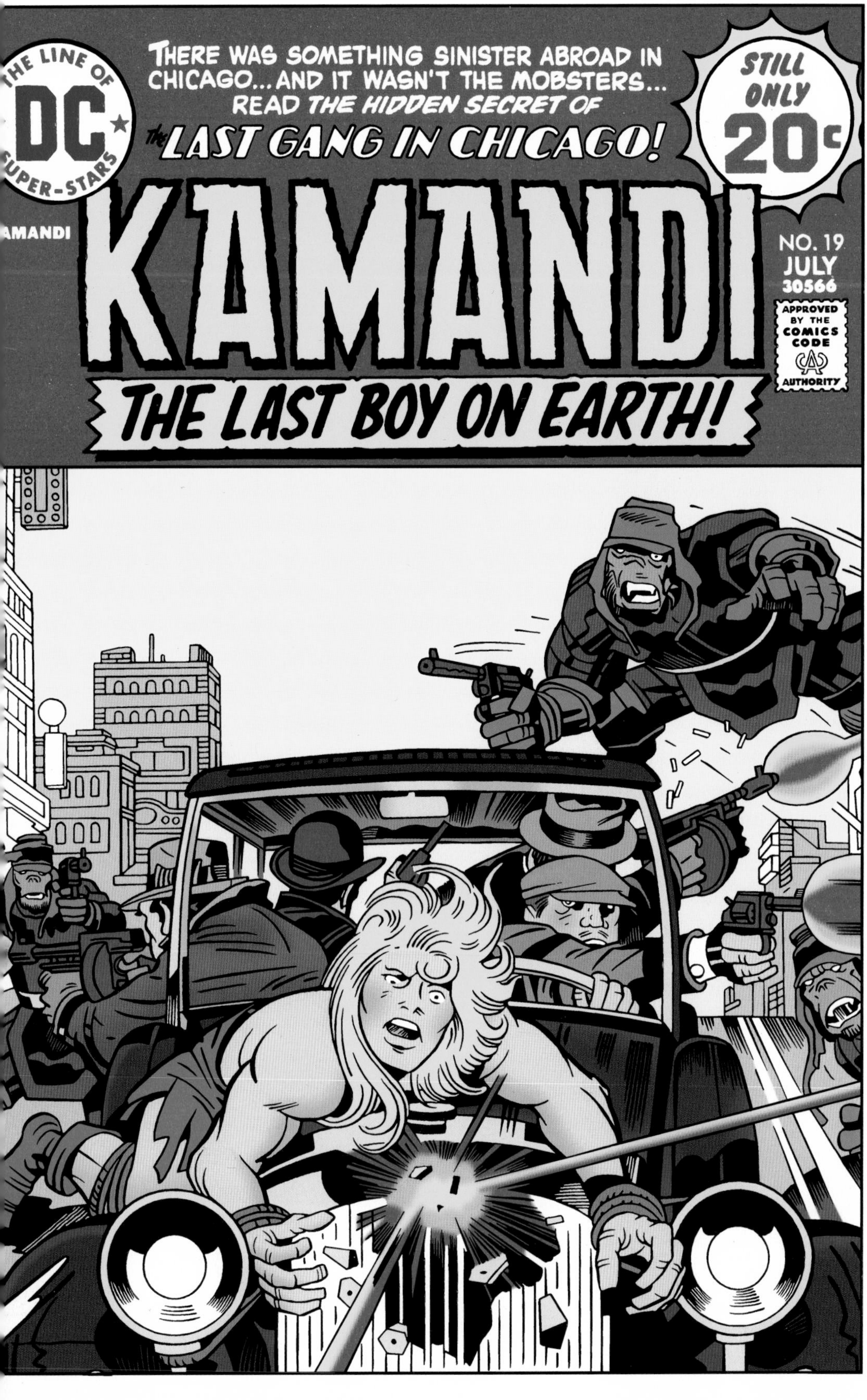
THE LINE OF DC SUPER-STARS
THERE WAS SOMETHING SINISTER ABROAD IN CHICAGO... AND IT WASN'T THE MOBSTERS... READ THE HIDDEN SECRET OF
THE LAST GANG IN CHICAGO!
STILL ONLY 20¢
KAMANDI
KAMANDI
NO. 19
JULY
30566
APPROVED BY THE COMICS CODE AUTHORITY
THE LAST BOY ON EARTH!

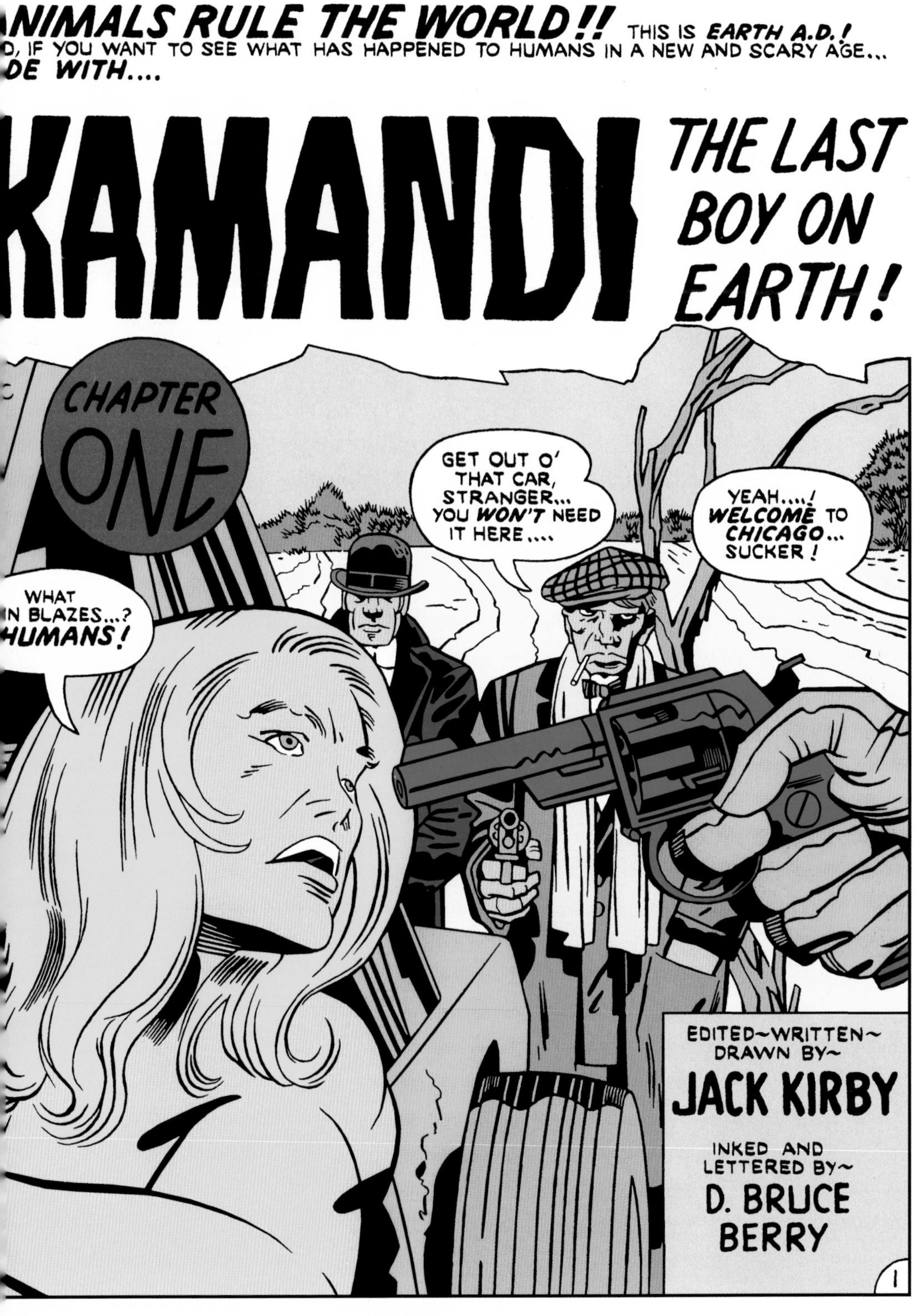
NIMALS RULE THE WORLD!! THIS IS EARTH A.D.!
D, IF YOU WANT TO SEE WHAT HAS HAPPENED TO HUMANS IN A NEW AND SCARY AGE...
DE WITH....
KAMANDI THE LAST BOY ON EARTH!
CHAPTER ONE
GET OUT O' THAT CAR, STRANGER... YOU WON'T NEED IT HERE....
YEAH....! WELCOME TO CHICAGO... SUCKER!
WHAT N BLAZES...? HUMANS!
EDITED~WRITTEN~ DRAWN BY~ JACK KIRBY
INKED AND LETTERED BY~ D. BRUCE BERRY
1

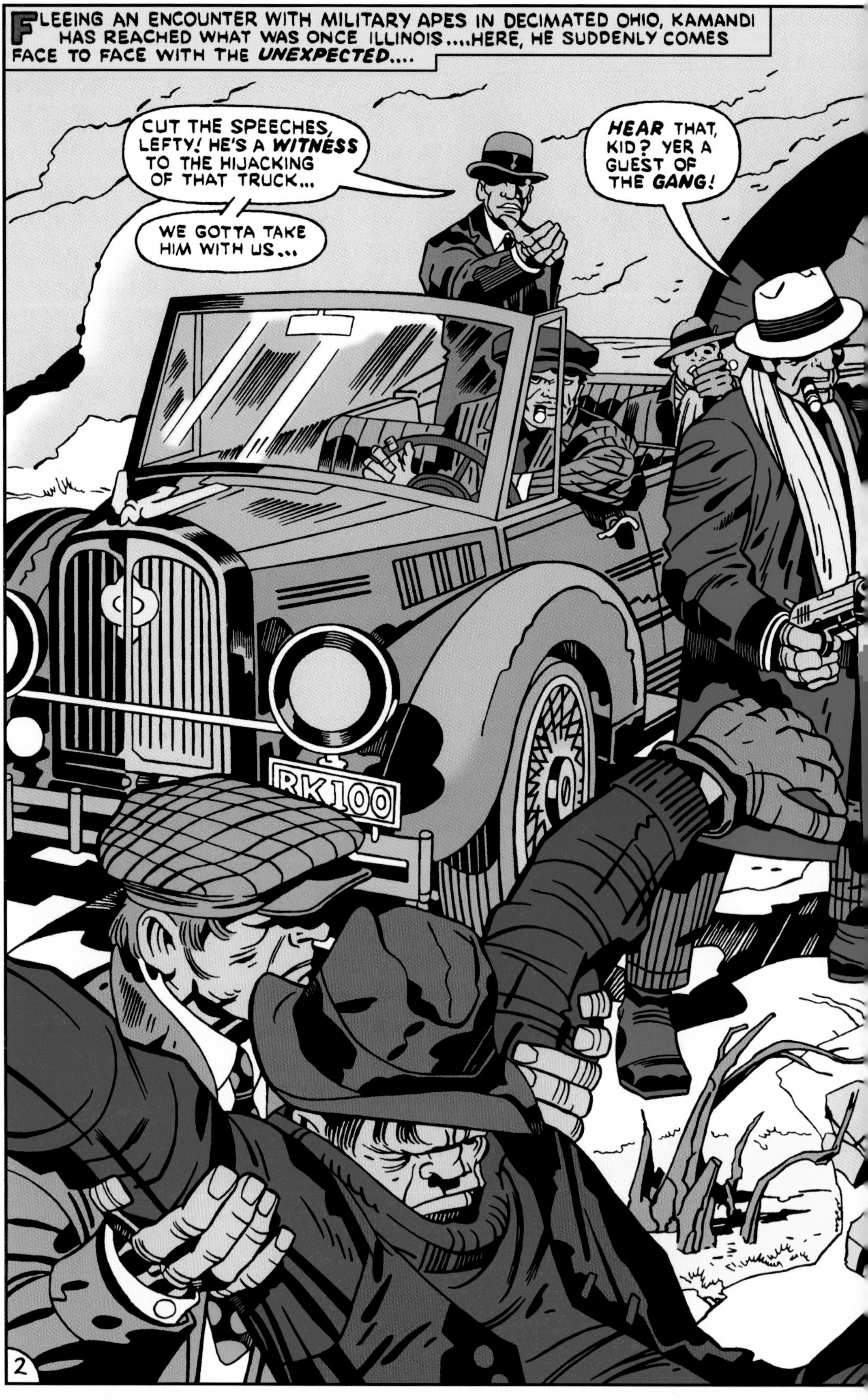
FLEEING AN ENCOUNTER WITH MILITARY APES IN DECIMATED OHIO, KAMANDI HAS REACHED WHAT WAS ONCE ILLINOIS....HERE, HE SUDDENLY COMES FACE TO FACE WITH THE UNEXPECTED....
CUT THE SPEECHES, LEFTY! HE'S A WITNESS TO THE HIJACKING OF THAT TRUCK...
WE GOTTA TAKE HIM WITH US...
HEAR THAT, KID? YER A GUEST OF THE GANG!
RK 100
2

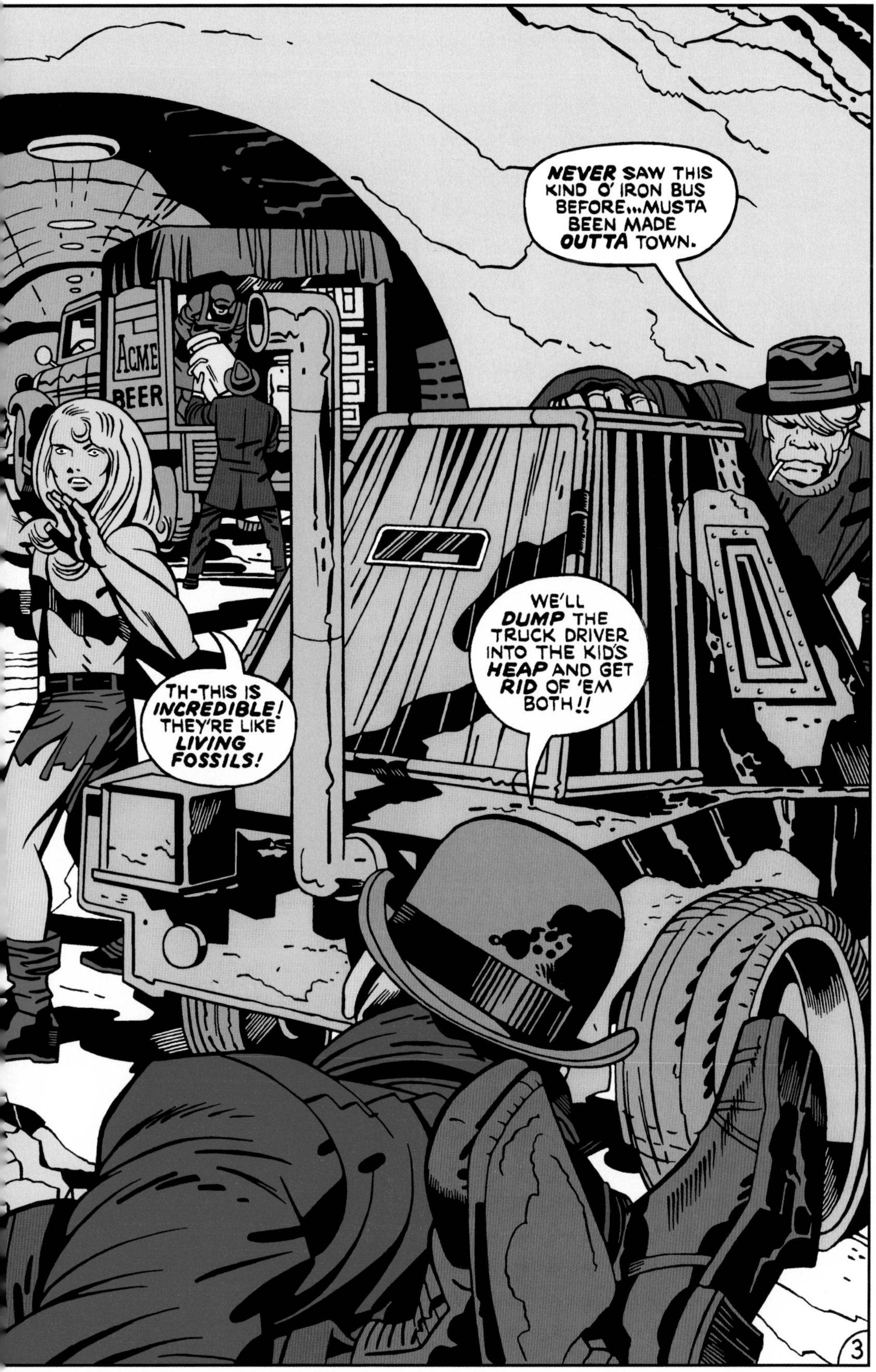
NEVER SAW THIS KIND O' IRON BUS BEFORE...MUSTA BEEN MADE OUTTA TOWN.
ACME BEER
WE'LL DUMP THE TRUCK DRIVER INTO THE KID'S HEAP AND GET RID OF 'EM BOTH!!
TH-THIS IS INCREDIBLE! THEY'RE LIKE LIVING FOSSILS!
3

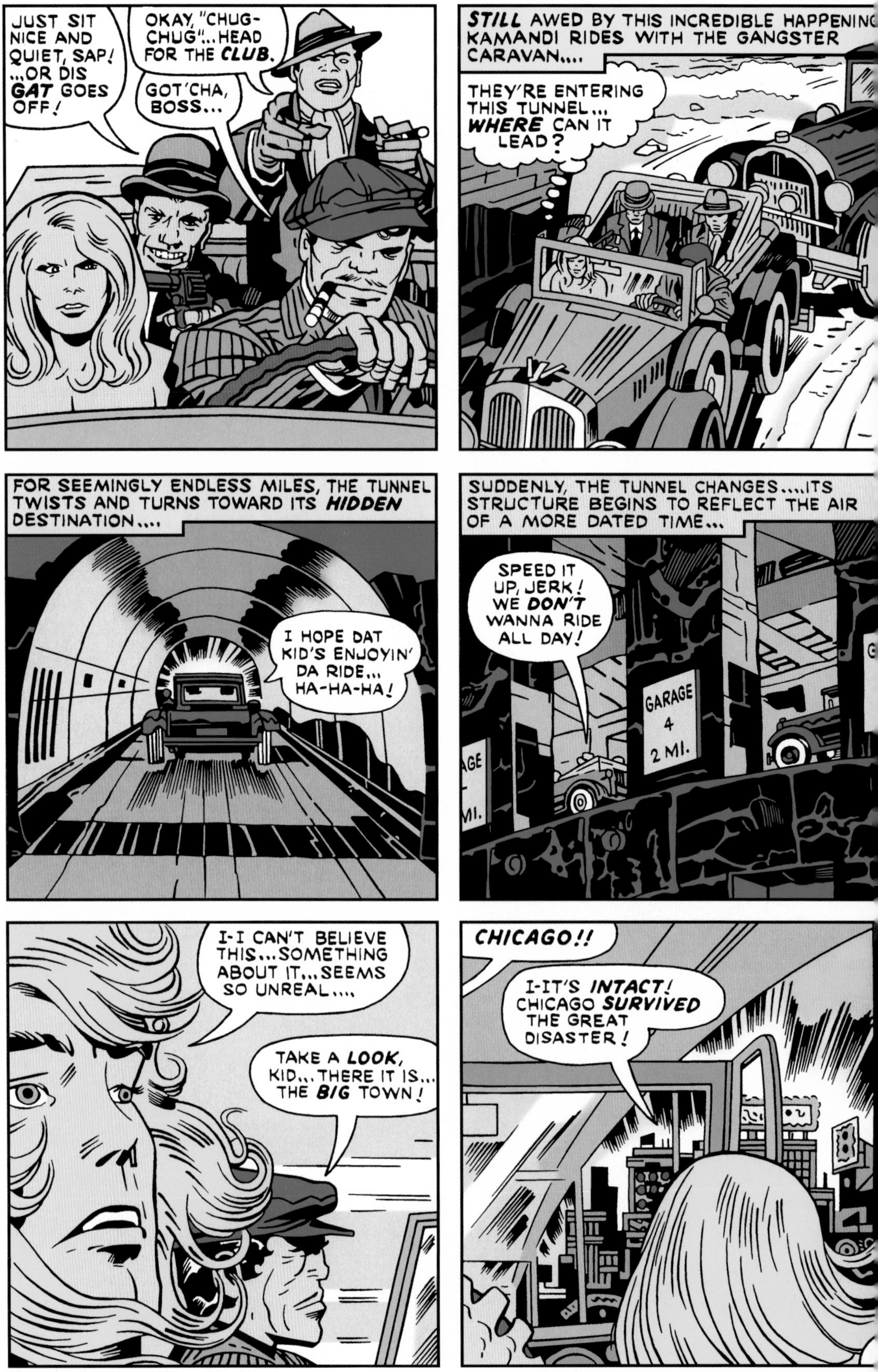
JUST SIT NICE AND QUIET, SAP! ...OR DIS GAT GOES OFF!
OKAY, "CHUG-CHUG"...HEAD FOR THE CLUB.
GOT'CHA, BOSS...
STILL AWED BY THIS INCREDIBLE HAPPENING KAMANDI RIDES WITH THE GANGSTER CARAVAN....
THEY'RE ENTERING THIS TUNNEL... WHERE CAN IT LEAD?
FOR SEEMINGLY ENDLESS MILES, THE TUNNEL TWISTS AND TURNS TOWARD ITS HIDDEN DESTINATION....
I HOPE DAT KID'S ENJOYIN' DA RIDE... HA-HA-HA!
SUDDENLY, THE TUNNEL CHANGES....ITS STRUCTURE BEGINS TO REFLECT THE AIR OF A MORE DATED TIME...
SPEED IT UP, JERK! WE DON'T WANNA RIDE ALL DAY!
GARAGE 4 2 MI.
I-I CAN'T BELIEVE THIS...SOMETHING ABOUT IT...SEEMS SO UNREAL....
TAKE A LOOK, KID... THERE IT IS... THE BIG TOWN!
CHICAGO!!
I-IT'S INTACT! CHICAGO SURVIVED THE GREAT DISASTER!

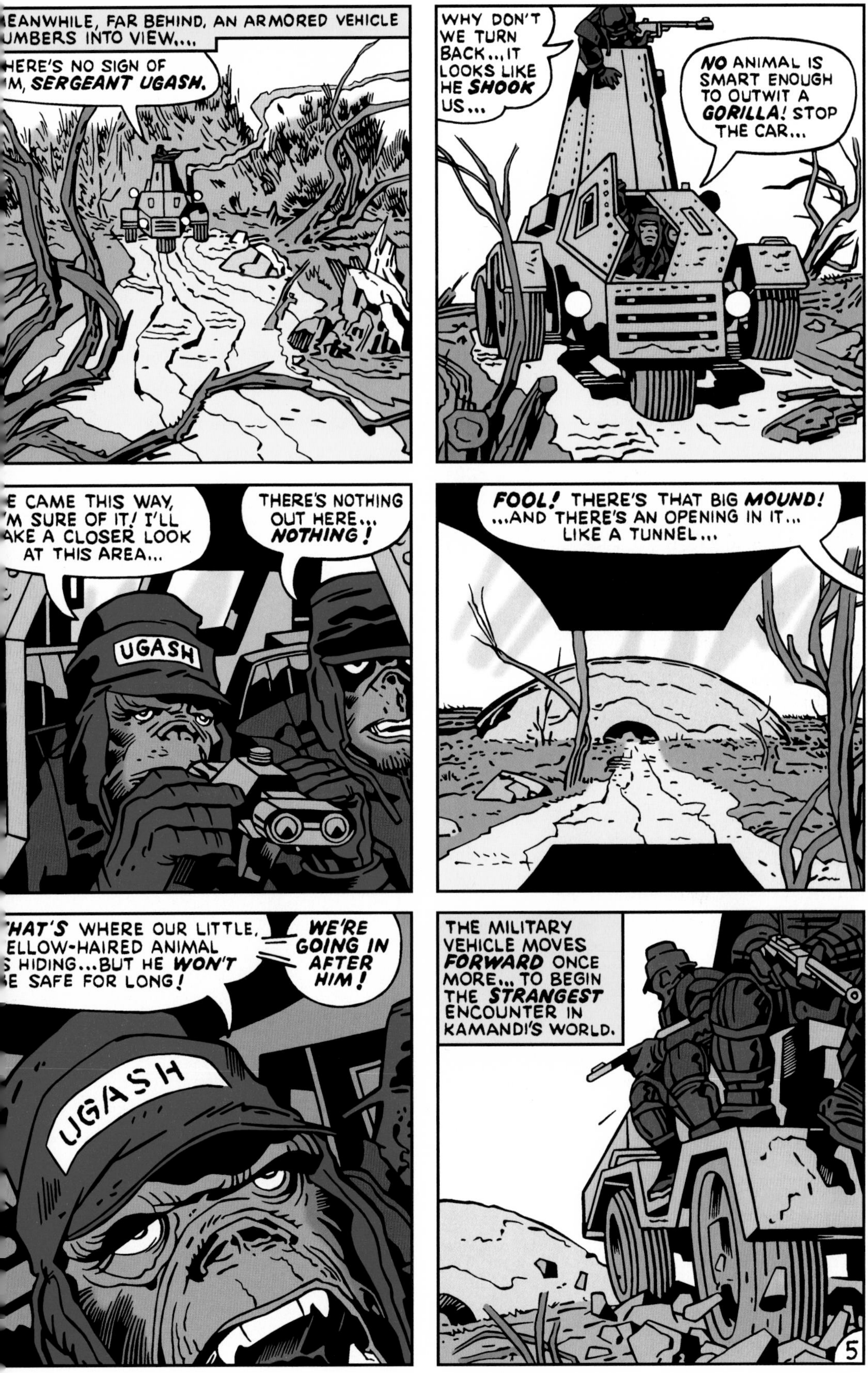
EANWHILE, FAR BEHIND, AN ARMORED VEHICLE
UMBERS INTO VIEW...
HERE'S NO SIGN OF
M, SERGEANT UGASH.
WHY DON'T WE TURN BACK... IT LOOKS LIKE HE SHOOK US...
NO ANIMAL IS SMART ENOUGH TO OUTWIT A GORILLA! STOP THE CAR...
E CAME THIS WAY,
M SURE OF IT! I'LL
AKE A CLOSER LOOK
AT THIS AREA...
THERE'S NOTHING OUT HERE... NOTHING!
UGASH
FOOL! THERE'S THAT BIG MOUND! ...AND THERE'S AN OPENING IN IT... LIKE A TUNNEL...
HAT'S WHERE OUR LITTLE,
ELLOW-HAIRED ANIMAL
S HIDING...BUT HE WON'T
E SAFE FOR LONG!
WE'RE GOING IN AFTER HIM!
UGASH
THE MILITARY VEHICLE MOVES FORWARD ONCE MORE... TO BEGIN THE STRANGEST ENCOUNTER IN KAMANDI'S WORLD.
5

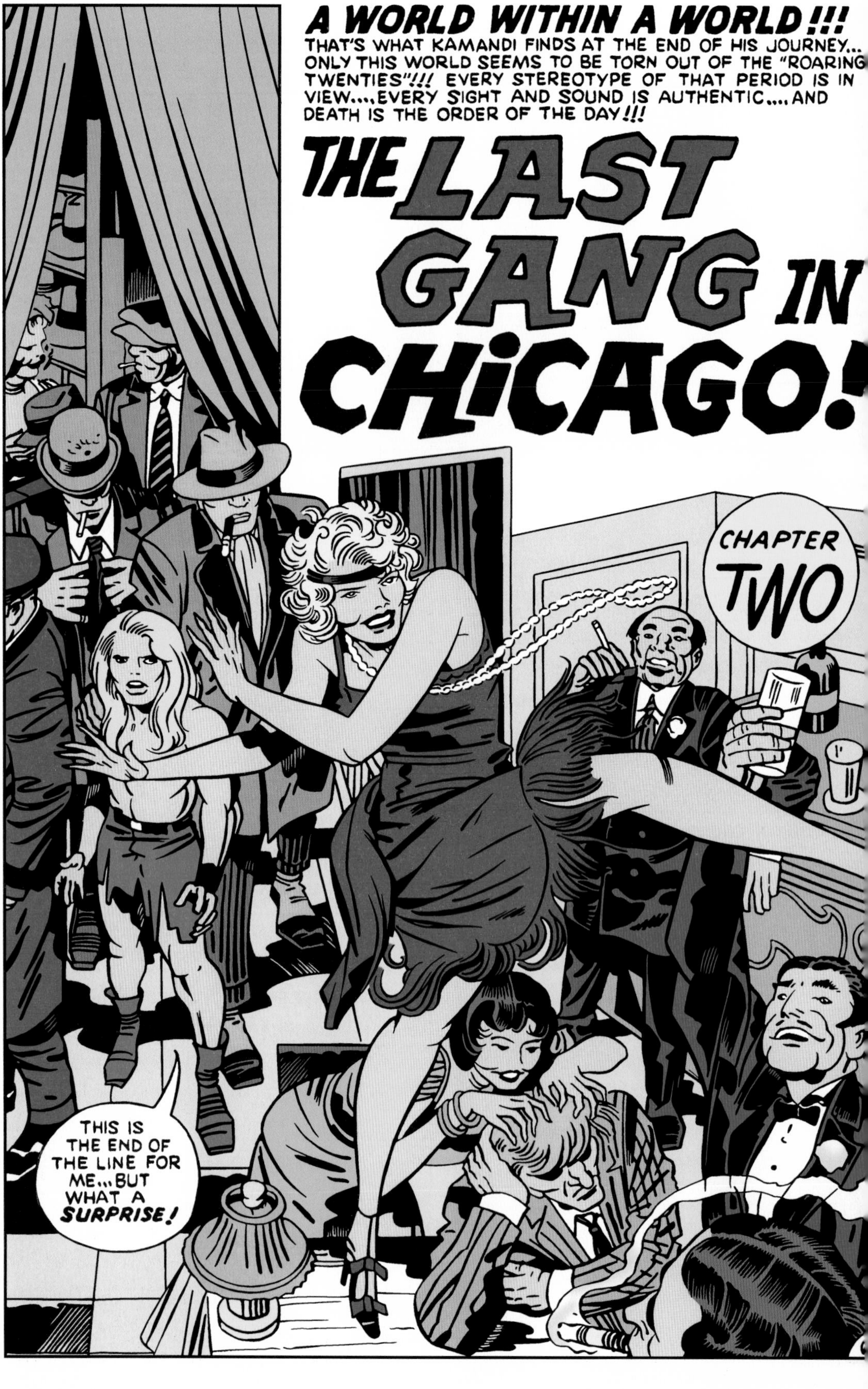
A WORLD WITHIN A WORLD!!!
THAT'S WHAT KAMANDI FINDS AT THE END OF HIS JOURNEY... ONLY THIS WORLD SEEMS TO BE TORN OUT OF THE "ROARING TWENTIES"!!! EVERY STEREOTYPE OF THAT PERIOD IS IN VIEW...,EVERY SIGHT AND SOUND IS AUTHENTIC.... AND DEATH IS THE ORDER OF THE DAY!!!
THE LAST GANG IN CHICAGO!
CHAPTER TWO
THIS IS THE END OF THE LINE FOR ME...BUT WHAT A SURPRISE!

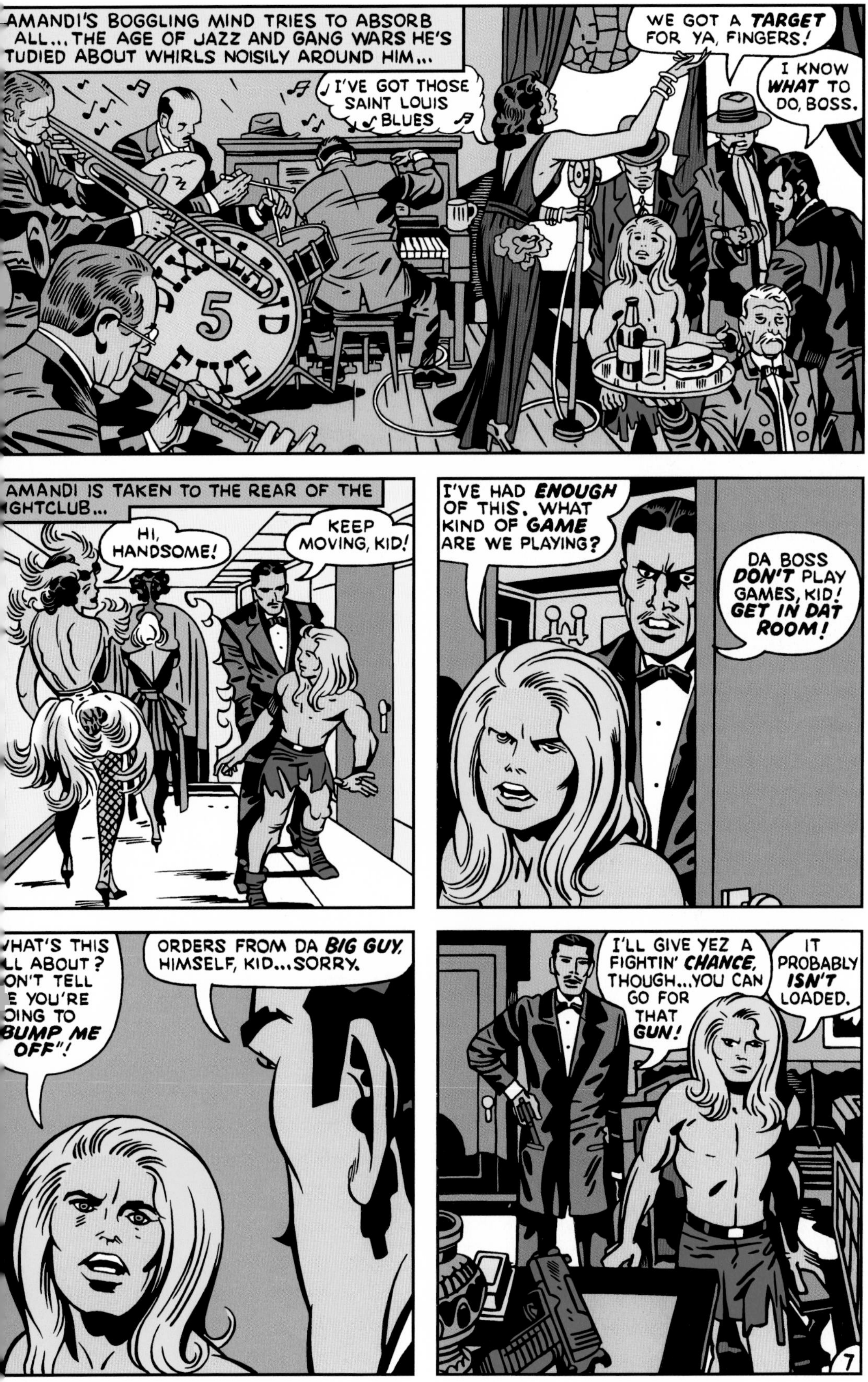
AMANDI'S BOGGLING MIND TRIES TO ABSORB ALL... THE AGE OF JAZZ AND GANG WARS HE'S TUDIED ABOUT WHIRLS NOISILY AROUND HIM...
I'VE GOT THOSE SAINT LOUIS BLUES
WE GOT A TARGET FOR YA, FINGERS!
I KNOW WHAT TO DO, BOSS.
AMANDI IS TAKEN TO THE REAR OF THE IGHTCLUB...
HI, HANDSOME!
KEEP MOVING, KID!
I'VE HAD ENOUGH OF THIS. WHAT KIND OF GAME ARE WE PLAYING?
DA BOSS DON'T PLAY GAMES, KID! GET IN DAT ROOM!
VHAT'S THIS LL ABOUT? ON'T TELL E YOU'RE OING TO BUMP ME OFF"!
ORDERS FROM DA BIG GUY, HIMSELF, KID... SORRY.
I'LL GIVE YEZ A FIGHTIN' CHANCE, THOUGH... YOU CAN GO FOR THAT GUN!
IT PROBABLY ISN'T LOADED.
7

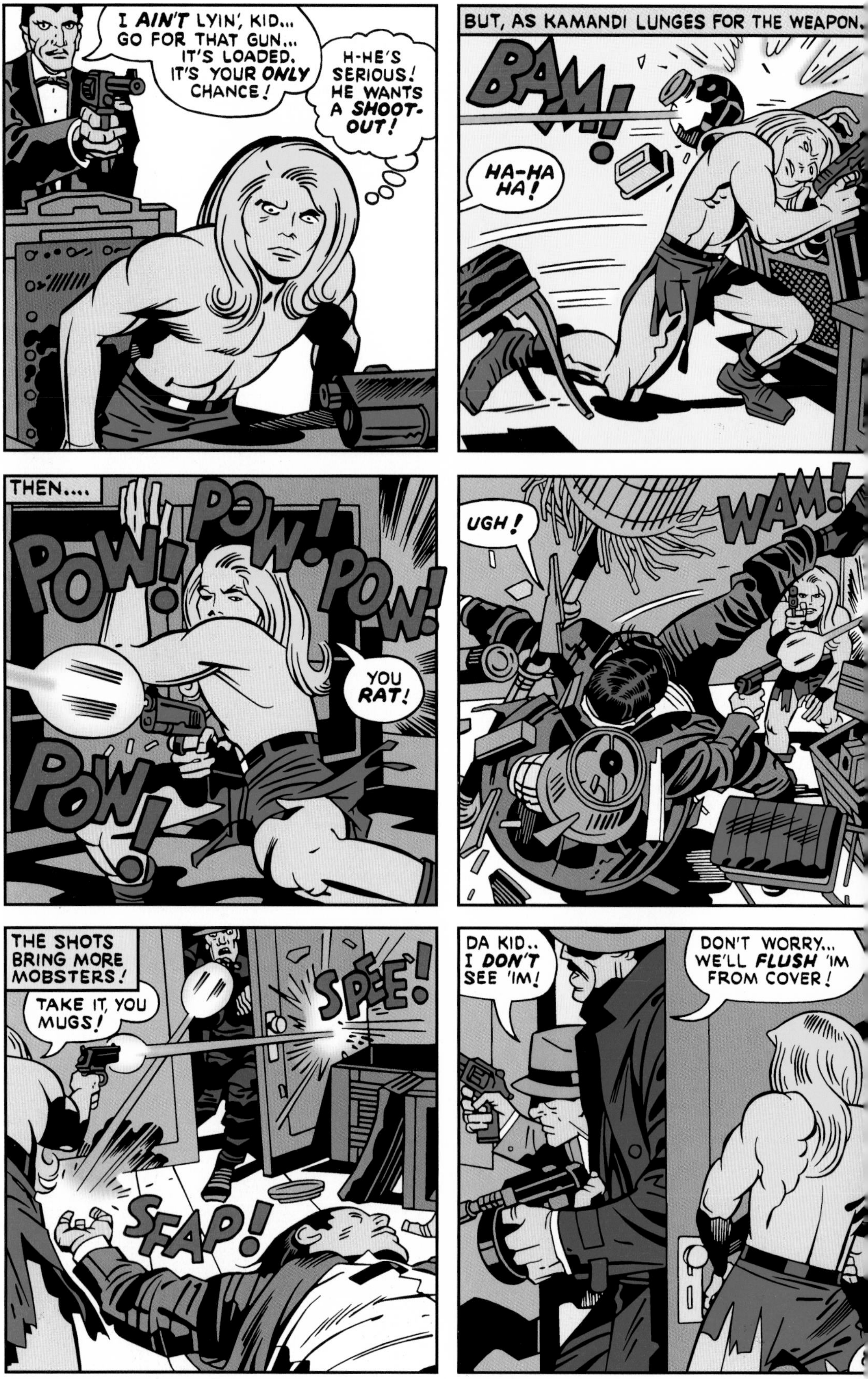
I AIN'T LYIN', KID... GO FOR THAT GUN... IT'S LOADED. IT'S YOUR ONLY CHANCE!
H-HE'S SERIOUS! HE WANTS A SHOOT-OUT!
BUT, AS KAMANDI LUNGES FOR THE WEAPON..
BAM!
HA-HA HA!
THEN....
POW! POW! POW!
YOU RAT!
POW!
UGH!
WAM!
THE SHOTS BRING MORE MOBSTERS!
TAKE IT, YOU MUGS!
SPEE!
SFAP!
DA KID.. I DON'T SEE 'IM!
DON'T WORRY... WE'LL FLUSH 'IM FROM COVER!

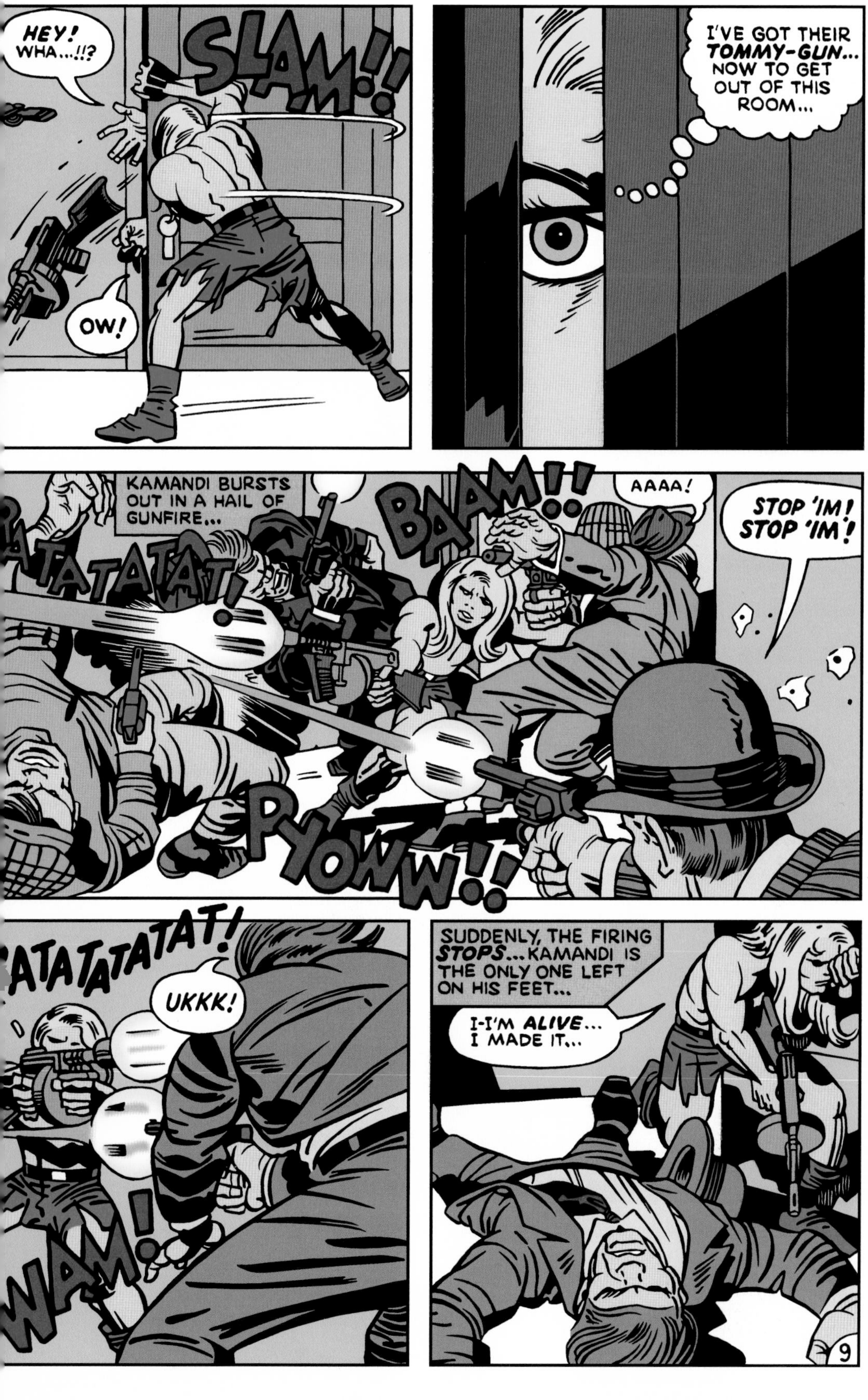
HEY! WHA...!!?
SLAM!!
OW!
I'VE GOT THEIR TOMMY-GUN... NOW TO GET OUT OF THIS ROOM...
KAMANDI BURSTS OUT IN A HAIL OF GUNFIRE...
TATATATATAT!
BAAM!!
AAAA!
STOP 'IM! STOP 'IM!
PYOWW!!
TATATATATAT!
UKKK!
WAM!
SUDDENLY, THE FIRING STOPS... KAMANDI IS THE ONLY ONE LEFT ON HIS FEET...
I-I'M ALIVE... I MADE IT...
9

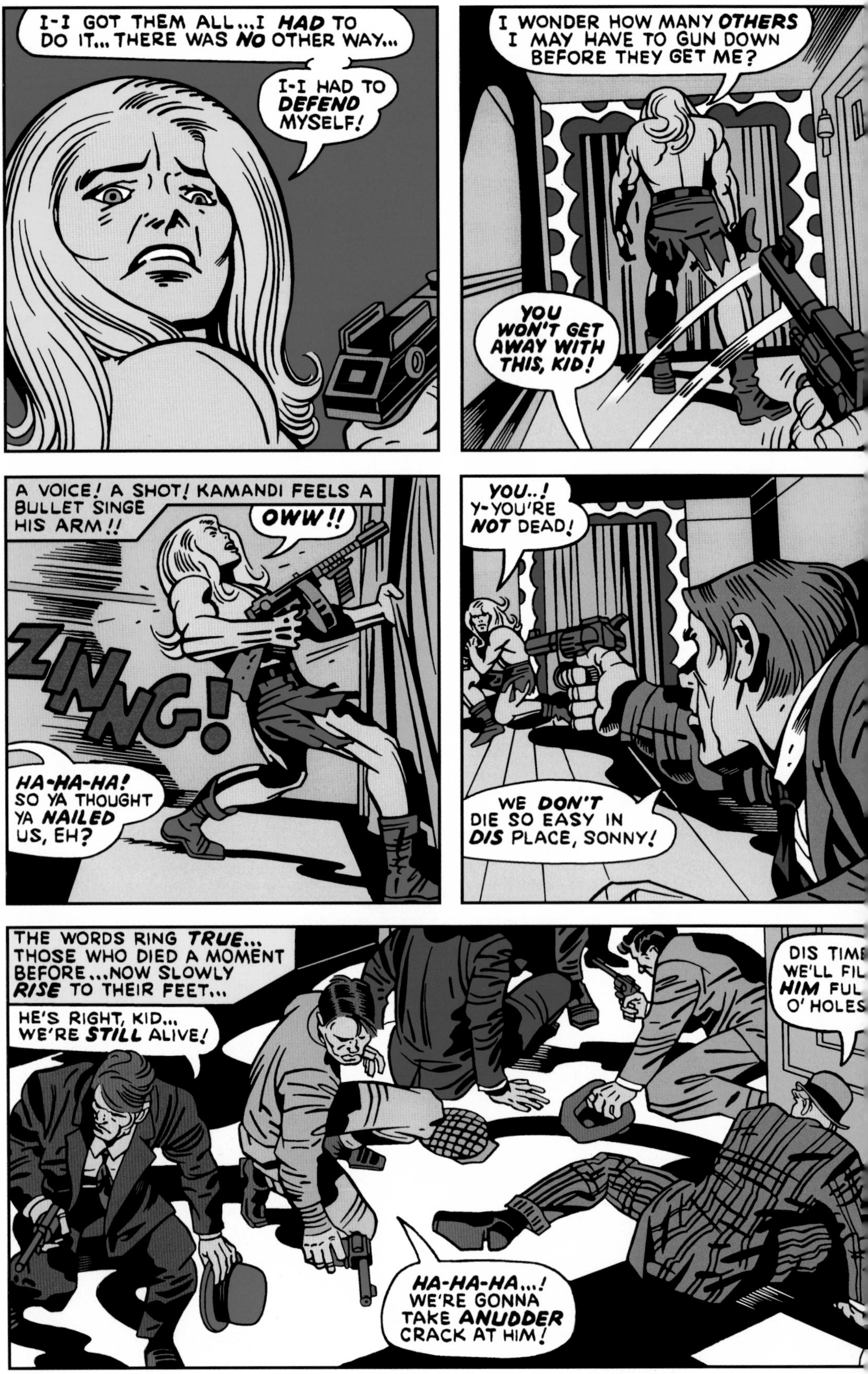
I-I GOT THEM ALL...I HAD TO DO IT... THERE WAS NO OTHER WAY...
I-I HAD TO DEFEND MYSELF!
I WONDER HOW MANY OTHERS I MAY HAVE TO GUN DOWN BEFORE THEY GET ME?
YOU WON'T GET AWAY WITH THIS, KID!
A VOICE! A SHOT! KAMANDI FEELS A BULLET SINGE HIS ARM!!
OWW!!
ZINNG!
HA-HA-HA! SO YA THOUGHT YA NAILED US, EH?
YOU..! Y-YOU'RE NOT DEAD!
WE DON'T DIE SO EASY IN DIS PLACE, SONNY!
THE WORDS RING TRUE... THOSE WHO DIED A MOMENT BEFORE...NOW SLOWLY RISE TO THEIR FEET...
HE'S RIGHT, KID... WE'RE STILL ALIVE!
HA-HA-HA...! WE'RE GONNA TAKE ANUDDER CRACK AT HIM!

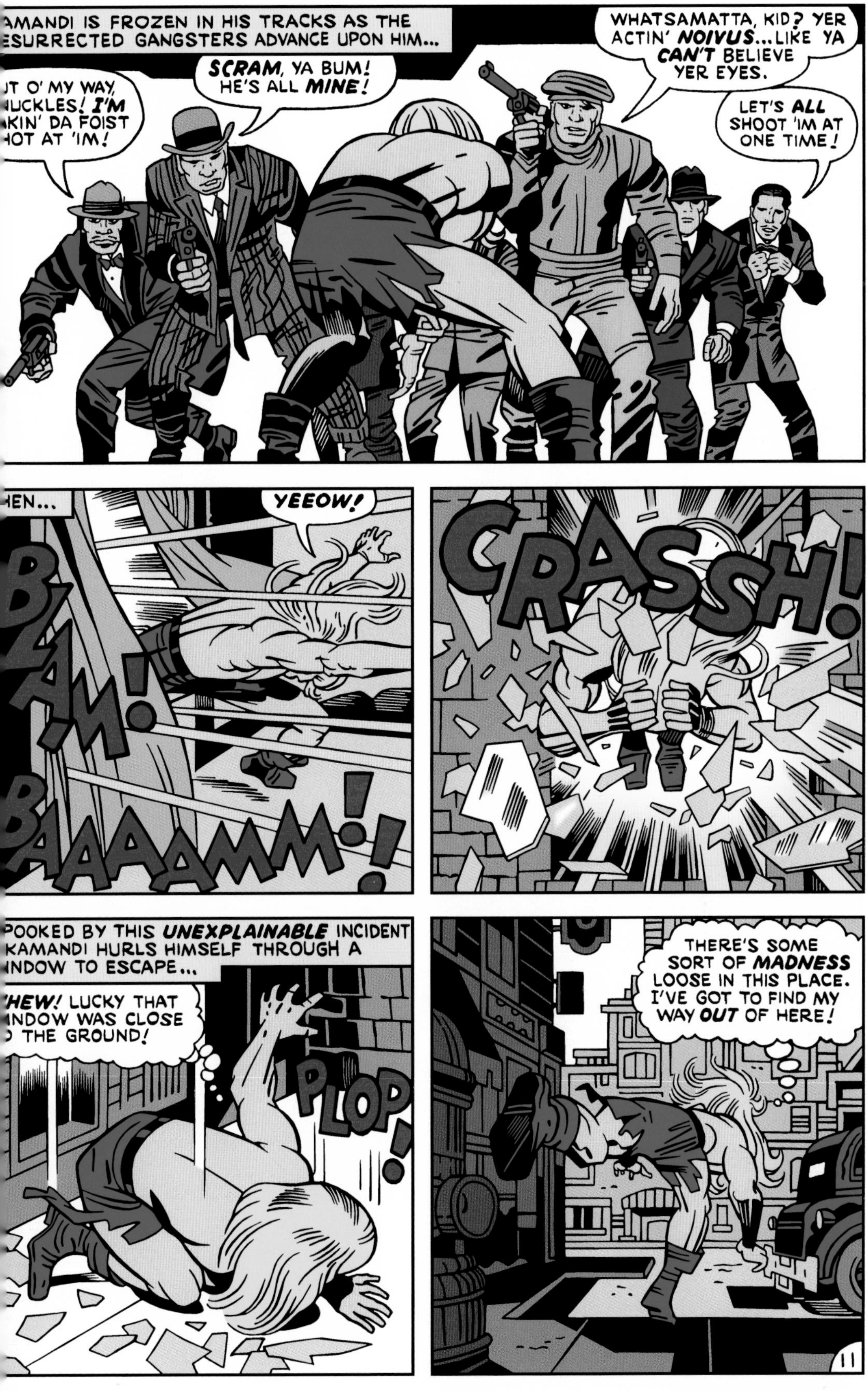
AMANDI IS FROZEN IN HIS TRACKS AS THE ESURRECTED GANGSTERS ADVANCE UPON HIM...
JT O' MY WAY, IUCKLES! I'M IKIN' DA FOIST HOT AT 'IM!
SCRAM, YA BUM! HE'S ALL MINE!
WHATSAMATTA, KID? YER ACTIN' NOIVUS...LIKE YA CAN'T BELIEVE YER EYES.
LET'S ALL SHOOT 'IM AT ONE TIME!
HEN...
YEEOW!
BLAM!
BAAAAMM!
CRASSH!
POOKED BY THIS UNEXPLAINABLE INCIDENT KAMANDI HURLS HIMSELF THROUGH A INDOW TO ESCAPE...
HEW! LUCKY THAT INDOW WAS CLOSE THE GROUND!
PLOP!
THERE'S SOME SORT OF MADNESS LOOSE IN THIS PLACE. I'VE GOT TO FIND MY WAY OUT OF HERE!
11

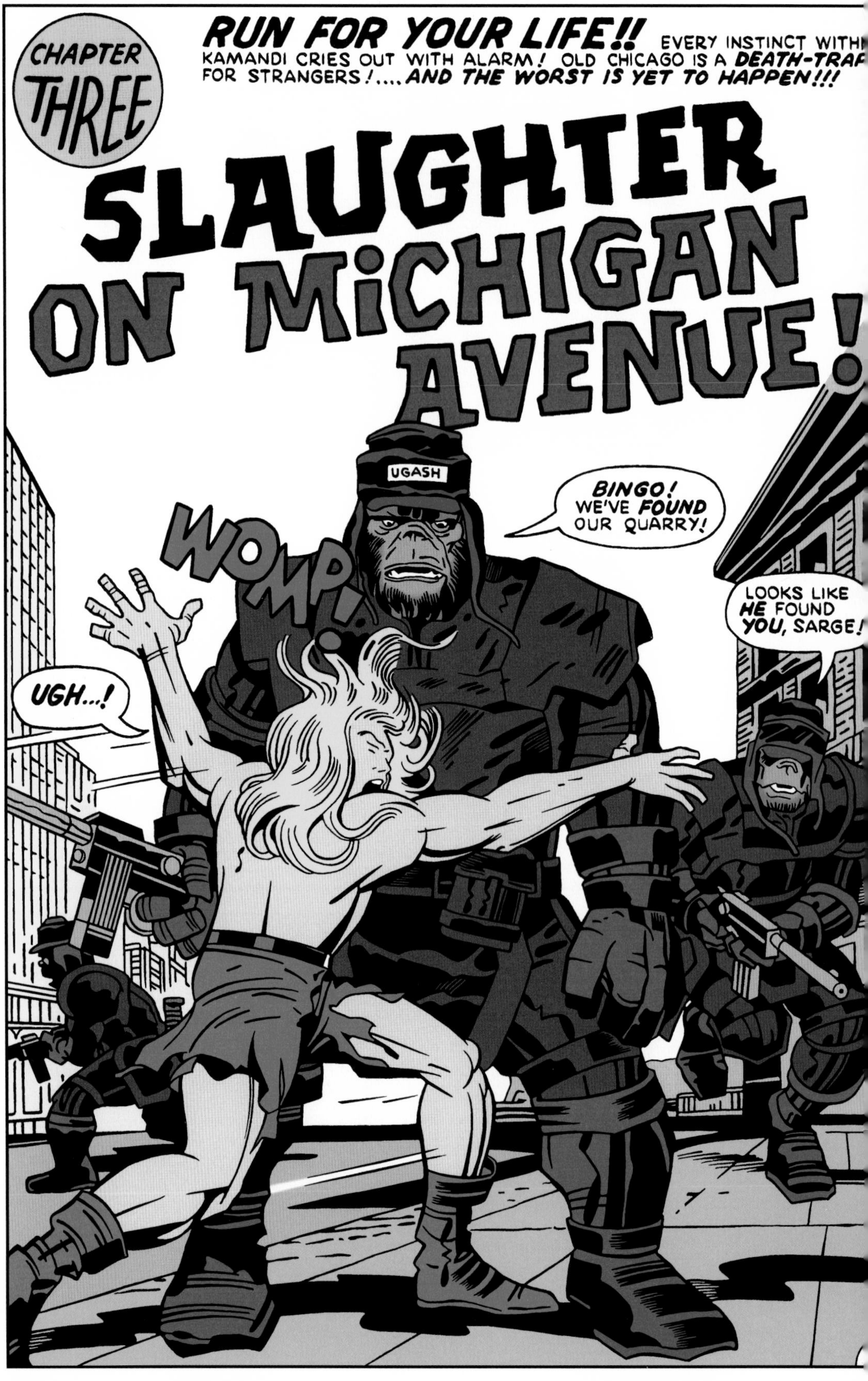
CHAPTER THREE
RUN FOR YOUR LIFE!! EVERY INSTINCT WITHI KAMANDI CRIES OUT WITH ALARM! OLD CHICAGO IS A DEATH-TRAP FOR STRANGERS!....AND THE WORST IS YET TO HAPPEN!!!
SLAUGHTER ON MICHIGAN AVENUE!
UGASH
BINGO! WE'VE FOUND OUR QUARRY!
WOMP!
LOOKS LIKE HE FOUND YOU, SARGE!
UGH...!

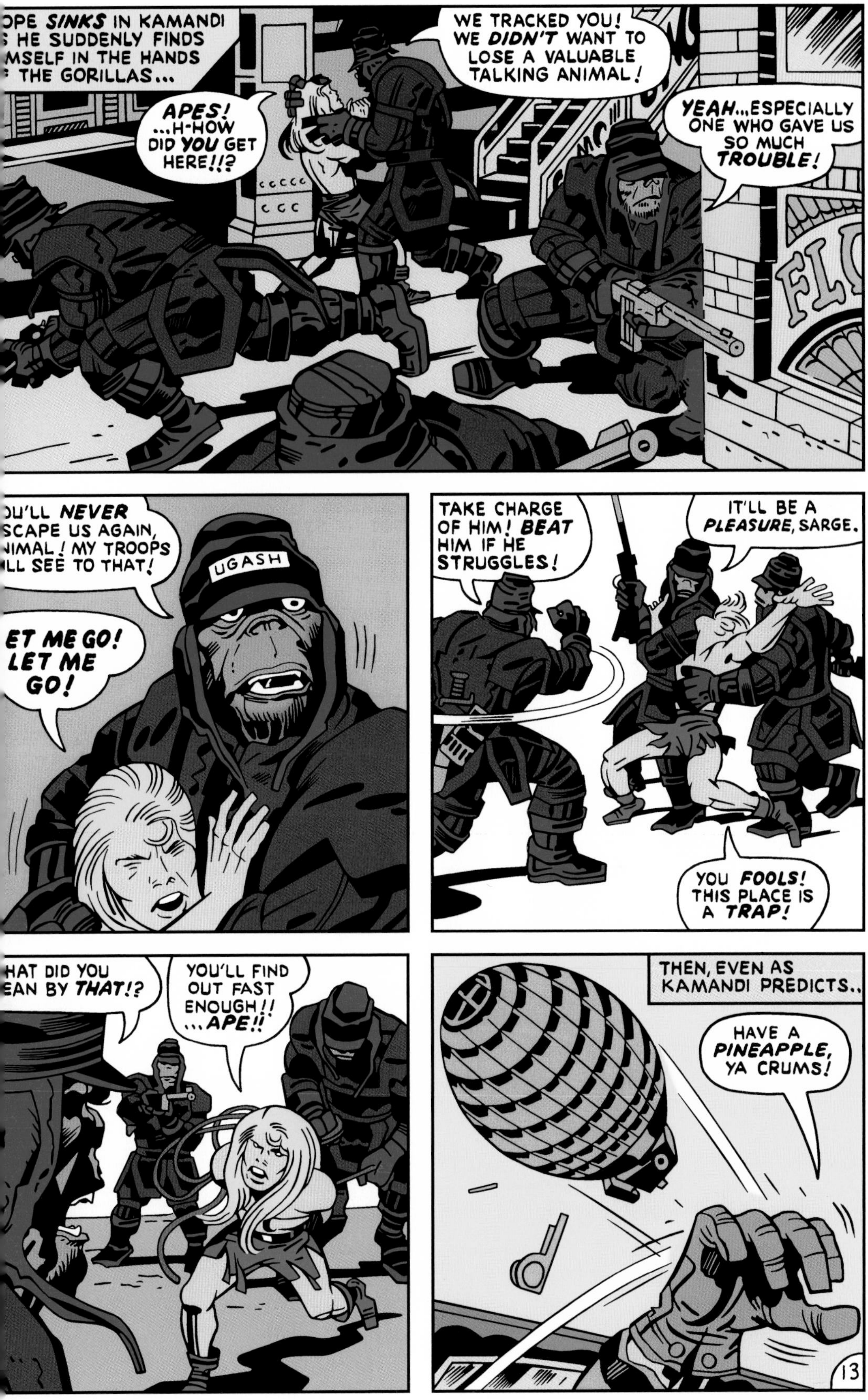
OPE SINKS IN KAMANDI
S HE SUDDENLY FINDS
MSELF IN THE HANDS
THE GORILLAS...
APES! ...H-HOW DID YOU GET HERE!!?
WE TRACKED YOU! WE DIDN'T WANT TO LOSE A VALUABLE TALKING ANIMAL!
YEAH...ESPECIALLY ONE WHO GAVE US SO MUCH TROUBLE!
OU'LL NEVER SCAPE US AGAIN, NIMAL! MY TROOPS LL SEE TO THAT!
UGASH
ET ME GO! LET ME GO!
TAKE CHARGE OF HIM! BEAT HIM IF HE STRUGGLES!
IT'LL BE A PLEASURE, SARGE.
YOU FOOLS! THIS PLACE IS A TRAP!
HAT DID YOU EAN BY THAT!?
YOU'LL FIND OUT FAST ENOUGH!! ...APE!!
THEN, EVEN AS KAMANDI PREDICTS..
HAVE A PINEAPPLE, YA CRUMS!
13

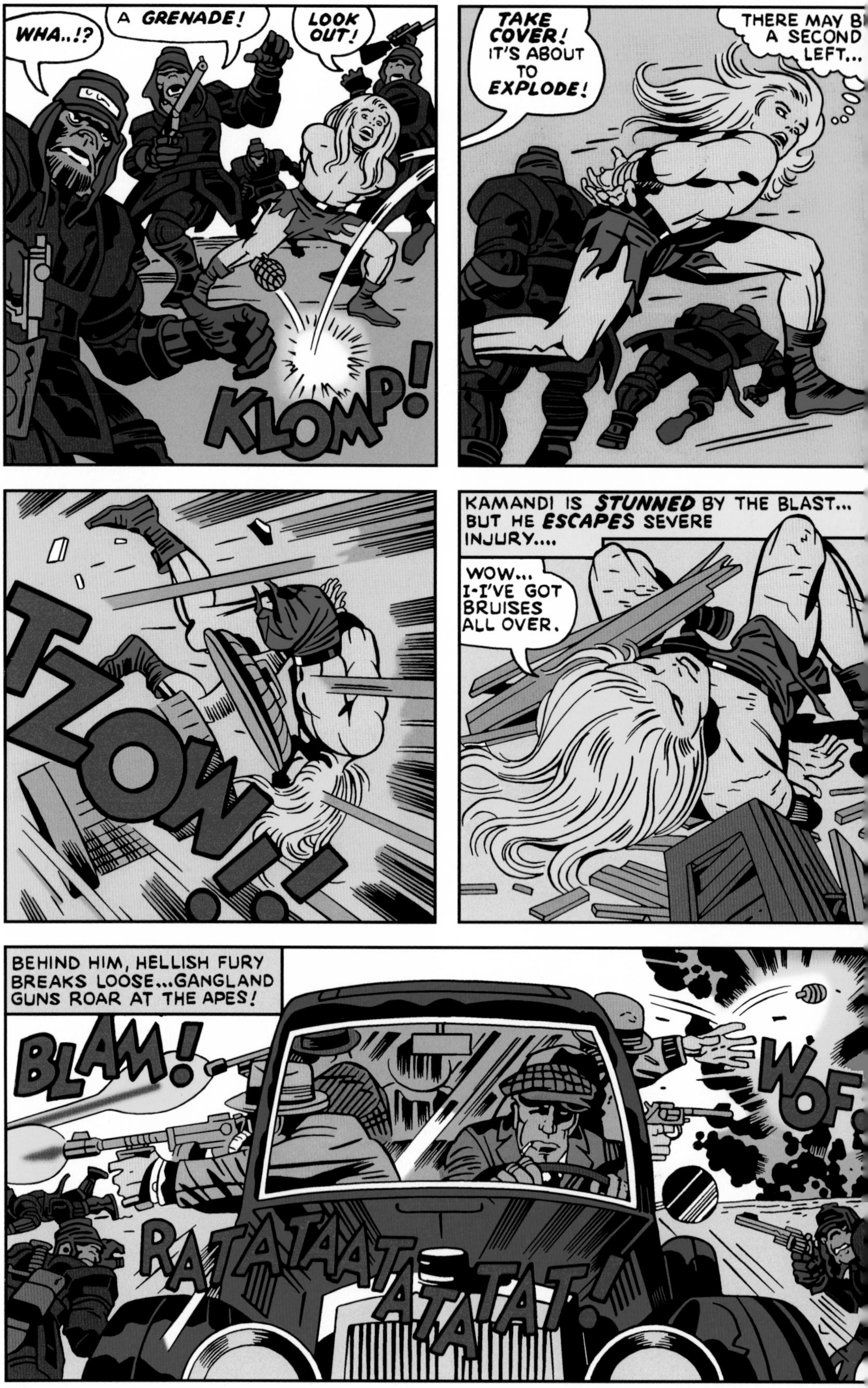
WHA..!?
A GRENADE!
LOOK OUT!
KLOMP!
TAKE COVER! IT'S ABOUT TO EXPLODE!
THERE MAY B
A SECOND
LEFT...
TZOW!!
KAMANDI IS STUNNED BY THE BLAST... BUT HE ESCAPES SEVERE INJURY....
WOW... I-I'VE GOT BRUISES ALL OVER.
BEHIND HIM, HELLISH FURY BREAKS LOOSE...GANGLAND GUNS ROAR AT THE APES!
BLAM!
WOF
RATATAAT ATATAT!

THE GORILLAS ARE CONFOUNDED AT THE SIGHT OF THE MOBSTERS...

POW!

POW!

TH-THIS TOWN IS RUN BY *KILLER-ANIMALS!*

AS FOR KAMANDI...

PSST! C'MERE, KID...

WH-WHO ARE *YOU*?

DON'T YOU SEE WHAT'S GOING ON? I'M GETTING OUT OF HERE...AND I SUGGEST *YOU* DO THE SAME!

SURE! ONLY *I* KNOW A SPOT WHERE YOU'LL LIKE THE ACTION *BETTER!*

I'D LIKE IT BETTER IF YOU'D *UNTIE* THESE ROPES!

ASK NO MORE. GENTLEMAN GEORGE IS A FRIEND TO *ALL!*

KAMANDI THEN FOLLOWS HIS NEW COMPANION.

WHERE ARE WE HEADING, ...PAL?

FOR THE *BIGGEST* POKER GAME IN TOWN. FOLLOW ME, KID.

BUT *WHY* DO WE HAVE TO SNEAK DOWN ALLEYS AND CELLARS?

TO *SHAKE* THE LAW...YOU KNOW GAMBLING'S ILLEGAL.

15

SOON...

STRANGE...I GET THE FEELING THAT *EVERYTHING* HAPPENING HERE IS A *PREPARED* SCENARIO TAKEN FROM OLD GANG MOVIES....

HERE WE ARE, KID...NOW YOU'LL MEET SOME *REAL* BIG SHOTS!

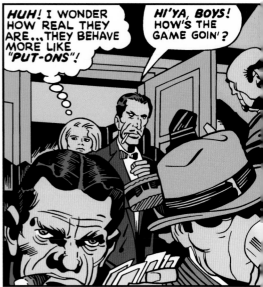

HUH! I WONDER HOW REAL THEY ARE...THEY BEHAVE MORE LIKE *"PUT-ONS"*!

HI'YA, *BOYS!* HOW'S THE GAME GOIN'?

IT'S GOIN' *ROTTEN,* GEORGE...I HOPE DIS KID CHANGES MY LUCK.

NO ONE'S LUCKIER'N DIS KID...I SEEN 'IM WALK THROUGH A *HAIL* O' BULLETS.

SAY! WE HEARD SOME SHOOTIN' OUTSIDE....

THAT'S BECAUSE YOUR TOWN'S BEEN *INVADED* BY GORILLAS!

HA-HA-HA... CHICAGO'S *FULLA* GORILLAS!

TAKE IT *EASY,* KID... IT HAPPENS ALLA TIME....JUST A LOTTA DA BOYS LETTIN' OFF STEAM...

NO, BIG SHOT! I'M TALKING ABOUT *REAL* GORILLAS! BUT THEY'RE OF A KIND YOU'VE OBVIOUSLY *NEVER* SEEN BEFORE.

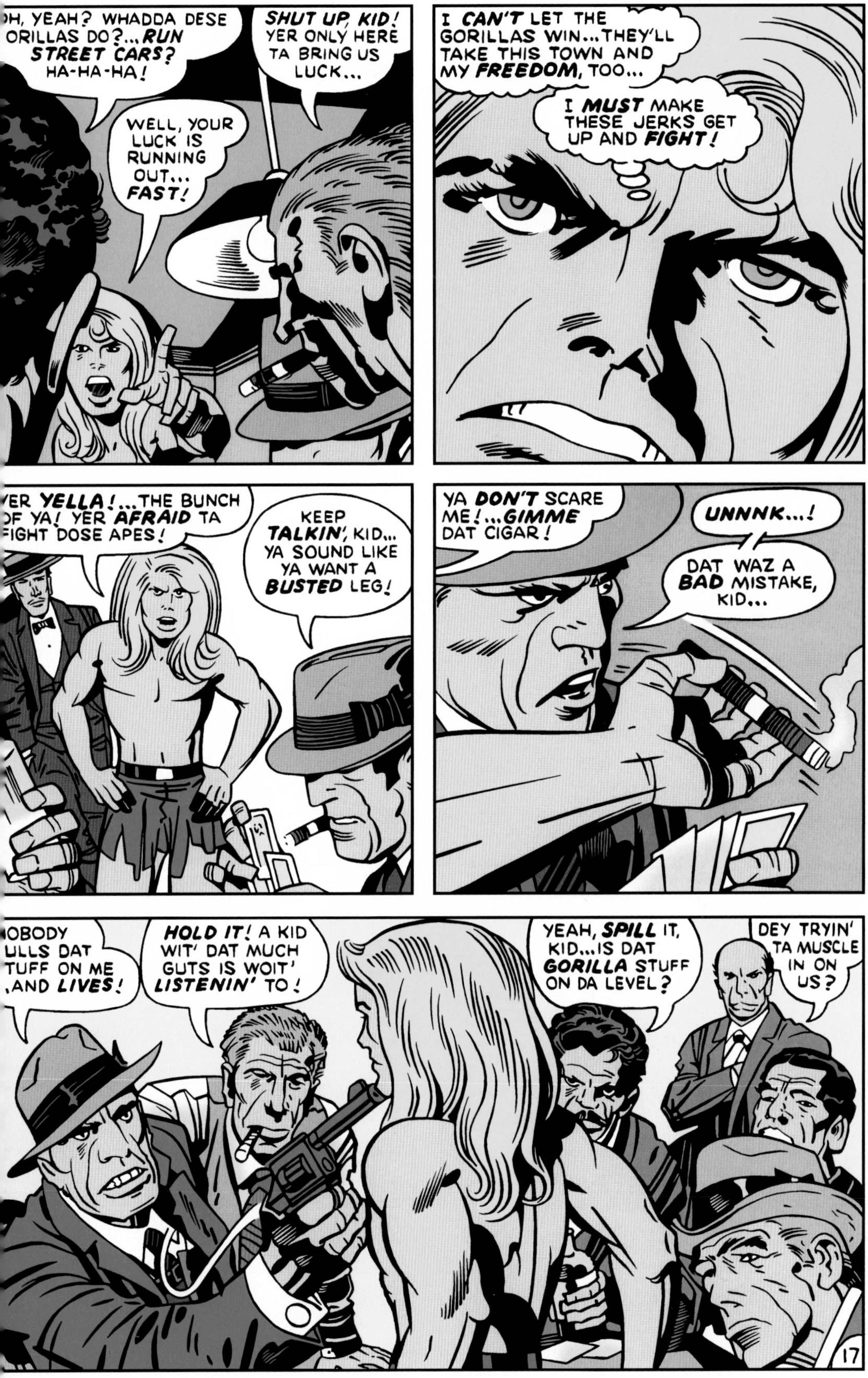
OH, YEAH? WHADDA DESE GORILLAS DO?...RUN STREET CARS? HA-HA-HA!
SHUT UP, KID! YER ONLY HERE TA BRING US LUCK...
WELL, YOUR LUCK IS RUNNING OUT... FAST!
I CAN'T LET THE GORILLAS WIN...THEY'LL TAKE THIS TOWN AND MY FREEDOM, TOO...
I MUST MAKE THESE JERKS GET UP AND FIGHT!
YER YELLA!...THE BUNCH OF YA! YER AFRAID TA FIGHT DOSE APES!
KEEP TALKIN', KID... YA SOUND LIKE YA WANT A BUSTED LEG!
YA DON'T SCARE ME!...GIMME DAT CIGAR!
UNNNK...!
DAT WAZ A BAD MISTAKE, KID...
NOBODY PULLS DAT STUFF ON ME ...AND LIVES!
HOLD IT! A KID WIT' DAT MUCH GUTS IS WOIT' LISTENIN' TO!
YEAH, SPILL IT, KID...IS DAT GORILLA STUFF ON DA LEVEL?
DEY TRYIN' TA MUSCLE IN ON US?
17

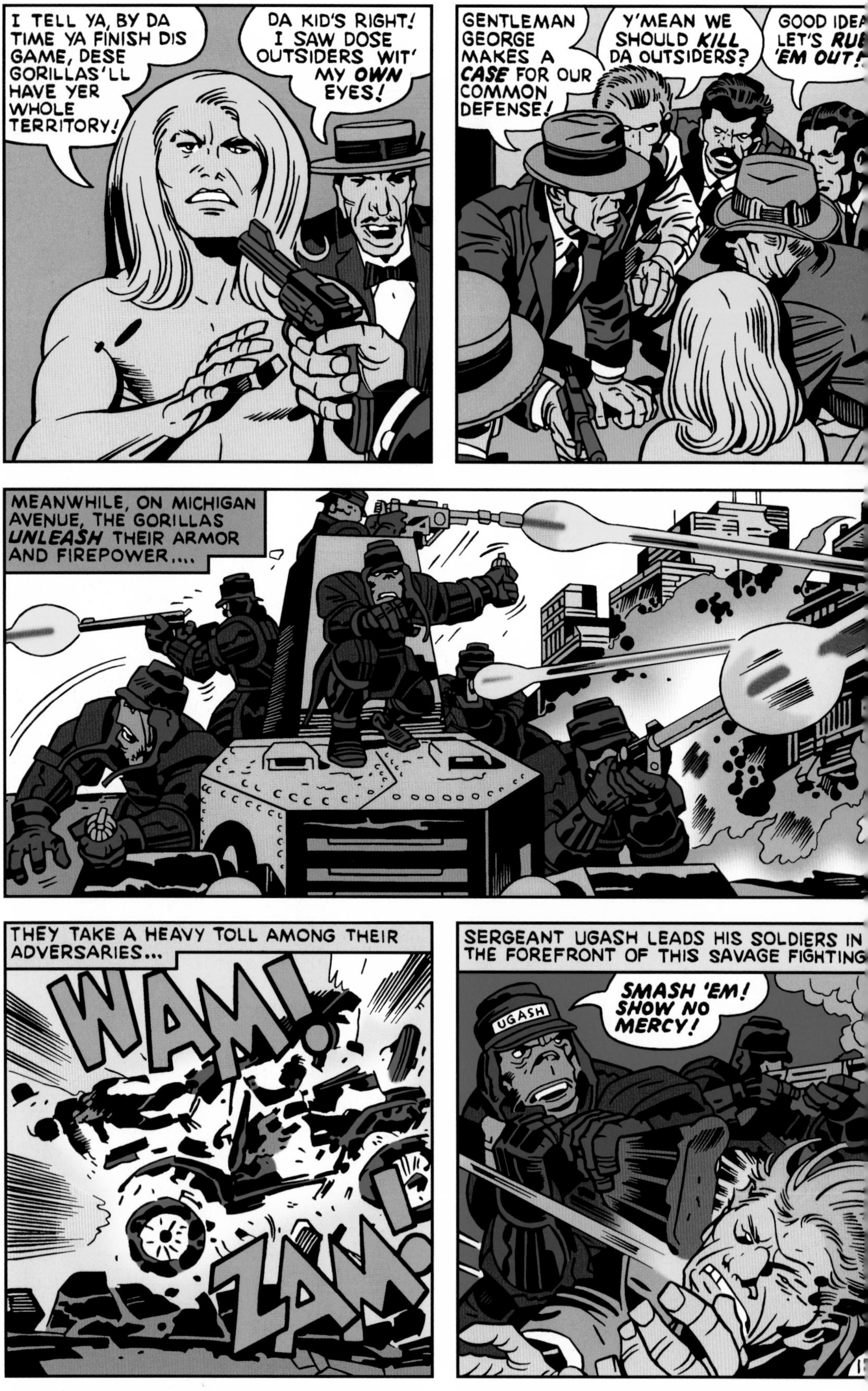
I TELL YA, BY DA TIME YA FINISH DIS GAME, DESE GORILLAS'LL HAVE YER WHOLE TERRITORY!
DA KID'S RIGHT! I SAW DOSE OUTSIDERS WIT' MY OWN EYES!
GENTLEMAN GEORGE MAKES A CASE FOR OUR COMMON DEFENSE!
Y'MEAN WE SHOULD KILL DA OUTSIDERS?
GOOD IDEA LET'S RU 'EM OUT!
MEANWHILE, ON MICHIGAN AVENUE, THE GORILLAS UNLEASH THEIR ARMOR AND FIREPOWER....
THEY TAKE A HEAVY TOLL AMONG THEIR ADVERSARIES...
WAM!
ZAM!
SERGEANT UGASH LEADS HIS SOLDIERS IN THE FOREFRONT OF THIS SAVAGE FIGHTING
UGASH
SMASH 'EM! SHOW NO MERCY!

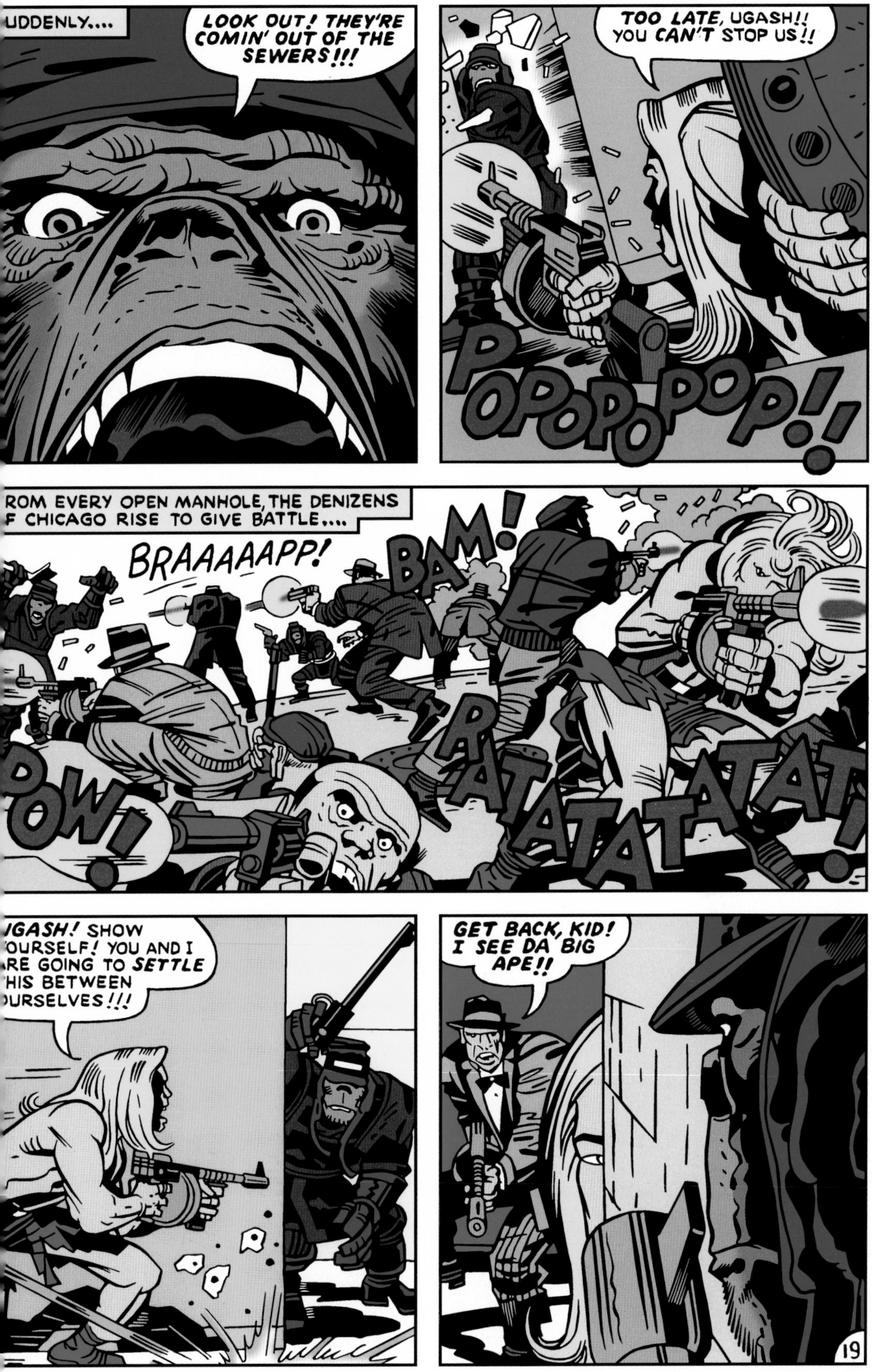
UDDENLY....
LOOK OUT! THEY'RE COMIN' OUT OF THE SEWERS!!!
TOO LATE, UGASH!! YOU CAN'T STOP US!!
POPOPOPOP!!
ROM EVERY OPEN MANHOLE, THE DENIZENS F CHICAGO RISE TO GIVE BATTLE....
BRAAAAAPP!
BAM!
RATATATATAT!
POW!
UGASH! SHOW YOURSELF! YOU AND I ARE GOING TO SETTLE THIS BETWEEN OURSELVES!!!
GET BACK, KID! I SEE DA BIG APE!!
19

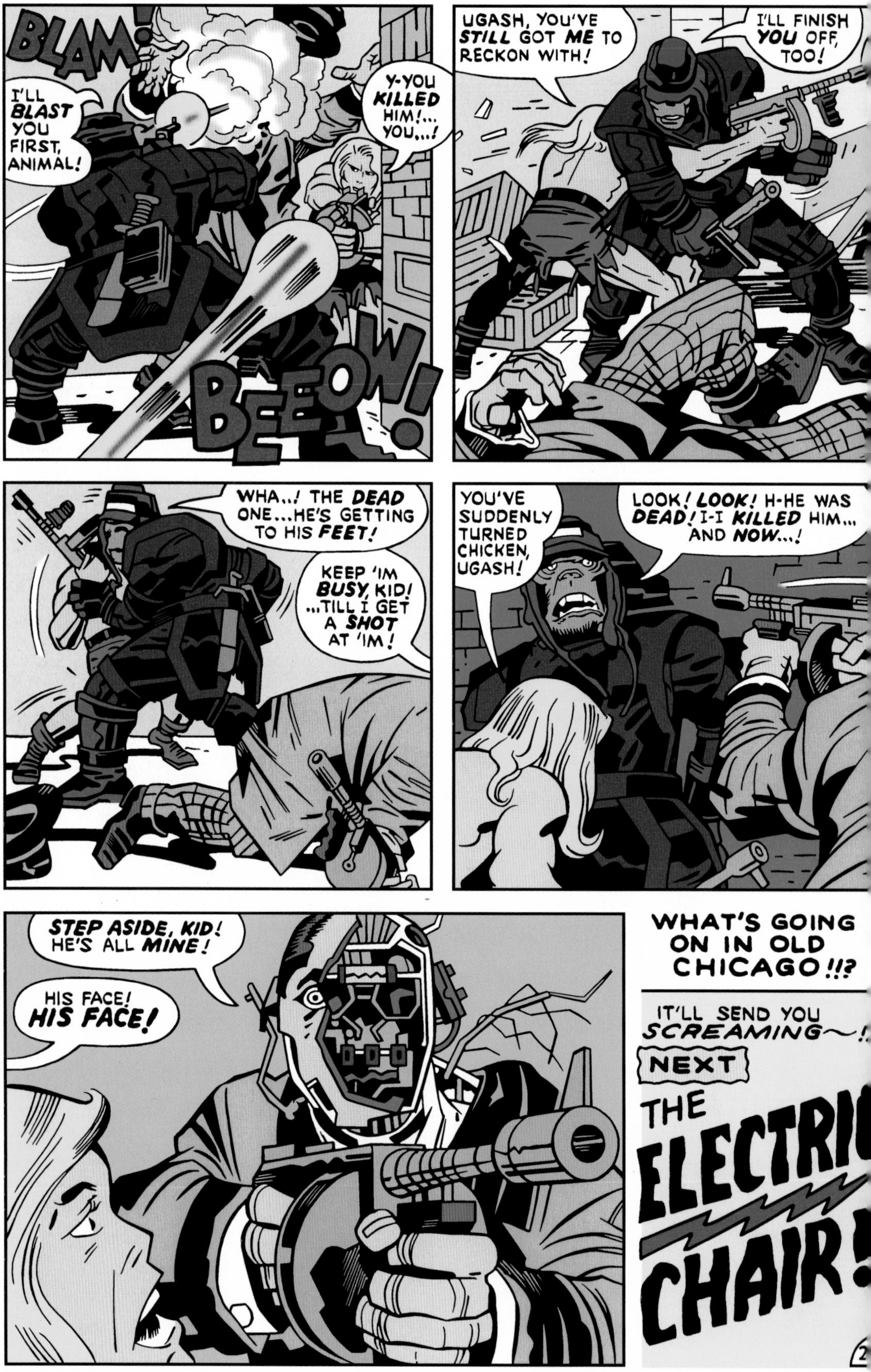
BLAM!
I'LL BLAST YOU FIRST, ANIMAL!
Y-YOU KILLED HIM!... YOU...!
BEEEOW!
UGASH, YOU'VE STILL GOT ME TO RECKON WITH!
I'LL FINISH YOU OFF, TOO!
WHA..! THE DEAD ONE...HE'S GETTING TO HIS FEET!
KEEP 'IM BUSY, KID! ...TILL I GET A SHOT AT 'IM!
YOU'VE SUDDENLY TURNED CHICKEN, UGASH!
LOOK! LOOK! H-HE WAS DEAD! I-I KILLED HIM... AND NOW...!
STEP ASIDE, KID! HE'S ALL MINE!
HIS FACE! HIS FACE!
WHAT'S GOING ON IN OLD CHICAGO!!?
IT'LL SEND YOU SCREAMING~!
NEXT
THE ELECTRI
CHAIR!

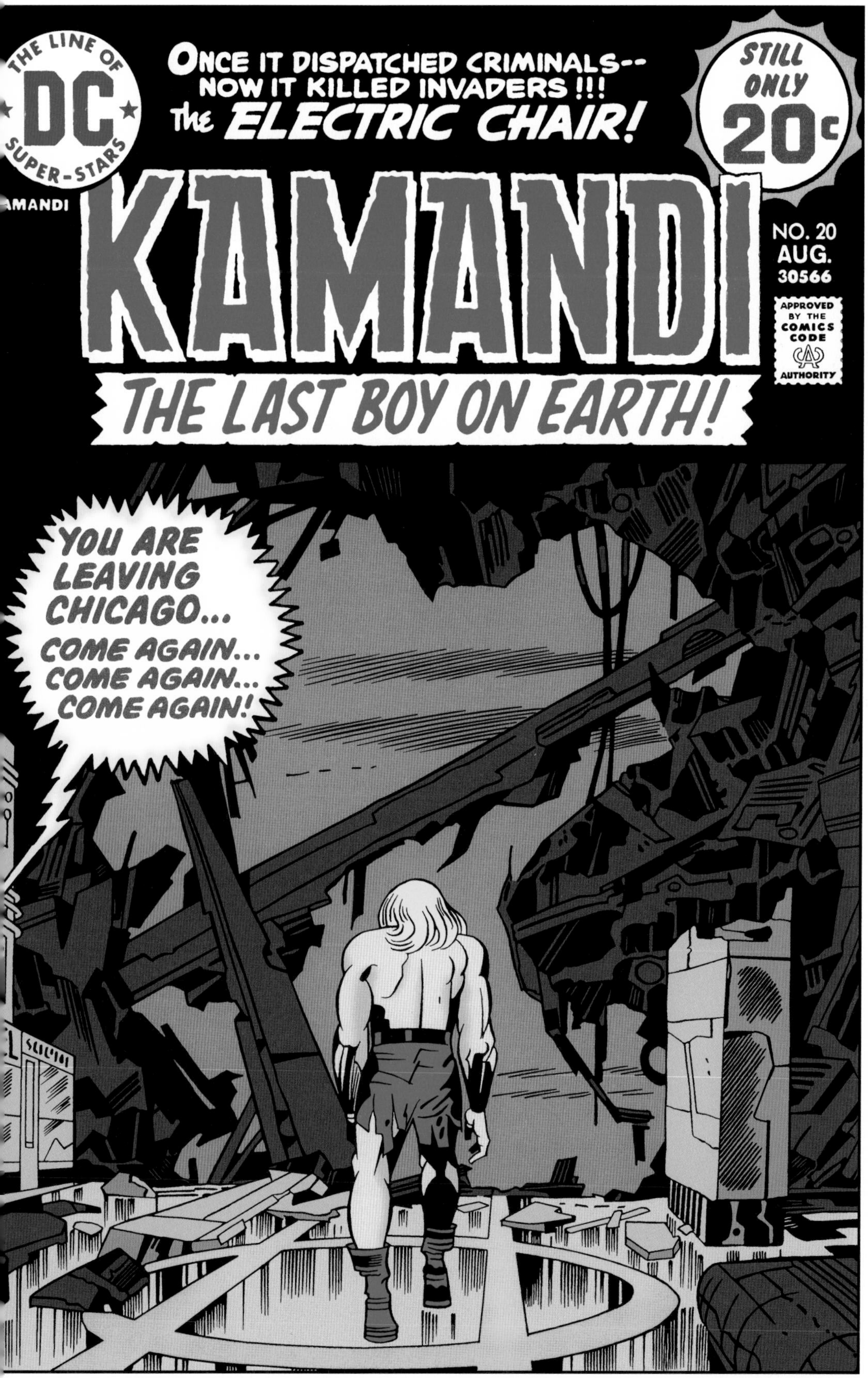
THE LINE OF DC SUPER-STARS
ONCE IT DISPATCHED CRIMINALS-- NOW IT KILLED INVADERS !!! The ELECTRIC CHAIR!
STILL ONLY 20¢
KAMANDI
NO. 20 AUG. 30566
APPROVED BY THE COMICS CODE AUTHORITY
KAMANDI
THE LAST BOY ON EARTH!
YOU ARE LEAVING CHICAGO... COME AGAIN... COME AGAIN... COME AGAIN!

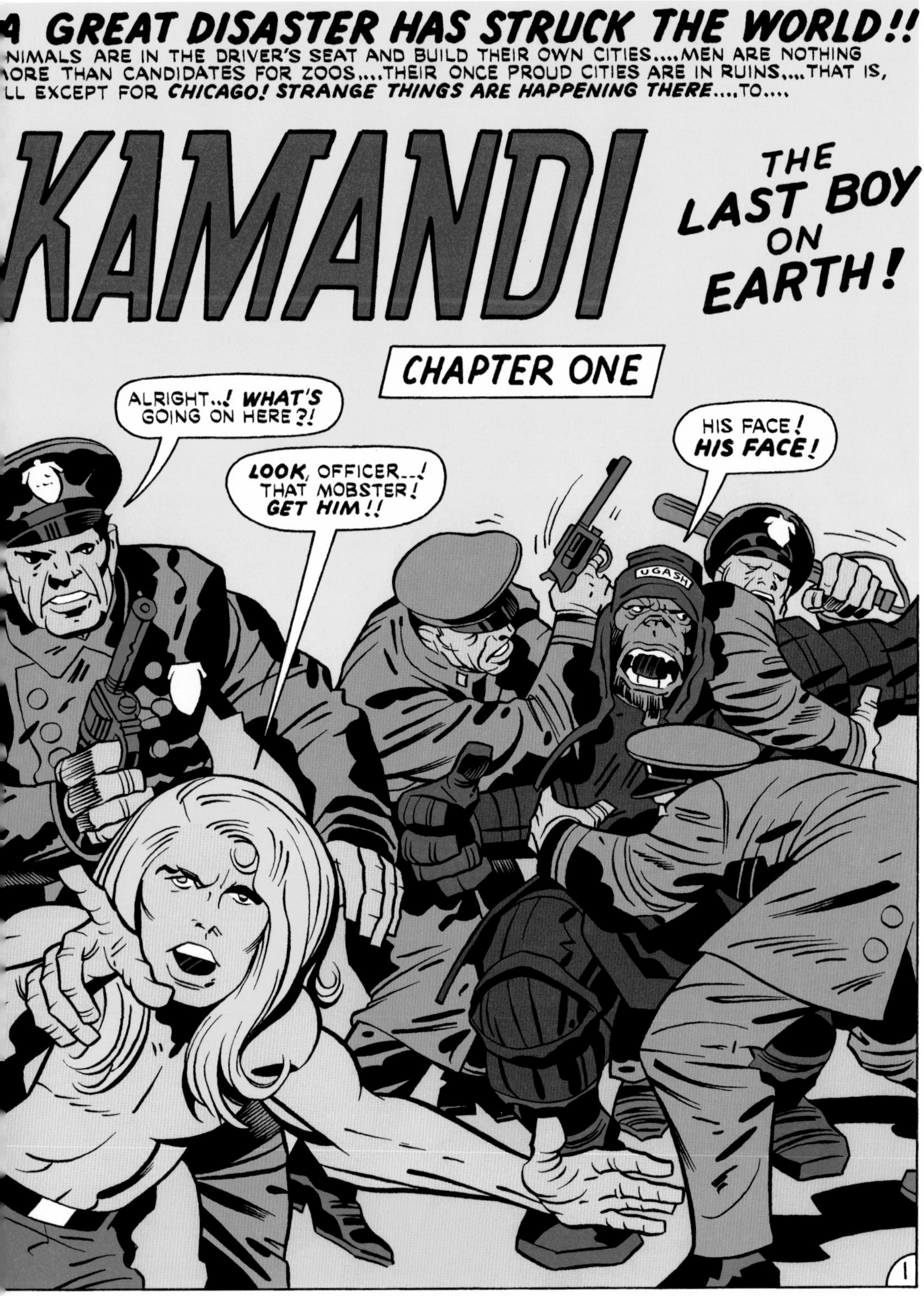
A GREAT DISASTER HAS STRUCK THE WORLD!!
NIMALS ARE IN THE DRIVER'S SEAT AND BUILD THEIR OWN CITIES....MEN ARE NOTHING MORE THAN CANDIDATES FOR ZOOS....THEIR ONCE PROUD CITIES ARE IN RUINS....THAT IS, LL EXCEPT FOR CHICAGO! STRANGE THINGS ARE HAPPENING THERE....TO....
KAMANDI
THE LAST BOY ON EARTH!
CHAPTER ONE
ALRIGHT..! WHAT'S GOING ON HERE?!
LOOK, OFFICER..! THAT MOBSTER! GET HIM!!
HIS FACE! HIS FACE!
UGASH
1

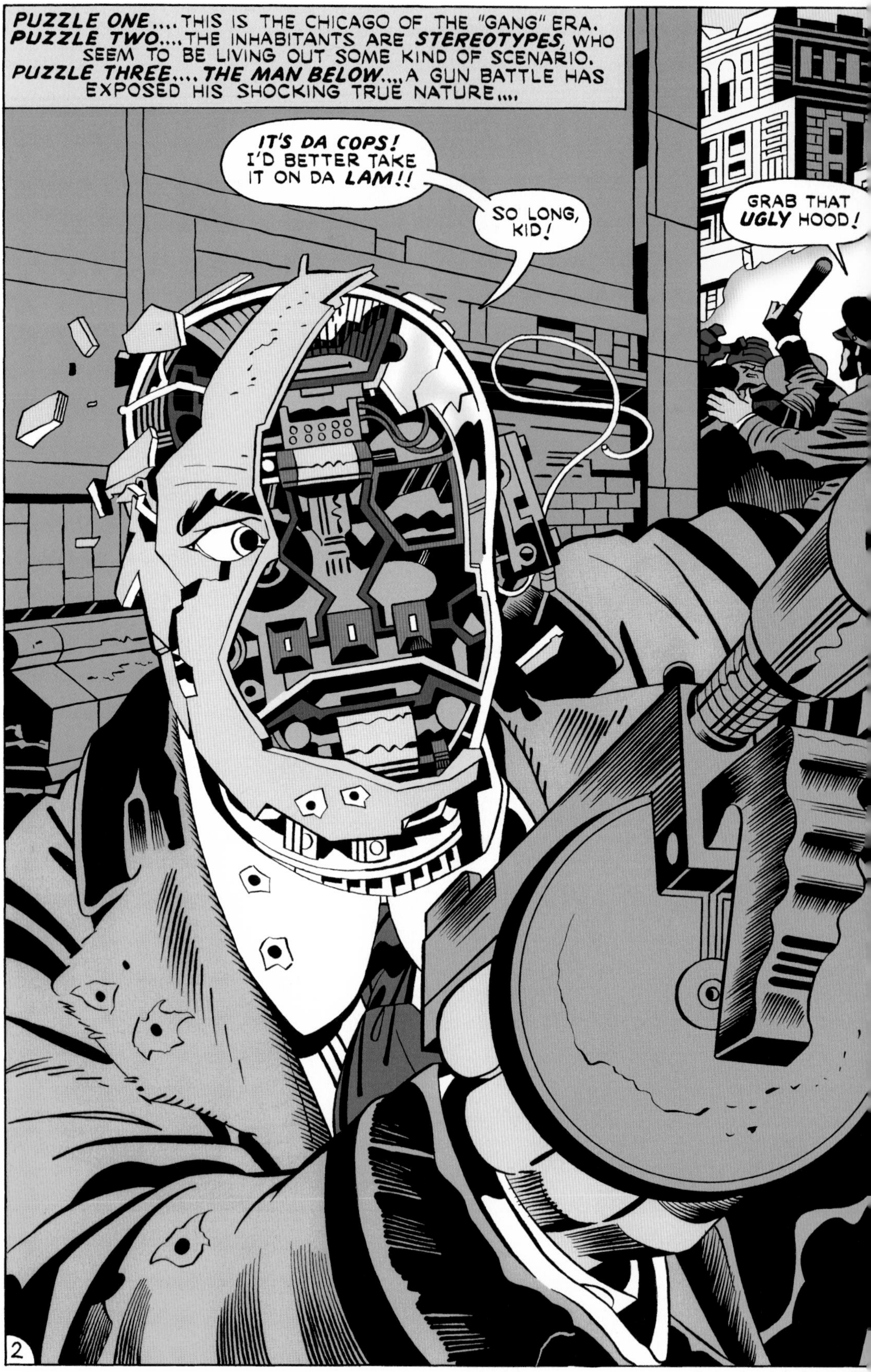
PUZZLE ONE.... THIS IS THE CHICAGO OF THE "GANG" ERA.
PUZZLE TWO.... THE INHABITANTS ARE STEREOTYPES, WHO SEEM TO BE LIVING OUT SOME KIND OF SCENARIO.
PUZZLE THREE.... THE MAN BELOW.... A GUN BATTLE HAS EXPOSED HIS SHOCKING TRUE NATURE....
IT'S DA COPS! I'D BETTER TAKE IT ON DA LAM!!
SO LONG, KID!
GRAB THAT UGLY HOOD!
2

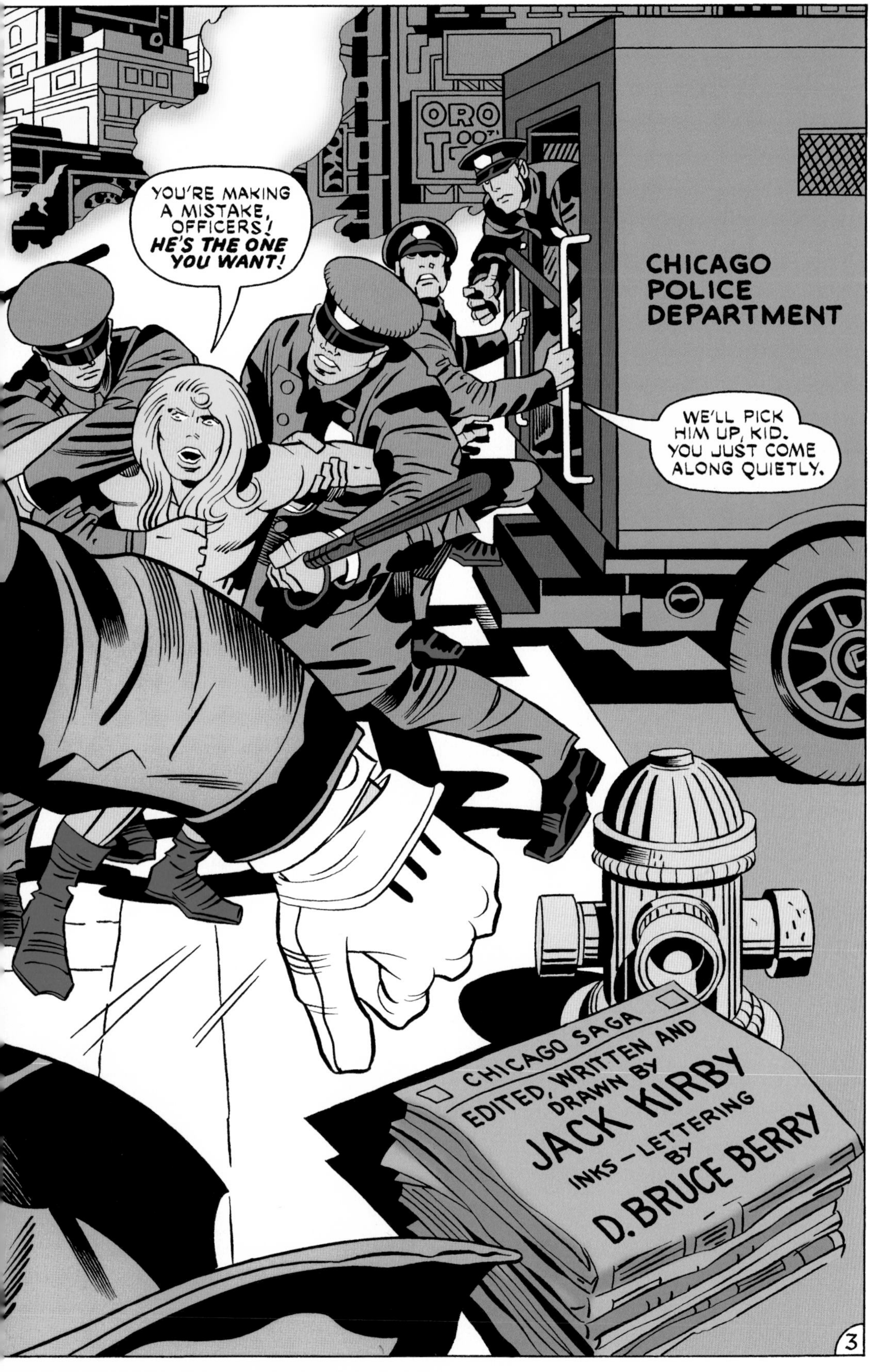

ORO
YOU'RE MAKING A MISTAKE, OFFICERS! **HE'S THE ONE YOU WANT!**
CHICAGO POLICE DEPARTMENT
WE'LL PICK HIM UP, KID. YOU JUST COME ALONG QUIETLY.
CHICAGO SAGA
EDITED, WRITTEN AND DRAWN BY
JACK KIRBY
INKS—LETTERING BY
D. BRUCE BERRY
3

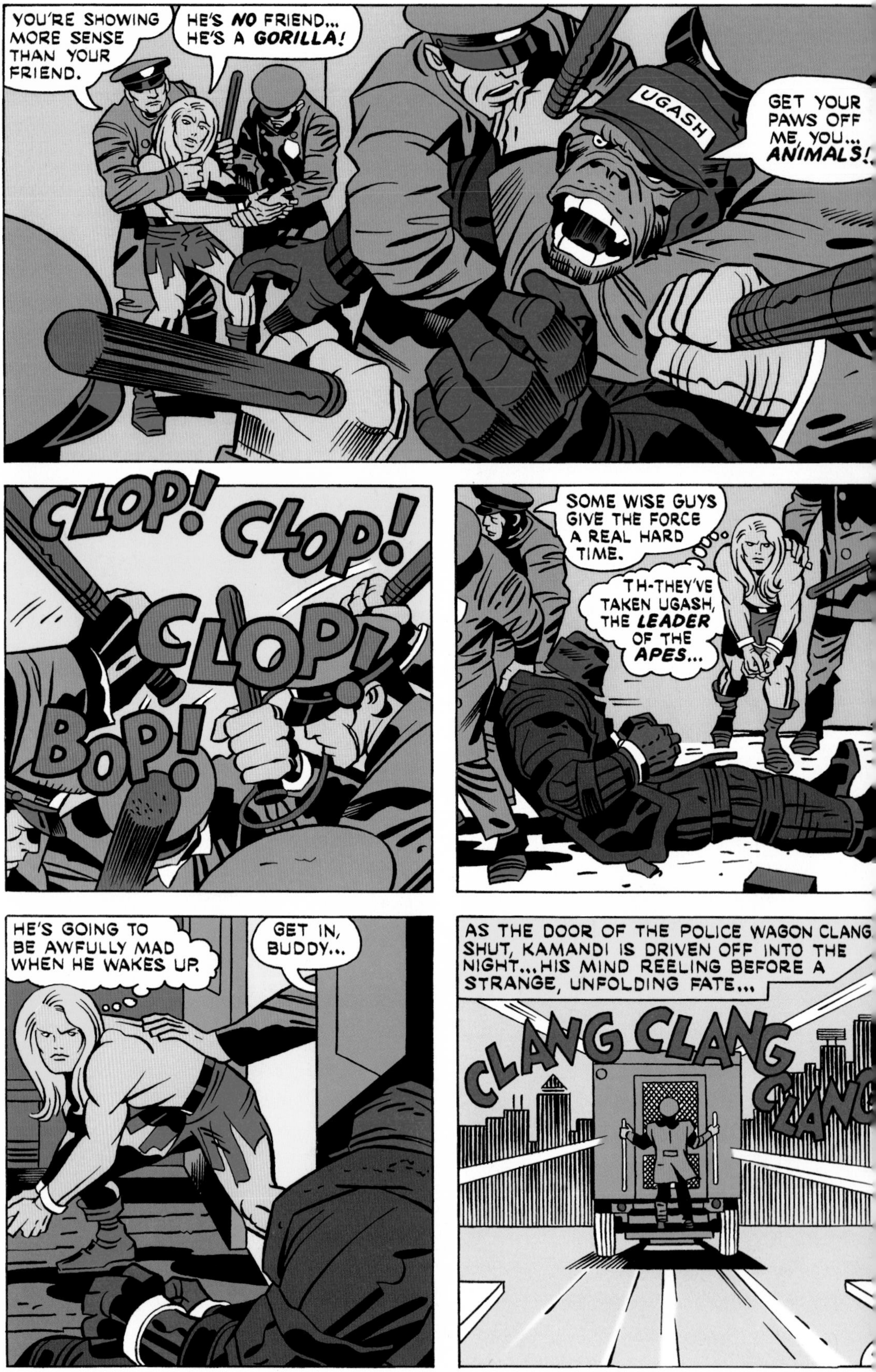
YOU'RE SHOWING MORE SENSE THAN YOUR FRIEND.
HE'S NO FRIEND... HE'S A GORILLA!
UGASH
GET YOUR PAWS OFF ME, YOU... ANIMALS!
CLOP! CLOP!
CLOP!
BOP!
SOME WISE GUYS GIVE THE FORCE A REAL HARD TIME.
TH-THEY'VE TAKEN UGASH, THE LEADER OF THE APES...
HE'S GOING TO BE AWFULLY MAD WHEN HE WAKES UP.
GET IN, BUDDY...
AS THE DOOR OF THE POLICE WAGON CLANGS SHUT, KAMANDI IS DRIVEN OFF INTO THE NIGHT... HIS MIND REELING BEFORE A STRANGE, UNFOLDING FATE...
CLANG CLANG

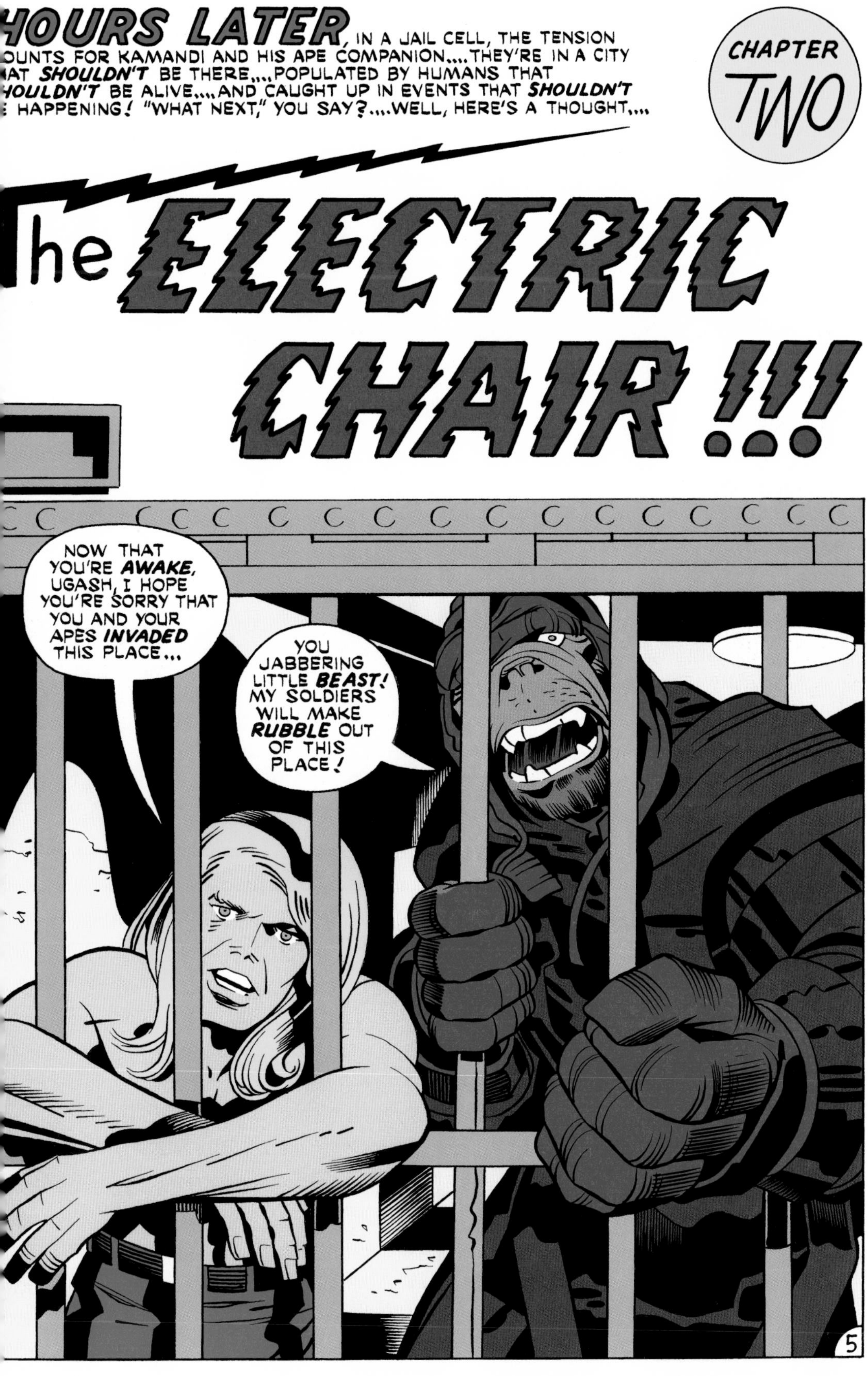
HOURS LATER, IN A JAIL CELL, THE TENSION
OUNTS FOR KAMANDI AND HIS APE COMPANION.... THEY'RE IN A CITY
AT SHOULDN'T BE THERE,... POPULATED BY HUMANS THAT
HOULDN'T BE ALIVE,... AND CAUGHT UP IN EVENTS THAT SHOULDN'T
HAPPENING! "WHAT NEXT," YOU SAY?.... WELL, HERE'S A THOUGHT,...
CHAPTER TWO
he ELECTRIC CHAIR!!!
NOW THAT YOU'RE AWAKE, UGASH, I HOPE YOU'RE SORRY THAT YOU AND YOUR APES INVADED THIS PLACE...
YOU JABBERING LITTLE BEAST! MY SOLDIERS WILL MAKE RUBBLE OUT OF THIS PLACE!
5

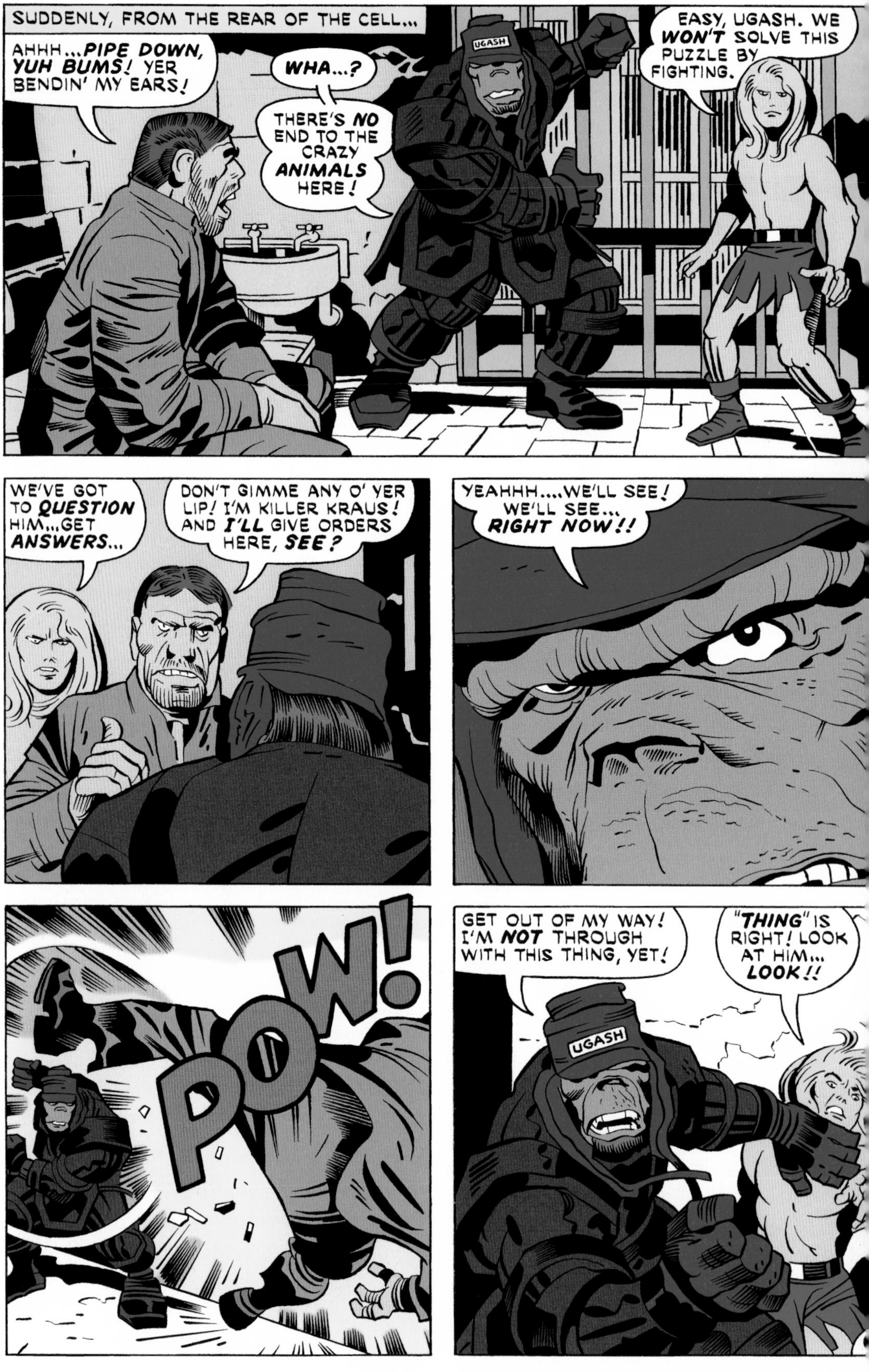
SUDDENLY, FROM THE REAR OF THE CELL...
AHHH...PIPE DOWN, YUH BUMS! YER BENDIN' MY EARS!
WHA...?
THERE'S NO END TO THE CRAZY ANIMALS HERE!
EASY, UGASH. WE WON'T SOLVE THIS PUZZLE BY FIGHTING.
UGASH
WE'VE GOT TO QUESTION HIM...GET ANSWERS...
DON'T GIMME ANY O' YER LIP! I'M KILLER KRAUS! AND I'LL GIVE ORDERS HERE, SEE?
YEAHHH....WE'LL SEE! WE'LL SEE... RIGHT NOW!!
POW!
GET OUT OF MY WAY! I'M NOT THROUGH WITH THIS THING, YET!
"THING" IS RIGHT! LOOK AT HIM... LOOK!!
UGASH

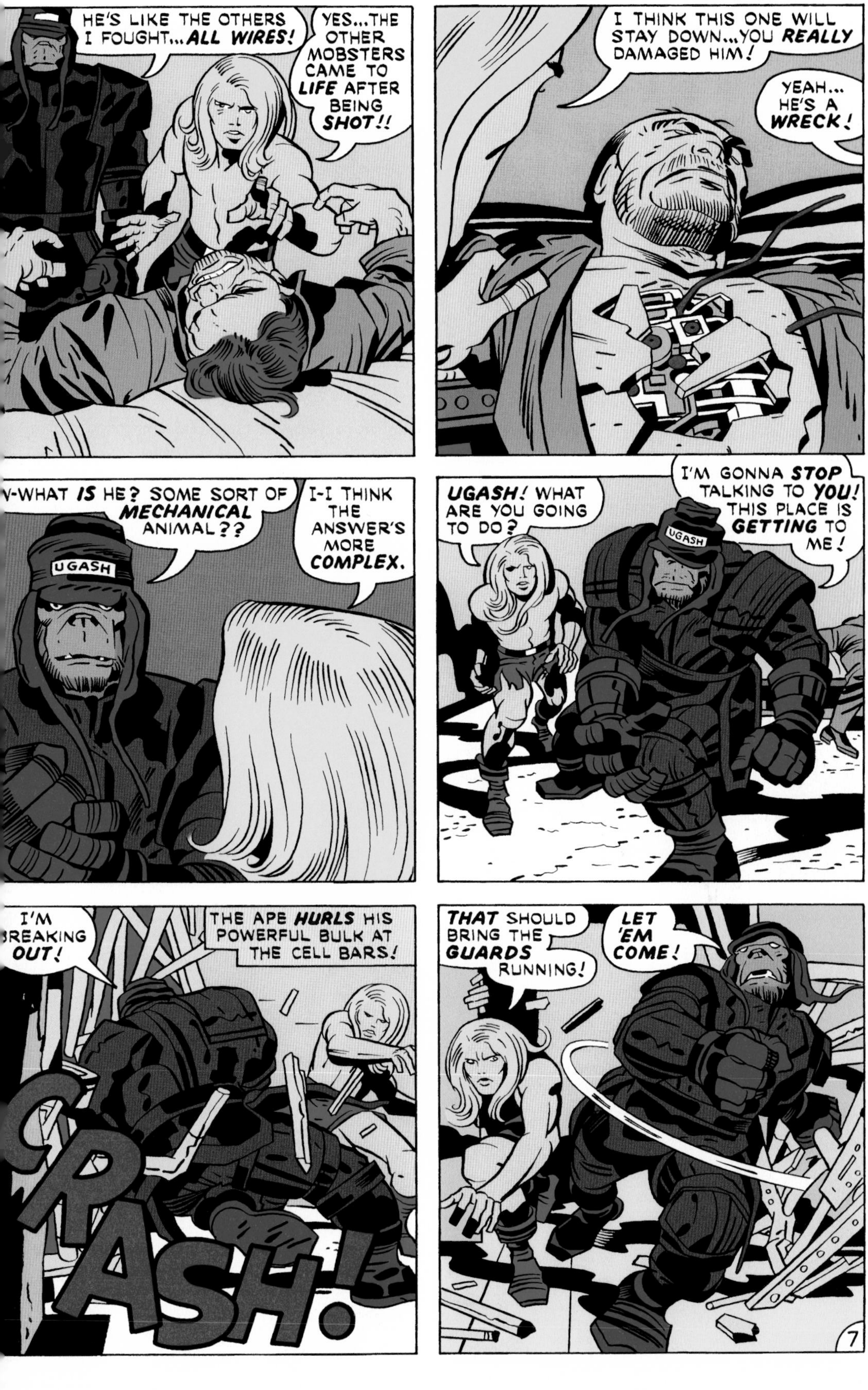
HE'S LIKE THE OTHERS I FOUGHT...ALL WIRES!
YES...THE OTHER MOBSTERS CAME TO LIFE AFTER BEING SHOT!!
I THINK THIS ONE WILL STAY DOWN...YOU REALLY DAMAGED HIM!
YEAH... HE'S A WRECK!
V-WHAT IS HE? SOME SORT OF MECHANICAL ANIMAL??
I-I THINK THE ANSWER'S MORE COMPLEX.
UGASH
UGASH! WHAT ARE YOU GOING TO DO?
I'M GONNA STOP TALKING TO YOU! THIS PLACE IS GETTING TO ME!
UGASH
I'M BREAKING OUT!
THE APE HURLS HIS POWERFUL BULK AT THE CELL BARS!
CRASH!
THAT SHOULD BRING THE GUARDS RUNNING!
LET 'EM COME!
7

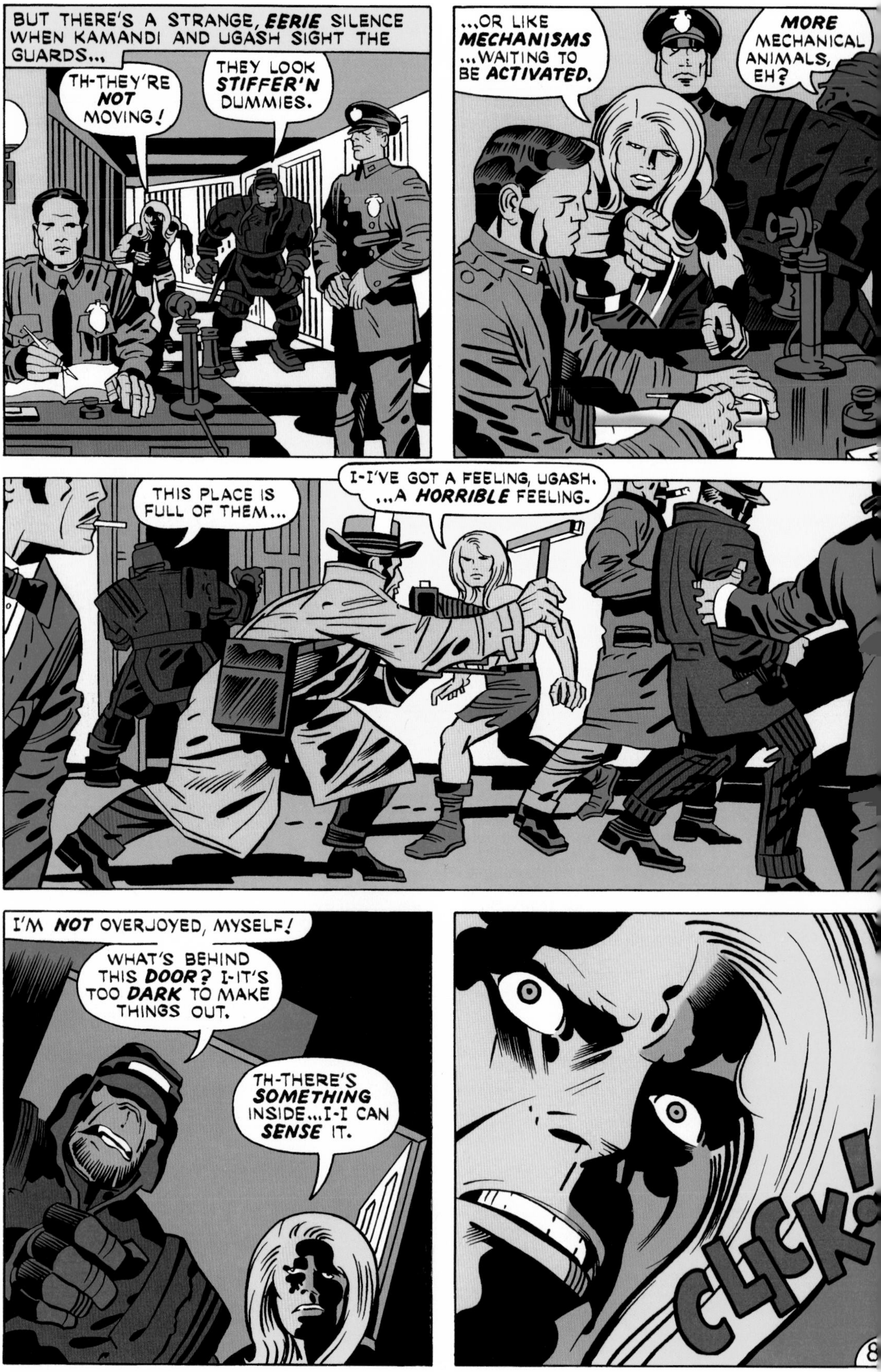
BUT THERE'S A STRANGE, EERIE SILENCE WHEN KAMANDI AND UGASH SIGHT THE GUARDS...
TH-THEY'RE NOT MOVING!
THEY LOOK STIFFER'N DUMMIES.
...OR LIKE MECHANISMS ...WAITING TO BE ACTIVATED.
MORE MECHANICAL ANIMALS, EH?
THIS PLACE IS FULL OF THEM...
I-I'VE GOT A FEELING, UGASH. ...A HORRIBLE FEELING.
I'M NOT OVERJOYED, MYSELF!
WHAT'S BEHIND THIS DOOR? I-IT'S TOO DARK TO MAKE THINGS OUT.
TH-THERE'S SOMETHING INSIDE...I-I CAN SENSE IT.
CLICK!

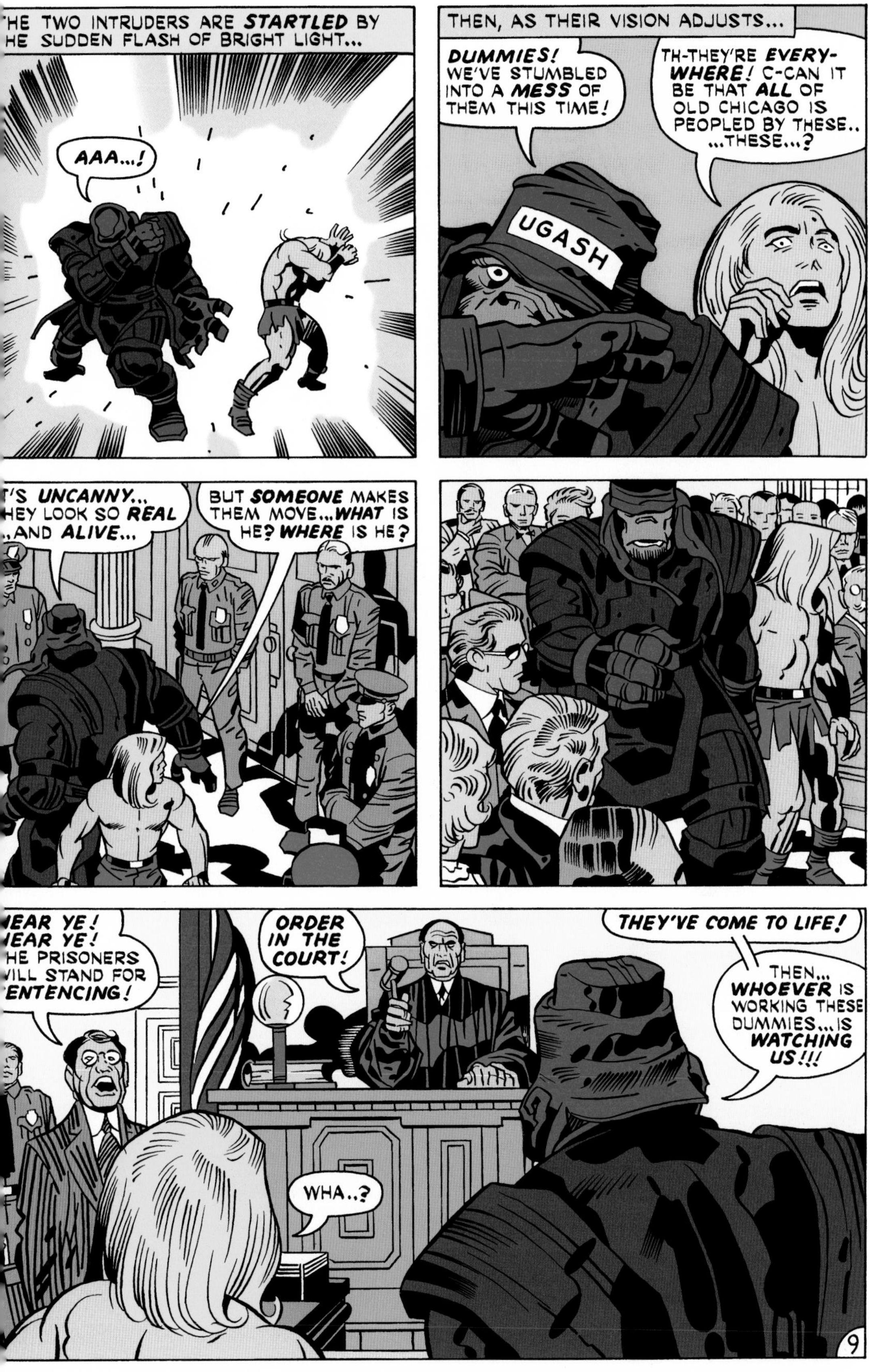
'HE TWO INTRUDERS ARE STARTLED BY
HE SUDDEN FLASH OF BRIGHT LIGHT...
AAA...!
THEN, AS THEIR VISION ADJUSTS...
DUMMIES! WE'VE STUMBLED INTO A MESS OF THEM THIS TIME!
TH-THEY'RE EVERY-WHERE! C-CAN IT BE THAT ALL OF OLD CHICAGO IS PEOPLED BY THESE.. ...THESE...?
UGASH
'S UNCANNY... HEY LOOK SO REAL ..AND ALIVE...
BUT SOMEONE MAKES THEM MOVE...WHAT IS HE? WHERE IS HE?
EAR YE! EAR YE! HE PRISONERS VILL STAND FOR ENTENCING!
ORDER IN THE COURT!
THEY'VE COME TO LIFE!
THEN... WHOEVER IS WORKING THESE DUMMIES... IS WATCHING US!!!
WHA..?
9

"**SOMEONE IS WATCHING YOU!!**" THAT'S **NOT** A NE[W] PHRASE....BUT, IN KAMANDI'S WORLD, IT CAN LEAD TO THE MOST BIZARRE AND HORRIFYING REVELATIONS....IT CAN SPELL **DOOM** FOR THE UNWARY....BECAUSE IT CAN WEAVE THAT DOOM AND SEAL IT! BECAUSE THERE'S....

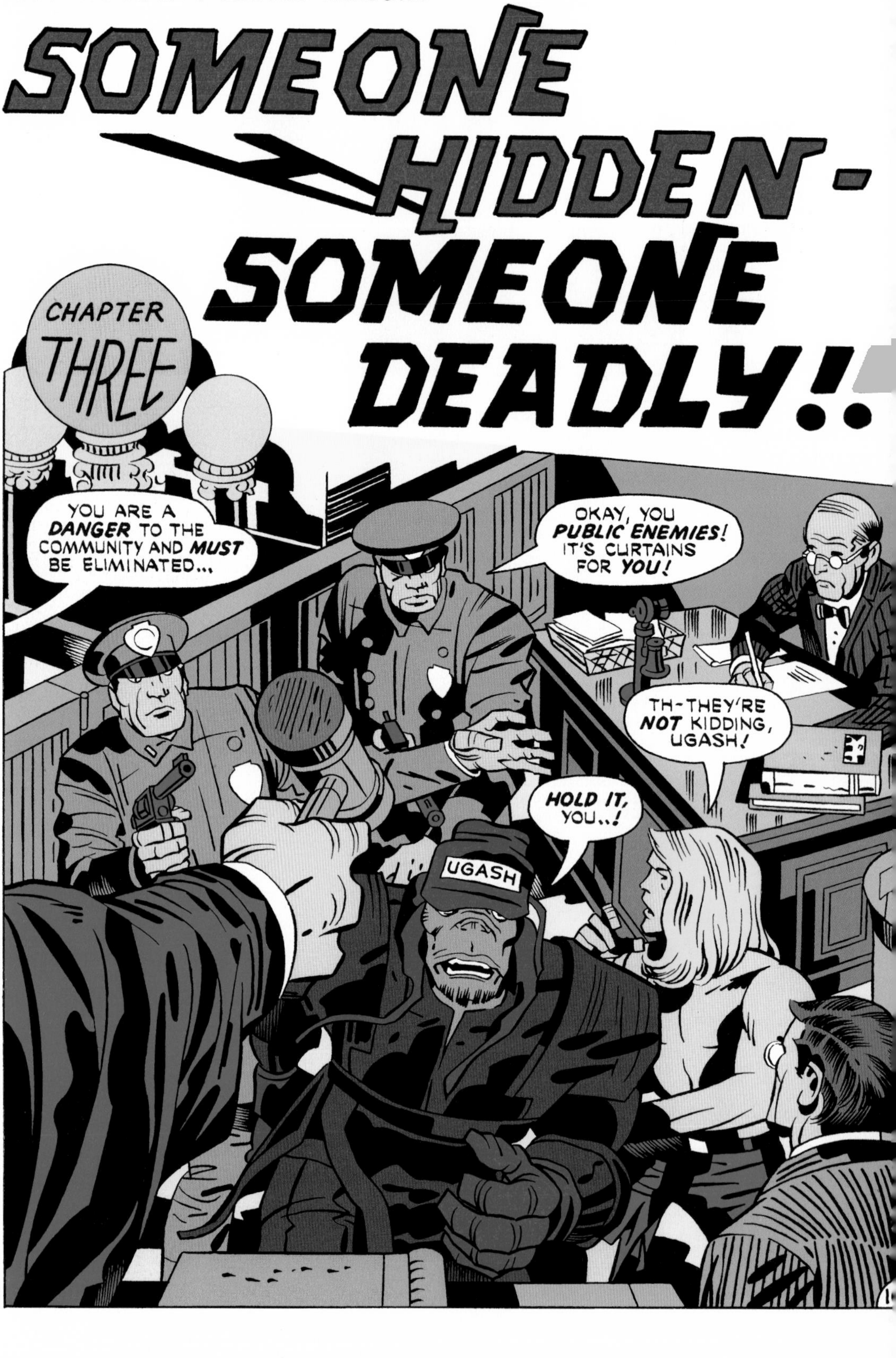
SOMEONE HIDDEN- SOMEONE DEADLY!!
CHAPTER THREE
YOU ARE A DANGER TO THE COMMUNITY AND MUST BE ELIMINATED...
OKAY, YOU PUBLIC ENEMIES! IT'S CURTAINS FOR YOU!
TH-THEY'RE NOT KIDDING, UGASH!
HOLD IT, YOU..!
UGASH

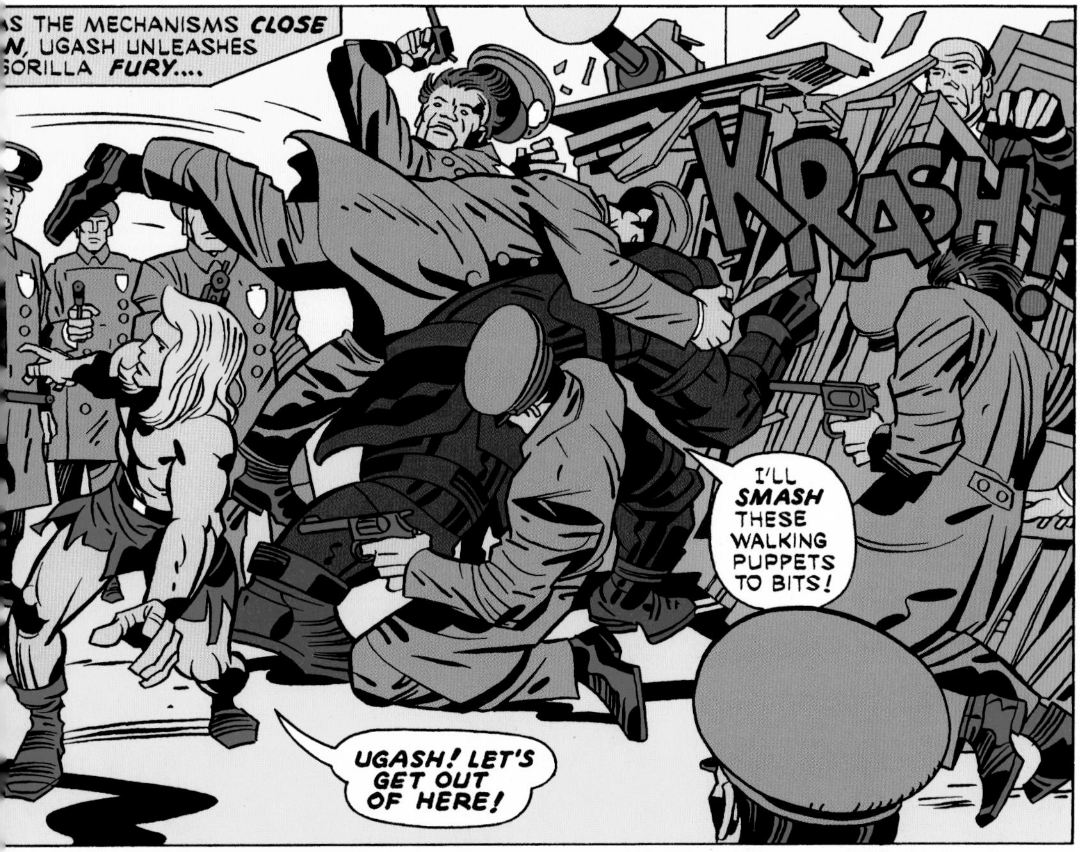
S THE MECHANISMS CLOSE
N, UGASH UNLEASHES
ORILLA FURY....
KRASH!
I'LL SMASH THESE WALKING PUPPETS TO BITS!
UGASH! LET'S GET OUT OF HERE!

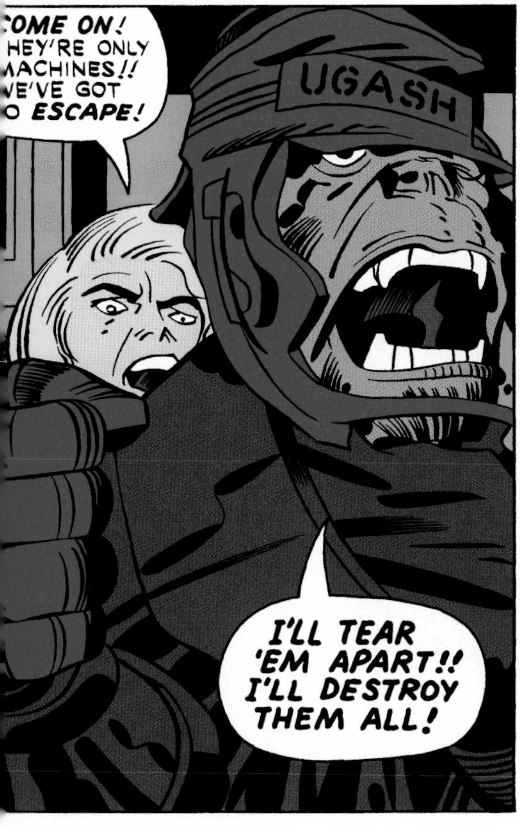
OME ON!
HEY'RE ONLY
ACHINES!!
E'VE GOT
O ESCAPE!
UGASH
I'LL TEAR 'EM APART!! I'LL DESTROY THEM ALL!

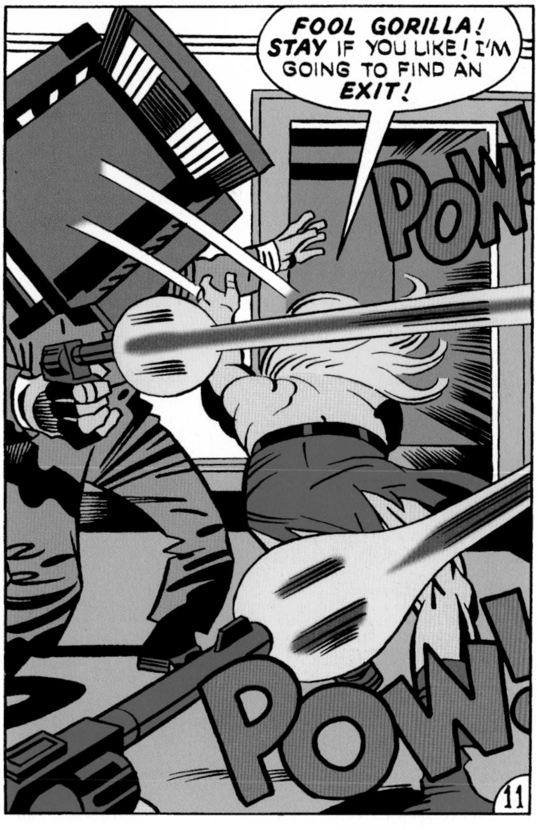
FOOL GORILLA! STAY IF YOU LIKE! I'M GOING TO FIND AN EXIT!
POW
POW
11

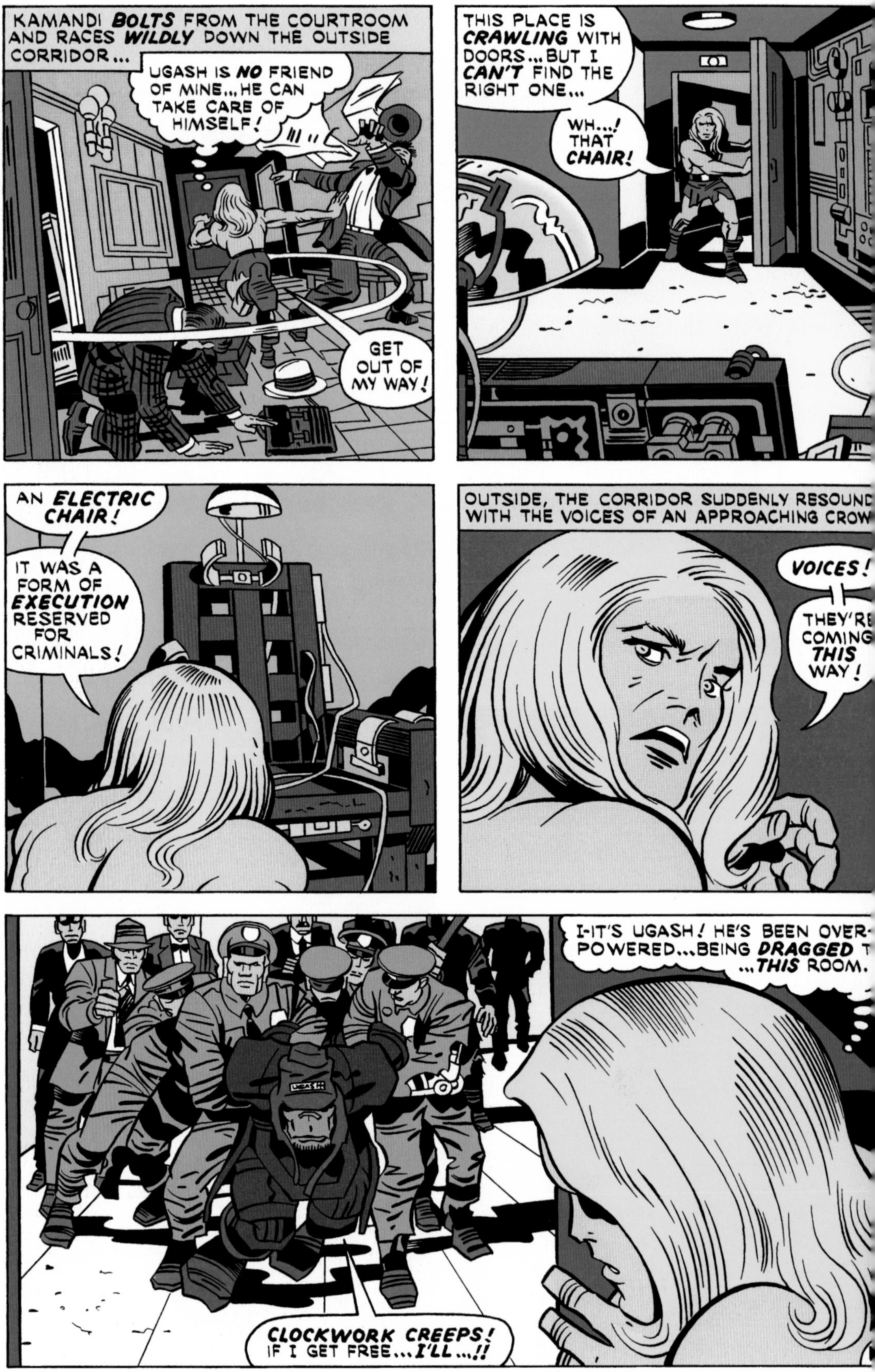
KAMANDI BOLTS FROM THE COURTROOM AND RACES WILDLY DOWN THE OUTSIDE CORRIDOR...
UGASH IS NO FRIEND OF MINE... HE CAN TAKE CARE OF HIMSELF!
GET OUT OF MY WAY!
THIS PLACE IS CRAWLING WITH DOORS... BUT I CAN'T FIND THE RIGHT ONE...
WH...! THAT CHAIR!
AN ELECTRIC CHAIR!
IT WAS A FORM OF EXECUTION RESERVED FOR CRIMINALS!
OUTSIDE, THE CORRIDOR SUDDENLY RESOUND
WITH THE VOICES OF AN APPROACHING CROW
VOICES!
THEY'RE COMING THIS WAY!
I-IT'S UGASH! HE'S BEEN OVER-POWERED... BEING DRAGGED T ...THIS ROOM.
CLOCKWORK CREEPS! IF I GET FREE... I'LL...!!

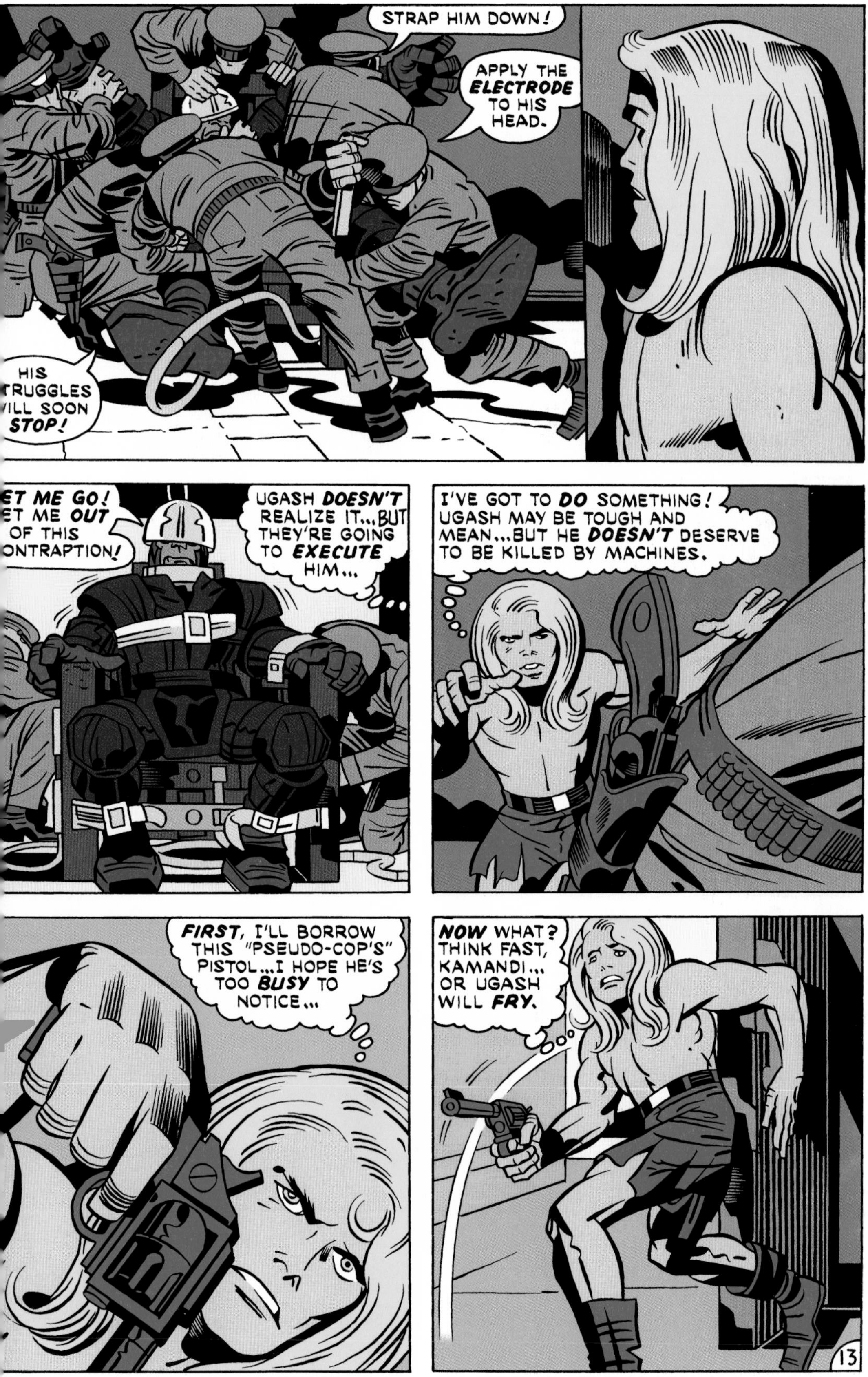
STRAP HIM DOWN!
APPLY THE ELECTRODE TO HIS HEAD.
HIS TRUGGLES VILL SOON STOP!
ET ME GO! ET ME OUT OF THIS ONTRAPTION!
UGASH DOESN'T REALIZE IT...BUT THEY'RE GOING TO EXECUTE HIM...
I'VE GOT TO DO SOMETHING! UGASH MAY BE TOUGH AND MEAN...BUT HE DOESN'T DESERVE TO BE KILLED BY MACHINES.
FIRST, I'LL BORROW THIS "PSEUDO-COP'S" PISTOL...I HOPE HE'S TOO BUSY TO NOTICE...
NOW WHAT? THINK FAST, KAMANDI... OR UGASH WILL FRY.
13

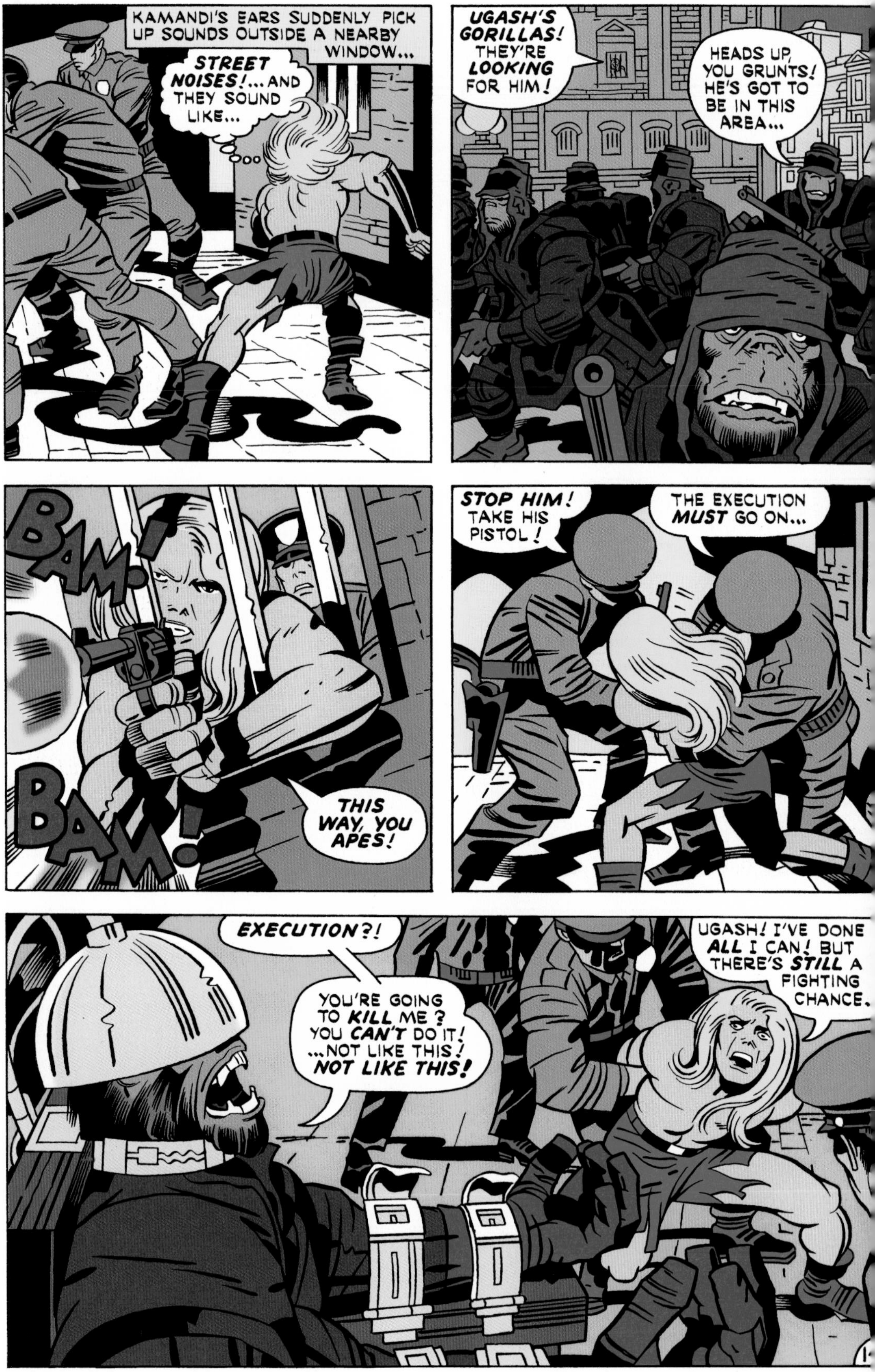
KAMANDI'S EARS SUDDENLY PICK UP SOUNDS OUTSIDE A NEARBY WINDOW...
STREET NOISES!... AND THEY SOUND LIKE...
UGASH'S GORILLAS! THEY'RE LOOKING FOR HIM!
HEADS UP, YOU GRUNTS! HE'S GOT TO BE IN THIS AREA...
BAM!
BAM!
THIS WAY, YOU APES!
STOP HIM! TAKE HIS PISTOL!
THE EXECUTION MUST GO ON...
EXECUTION?!
YOU'RE GOING TO KILL ME? YOU CAN'T DO IT! ...NOT LIKE THIS! NOT LIKE THIS!
UGASH! I'VE DONE ALL I CAN! BUT THERE'S STILL A FIGHTING CHANCE.

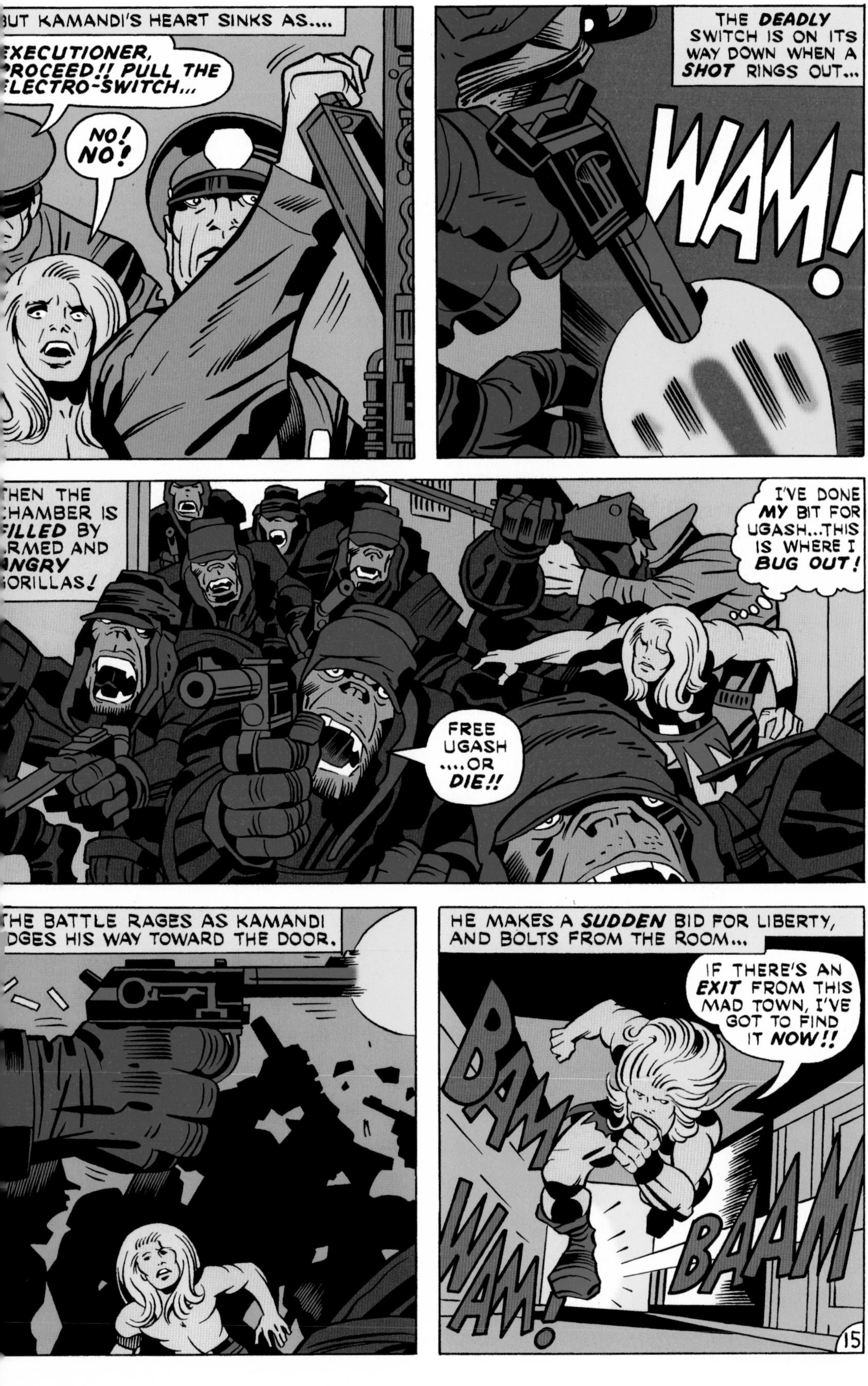
BUT KAMANDI'S HEART SINKS AS....
EXECUTIONER, PROCEED!! PULL THE ELECTRO-SWITCH...
NO! NO!
THE DEADLY SWITCH IS ON ITS WAY DOWN WHEN A SHOT RINGS OUT...
WAM!
THEN THE CHAMBER IS FILLED BY ARMED AND ANGRY GORILLAS!
I'VE DONE MY BIT FOR UGASH...THIS IS WHERE I BUG OUT!
FREE UGASH ....OR DIE!!
THE BATTLE RAGES AS KAMANDI EDGES HIS WAY TOWARD THE DOOR.
HE MAKES A SUDDEN BID FOR LIBERTY, AND BOLTS FROM THE ROOM...
IF THERE'S AN EXIT FROM THIS MAD TOWN, I'VE GOT TO FIND IT NOW!!
BAM
WAM!
BAAM
15

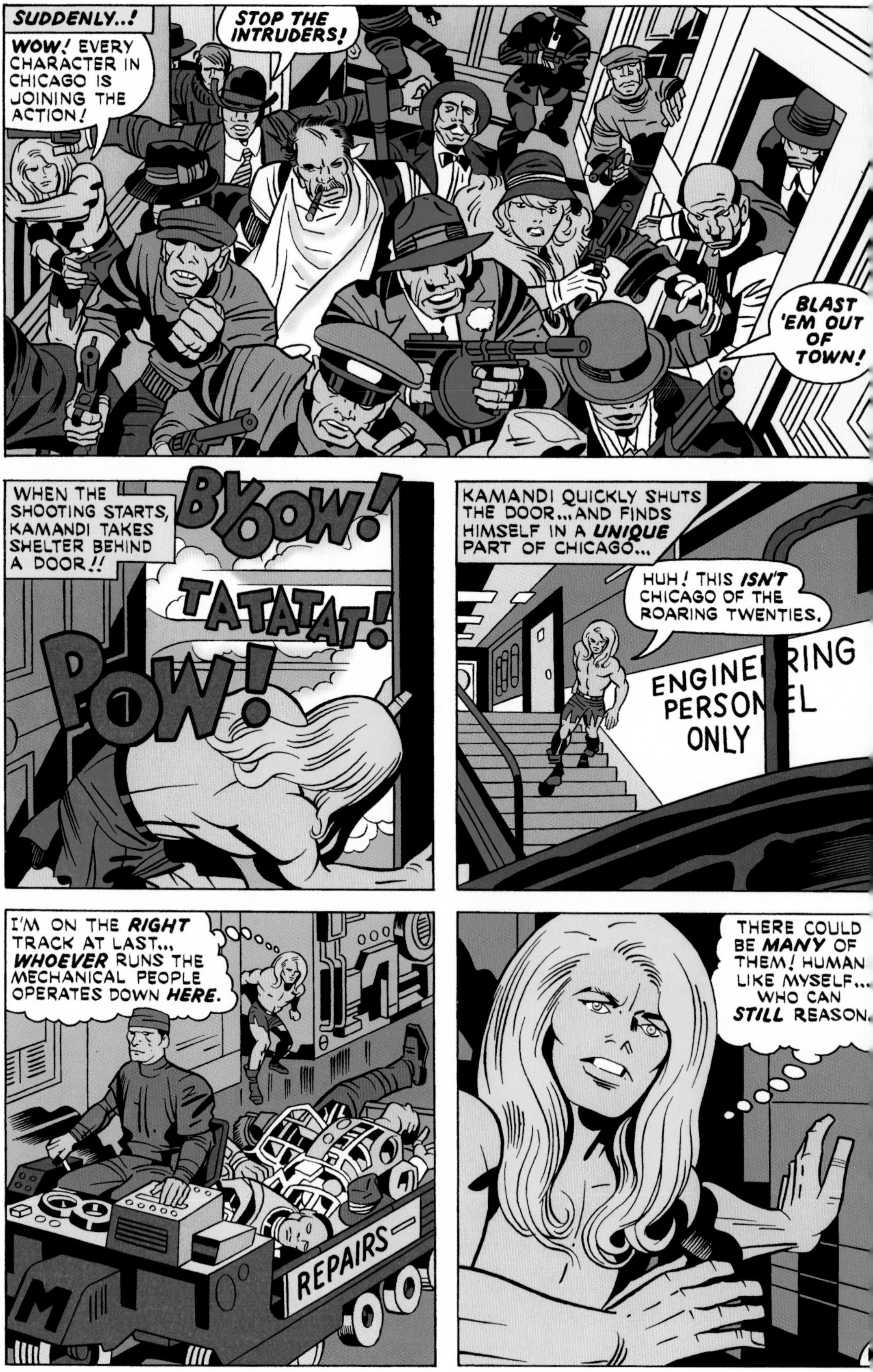
SUDDENLY..!
WOW! EVERY CHARACTER IN CHICAGO IS JOINING THE ACTION!
STOP THE INTRUDERS!
BLAST 'EM OUT OF TOWN!
WHEN THE SHOOTING STARTS, KAMANDI TAKES SHELTER BEHIND A DOOR!!
BYOOW!
TATATAT!
POW!
KAMANDI QUICKLY SHUTS THE DOOR...AND FINDS HIMSELF IN A UNIQUE PART OF CHICAGO...
HUH! THIS ISN'T CHICAGO OF THE ROARING TWENTIES.
ENGINE RING
PERSON EL
ONLY
I'M ON THE RIGHT TRACK AT LAST... WHOEVER RUNS THE MECHANICAL PEOPLE OPERATES DOWN HERE.
REPAIRS
M
THERE COULD BE MANY OF THEM! HUMAN LIKE MYSELF... WHO CAN STILL REASON.

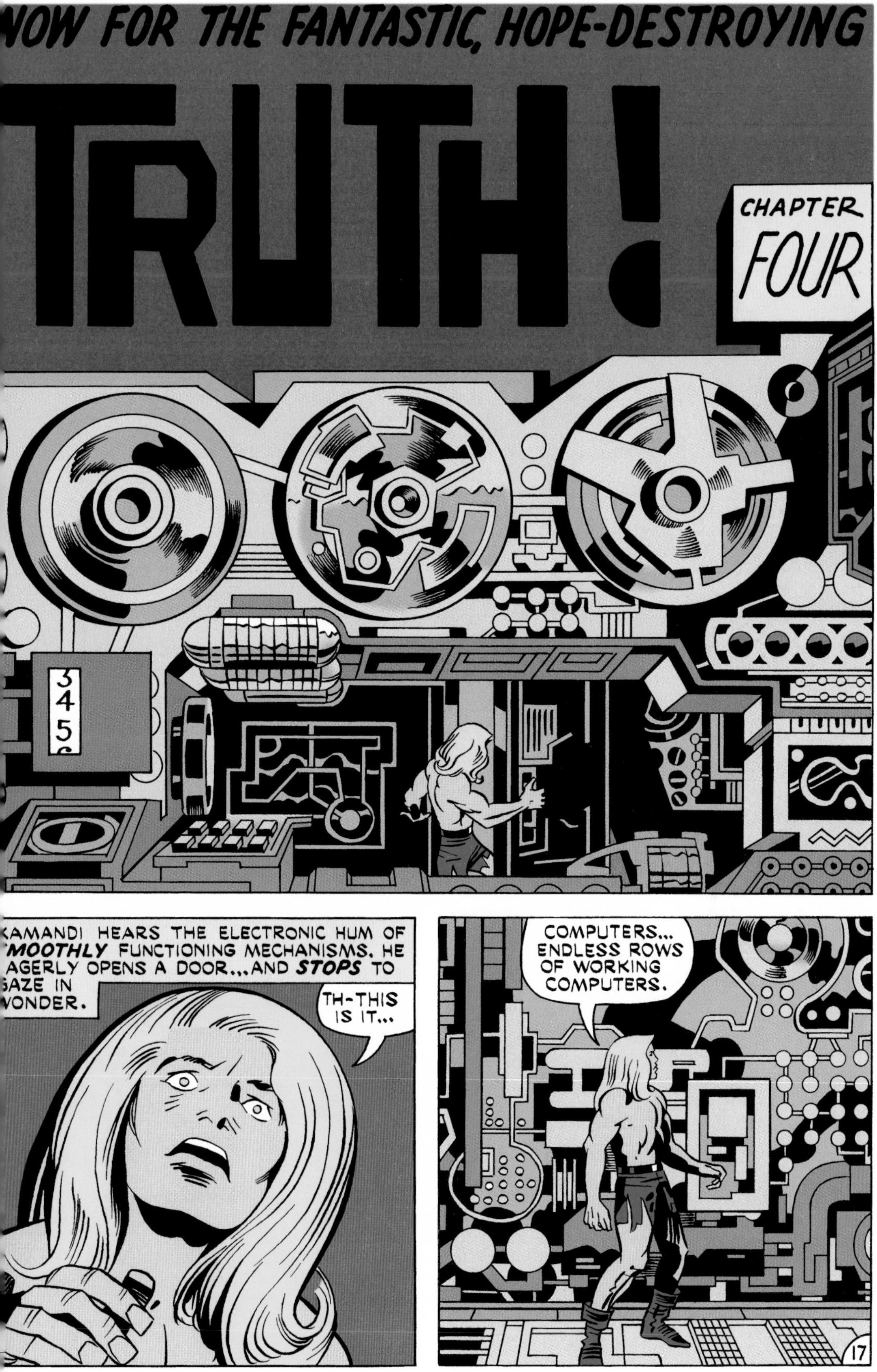

NOW FOR THE FANTASTIC, HOPE-DESTROYING

TRUTH!

CHAPTER FOUR

KAMANDI HEARS THE ELECTRONIC HUM OF SMOOTHLY FUNCTIONING MECHANISMS. HE EAGERLY OPENS A DOOR... AND STOPS TO GAZE IN WONDER.

TH-THIS IS IT...

COMPUTERS... ENDLESS ROWS OF WORKING COMPUTERS.

17

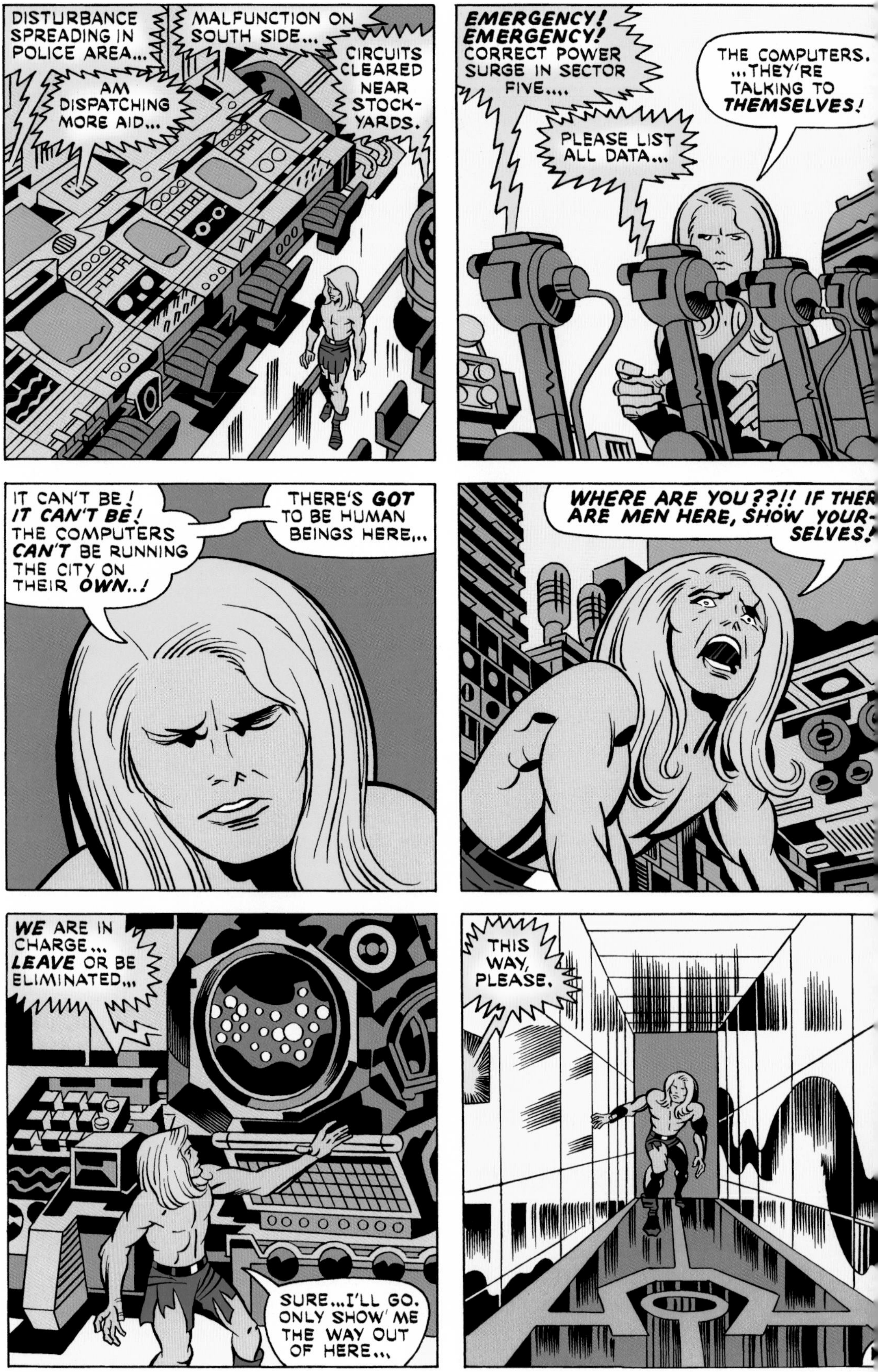
DISTURBANCE SPREADING IN POLICE AREA...
MALFUNCTION ON SOUTH SIDE...
CIRCUITS CLEARED NEAR STOCK-YARDS.
AM DISPATCHING MORE AID...
EMERGENCY! EMERGENCY! CORRECT POWER SURGE IN SECTOR FIVE....
THE COMPUTERS. ...THEY'RE TALKING TO THEMSELVES!
PLEASE LIST ALL DATA...
IT CAN'T BE! IT CAN'T BE! THE COMPUTERS CAN'T BE RUNNING THE CITY ON THEIR OWN..!
THERE'S GOT TO BE HUMAN BEINGS HERE...
WHERE ARE YOU??!! IF THER ARE MEN HERE, SHOW YOUR-SELVES!
WE ARE IN CHARGE... LEAVE OR BE ELIMINATED...
SURE...I'LL GO. ONLY SHOW ME THE WAY OUT OF HERE...
THIS WAY, PLEASE.

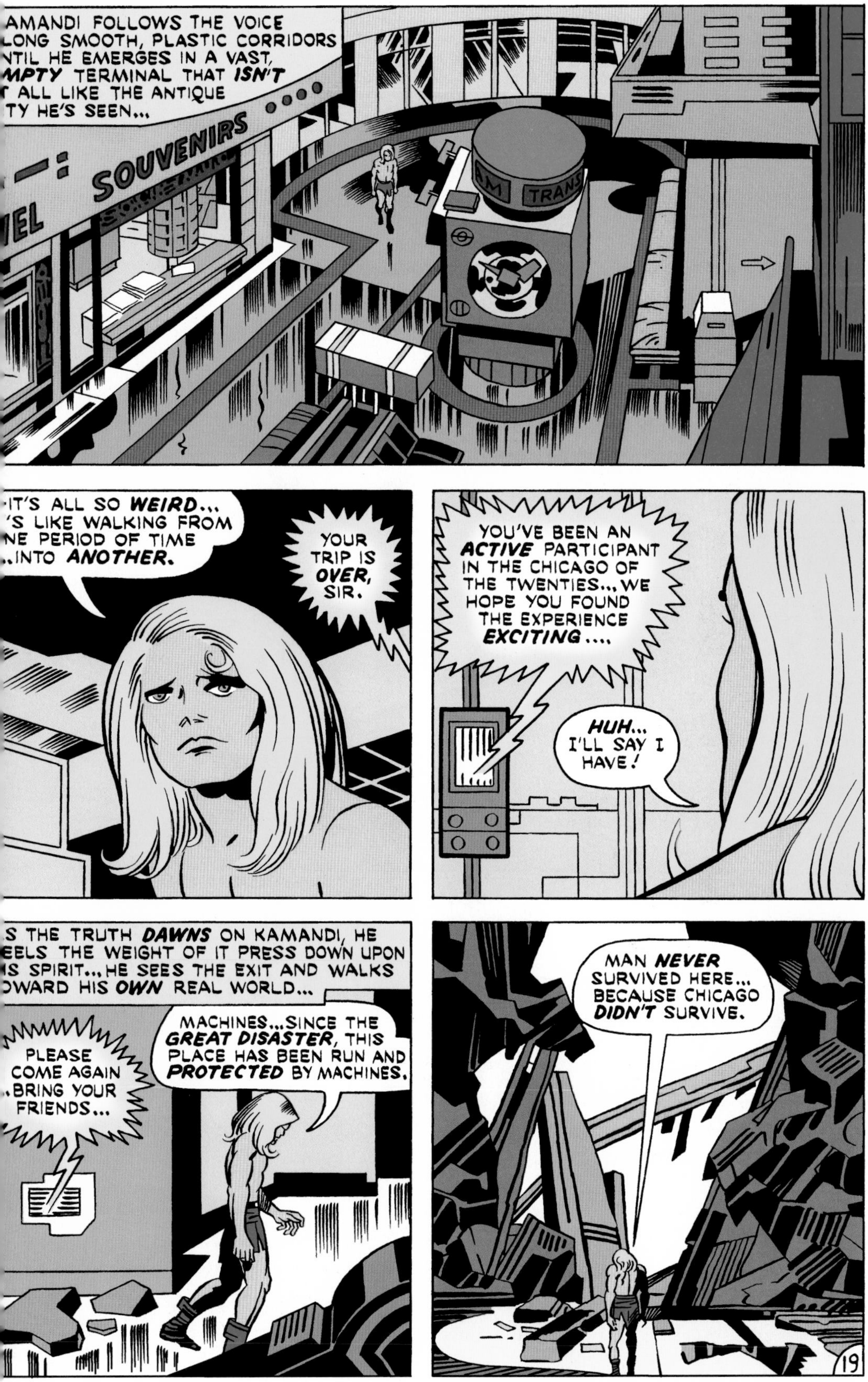
AMANDI FOLLOWS THE VOICE
LONG SMOOTH, PLASTIC CORRIDORS
NTIL HE EMERGES IN A VAST,
MPTY TERMINAL THAT ISN'T
ALL LIKE THE ANTIQUE
TY HE'S SEEN...
SOUVENIRS
EL
TRANS
IT'S ALL SO WEIRD...
'S LIKE WALKING FROM
NE PERIOD OF TIME
..INTO ANOTHER.
YOUR TRIP IS OVER, SIR.
YOU'VE BEEN AN ACTIVE PARTICIPANT IN THE CHICAGO OF THE TWENTIES...,WE HOPE YOU FOUND THE EXPERIENCE EXCITING....
HUH... I'LL SAY I HAVE!
S THE TRUTH DAWNS ON KAMANDI, HE
EELS THE WEIGHT OF IT PRESS DOWN UPON
S SPIRIT...HE SEES THE EXIT AND WALKS
OWARD HIS OWN REAL WORLD...
PLEASE COME AGAIN ..BRING YOUR FRIENDS...
MACHINES...SINCE THE GREAT DISASTER, THIS PLACE HAS BEEN RUN AND PROTECTED BY MACHINES.
MAN NEVER SURVIVED HERE... BECAUSE CHICAGO DIDN'T SURVIVE.
19

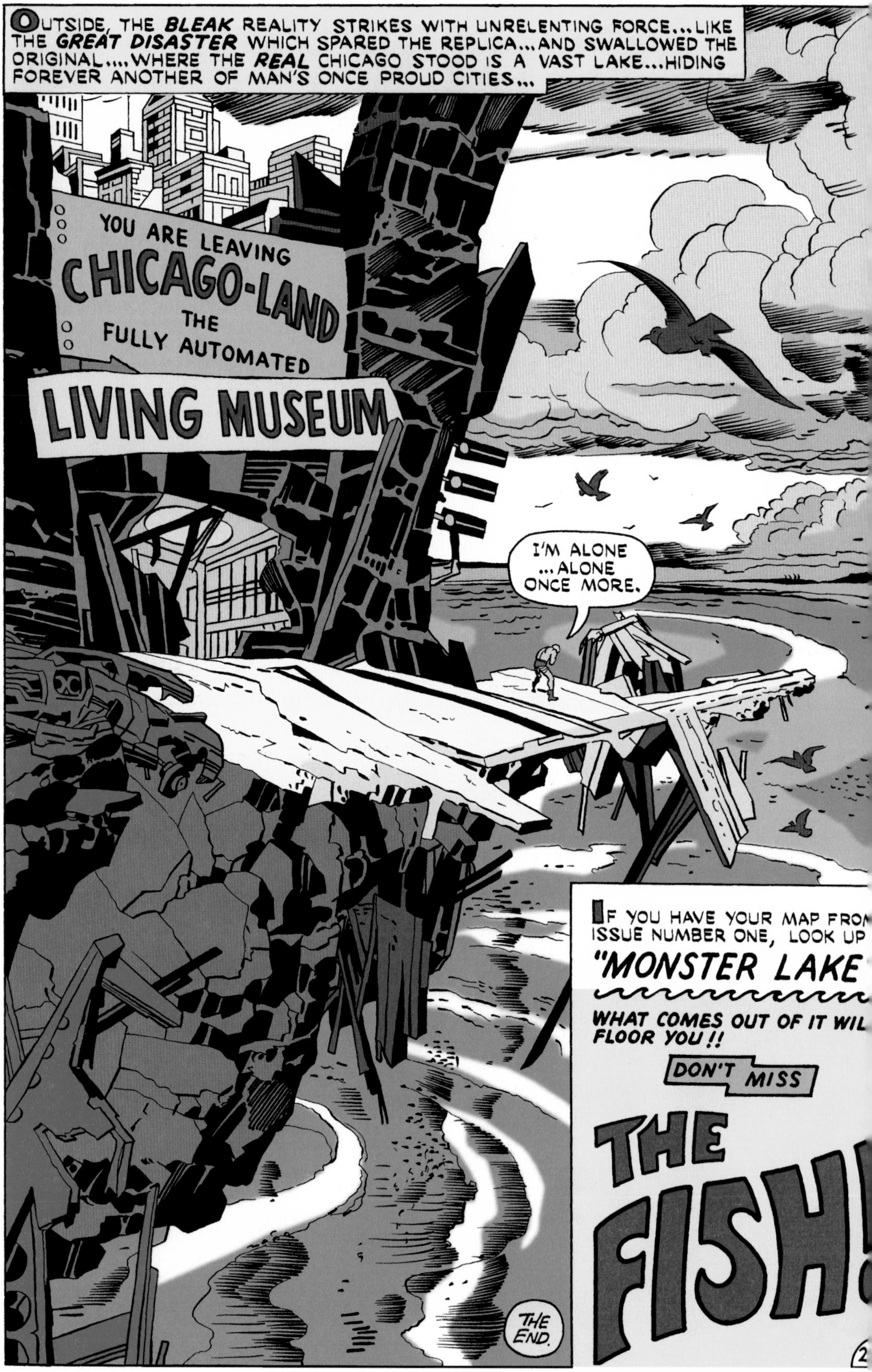
OUTSIDE, THE BLEAK REALITY STRIKES WITH UNRELENTING FORCE...LIKE THE GREAT DISASTER WHICH SPARED THE REPLICA...AND SWALLOWED THE ORIGINAL....WHERE THE REAL CHICAGO STOOD IS A VAST LAKE...HIDING FOREVER ANOTHER OF MAN'S ONCE PROUD CITIES...
YOU ARE LEAVING CHICAGO-LAND THE FULLY AUTOMATED
LIVING MUSEUM
I'M ALONE ...ALONE ONCE MORE.
IF YOU HAVE YOUR MAP FROM ISSUE NUMBER ONE, LOOK UP "MONSTER LAKE
WHAT COMES OUT OF IT WIL FLOOR YOU!!
DON'T MISS
THE FISH
THE END.

JACK KIRBY

A true giant in the world of comics, Jack "The King" Kirby began his comics career in 1937 at the age of 20 and worked in the field for nearly six decades. During comics' Golden Age, Kirby (along with his partner Joe Simon) drew and/or created innumerable features, including Captain America, the Young Allies, Sandman, the Newsboy Legion and Manhunter. During the 1950s, Kirby and Simon continued to pour out stories and concepts, including the DC Comics titles THE FIGHTING AMERICAN and BOYS' RANCH, as well as creating the romance comics genre with their groundbreaking title *Young Romance* for Prize Comics. In 1961, the first issue of Marvel Comics' *The Fantastic Four* — a collaboration between Kirby and Marvel editor-in-chief Stan Lee — cemented Kirby's reputation as comics' preeminent creator. Throughout the 1960s, Kirby and Lee laid the groundwork for the Marvel Universe that flourishes to this day. Kirby returned to DC in 1971 with his classic "Fourth World Trilogy" — THE NEW GODS, MISTER MIRACLE and THE FOREVER PEOPLE — which was followed by THE DEMON, OMAC and KAMANDI. He continued working and innovating in comics until his death in 1994

MIKE ROYER

Mike Royer began his comics career assisting the legendary Russ Manning in the 1960s on *Magnus, Robot Fighter* and *Tarzan* for Gold Key. In the 1970s he went on to ink and letter Manning's *Tarzan* and *Star Wars* syndicated newspaper strips.

During this same period, Royer also pencilled and inked stories on his own for the Warren anthologies *Creepy, Eerie* and *Vampirella*. However, his best-known works are undoubtedly his numerous collaborations with Jack Kirby on THE NEW GODS, THE FOREVER PEOPLE, MISTER MIRACLE, THE DEMON and KAMANDI for DC Comics, as well as *Captain America, The Eternals* and many other titles for Marvel Comics.

Following his partnership with Kirby, in 1979 Royer began a long association with the Walt Disney Company, where he worked in the creative department of the Consumer Products/Licensing division. In 1993 Royer left his staff position to freelance for the Disney Stores creative group. He continues to freelance for various companies from his home in Oregon.

D. BRUCE BERRY

A longtime participant in the worlds of comics and science fiction fandom, D. Bruce Berry began his relatively brief inking career assisting Mike Royer on Jack Kirby's prolific pencil work for DC in the early 1970s. Over the next ten years, Berry contributed work to the DC titles KAMANDI, OMAC and OUR FIGHTING FORCES as well as Marvel's *Captain America* and Pacific Comics' *Silver Star*. He also worked on such magazines as *Other Worlds, Imaginative Tales* and *Fantasy Illustrated*, and in 1975 he co-wrote the novel *Genetic Bomb* with Andrew J. Offutt. Beyond the fields of genre entertainment, Berry has also enjoyed a long career providing art for the advertising industry.

SOME BIOGRAPHICAL RESEARCH PROVIDED BY CRAIG DELICH AND MARK EVANIER.